Globalization and National Security

EDITED BY Jonathan Kirshner

Routledge
Taylor & Francis Group
New York   London

Routledge is an imprint of the
Taylor & Francis Group, an informa business

Routledge
Taylor & Francis Group
270 Madison Avenue
New York, NY 10016

Routledge
Taylor & Francis Group
2 Park Square
Milton Park, Abingdon
Oxon OX14 4RN

© 2006 by Taylor & Francis Group, LLC
Routledge is an imprint of Taylor & Francis Group, an Informa business

Printed in the United States of America on acid-free paper
10 9 8 7 6 5 4 3 2

International Standard Book Number-10: 0-415-95511-4 (Softcover) 0-415-95510-6 (Hardcover)
International Standard Book Number-13: 978-0-415-95511-9 (Softcover) 978-0-415-95510-2 (Hardcover)

Library of Congress Cataloging-in-Publication Data

Globalization and national security / edited by Jonathan Kirshner.
    p. cm.
Includes bibliographical references and index.
ISBN 0-415-95510-6 (hardback : alk. paper) -- ISBN 0-415-95511-4 (pbk. : alk. paper) 1. Globalization. 2. National security. I. Kirshner, Jonathan.

JZ1318.G5777 2006
355'.033--dc22   2006007359

Visit the Taylor & Francis Web site at
http://www.taylorandfrancis.com

and the Routledge Web site at
http://www.routledge-ny.com

CONTENTS

ACKNOWLEDGMENTS

The chapters in this volume were developed over the course of two workshops, in November 2003 and June 2004, under the auspices of the Economics and National Security Program of the John M. Olin Institute for Strategic Studies at Harvard University. We thank Stephen Rosen, director of the Olin Institute, for his support of the program and this project.

Some of the chapters-in-progress were also presented at the 2004 annual convention of the International Studies Association in Montreal. Over the course of these meetings and workshops, we benefited tremendously from the comments and participation of numerous discussants who were extremely helpful in improving the chapters individually and the project as a whole. We thank Rawi Abdelal, Robert Art, Nora Bensahel, Tom Berger, Stephen Brooks, Ronald Deibert, Peter Dombrowski, Yinan He, Peter Liberman, Sean Lynn-Jones, Kevin Narizny, Jeremy Pressman, Dick Samuels, and Chris Way for bringing our workshops to life and keeping us on our toes.

We would also like to thank Ann Townes and Hamutal Bernstein at the Olin Institute, Robert Tempio at Routledge, and two anonymous referees.

1

GLOBALIZATION AND NATIONAL SECURITY

Jonathan Kirshner

WHAT ARE THE CONSEQUENCES OF GLOBALIZATION for national security? Although there is an enormous and still burgeoning literature on globalization, the answer to this crucial question remains unclear.[1] Part of the reason for this is that much of the debate has recaptured a traditional divide among international relations (IR) scholars, with one side resolutely challenging the relative novelty of contemporary globalization and defending the primacy of the state; while at the other end of the spectrum, suggestions of a brave new borderless world fill the air.[2] This volume does not address those debates, but rather, engages the question: What are the consequences of globalization (however novel) for national security (traditionally defined)? It argues that even while retaining the state-centric perspective, globalization changes the nature of the game, even if the actors are assumed to retain the same goals they have always pursued. Failure to account for the influence of globalization will make it increasingly difficult to understand changes in the balance of power, prospects for war, and strategic choices embraced by states. Switching from polo on horseback to water polo does not change the principals or their objectives, but the contest is still profoundly transformed by the change in setting. Some players, for example, might have been much better riders than they are swimmers.[3]

Some definitions are in order.[4] *Globalization* (as used here) is shorthand for an array of phenomena that derive from unorganized and stateless forces but that generate pressures that are felt by states. It is important to note that in this usage, globalization is not simply an extreme form of "interdependence," which concerns the political consequences of relationships between two (or more) states.[5] Nor is globalization a synonym for subnational, transnational, regional, or supranational forms of political organization. Rather, in contrast, the forces of globalization as defined here are in their purest incarnations disorganized and purposeless, the powerful but uncoordinated consequences of individual behavior and technological change. An illustration of globalization, by this definition, is the financial crisis that forced France's socialists to reverse their economic strategy in 1982. The crisis was not the result (as far as the evidence to date shows) of coordinated political action by agents within France or by other states, but by uncoordinated capital flight.[6]

However, although such market pressures are the most obvious exemplars of globalization, they are not the only forces of globalization captured by this definition, which includes any relatively general phenomenon that is stateless and uncoordinated, and that has little inherent regard for national borders. Some (but not all) forms of technological and social change also fit this description, most obviously with regard to the political consequences of the spread of information technology and of ideas.

National security refers to organized political violence that speaks to the vital interests of at least one state. The consequences of globalization for national security, however, need not be limited to war or insurgency, but include as well how forces of globalization affect the balance of power, change the offense-defense balance or other factors that might affect the security dilemma and the likelihood of war, or transform the ability of the state to defend its own interests.

The conjunction *and* (from the phrase "globalization and national security") also plays a critical role in this volume. The focus here, as noted above, is on the consequences *of* globalization *for* national security. This is both restricting and liberating. It is restricting for obvious reasons. But it also provides the mechanism through which a broad range of phenomena can be introduced into the mix. For example, the consequences of U.S. preponderance, or the prospects for a "clash of civilizations," or the spread of terrorism, to take three examples that will appear in the pages that follow, are *not* in and of themselves objects of inquiry under the definitions just prescribed. Terrorism, after all, could and did exist in the absence of globalization. However, when issues such as these are in turn linked (*tightly and explicitly*) to forces of globalization (i.e., how the processes of globalization affect the nature or spread of terrorism) they are certainly relevant here; as long as these links are explicit and elucidated, in practical terms there are relatively few constraints on the types of concerns that can be addressed. Similarly, although transnational organizations or international institutions were specifically excluded above from the definition of globalization, it can still be readily argued that globalization has increased the importance of such actors for national security. Tight and explicit links to globalization with specific implications for national security thus allow numerous phenomena to be put on the table. In sum, this definition of "globalization and national security" is in many ways fairly broad; however, ultimately, it is rooted in and delimited by a traditional conception of security concerns. This conception does exclude a large set of issues, such as those often placed under the rubric of "new security," including global challenges such as environmental degradation or broader conceptions of "human security."

OVERVIEW

This chapter proceeds in two principal parts. First, it addresses the political context of globalization (especially the role of unipolarity and U.S. power) and then considers three broad ways in which security can be affected by globalization: by reshaping *state capacity,* recasting *relative power,* and revising the calculations associated with *international conflict.* Obviously, given the definition employed above, globalization will reduce or at the very least change the capabilities and autonomy of the state vis-à-vis nonstate actors.[7] Because the consequences for capacity and autonomy will vary from state to state, globalization will also affect the balance of power between states, relatively empowering some at the expense of others. Globalization will also change the nature of conflict, generating new axes of strife, privileging distinct expressions of violence, and affecting the likelihood of war.

Second, this chapter considers the processes of globalization and how they can affect state capacity, the balance of power, and the nature of conflict. These processes are also bundled together in three groups, which to some extent inevitably overlap and are mutually reinforcing, but are nevertheless purposefully designed to call attention to three distinct conduits through which the pressures of globalization are transmitted through the system: via the intensification of *economic exchange,* the flow of *information,* and *marketization*—the expansion of the set of social relations governed by market forces. A brief conclusion describes how each chapter in the volume is integrated into this general framework.

UNIPOLARITY, GLOBALIZATION, AND SECURITY

The contemporary international system is influenced by two "mock-systemic" effects: unipolarity and globalization. These are systemic forces in that to a large extent they affect all states uniformly (though, because states are, at a minimum, differently situated, there is variation in the relative significance of and range of response to those forces). However, they are not systemic in the pure sense of the concept because, in both cases, they are shaped by state choices, especially those of the United States.[8] Indeed, regarding unipolarity, the mock-systemic effect that is felt by other states is not so much a direct function of the distribution of power, as with (arguably) bipolarity, but rather the doctrinal foreign policy choices of the United States.

This is a bit of a paradox—systemic explanations normally rest on the consequences of essentially uniform (or at least unidirectional) pressures faced by relatively like units distinguished principally by their relative capabilities—a conception of world politics as a function of constrained choice where position trumps preference. Thus highlighting the distribution of power (in this case, American predominance) as a causal variable would appear to privilege the perspective that state behavior is constrained by systemic imperatives, just as individual firms must respond to the dictates imposed by the market. But this analogy has always been imperfect, as even oligopolists (surely more analogous to states in international relations than small firms are) are not pure "price takers," but can influence their environment through their behavior.[9] And the greater the concentration of power—market or political—the broader the discretion enjoyed by the biggest players. Thus the extraordinary preponderance of U.S. power presents us with a state virtually uninhibited by traditional systemic constraints. Unnaturally unconstrained by its position, the United States has the luxury of choosing from a large menu of policy choices. To the extent that those choices reflect a coherent underlying purpose or doctrine—such as the Bush Doctrine of preventive war or the promotion of global economic liberalization—that policy choice is transmitted throughout and shapes the nature of the system as a "mock systemic" effect.[10]

One such policy choice of the United States is the embrace of, or at the very least a policy of purposeful benign permissiveness regarding, the forces of globalization. Technology may make it much easier to transmit information, or more difficult to control capital flows, but if the world's only superpower had different policy preferences, say those of caution, closure, and control, then the pressures of globalization, while still present and powerful, would not be as pervasive.[11] Finance may be unbound, but financial deregulation was (and remains) to a large extent the result of decisions by great powers pursuing their perceived national interests; similarly, although it may be more difficult for authorities to control what their citizens read, see, and share with others, states—especially the most powerful states—nevertheless play a central role in negotiations regarding media spaces and information policies, which establish the legal, technical, and political market structures that shape the ways in which information flows.[12] In sum, it would be a serious mistake to overlook the political foundations of globalization or to lose sight of the fact that globalization is not politically neutral. As one journalist neatly observed, "Globalization is the narcissism of a superpower in a one superpower world."[13]

At the same time, it is also crucial to be sensitive to the limitations of the influence both of unipolarity and of globalization. Although the United States is indeed at the center of a unipolar political order, the military predominance reflected in unipolarity translates only uneasily to economic "hegemony"—on the economic front, there are more chinks in the American armor—unchallenged on the battlefield, the United States is nonetheless saddled by national debt, fiscal deficits, and record trade imbalances. Second, and more important, both unipolarity and hegemony are largely measures of relative state capacities without regard to other challenges (and opportunities) faced by states. Thus although the enormous U.S. economy is "hegemonic" compared to other national economies (and its military unrivaled by any other state), it nevertheless is constrained by the pressures of globalization in ways that economic hegemons (and military superpowers) of the past (such as the United States after the Second World War) were not. Therefore, even though the United States has purposefully promoted globalization and has flourished in that context, this does not alter the fact that America itself is also "not immune to the powerful forces of globalization."[14]

Finally, it is also important not to overstate the consequences of globalization. The pressures of globalization, however powerful, do not present iron laws, but rather they change the cost-benefit calculus of various policy choices. Resistance to globalization—efforts by states to keep borders (more or less) closed to flows of data, money, and people—is certainly possible; the "level" of globalization does not operate by fiat imposing openness upon all so much as it raises in general the opportunity costs of such closure.

In sum, globalization does not derive of thin air but is, at a minimum, the result of a politically permissive environment. It is neither inevitable nor irreversible.[15] Nevertheless, it is here now, and it must be reckoned with in any understanding of national security.

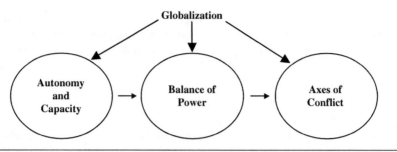

Figure 1.1 How globalization affects national security.

CONSEQUENCES FOR SECURITY

Globalization influences traditional security concerns in three principal ways (see Figure 1.1). It affects state capacity and autonomy—that is, the relative power of the state vis-à-vis nonstate actors, social forces, and market pressures. It also affects the balance of power between states, because even if changes in the system left each state absolutely less able to advance its interests, there would still be a reshuffling of relative capabilities. Finally, by creating new sources of conflict between states, new opportunities for entrepreneurs of political violence, and by reshaping the costs and benefits of both warfare and conquest, the forces of globalization can recast the nature of armed conflict.

State Capacity and Autonomy

To a large extent, the most obvious consequence of globalization is the diminishing of the power and influence of the sovereign state. This is plainly visible in the reduction of macroeconomic policy autonomy that has accompanied the globalization of finance, although the extent of that diminished capacity remains open to debate. But the ability to manage the macroeconomy, with consequences for the state's capacity to manipulate domestic politics and its ability to garner resources for war, is inhibited (or at the very least altered[16]) by the breathtaking pace of capital mobility. Changes in the scale of production (upward as the global production economy is more integrated), and with the fragmentation of that production within and between firms across borders, will likely undermine the traditional preference of states for relative autarky in defense production.[17] These changes could affect not only decisions about procurement for defense but also those regarding military alliances.

The dramatic expansion in communications technology—of television and satellites and cellular telephones, faxes, computers, and the Internet, collectively often labeled the "hypermedia environment"—are routinely cited as examples of state decline. And to some extent they are. However, and the point is a general one, these changes may be more significant for the ways in which they transform rather than reduce state capacity. Government authorities are especially well suited to use new technologies to their own advantage—indeed, enhanced surveillance technologies can empower the state, extending its reach further than before.[18] Or the changes in modes of communication might shift the nature rather than the extent of state control, from one of inward looking legal regulation toward outward oriented multilaterally negotiated agreements.[19] Most broadly, as Ronald Deibert has argued, these changes affect the relative power of social forces, because "social forces whose interests match a communications environment will be favored while those whose interests do not will be disfavored." For example, this will empower some firms (compared with other firms and states), because "the hypermedia environment ... favors the transnationalization of production" both within and among multiple firms, facilitating strategic alliances, joint ventures, and joint production.[20]

The Balance of Power

The hypermedia environment not only changes the relative power of social forces, it also affects the relative power of states.[21] Those authoritarian states that have traditionally tried to retain a tight control on information—Syria, which into the 1990s required that all typewriters be registered with the state and prohibited the use of fax machines until the end of the decade, would be one such example—should find the globalized information environment more subversive of their authority than other states with a more laissez-faire attitude toward the flow of information. This may provide a strategic advantage to more politically liberal regimes, less radically challenged by these developments. In a parallel fashion, the pressures and opportunities presented by the relatively open, outward oriented international trade and production environment associated with globalization will present fewer and relatively less intense challenges to those states that have already embraced strategies of economic liberalization. Other states, once again, in particular, authoritarian "bunker" states but also including "clientelist" regimes that lean heavily on the use of distributing economic rents and protectionism to reward political allies, might find themselves backed into a corner. An environment with more pressure for economic reform is especially challenging for these types of governments because such reforms can undercut core political bargains upon which regime maintenance rests.[22]

Even with regard to the liberalization of finance, which remains the poster child for the general transfer of influence from states to markets, the effects of globalization cut heterogeneously within and differentially across national economies. As will be discussed below, despite the fact that even the enormous U.S. economy is now more beholden to the whims of international financial markets, given its deep capital markets, powerful financial institutions, and enormous influence with the International Monetary Fund (IMF), globalized finance enhances the relative power of the United States compared to virtually every other state in the world. If anything, the globalization of finance is an even more politicized project than the liberalization of production: those who were (properly) taught that markets generally work and free trade is largely a good thing might be surprised to learn that there is simply no solid evidence to support the view that completely unregulated capital flows are economically efficient. Politics rather than economics accounts for capital deregulation.[23]

The Nature of Conflict

Globalization also can reshape the nature of conflict and the style and pattern of organized political violence. Not surprisingly, the powerful and indefatigable economic, political, and cultural pressures associated with globalization give rise to new conflicts between groups. The pressures for convergence on all these fronts create new vulnerabilities, generate demands for insulation, and elicit calls for resistance. These forces are destabilizing—in the value neutral sense of the term—meaning that they disrupt traditional patterns of activity as well as local norms, arrangements, and understandings. These redistributions will often widen disparities between individuals, groups, and states, changes (and their consequences) which will be more salient by the highly interconnected information environment. As Stanley Hoffman has observed, "Globalization, far from spreading peace, thus seems to foster conflicts and resentments." Times of dramatic change, even when largely for the better, are often associated with political instability, as the more rapid progress of some as opposed to others gives rise to what Albert Hirschman dubbed the "tunnel effect" of changing expectations. This can be especially destabilizing if the winners are disproportionately represented by distinct regions, interests, or an identifiable minority group.[24]

Not surprisingly, given that American unipolarity has both extended the political influence and engagement of the United States throughout the world and also fostered the permissive environment in which globalization has flourished, disentangling globalization from

Americanization is not always easy or obvious, or for some, politically shrewd. As a result, some of the backlash against globalization finds its expression in anti-Americanism, as well as broader opposition to Western cultural and economic values. An increase in violent anti-American terrorism as a consequence of unipolarity and globalization captures this entire package. As Martha Crenshaw has argued, given U.S. support for regimes with embittered domestic oppositions, some terrorism can be seen "as a strategic reaction to American power in the context of globalized civil war" (a function of unipolarity), by forces "who appeal to Islamic values and have formed transnational ties and allegiances" (a political-strategic response to and tactical exploitation of globalization).[25]

Globalization can also affect the expression of violence and warfare. It may, for example, increase the likelihood of acts of terror designed to result in mass casualties. Terrorism practiced locally arguably faces an inverse U-shaped function regarding civilian casualties: initially, more casualties would translate into more attention and credibility, but at some threshold too many deaths could undermine indigenous support for the terrorist group and its goals. Globalized terrorist networks, on the other hand, can find sources of recruitment, financing, and legitimacy from areas outside their targets, removing one disincentive to avoid mass casualties.[26] More generally, Mary Kaldor argues that globalization has led to nothing less than a "revolution in the social relations of warfare." Rather than classical state-against-state warfare, weak states and information interconnectedness will combine to fuel movements that undermine the state from below, with smaller scale, open ended conflicts maintained by external support, criminal networks, and plunder. Collectively, the processes of globalization contribute to violent uprisings by making weak states weaker and creating opportunities that strengthen their armed opponents.[27]

Finally, the processes of globalization can affect the likelihood of war. The fragmentation of the production process and increased importance of "knowledge based economies" in the context of an international economy that is open to both trade and foreign direct investment has arguably reduced the gains from territorial conquest by limiting that which can be extracted by force and increasing that product which is more efficiently garnered though exchange rather than warfare.[28] As I will argue below, financial globalization also makes the resort to arms by states less likely (ceteris paribus) because the macroeconomic discipline demanded by world financial markets, lending institutions, and powerful credit agencies is incompatible with military adventurism. However, the previous discussion should make clear that once again, the logic of globalization does not cut uniformly in one direction. Globalization has arguably increased the incentives and opportunities for terrorism, exacerbated ethnic conflict, and left relatively weak states more vulnerable to attack from both within and without. In many settings, the ease of transnational communications and travel is less likely to bring people together than it is to set them apart—undermining national cohesion and identity from within and providing an impetus to violent insurgency and separatist movements.[29]

GLOBALIZATION—THREE CONDUITS OF TRANSMISSION

"Globalization" is shorthand for an array of phenomena defined above as the rise and influence of stateless and unorganized forces. But these pressures and their implications are not uniform. There are three distinct conduits that transmit the forces of globalization: those associated with the intensification of economic exchange—in the real economy production, trade, factor mobility, and, importantly and distinctly, on the monetary side of the economy, in world financial markets; the flow of information, with its implications for the state-society relations and new strategic threats such as cyberwarfare; and via marketization—the encroachment of the market sphere and the related pressures on cultural and identity politics (see Table 1.1).

EXCHANGE

Globalization is often thought of as first and foremost an economic phenomenon—the increase in the volume and intensity of cross-border market transactions. Once again, it should be noted that this observation does not rest on claims of novelty or irreversibility: borders still

Table 1.1 The Conduits of Globalization

Exchange	Information	Marketization
Increase in the volume and intensity of economic transactions	Increase in the ease, speed, and forms of communication	Increase in the range of activities governed by economic forces
Fragmentations of production; permeability of borders	Intelligence and cyberwarfare	Encroachment of the market sphere
Capital deregulation; crisis, rivalry, and war	Control, surveillance, and state–society relations	The market for identity

powerfully shape the pattern of economic exchange; capital mobility has been very high in the past; and, although people can travel great distances much more quickly than before, the nineteenth century witnessed more epoch-shaping waves of human traffic. Nevertheless, the past quarter century has witnessed the expansion of international commerce to a remarkable extent in both the real and the monetary sides of the economy, with significant consequences for national security.

The Fragmentation of Production and Trade

Levels of trade, cross-border investment, and production are not simply rising, they are also changing qualitatively in a manner that is contributing to the denationalization of production. In the permissive environment of globalization, firms have dramatically increased intrafirm international trade, joint ventures and alliances, and subcontracting to an extent that in many cases it is hard to characterize a large percentage of global trade and production as "international" given the blurring, melding, and fragmenting of much of the world's business enterprises. As Stephen Brooks has observed, of all the trends associated with globalization, the globalization of production "is the most historically unprecedented."[30] This matters in a general sense, as it again further challenges state autonomy with regard to the regulation of economic activity and also tends to complicate the pristine definition of the "national interest." It also compromises efforts at defense autonomy, complicates the practice of economic sanctions, and undermines strategic industrial targeting.

The easing of movements in the real economy also creates new challenges for states wishing to regulate illicit cross-border economic traffic. Under globalization it is more difficult to resist unwanted (from the perspective of the state) cross-border economic flows, including activities relating to human traffic (migration) and physical goods such as recreational drugs, guns, or other forbidden products. Given that these activities are largely outside the law they also attract and give rise to networks of organized criminal elements that can form transnational alliances, and that engage in "money laundering," the recycling of funds that illicitly finance their activities or are generated as profits from them.[31]

These extralegal creatures of globalization lend themselves quite naturally to the activities of violent organized nonstate political actors. Terrorists, for example, who also have money to circulate and launder, take full advantage of the global media environment—such as Web sites, faxes, and cell phones—employed by global business networks, and recognize opportunities to cooperate with transnational criminal enterprises. Ironically, while many terrorist networks articulate anti-globalization rhetoric, they are often "dependent on its financial and communications infrastructure." The al-Qaeda network, for example, "looked less like a cult of religious zealots than a far reaching and profitable business enterprise."[32]

Finance, Power, and War

The national security consequences of financial globalization are profound. They are also less well appreciated and merit special attention here for this reason. Although integrated world capital markets and financial globalization have arguably existed previously in history, such as in the decades preceding the First World War, nothing quite captures the frenzied interconnectedness of contemporary globalization quite the way the qualitative and quantitative explosion of world finance in the last quarter of the twentieth century does. In 1979, the daily turnover in world currency markets reached an unprecedented $100 billion; in 1989, it had quadrupled to $400 billion; and then sometime in the 1990s, daily turnover exceeded $1 trillion, after which, like McDonalds once they reached the "over 100 billion served" mark, there seemed little point in counting further. Other changes in international finance, less spectacular, are just as significant and more novel. Overseas investment funds, for example, principally pensions and insurance company holdings, were in 1995 valued at over $20 trillion, or more than the combined gross domestic product (GDP) of the Group of Seven (G7; Canada, France, Germany, Italy, Japan, the United Kingdom, and the United States).[33]

But the awesome power of financial markets does not imply the eclipsing of politics. To the contrary, finance is the political wolf lurking within the herd of economic sheep. Although all states generally have less macroeconomic policy autonomy than before and must be more sensitive to how their policy choices will be received by the world financial community, the business of finance remains concentrated in a few national centers, and the deregulation of capital was a purposeful, politically motivated process. The consequences of financial globalization speak to the balance of power, state autonomy and the prospects for political competition, and the likelihood of war.[34]

The Balance of Power and the Political Nonneutrality of Financial Crises Any brief survey of international finance under globalization makes clear that the system as a whole is crisis prone and that there is more, rather than less, politically consequential currency instability.[35]

The shift to a financial system where crises are unanticipated, more common, and spread more easily is even more notable given that it is not at all apparent that completely unregulated finance is economically efficient. As a noted champion of free trade, Jagdish Bhagwati, concluded, "the weight of evidence and the force of logic point in the opposite direction, toward restraints on capital flows."[36] Recent studies have supported Bhagwati's argument that there is no empirical evidence to support the contention that completely unregulated capital is the optimal policy, and that there are good reasons to be cautious about dismantling all controls that mediate the flow of capital. Capital account liberalization is associated with an increased likelihood of financial crisis, and such crises may occur even when the government is following "sound" policies.[37] And even when the market's response does reflect an identifiable need for discipline (a benefit of free capital markets often emphasized by proponents of liberalization), the market correction is likely to be inefficient—that is, "too much too late."[38]

Despite this, however, both the United States and the IMF aggressively promoted complete and comprehensive financial liberalization, even in the wake of spectacular and unanticipated disruptions such as the East Asian Financial Crisis. For although a world of completely unregulated capital is risky, it is relatively the least risky for the United States. Given the hegemonic position of the American economy, and with its deep and sound capital markets, the United States is likely to suffer less than others in an international financial crisis. In fact, it may attract capital during a crisis as investors "flee to quality." Thus the United States will bear a disproportionately small share of the costs from a system prone to financial crisis. And when crises do occur, given its resources and influence in international institutions such as the IMF, the United States can set conditions for those who seek help (or it can choose not to assist those in distress). As Susan Strange has argued, global financial integration has enhanced U.S. structural power at the expense of other states.[39]

All of these elements can be illustrated with the experience of Korea during the 1997 Asian Financial Crisis. After the crisis reached its shores, Korea received unprecedented financial support from the IMF. In exchange for that support, however, Korea agreed to a comprehensive set of conditions.[40] These conditions fell into two categories—one group of reforms was obviously related to the financial crisis—such as the restructuring, prudential regulation, and transparency of the banking and financial sector. But a second set of reforms demanded in exchange for IMF assistance—the elimination of ceilings on foreign holdings of bonds and equities, abolishing restrictions on foreign ownership of land, dismantling of trade barriers, acceleration of capital account liberalization, and a reduction on the restrictions on corporate borrowing abroad—were, as mainstream economists observed, clearly unrelated to the risk of financial crisis.[41]

Those IMF demands did include, however, many items that the United States had been pressing for unsuccessfully in bilateral negotiations over the course of several decades. Much to the consternation of the Americans, Korea had always restricted foreign direct investment (FDI) and also protected its financial service sector from foreign competition. U.S. export interests had also long been pressing for greater access to the Korean market, another requirement of the IMF agreement. The inclusion of these items as conditions of IMF support have been characterized as "a crude political power play," an assessment buttressed by the statements of senior U.S. official at the time.[42] As this episode illustrates, the benefits and burdens of financial globalization are not distributed uniformly throughout the system, but rather recast the distribution of power between states.

Autonomy, Currency Conflict, and Rivalry   Financial globalization (and unipolarity) will also increase conflicts between states that derive from the monetary competition between them. Ironically, the relative increase in U.S. power as expressed in the shift from bipolarity to unipolarity has increased generally the likelihood of economic conflict among the former participants in the anti-Soviet coalition: the United States, Western Europe, and Japan. The source of this emerging conflict is often misattributed; especially with regard to monetary cooperation, it is not that U.S. hegemony at the center of a stable Cold War–alliance system allowed the Americans in particular to disregard concerns for "relative gains." The pursuit of relative gains is not a function of anarchy, but rather it is virtually inherent in the process of negotiation between civil parties within states where there can be no plausible link back to fears of anarchy.[43] Rather, during the Cold War, shared concerns for security provided an emergency brake on the economic conflict—all sides had strong incentives not to let such conflicts get out of hand lest they undermine crucial military alliances. Without this fear to rein in behavior, economic conflicts will become more uninhibited.

Financial globalization, in particular the pressures it generates for macroeconomic convergence and the reduction of policy autonomy, coupled with the greater financial instability noted above, creates incentives for states that issue currencies used internationally to cultivate spheres of monetary influence, enhancing, to some extent, their autonomy and discretion. Smaller states will likely associate with one currency group following political and regional patterns of trade logics to minimize fluctuations in exchange values that would disrupt trade. Given globalization, it is highly unlikely that arrangements will be closed and discriminatory[44] but these arrangements will have political consequences and shape axes of potential conflict.

The formation of the euro as well as increased discussion within Japan about whether the time has come to push for a larger role for the yen as an international currency reflect these new realities.[45] Since the late 1980s, Japan had harbored aspirations to a greater leadership role in international monetary affairs, in order to enhance its international influence but also to circumscribe U.S. monetary power.[46] These ambitions were put on the back burner with Japan's sustained economic malaise in the 1990s, but the Asian financial crisis created both an opportunity and an incentive to revisit the question of the internationalization of the yen and Japan's monetary leadership in Asia more broadly. Encouraging other states in Asia to link to the yen rather than to the dollar, advocates argue, will afford greater stability to the region and "promote the national interests of Japan." Such a push would also promote Tokyo as a financial center and enhance the international position of Japan's financial institutions.[47] These objectives reflect reactions to both unipolarity and financial globalization—yen internationalization and Asian monetary leadership would circumscribe American power and hold the promise of greater insulation from global financial instability.[48]

The most celebrated (and ill-fated) outcome of Japan's new assertiveness was Tokyo's proposal, floated in the summer of 1997, for an Asian Monetary Fund (AMF). The concept was never fully developed but would have been bankrolled by $50 billion from Japan with an additional $50 billion in contributions from other Asian countries and, crucially, would have provided emergency assistance to Asian states facing financial crisis loans without the types of conditions associated with IMF assistance.[49]

Leaders in both Tokyo and Washington understood that the stakes over the AMF were more geopolitical than economic—an effort to expand Japan's influence in the region at the expense of U.S. interests. Thus the Japanese Ministry of Finance quietly coordinated its proposal exclusively with other Asian nations, leaving the United States to be "caught by surprise" by the plan, which only heightened the tensions— as one account stated simply, "American officials were enraged."[50] In the end, the original AMF proposal never got very far—most importantly due to "heated" and "vehement" U.S. opposition.[51] But other factors played a role as well, including the strong opposition of China. Beijing also interpreted the AMF proposal in geopolitical terms. Pursuing its own strategy of expanding political influence through the cultivation of economic ties, China saw the AMF as an effort by Japan to assert regional leadership at the expense of its chief Asian rival.[52]

The demise of the AMF proposal did not end Japan's increased interest in asserting monetary leadership, and Tokyo has continued to play a more active role in the region's financial arrangements.[53] Similarly, the ambitions of some in Europe for the euro "to challenge the U.S. dollar as the currency of choice" are more likely to gather rather than lose momentum. Experts debate how well suited the euro is to challenge the dollar as the "world's currency," and whether or not the euro will be able to compete with the dollar for influence in the near term as opposed to the long run. However, as Martin Feldstein has argued, there is "no doubt" that the real rationale for European Monetary Union (EMU) is "political, not economic," as the aggregation of European resources provides some insulation from global instability, and holds the potential of offering an essential element to any political counterweight to the United States. This will become increasingly important if the divergent foreign policy visions of the European Union and the United States create increasingly greater political space between the two entities.[54]

Finance and War—The High Politics of Low Inflation   Finally, financial globalization will also affect the likelihood of war generally in the international system by creating a new disincentive for states to risk both militarized crises and war.[55] This is because all states are now more beholden to the preferences of the "international financial community," which is simply another phrase for the power of "financial globalization"—the consequences of the collective behavior of thousands of individual agents making their best informed guesses about the future value and attractiveness of various paper assets such as national currencies. How are these guesses formed? What does finance want? Simply put, low inflation and policies designed to keep inflation low, balanced government budgets, attractive real interest rates, open and unfettered interaction with international financial markets, and relative strength and stability in the exchange rate. These policies protect the value of financial assets, signal to observers that the government is committed to preserving the value of those assets in the future, and provide an environment in which finance is able to profit and thrive.

But war and policies that risk war threaten every aspect of this macroeconomic environment. The expansion of government spending and risk of inflation, depreciation, and disruption of international financial relations that accompanies measures that risk war are more likely to result in punishing capital flight and downgrading of creditworthiness by international agencies. None of this, to be clear, prevents states from initiating international conflicts. But financial globalization does, ceteris paribus, raise both the costs and opportunity costs of choosing such a path. Additionally, this also suggests that states with a greater sensitivity to the interests of finance, both at home and abroad, will be more inhibited by these concerns than states that are not, another mechanism via which globalization can affect the pattern of global military disputes.

INFORMATION AND THE HYPERMEDIA ENVIRONMENT

Along with financial globalization, the information revolution and the associated vision of a "global village" linked by communications technology is the most common signifier of globalization. There have been information revolutions in the past—and now, as then, this transformation has profound consequences for both military security and state power as it relates to state-society relations.[56]

Security and Cyberwarfare

The increasing importance of the Internet, and of information technology more generally, also begs the question of how warfare itself might be changed. Information dominance—for intelligence, surveillance, reconnaissance, and real-time military operations—enhances the relative power of great powers and especially of the United States, which enjoys considerable advantages in these areas.[57] At the same time, both civilian and military dependence on computers and other forms of information technology may raise new vulnerabilities. Techniques of cyberwarfare are understandably attractive to belligerents at war, insurgencies, and separatist movements, as well as terrorists.[58]

Russia, India, China, and the United States are the states most commonly mentioned as "rapidly developing" cyberwar capacities, with several others also revealing some interest. The hope that such techniques might be able to disrupt military command and control is especially appealing to many states in a unipolar world with its teched-up superpower; China in particular is cited for its interest in cybertactics as a strategy of asymmetric warfare. The governments of Indonesia, Sri Lanka, and Mexico have each reportedly had their computer systems attacked by insurgents. In theory, at least, the United States looks vulnerable to cyberterrorism—the department of defense uses two million computers and operates more than 10,000 local area networks; the computers associated with the air traffic system would presumably also offer a tempting target. More vulnerable in practice might be "softer" civilian systems—the disruption of communications nodes, power grids, or financial systems all dependent on computer networks would not likely cause permanent harm to the economy, but they could advance the political objectives of terrorist groups and might effectively be combined with more violent operations. Captured al-Qaeda computers did reveal plans to attack the computer systems of "critical infrastructure" such as dams and power grids.[59]

The disruptive effects of information warfare by terrorists or insurgent groups, however, will likely be of less sustained significance than the political and military opportunities and vulnerabilities created by the hypermedia environment. It is now necessary to factor in the information environment to accurately assess state power, capacity, and international relations. As with globalized finance, the consequences for national security will be seen more in the recasting and redistribution of state power than in its diminution.

Communication Control and State-Society Relations

The proliferation of communications technology also points to a larger set of questions about the role of information in defining the relationship between state and society. In the late 1970s, fundamentalist opponents of the shah of Iran combined state of the art media technology—mass-produced audio cassette tapes and photocopy machines—to spread Khomeini's revolutionary messages. Thousands of tapes distributed through bazaars and other social and religious networks proved untraceable and irrepressible, as were British Broadcasting Corporation (BBC) radio reports that limited the government's information monopoly. These technologies were understood to undermine the state's authoritarian control and to have contributed to the shah's overthrow.[60]

When the shah left Iran for the last time, there was no Cable News Network (CNN), no Internet, no fax machines, no cell phones—in retrospect, it is remarkable how much has changed in a relatively short period of time. It is not unreasonable to assume that if the power of the state to control information was receding way back in the stone age of the 1970s, it must be almost completely withered away by now, with predictable consequences for state autonomy and capacity. However, as Geoffrey Herrera has argued, although the new media environment does challenge state power, a number of factors as yet still unknown will determine the balance of power between states, firms, and individuals. Much depends on choices of technology, which will define the general properties of a "mature digital information network" that will fall between two idealized types: one that is open, universal, and anonymous, the other fragmented, proprietary, and monitored.[61]

Thus, even if the state is on the high-tech ropes it is not yet down, furthermore, some aspects of these technologies will relatively enhance state power; and presumably states—as motivated, resourceful institutions—will engage proactively the new information environment with a keen sense of interest and strategy. Rather than sit passively, states can take measures designed to protect their own information space and to try and influence media structures outside of their own borders. Once again, the redistribution of power between various states based on these efforts is at least as important for international relations as any general erosion of state power that occurs. The control of key orbital slots, for example, can affect what types of satellite transmissions will be seen where. The government of Singapore has taken this one step further, envisioning a cable system so modern and comprehensive that satellite could not hope to compete with it—as a wired society is much easier to monitor and control than a wireless one. Iran, Burma, and Malaysia share Singapore's strategy of banning private ownership of satellite dishes—though in all cases these efforts have met with mixed success.[62]

The Internet in particular is seen as a threat to the state, empowering opposition groups. Political opponents of the Suharto regime in Indonesia, for example, used both Web sites and e-mail lists to communicate with supporters, rally international support, and organize forms of resistance. Other insurgent movements in Burma and Mexico have employed these tactics.[63] But the power of the Internet cuts both ways—states can employ both reactive and proactive strategies for addressing the challenges raised by the Internet. Reactive strategies involve restrictions on Internet use, filters to block proscribed sites, and, perhaps most significantly, monitoring. Monitoring is relatively easy, and at the same time difficult to detect, which could offer an effective incentive for individuals to self-censor their own behavior. Chillingly, states can also employ technology to track what sites specific computers have visited. Proactive strategies include using the Internet as a conduit for government authority, information, and propaganda, as well as the construction of closed, government run national intranets. Many authoritarian regimes have employed these techniques successfully.[64]

The hypermedia environment, which tends to "unbundle" and "deterritorialize" information flows, allows social movements with goals different from or in direct opposition to authorities the ability to communicate, coordinate, and promote their interests to a greater extent than in the past. But governments throughout history have found ways to dominate most forms of mass media, even those that appeared revolutionary at the time (such as the telegraph, telephone, mass circulation newspaper, radio, and television). Technology has made it possible for governments to track and monitor individuals to an unprecedented extent—through surveillance, data collection, telecommunications intercepts, and more—yet they are less able to control the access to and flow of information than ever before. Two sets of tensions will influence the ultimate rebalancing of power between states, firms, and individuals: as already discussed, technological choices (such as wires or wireless), but also, the classic dilemma of the state to balance its concerns for security with its needs to ensure adequate economic growth, the very foundation of future state power. Unlike some other authoritarian regimes, for example, China is promoting the use of the Internet as an essential part of its strategy of liberalization and the need to enhance international competitiveness. Negotiating the pursuit of wealth and power—inextricably linked in the long run but often competing in the short run—is a dilemma that does not derive from globalization, but is further complicated by it.[65]

MARKETIZATION

The least appreciated conduit of globalization is the way social relations themselves are affected by marketization—the consequence not simply of more powerful markets, but of economic forces reshaping a broader range of human activity. New challenges for state autonomy and national security emerge as the market sphere expands; new axes of conflict are created as market forces disrupt non-market-based forms of human organization and challenge both interests and identities.

The Encroachment of the Market Sphere

The tension between market and authority is nothing new; indeed, it rests at the core of all inquires into political economy, even in closed economy "desert island" fables. States have a value-conscious vision of economic exchange and may proscribe activities such as gambling or the sale of sex and alcohol; regulate the employment of child labor; and set limits on some prices, such as minimum wages or rent controls. Markets, on the other hand, are indifferent to such preferences; they are efficient, amoral, and remarkably sensitive to changes in supply and demand. Thus, authority and market are to some extent inherently in tension. Globalization, however, greatly complicates matters, as the legal authority of the state stops at the border, which is itself a political invention of little inherent interest to market forces.

Globalization not only affects the static balance in this continuous tug-of-war between market and authority, it also produces an environment conducive to the expansion of the market sphere.[66] This is an extremely important distinction—this chapter has considered the intensity of economic exchange—the remarkable fragmentation of production and trade, and the breathtaking growth in the size and swiftness of global capital markets. But marketization is not about *how much* is exchanged; it is about *what* is up for sale. This is a distinct phenomenon, and one not really about "economics" but rather more about society and politics, and thus in many ways is an even more politically charged consequence of globalization.

The assessment of what spheres of human exchange are appropriately supervised by the market (say, the price of cars, advertising rates, or movie stars' salaries) and what is not (grades in school, literary awards, or human organ donations) differs to some extent from one society to another, but both within and between political communities these can be hotly contested political boundaries. These boundaries also shift over time. Once upon a time, for example, television network news divisions were understood to be outside the market sphere; as part of the public service responsibility of broadcasting, typically the news division was simply assigned a budget and it was assumed that the news would lose money. Nowadays, network news programs are expected to make money, and in some cases are increasingly understood and organized as another form of entertainment.[67]

The encroachment of the market also surfaces in the realm of security, as the same incentives, pressures for efficiency, and economies of scale faced by the producers of consumer goods are felt by defense contractors, and with similar results. The commercialization and globalization of the defense industry will likely interfere with efforts to stem the proliferation of some types of conventional weapons, and the diffusion of military technology could provide an advantage to smaller states resisting the military operations of great powers.[68]

Additionally, marketization has even contributed to the privatization of defense itself, with more functions of military security subcontracted to the private sector or even subcontracted to foreign suppliers. A number of factors have contributed to the rise of the "privatized military industry"—the end of the Cold War left a surplus of small (and not so small) arms on the market, not to mention the downsizing of armed forces. Low intensity warfare, highly specialized expertise, and reduced government capacity in weak states have also created conditions ripe for the rise of this industry. Such marketization, as Deborah Avant has argued, "almost inevitably redistributes power over the control of violence both within governments and between states and non-state actors."[69]

The Market for Identity

Related to the encroachment of the market sphere are the consequences of and reactions to the tendency for globalization to be associated with the expansion of Western culture and cultural values and of Western economic values, such as consumerism. There are throughout the world (and, it should be noted, within the "west" itself) numerous anticonsumerist philosophies, which are not enchanted with and are to some extent threatened by the materialism that often accompanies globalization.[70] As a result, some of these movements "have become sources of resistance and alternatives to materialism." To be sure, this antimarket resentment is often manipulated by powerful vested interests seeking to resist implementing political and economic reforms.[71] But this in no way diminishes the fact that the perceived encroachment of consumerist culture as transmitted by globalization represents an important political fault line in world politics.

The perceived globalization of Western economic values and especially of consumerism are consequential not solely for their economic implications: The forces of globalization, especially as they are transmitted through global communications networks, are also on balance conduits of Western cultural values. The political and potential security implications of these influences and the resistance to them should not be underestimated. There are circumstances under which increased cultural contact can contribute to disharmony rather than to greater mutual understanding and respect.[72]

American and Western cultural dominance can be exaggerated, as a result of the global dominance of Hollywood. But mass entertainment films have very high fixed costs and the industry is sensitive to economies of both scope and scale, factors that have contributed to U.S. dominance in cinema that do not necessarily extend to the same extent to other entertainment outlets. Even in some markets where American films dominate (such as the larger Latin American economies), despite privatization, liberalization, and deregulation, local and regional television programming can do quite well. Local music still dominates world markets, and American books do not share the same success of

Hollywood movies, even in relatively small, close, culturally similar Canada. Furthermore, technological changes such as digital film technology may lower costs of production (and higher fixed costs are in general associated with the concentration of production), suggesting that technological change and the diffusion of technology via the processes of globalization might cut against American and Western advantages in this area. Finally, it should be noted that globalized entertainment is a two-way street—Hollywood studios now earn half of their income from foreign markets, and the need to be attentive to how a product will sell abroad shapes the product. As in other spheres, the United States is not immune from the forces of globalization, even in sectors where it enjoys the greatest comparative advantages.[73]

However, these important observations simply qualify rather than undercut arguments about the significance of contemporary media, entertainment, and information flows. The entertainment industry is a large and growing sector: In the United States, 5.4 percent of household spending—almost $500 billion—is devoted to entertainment. Globally the media industry is dominated by about ten Western (mostly American) vertically integrated media conglomerates.[74] The greater permeability of all societies to foreign cultural products, and, as a consequence, of foreign cultural values, remains a consequence of globalization, and one that can be an important source of conflict within and between societies. Satellite transmission of news and television programs is extremely difficult to curtail. China banned the private ownership of satellites in 1990; but in 1994, there were estimated to be over 11 million households that owned dishes, providing access for over 30 million people to Rupert Murdoch's Star TV. Iran's legendary love-hate relationship with the TV show *Baywatch*—condemned by authority, beloved by millions—is admittedly amusing, but that which is perceived as an affront to critical sensibility in the West is nevertheless an affront to cultural values elsewhere, and, more seriously, is suggestive of more significant underlying political issues. Even though satellite dishes are banned in Iran, they sell in the black market for as little as $400.[75]

What is at stake here is not good taste, however sobering it may be to learn that in the mid-1990s, *Baywatch* was seen in 144 countries with a reputed following of one billion viewers.[76] Rather, it is that the process of marketization and the challenges posed to competing value systems create new axes for international conflict. Global television viewing, which has been increasing for decades, continues to expand at a rapid pace; TV shows tend to be supported by advertising that is implicitly (or perhaps explicitly) associated with the values of secular capitalism: universalism, materialism, and consumerism.[77] But many national, social, and cultural movements have competing core values and can view these challenges with great alarm. Religion is an obvious example of this—as Timur Kuran has argued, otherwise diverse faiths, such as Hinduism, Buddhism, Christianity, and Islamism, all share "a common aspiration to ground economic prescriptions in normative religious sources" and "insist on the inseparability of economics from other realms of human activity"; these aspirations, of course, represent the very antithesis of marketization. It is therefore not surprising that many religious movements, to varying extents, see themselves as pushing back against globalization; or that those who see themselves as marginalized by or victims of globalization increasingly find antiglobalist identity politics appealing.[78] These forces contribute to the formation of new axes of contemporary political conflicts and help reconstitute the configuration of political coalitions, in ways that are not readily apparent until the influences of globalization are put on the table.

NATIONAL SECURITY IN A GLOBALIZED WORLD

A self-reinforcing triumvirate: a politically permissive environment, economic liberalization, and technological change, have unleashed powerful forces of globalization—unorganized, stateless pressures— that have important consequences for national security, however narrowly defined. It is not necessary to argue that contemporary globalization is unprecedented, irreversible, or irresistible, or that it will inevitably lead to the demise of the state, to reach this conclusion. It is simply to recognize that the intensification of economic exchange, the information revolution, and pressures for marketization are changing (though not always diminishing) the nature of state power and state capacity, affecting the balance of power between states, and creating new sources of and axes of conflict between them. Baseball and basketball are both zero-sum games played by self-interested teams seeking victory. But it is crucial to know which game is being played to understand the strategies chosen and course and even likely outcomes of the competition. The world's greatest basketball player, after all, turned out to be a mediocre double-A baseball player.

The next section of this book contains three chapters that consider more closely some aspects of the "processes" of globalization—exchange, information, and marketization. Fiona B. Adamson (chapter 2) considers one element of economic exchange, migration, in the context of a much broader discussion of the consequences of increased human mobility for issues of national security. Geoffrey L. Herrera (chapter 3) looks closely and carefully at the political ramifications of the new information technologies—which actors gain greater political advantage and why—and the way in which state power and international relations are being reshaped by these changes. Deborah Avant (chapter 4) offers an illustration of marketization inextricably bound with security: the privatization of force, a phenomenon with great contemporary practical relevance that is at the same time a harbinger of sustained, systematic consequences for the use of force more generally.

This section is then followed by six chapters that address specific countries or regions. These contributions address a myriad of issues relating to globalization and national security, but they link extensively with each other, and draw upon the introductory chapter and the process chapters, illustrating the core shared themes of the volume as a whole. Karl P. Mueller's analysis (chapter 5) of the United States explores further the relationship between globalization and unipolarity, an issue that then resurfaces repeatedly in subsequent chapters. Marc Lynch's discussion (chapter 6) on the Middle East engages not only marketization and migration, but shares, with Adam Segal's analysis (chapter 10) of China, the issue of how authoritarian regimes confront the challenges posed by the hypermedia environment. Alexander Cooley's consideration (chapter 7) of the former Soviet space mines the intersection of processes raised by Avant and Adamson and illustrates the consequences of globalization's tendency to erode the difference between legitimate and illicit exchange and between formal and informal institutional authority.

Over the course of the pages that follow, all of the chapters combine and recombine with each other, intersecting across different dimensions. Rachel Epstein (chapter 8) on Europe and Paul Midford (chapter 9) on Japan, for example, each address the issue of economies of scale and defense production, which in turn relate to themes raised in Segal's chapter on China. But in other passages, these chapters part company and find linkages elsewhere: Epstein's emphasis on the political stakes for Europe returns to the question of American preponderance; Midford's emphasis on Japan's quest for autonomy revisits the financial diplomacy raised in the introduction; while Segal observes the unique way in which China faces globalization as both a great power and a developing state. More generally, a variety of commonalities and touchstones are explored by each of the authors in their respective chapters. In the conclusion, the central themes of the volume are reintroduced in the context of those contributions, and future prospects are considered.

NOTES

1. For representative entry points into this vast literature, see David Held, Anthony McGrew, David Goldblatt, and Jonathan Perraton, *Global Transformations: Politics, Economics and Culture* (Palo Alto, CA: Stanford University Press, 1999); Jan Aart Scholte, *Globalization: A Critical Introduction* (New York: Palgrave, 2000); John Micklethwait and Adrian Wooldridge, *A Future Perfect: The Challenge and Hidden Promise of Globalization* (New York: Crown Business, 2000).
2. Kenneth Waltz, "Globalization and Governance," *PS: Political Science and Politics* 32(4) (December 1999): 693–700; Robert Gilpin, *Global Political Economy: Understanding the International Economic Order* (Princeton, NJ: Princeton University Press, 2001), especially 362–376; Thomas Friedman, *The Lexus and the Olive Tree: Understanding Globalization*, rev. ed. (New York: Anchor Books, 2000); Kenichi Ohmae, *Invisible Continent: Four Strategic Imperatives of the New Economy* (New York: Harper Collins, 2000).
3. This, in the terminology of Held et al. in *Global Transformations*, is a "transformalist" perspective, which is contrasted with the "hyperglobalist" and "skeptical" theses.
4. These definitions are not introduced with the claim that other definitions are untenable; indeed, there are a number of reasonable ways to define globalization, which is why it is necessary to be especially clear about the one that will be used here.
5. On interdependence, see for example Robert Keohane and Joseph Nye, *Power and Interdependence: World Politics in Transition* (Boston: Little Brown, 1977); Edward D. Mansfield and Brian M. Pollins, eds., *Economic Interdependence and International Conflict: New Perspectives on an Enduring Debate* (Ann Arbor: University of Michigan Press, 2003).
6. Note that, as discussed below, this need not imply "globalization rules": France's socialists had the option, and debated seriously, of imposing a broader system of comprehensive controls to stem the crisis without reversing policy. But it was decided that costs of this (possibly unraveling a set of larger European agreements) were too high. See Michael Loriaux, *France After Hegemony: International Change and Financial Reform* (Ithaca, NY: Cornell University Press, 1991); Jeffrey Sachs and Charles Wyplosz, "The Economic Consequences of President Mitterrand," *Economic Policy* (April 1986): 262–306.
7. Jonathan Kirshner, "Political Economy in Security Studies After the Cold War," *Review of International Political Economy* 5(1) (Spring 1998): 73–74, 78–79.
8. There is a growing literature on the meaning and implications of contemporary unipolarity. A good starting point is G. John Ikenberry, ed., *America Unrivaled: The Future of the Balance of Power* (Ithaca, NY: Cornell University Press, 2002); see also Stephen Brooks and William Wolforth, "American Primacy in Perspective," *Foreign Affairs* 81(4) (July–August, 2002): 20–33.
9. For a good discussion of these issues, see Joseph S. Nye, Jr., "Neorealism and Neoliberalism," *World Politics* 40(2) (January 1988): especially 235, 242, 243.
10. On the policy preferences of the Bush administration, see "The National Security Strategy of the United States of America," the White House, Washington, D.C., September 2002, www.whitehouse.gov/nsc/nss.html. Note, for example, those foreign policies of the Bush administration that would not have been introduced by would-be President Gore are attributable to unpredictable quirks in the American electoral process and not to systemic imperatives.
11. On this point more generally, see Peter Katzenstein, *A World of Regions: Asia and Europe* (Ithaca, NY: Cornell University Press, 2005).

12. Eric Helleiner, *States and the Reemergence of Global Finance* (Princeton, NJ: Princeton University Press, 1994; cf. John Goodman and Louis Pauly, "The Obsolescence of Capital Controls? Economic Management in the Age of Global Markets," *World Politics* 46(1) (1993): 50–82; Monroe E. Price, *Media and Sovereignty: The Global Information Revolution and Its Challenge to State Power* (Cambridge, MA: MIT Press, 2002), 227, 230.

13. Peter Beinart, "An Illusion for our Time: The False Promise of Globalization," *The New Republic*, October 20, 1997, 20 (quote).

14. Jean-Marie Guehenno, "The Impact of Globalization on Strategy," *Survival* 40(4) (Winter 1998–99): 16 (quote).

15. Harold James, *The End of Globalization: Lessons from the Great Depression* (Cambridge, MA: Harvard University Press, 2001); Kevin H. O'Rourke and Jeffrey G. Williamson, *Globalization and History: The Evolution of a Nineteenth Century Atlantic Economy* (Cambridge, MA: MIT Press, 1999). It is worth noting, on the other hand, that similar "levels" of globalization can be of different qualitative significance. See Michael Bordo, Barry Eichengreen, and Douglas Irwin, "Is Globalization Today Really Different than Globalization a Hundred Years Ago?", NBER Working Paper No. 7195 (Cambridge, MA: NBER, 1999).

16. For example, states may be less able to rely on monetary policy and more dependent on fiscal policy.

17. See the various essays in "Searching for Security in a Global Economy," *Daedalus* 120(4) (Fall 1991).

18. Charlotte Twight, *Watching You: Systematic Federal Surveillance of Ordinary Americans*, Cato Institute Briefing Papers No. 69 (Washington, DC: Cato Institute, 2001); David Lyon, "Editorial. Surveillance Studies: Understanding Visibility, Mobility and the Phenetic Fix," *Surveillance and Society* 1(1) (2002): 1–7.

19. Price, *Media and Sovereignty*, 3.

20. Ronald J. Deibert, *Parchment, Printing and Hypermedia: Communication in World Order Transformation* (New York: Columbia University Press, 1997), 2, 67 (first quote), 137, 142 (second quote). Deibert also explores the ways in which changes in the modes of communication change elements of collective mentality, or the "web of beliefs" (see, e.g., 36, 38, 95, and 177ff.), an important consideration not emphasized here.

21. As Deibert argues, "Such an environment clearly favors those security arrangements … that are open to the outside world while disadvantaging those … premised on closure." Ibid., 174.

22. Clement M. Henry and Robert Springborg, *Globalization and the Politics of Development in the Middle East* (Cambridge: Cambridge University Press, 2001), 100, 121, 127, 134, 161, 192–193. Henry and Springborg present these challenges more starkly, arguing "the danger to a bunker economy is that adjustment to the global economy, however necessary, will undermine it," 122.

23. See Jonathan Kirshner, "The Inescapable Politics of Money," in Jonathan Kirshner, ed., *Monetary Orders: Ambiguous Economics, Ubiquitous Politics* (Ithaca, NY: Cornell University Press, 2003).

24. Stanley Hoffman, "Clash of Globalizations," *Foreign Affairs* 81(4) (July/August 2002): 111; Audrey Kurth Cronin, "Behind the Curve: Globalization and International Terrorism," *International Security* 27(3) (Winter 2002/03): 53; Albert O. Hirschman, "The Changing Tolerance for Income Inequality in the Course of Economic Development," *Quarterly Journal of Economics* 87(4) (November 1973): 544–566. For the argument that market liberalization and democracy contribute to ethnic instability and violence in many developing states with "market-dominant-minorities," see

Amy Chua, *World on Fire: How Exporting Free Market Democracy Breeds Ethnic Hatred and Global Instability* (New York: Anchor, 2004), especially 10, 16, 125, 132.

25. Martha Crenshaw, "Why America? The Globalization of Civil War," *Current History* 100 (December 2001), 425 (quote), 429 (quote); see also Michael T. Clare, "Waging Post-Industrial Warfare on the Global Battlefield," *Current History* (December 2001): 435, 437; Cronin, "Behind the Curve," 53.

26. Martha Crenshaw and Maryann Cusimano Love, "Networked Terror," in *Beyond Sovereignty: Issues for a Global Agenda,* ed. Maryann Cusimano Love, 2nd ed. (Belmont, CA: Wadsworth/Thomson, 2003), 127.

27. Mary Kaldor, *New and Old Wars: Organized Violence in a Globalized Era* (Palo Alto, CA: Stanford University Press, 2001), 2, 3 (quote), 9, 90, 110; see also John Mackinlay, *Globalization and Insurgency,* Adelphi Paper 352 (London: International Institute for Strategic Studies, 2002), 27.

28. Stephen G. Brooks, "The Globalization of Production and the Changing Benefits of Conquest," *Journal of Conflict Resolution* 43(5) (October 1999): 646–670. Cf. Peter Liberman, *Does Conquest Pay: The Exploitation of Occupied Industrial Societies* (Princeton, NJ: Princeton University Press, 1996).

29. "Because of globalization, terrorists have access to more powerful techniques, more targets, more territory, more means of recruitment, and more exploitable sources of rage than ever before," Cronin, "Behind the Curve," 53; see also Hoffman, "Clash of Globalizations," 112. On globalization and separatism, see Walter Connor, "Nation-Building or Nation-Destroying?" *World Politics* 24(3) (April 1972): 329; also Kaldor, *New and Old Wars,* 4, 70, 110; Chua, *World on Fire,* 187; Mackinlay, *Globalization and Insurgency,* 93.

30. Brooks, "The Globalization of Production," 654; Deibert, *Parchment, Printing and Hypermedia,* 26.

31. See Peter Andreas, *Border Games: Policing the US-Mexico Divide* (Ithaca, NY: Cornell University Press, 2001); Saskia Sassen, *Globalization and Its Discontents: Essays on the New Mobility of People and Money* (New York: New Press, 1998), sec. I, 3–76; Susan Strange, *Mad Money: When Markets Outgrow Governments* (Ann Arbor: University of Michigan Press, 1998), chap. 7, 97–122.

32. Crenshaw and Love, "Networked Terror," 127–128; Kaldor, *New and Old Wars,* 2, 9, 105; Clare, "Waging Post-Industrial Warfare," 437 (first quote); Crenshaw, "Why America," 431 (second quote).

33. Ron Martin, "Stateless Monies, Global Financial Integration and National Economic Autonomy: The End of Geography?" in *Money, Power and Space,* eds. Stuart Corbridge, Ron Martin, and Nigel Thrift (Oxford: Blackwell, 1994), 258, 260; Herbert Dieter, "World Economy—Structures and Trends," in *Global Trends and Global Governance,* eds. Paul Kennedy, Dirk Messner, and Franz Nuscheler (London: Pluto Press, 2002), 71–72; J. Carter Beese Jr., "U.S. Capital Markets Leadership in the Changing Global Economy," in *Economic Strategy and National Security: A Next Generation Approach,* ed. Patrick J. DeSouza (Boulder, CO: Westview Press, 2000), 189; see also Susan Roberts, "Fictitious Capital, Fictitious Spaces: the Geography of Offshore Financial Flows," also in Corbridge, Martin, and Thrift, *Money, Power and Space.* On previous episodes of financial globalization, see O'Rourke and Williamson, *Globalization and History,* 213–223, and Robert Zevin, "Are World Financial Markets More Open? If So Why and With What Effects," in *Financial Openness and National Autonomy: Opportunities and Constraints,* eds. Tariq Banuri and Juliet B. Schor (Oxford: Clarendon Press, 1992).

34. Martin, "Stateless Monies," 255, 264, 271, 274; see also Helleiner, *States and the Reemergence of Global Finance;* Kirshner, "The Inescapable Politics of Money."
35. See for example Barry Eichengreen, *Financial Crises* (Oxford: Oxford University Press, 2002); John Eatwell and Lance Taylor, *Global Finance at Risk* (New York: The New Press, 2000); Alexandre Lamfalussy, *Financial Crises in Emerging Markets: An Essay on Financial Globalisation and Fragility* (New Haven, CT: Yale University Press, 2002).
36. Jagdish Bhagwati, "The Capital Myth," *Foreign Affairs* 77(3) (May/June 1998): 9, 12 (quote); Dani Rodrik, "Who Needs Capital Account Convertibility?" in *Should the IMF Pursue Capital Account Convertibility?* ed. Peter Kenen, Essays in International Finance, International Finance 207 (Princeton, NJ: Princeton University Press, 1998), 61; Richard N. Cooper, "Should Capital Controls Be Banished?," *Brookings Papers on Economic Activity* 1 (1999): 99; also Cooper, "Should Capital Account Convertibility Be a World Objective?" in Kenen, *Should the IMF Pursue Capital Account Convertibility?*
37. Mark Blyth, "The Political Power of Financial Ideas: Transparency, Risk and Distribution in Global Finance," in Kirshner, *Monetary Orders.*
38. John Williamson and Molly Mahar, *A Survey of Financial Liberalization,* Essays in International Finance 211 (Princeton, NJ: Princeton University Press, 1998); Ariel Buria, *An Alternative Approach to Financial Crises,* Essays in International Finance 212 (Princeton, NJ: Princeton University Press, 1999); Thomas D. Willett, *International Financial Markets as Sources of Crises or Discipline: The Too Much Too Late Hypothesis,* Essays in International Finance 218 (Princeton, NJ: Princeton University Press, 2000).
39. Blyth, "The Political Power of Financial Ideas"; Jonathan Kirshner, "Explaining Choices About Money: Disentangling Power, Ideas and Conflict," and Ilene Grabel, "Ideology, Power and the Rise of Independent Monetary Institutions in Emerging Economies," both in Kirshner, *Monetary Orders;* Susan Strange, "Finance, Information and Power," *Review of International Studies* 16(3) (July 1990), reprinted in *Authority and Markets: Susan Strange's Writings on International Political Economy,* eds. Roger Tooze and Christopher May (New York: Palgrave Macmillan, 2002), 71, 79.
40. See Uk Heo, "South Korea: Democratization, Financial Crisis, and the Decline of the Developmental State," in *The Political Economy of International Financial Crises: Interest Groups, Ideologies, Institutions,* eds. Shale Horowitz and Uk Heo (London: Rowman and Littlefield, 2001); see also Kiseok Hong and Jong-Wha Lee, "Korea: Returning to Sustainable Growth?" in *The Asian Financial Crisis: Lessons for a Resilient Asia,* eds. Wing Thye Woo, Jeffrey Sachs, and Klaus Schwab (Cambridge, MA: MIT Press, 2000).
41. Martin Feldstein argued the Korean economy, "an economy to envy," was suffering from a crisis of "temporary illiquidity rather than fundamental insolvency" in "Refocusing the IMF," *Foreign Affairs* 77(2) (1998): 24, 27, 32; W. Max Corden concurred, noting that the second category of IMF demands would not "either help resolve the crisis or prevent a future one." ("The World Financial Crisis: Are the IMF Prescriptions Right?" in Horowitz and Heo, *The Political Economy of International Financial Crisis,* 59).
42. Joseph E. Stiglitz, "Failure of the Fund: Rethinking the IMF Response," *Harvard International Review* 23 (2) (Summer 2001): 17 (quote), 18. See also Robert Gilpin, *The Challenge of Global Capitalism: The World Economy in the 21st Century* (Princeton, NJ: Princeton University Press, 2000), 157, 159; John A. Mathews, "Fashioning a New Korean Model out of the Crisis: The Rebuilding of Institutional Capabilities," *Cambridge Journal of Economics* 22 (1998): 752; Donald Kirk, *Korean Crisis: Unraveling of the Miracle in the IMF Era* (New York: Palgrave, 1999), 35, 36–38, 43, 46. U.S. Treasury Secretary Lawrence Summers said that "the IMF has done more to promote

America's trade and investment agenda in East Asia than 30 years of bilateral trade negotiations," quoted in David Hale, "Dodging the Bullet—This Time," *Brookings Review* (Summer 1998): 24, see also 26; U.S. Trade Representative Mickey Kantor referred to the IMF as a "battering ram" used to open Asian markets, quoted in *International Herald Tribune,* January 14, 1998.

43. The collective bargaining agreement of the National Basketball Association, for example, sets player's salaries at 48.04 percent of basketball related income (BRI). C. F. Joanne Gowa, "Bipolarity, Multipolarity and Free Trade," *American Political Science Review* 85(4) (December 1984): 1245–1256; and Joseph Grieco, "Understanding the Problem of International Cooperation: The Limits of Neoliberal Institutionalism and the Future of Realist Theory," in *Neorealism and Neoliberalism: The Contemporary Debate,* ed. David Baldwin (New York: Columbia University Press, 1993).

44. Katzenstein, *A World of Regions.*

45. C. Fred Bergsten, "America's Two Front Economic Conflict," *Foreign Affairs* 80(2) (March/April 2001): 16–27.

46. On Japan's increasing assertiveness in the late 1980s, see Eric Helleiner, "Japan and the Changing Global Financial Order," *International Journal* 47 (Spring 1992): especially 434–437.

47. Council on Foreign Exchange and Other Transactions, "Internationalization of the Yen for the 21st Century," Report 20, April 1999, http://www.mof.go.jp/english/if/e1b064a.htm, especially 4 (quote), 5, 7. See also William Grimes, "The Internationalization of the Yen and the New Politics of Monetary Insulation," in Kirshner, *Monetary Orders*; Jennifer Holt Dwyer, "U.S.-Japan Financial-Market Relations in an Era of Global Dominance," in *New Perspectives of U.S.-Japan Relations,* ed. Gerald L. Curtis (Tokyo: Japan Center for International Exchange, 2000), 92, 116.

48. Saori N. Katada, "Japan and Asian Monetary Regionalization: Cultivating a New Regional Leadership Role After the Asian Financial Crisis," *Geopolitics* 7(1) (Summer 2002): especially 86; Grimes, "Internationalization of the Yen," 173, 181, 185; See also Paul Bowles, "Asia's Post-Crisis Regionalism: Bringing the State Back In, Keeping the (United) States Out," *Review of International Political Economy* 9(2) (Summer 2002): 231, 248.

49. Eric Altbach, "The Asian Monetary Fund Proposal: A Case Study of Japanese Regional Leadership," *JEI Report* 47 (December 19, 1997); C. Fred Bergsten, *Reviving the "Asian Monetary Fund,"* International Economics Policy Briefs 98-8 (Washington, DC: Institute for International Economics, 1998): 1–14.

50. Michael J. Green, *Japan's Reluctant Realism: Foreign Policy Challenges in an Era of Uncertain Power* (New York: Palgrave, 2001), 230–231, 245 (first quote), 248; Paul Bluestein, *The Chastening: Inside the Crisis that Rocked the Global Financial System and Humbled the IMF* (New York: Public Affairs, 2001), 165–166.

51. Eric Helleiner, "Still an Extraordinary Power, but for How Much Longer? The United States in World Finance," in *Strange Power: Shaping the Parameters of International Relations and International Political Economy,* ed. Thomas C. Lawton, James N. Rosneau, and Amy C. Verdun (Aldershot: Ashgate, 2000), 236; Philip Y. Lipscy, "Japan's Asian Monetary Fund Proposal," *Stanford Journal of East Asian Affairs* 3(1) (Spring 2003): 93; Christopher B. Johnstone, "Paradigms Lost: Japan's Asia Policy in a Time of Growing Chinese Power," *Contemporary Southeast Asia* 21(3) (December 1999): 377; Altbach, "Asian Monetary Fund," 2, 10 (quotes).

52. Katada, "Japan and Asian Monetary Regionalization," 87, 104, 105; Grimes, "Internationalization of the Yen," 173; Johnstone, "Paradigms Lost," 381; Green, *Japan's Reluctant Realism,* 230. For an example of China's ambitions, see Jane Perlez, "With U.S. Busy, China is Romping with Neighbors," *New York Times,* December 3, 2003.

53. Saori Katada, "Determining Factors in Japan's Cooperation and Non-Cooperation with the United States: The Case of the Asian Financial Crisis Management, 1997–1999," in *Japanese Foreign Policy in Asia and the Pacific: Domestic Interests, American Pressure, and Regional Integration*, eds. Akitoshi Miyashita and Yoichiro Sato (New York: Palgrave, 2001), 161, 169. Katada argues that domestic financial concerns that surfaced in Japan in 1997 also contributed to the demise of the AMF, suggesting that Japan would reassert its international ambitions as domestic economic pressures eased (162). See also Hughes, "Japanese Policy and East Asian Currency Crisis," 245–247; Bowles, "Asia's Post Crisis Regionalism," 239, 240; Lipscy, "Japan's Asian Monetary Fund Proposal," 96, 97; Council on Foreign Exchange, "Internationalization of the Yen."

54. Norbert Walter, "The Euro: Second to (N)one," *German Issues* 23 (1999): 24 (first quote); Martin Feldstein, "The EMU and International Conflict," *Foreign Affairs* 76(6) (November/December 1997): 60 (quote), 72, 73; see also Hubert Zimmerman, "Ever Challenging the Buck? The Euro and the Question of Power in International Monetary Governance" (unpublished paper, Cornell University, 2003). On how soon the euro will challenge the dollar, see C. Fred Bergsten, "The Euro Versus the Dollar: Will There Be a Struggle for Dominance," paper presented at the American Economic Association, January 4, 2002 (argues for sooner); Benjamin J. Cohen, "Global Currency Rivalry: Can the Euro Ever Challenge the Dollar," *Journal of Common Market Studies* 41(4) (2003): 575–595 (argues for later). On the possibility of emerging rifts between the United States and Europe, see Charles Kupchan, *The End of the American Era* (New York: Knopf, 2002).

55. I elaborate this argument in "Appeasing Bankers: Financial Caution on the Road to War" (unpublished manuscript).

56. Harold Innis, *Empire and Communications* (Oxford: Oxford University Press, 1950); see also Peter J. Hugill, *Global Communications Since 1844: Geopolitics and Technology* (Baltimore, MD: Johns Hopkins University Press, 1999).

57. Joseph S. Nye, Jr., and William Owens, "America's Information Edge," *Foreign Affairs* 75(2) (March/April 1996): 20–36; Peter Wilkin, *The Political Economy of Global Communication* (London: Pluto Press, 2001), 36; See also Jeremy Shapiro, "Information and War: Is it a Revolution?" in *Strategic Appraisal: The Changing Role of Information in Warfare*, eds. Zalmay Khalilzad and John White (Santa Monica, CA: RAND, 1999).

58. See Zalmay Khalilzad, "Defense in a Wired World: Protection, Deterrence, and Prevention," in Khalilzad and White, *Strategic Appraisal*, especially 407.

59. Lawrence Greenberg, "Danger.com: National Security in a Wired World," in DeSouza, *Economic Strategy and National Security*, 303–305; Steven A. Hildreth, "Cyberwarfare," Congressional Research Service Report RL30735 (June 19, 2001), 2, 12, 15; Shanthi Kalathil and Taylor C. Boas, "The Internet and State Control in Authoritarian Regimes: China, Cuba and the Counterrevolution," Carnegie Endowment Information Revolution and World Politics Project, Working Paper 21 (July 2001), 10; Richard Love, "The Cyberthreat Continuum," in Cusimano Love, *Beyond Sovereignty*, 196, 203.

60. Annabelle Sreberny-Mohammadi, "Small Media for a Big Revolution: Iran," *Politics, Culture and Society* 3(3) (Spring 1990): 341–371.

61. Geoffrey L. Herrera, "The Politics of Bandwidth: International Political Implications of a Global Digital Information Network," *Review of International Studies* 28 (2002): 93, 95, 103 (quote); see also Lawrence Lessig, *Code: And Other Laws of Cyberspace* (New York: Basic Books, 1999), especially 43–44.

62. Price, *Media and Sovereignty*, 19, 73, 90; Gary Rodan, "The Internet and Political Control in Singapore," *Political Science Quarterly* 113(1) (1998): 70, 72; Diebert, *Parchment, Printing and Hypermedia*, 168; Wilkin, *Political Economy of Global Communication*, 44.

63. Shanthi Kalathil, "The Internet and Asia: Broadband or Broad Bans?" *Foreign Service Journal* (February 2001): 21–36.

64. Kalathil and Boas, "The Internet and State Control in Authoritarian Regimes," 2, 3, 9, 14; Michael Chase and James C. Mulvenon, *You've Got Dissent! Chinese Use of the Internet and Beijing's Counter-Strategies* (Santa Monica, CA: RAND, 2002), 3, 49, 63, 87; Rodan, "The Internet and Political Control," 74, 76, 81, 86.

65. Deibert, *Parchment, Printing and Hypermedia*, 158, 164, 167; Herrera, "The Politics of Bandwidth"; Stephen Gill, "The Global Panopticon? The Neoliberal State, Economic Life, and Democratic Surveillance," *Alternatives* 2 (1995): 2, 12; Kalathil and Boas, "The Internet and State Control," 15–16; Rodan, "The Internet and Political Control," 89; see also Nina Hachigian, "China's Cyber-Strategy," *Foreign Affairs* 80(2) (March/April 2001): 118–133; and Kirshner, "Political Economy in Security Studies," 65–66.

66. This is an important theme in Benjamin J. Barber, *Jihan vs. McWorld* (New York: Ballentine Books, 2001), see especially xxx, xxxi, 237, 243.

67. See for example Walter S. Salant, *Salant, CBS and the Battle for the Soul of Broadcast Journalism: The Memoirs of Richard S. Salant* (Boulder, CO: Westview Press, 1998); Bonnie Anderson, *News Flash: Journalism, Infotainment and the Bottom-Line Business of News* (Hoboken, NJ: Wiley, 2004).

68. Richard A. Bitzinger, "The Globalization of the Arms Industry: The Next Proliferation Challenge," *International Security* 19(2) (Fall 1994): 170–198; William Keller, *Arm in Arm: The Political Economy of the Global Arms Trade* (New York: Basic Books, 1995); see also Catherine M. Alexander, "National Security Issues in a Wired World," in *Digital Democracy: Policy and Politics in the Wired World*, eds. Cynthia J. Alexander and Leslie A. Pal (Oxford: Oxford University Press, 1998), and Ashton B. Carter, "Adapting US Defense to Future Needs," *Survival* 41(4) (Winter 1999–2000): 112, 114. On the significance of the diffusion of military technology more generally, see Robert Gilpin, *War and Change in World Politics* (Cambridge: Cambridge University Press, 1981), 162.

69. See P. W. Singer, "Corporate Warriors: The Rise of Privatized Military Industry and Its Ramifications for National Security," *International Security* 26(3) (Winter 2001/02): 187, 193–195; Deborah Avant, *The Market for Force: The Consequences of Privatizing Security* (Cambridge: Cambridge University Press, 2005).

70. On the deleterious consequences of materialism that is associated with capitalism, see Daniel Bell, *The Cultural Contradictions of Capitalism* (New York: Basic Books, 1996 [1976]), 84.

71. Mustapha Kamal Pasha, "Globalization, Islam, and Resistance," in *Globalization and the Politics of Resistance*, ed. Barry K. Gills (London: Macmillan, 2000), 250 (quote), see also 242; Michael Mousseau, "Market Civilization and Its Clash with Terror," *International Security* 27(3) (Winter 2002/03): 6, 19, 24; Mousseau argued that this is why, even though those at the bottom of the economic ladder are the most vulnerable to the negative consequences of globalization, it is the protected patrons and their clients who have the most to lose, which is "why leaders of terrorist organizations frequently come from privileged backgrounds" (19).

72. Connor, "Nation-Building or Nation-Destroying?" 347.

73. Tyler Cowen, *Creative Destruction: How Globalization Is Changing the World's Cultures* (Princeton, NJ: Princeton University Press, 2002), 8, 9, 78, 83, 99. Note that Cowen is an optimist regarding culture and globalization, arguing from a Shumpeterian perspective that challenge and change is revitalizing and encourages creativity, and from a Ricardian perspective that exchange between small and large dramatically expands the choices and opportunities available to the small. Cowen recognizes that some things will be lost, but on balance sees clear net benefits from the processes of cultural globalization, see, e.g., 11, 103, 106. See also Elizabeth Fox and Silvio Waisbord, "Latin Politics, Global Media," in *Latin Politics, Global Media,* eds. Elizabeth Fox and Silvio Waisbord (Austin: University of Texas Press, 2002), 6, 19; Silvio R. Waisbord, "The Ties that Still Bind: Media and National Cultures in Latin America," *Canadian Journal of Communication* 23(3) (1998): 3; Charles R. Acland, *Screen Traffic: Movies, Multiplexes and Global Culture* (Durham, NC: Duke University Press, 2003), 18, 26.

74. John Hannigan, "The Global Entertainment Economy," in *Street Protests and Fantasy Parks: Globalization, Culture and the State,* eds. David R. Cameron and Janice Gross Stein (Vancouver: UBC Press, 2002), 20; Edward S. Herman and Robert W. McChesney, *The Global Media: The New Missionaries of Global Capitalism* (London: Cassell, 1997), 104.

75. Ronald J. Diebert, "Altered Worlds: Social Forces in the Hypermedia Environment," in Alexander and Pal, *Digital Democracy,* 37.

76. Thomas L. McPhail, *Global Communication: Theories, Stakeholders and Trends* (Boston: Allyn and Bacon, 2002), 99. It should be noted that globalization can be culturally uplifting as well; Western film festivals such as those in Cannes and New York are important outlets for Iranian films. Hamid Dabashi, *Close Up: Iranian Cinema, Past, Present, and Future* (London: Verso, 2001), 259, 276.

77. Herman and McChesney, *The Global Media,* 39, 67, 153, 155; see also Vincent Cable, "The Diminished Nation-State: A Study in the Loss of Economic Power," *Daedalus* 124(2) (Spring 1995), 24; Robert W. McChesney, "The New Global Media," *The Nation,* November 29, 1999; see also Barber, *Jihad vs. McWorld,* 17.

78. Timur Kuran, "Fundamentalisms and the Economy," in *Fundamentalisms and the State,* eds. Martin E. Marty and R. Scott Appelby (Chicago: University of Chicago Press, 1993), 290, 299; see also Nikki R. Keddie, "The New Religious Politics: Where, When and Why do 'Fundamentalisms' Appear," *Comparative Studies in Society and History* 40(4) (October 1998): especially 699, 700; Peter Beyer, *Religion and Globalization* (London: Sage, 1994), 97, 105.

2

INTERNATIONAL MIGRATION IN A GLOBALIZING WORLD[*]

Assessing Impacts on National Security

Fiona B. Adamson

THE MOBILITY OF PEOPLE ACROSS NATIONAL BORDERS, like the mobility of other factors, such as capital, ideas, and goods, is a key component of globalization. Just as increased levels of economic exchange, the emergence of new technologies, and growing marketization all impact on the security environment facing states, so, too, does the flow of people across borders. International migration is itself a form of cross-border exchange—driven by global economic and market pressures that create incentives for human mobility, which are in turn reinforced by greater access to new and cheaper forms of global transportation and communication. The migration of people across national borders is thus a prime example of how the rise of stateless forces alters the milieu in which state actors formulate and implement security policy.

Yet, asking how migration and the mobility of people across borders affect "national security" is, at first glance, a bit of a strange question. In most respects, the fact that the world is increasingly mobile has no great impact on national security, as traditionally defined. The majority of those who cross international borders every day do so for a vacation or a business meeting. Others cross national borders to obtain an education, to find a job and support their family, or to escape political

---

* A modified version of this chapter was published as "Crossing Borders: International Migration and National Security," *International Security* 31(1) (Summer 2006).

35

persecution or violent conflicts in their home country. If one were to ask everyone on this planet about the relationship between migration and their own security, it is likely that most people would feel more threatened, on a personal level, by the overall lack of opportunities to travel and migrate, and the difficulty of crossing international borders, than they would be by the overall rise in human mobility on the planet over the past decades. As compared to other factors affecting state security interests, such as weapons of mass destruction, hostile states, or international terrorism, the "threat" posed by international migration would appear to be rather insignificant.

At the same time, however, to dismiss international migration flows as being wholly irrelevant to issues of national security would be foolhardy. Anyone wishing to do so would have to turn a blind eye to the ways in which migration and national security have become inextricably linked in the post-9/11 environment. The fact that 19 hijackers from overseas were able to enter, live, and train in the United States in preparation for carrying out attacks on the World Trade Center and Pentagon could not but raise concerns about the links between the mobility of people and international terrorism. In the period since the attacks, the management of migration has become a top national security priority for the United States, with concerns about migration helping to drive the largest reorganization of the U.S. government since the National Security Act of 1947.[1]

Even before 9/11, though, interest in the relationship between globalization, migration, and security had emerged in both the policy world and in some areas of the security studies literature.[2] Migration was at the top of the European security agenda throughout the 1990s.[3] The end of the Cold War and bipolarity led to a transformation in both the nature and function of national boundaries in ways that increasingly securitize migration and have led to greater policing of national borders.[4] Concerns about the security impacts of massive refugee flows, and the roles that mobilized diasporas and targeted labor remittances play in fueling violent conflicts around the globe, were being actively discussed long before 9/11.[5]

In addition, migration and migrants have had a long history of being closely linked to traditional national security concerns. States traditionally forge their national immigration policies in response to a set of security interests, in addition to their broader economic interests.[6] Historically, in the United States and other countries, migrants have often been viewed with suspicion during times of war or crisis—as national security threats because of the possibility that they may have dual political loyalties or represent a "fifth column" in a conflict.[7]

Such concerns in the past have often been dismissed as being issues of domestic politics by mainstream security studies. However, like other issues that have come to the fore since 9/11, such as terrorism, border control, organized crime, failed states, and nonstate actors, migration has moved up the "status hierarchy" in security studies of late. Skeptical of such matters as "soft security issues" or "new security issues" during the 1990s, even the most die-hard state-centric scholars of security are now hard-pressed to ignore the impact that international migration and the rise of other stateless forces has in shaping the international security environment facing states. Globalization, it appears, is a process that can no longer be discounted by scholars in mainstream security studies.

In this chapter, I examine international migration as a component of globalization, treating it as an independent variable and hypothesizing its various impacts on national security. A definition of what constitutes national security, for our purposes, has been provided in the introduction to this volume.[8] International migration as used here will broadly denote the movement of people across state borders.[9] It is difficult, of course, to make universal claims about migration and national security, as this relationship is always mediated by a set of intervening variables— most importantly, state policy and a state's capacity to implement such policy—which varies substantially, as the country- and region-specific chapters in this volume illustrate. Nevertheless, much leverage can be gained by looking for generalizable patterns of how migration flows affect the three components of national security identified by Kirshner in his introduction to this volume: the capacity and autonomy of states, the balance of power, and the nature of violent conflict.

The rest of this chapter is organized into four main sections. In the first section, I unpack the independent variable by examining what specific categories of phenomena the terms "international migration" and "mobility of people across national borders" refer to. I provide a brief overview of the volume, types, and causes of contemporary migration flows. If we wish to come to general conclusions regarding the impact of migration and human mobility on national security, it is necessary to first acknowledge that people cross borders for a variety of different reasons, and that states generally devise immigration policies to encourage some forms of border crossing and not others. The general impact of migration on national security is therefore highly dependent on the efficacy of a particular state's policy to shape migration flows in ways that encourage some categories of border crossing and deter others.

The second, third, and fourth sections of the chapter each discuss the ways in which immigration may impact one of three dimensions of national security—state capacity and autonomy, the balance of power, and the nature of conflict. In the section on state capacity and autonomy, I examine the impact of migration in the areas of border control and national identity. With regard to migration and the balance of power, I look at impacts on states' abilities to exercise and project economic, military, and diplomatic power. Finally, in the section on the nature of conflict, I examine the relationship between migration and three forms of security threats to states: internal conflicts, organized crime, and international terrorism. I conclude with a summary of my overall findings derived from the analysis in each section and a discussion of their implications.

GLOBALIZATION, INTERNATIONAL MIGRATION, AND CROSS-BORDER MOBILITY

Migration is not a new phenomenon. It is, however, more than ever before, a global phenomenon and is closely related to a number of other globalization processes in both its causes and effects. Most salient here are the globalization of trade, production, and increased global economic integration—processes that contribute to local economic dislocations and the emergence of new and more mobile pools of labor, while simultaneously creating stronger ties and networks among advanced industrial and developing economies that provide new avenues and opportunities for migration.[10] These processes are then reinforced by cheaper and more accessible forms of transportation and communication technologies, as well as an emerging global infrastructure of services that link national economies and that undergird the formation of international migration networks.[11]

"Like other flows, whether financial or commercial, flows of ideas or information," notes a 2003 report, "the rising tide of people crossing frontiers is among the most reliable indicators of the intensity of globalization."[12] Every corner of the globe is now affected by the flow of people across borders and "there is now almost no state or part of the world that is not importing or exporting labor."[13] States that in the past were countries of emigration have now become countries of immigration, and states that once declared that they were "not countries of immigration" have amended long-standing migration and citizenship policies to adjust to the realities of contemporary migration flows.[14] As Midford points out in this volume, even Japan, one of the most homogenous states in the world, has experienced increased rates of migration in recent years.

An indication of the contemporary significance of migration as one component of the larger process of globalization can be acquired through an examination of some basic migration statistics. According to the United Nations, there are now 180 million people living outside their country of birth, which is up from 80 million three decades ago. The number of people who migrate across national borders in any given year is between 5 and 10 million.[15] One out of every 35 persons in the world is a migrant, or about 2.9 percent of the globe. If all migrants in the world formed a single state, it would be the world's fifth most populous country.[16] Migration to both Europe and the United States has continued to increase over the past two decades.[17] In the year 2000, 40 percent of all international migrants were living in Western industrialized countries.[18] In Europe, there are approximately 19 million noncitizens within the European Union (EU).[19] (See Table 2.1 and Table 2.2.)

Many countries have significant portions of their populations abroad and rely on them heavily as a source of foreign exchange. Lynch in his contribution to this volume notes the important role that migration plays in the economic life of states in the Middle East. For example, 1 in 10 Moroccans live outside of Morocco, and 8 percent of Tunisians live outside Tunisia.[20] In some of the Gulf states, up to 70 percent of the labor force is composed of migrant labor.[21]

A range of factors have contributed to the overall increase in migration rates over the past several decades. These include declining transportation costs and the ease of travel; continuing levels of economic inequality among states; the fall of the Iron Curtain and the opening up of borders in the former Soviet bloc; the loosening of emigration restrictions in other states, such as China;[22] refugee-generating conflict and violence, such as in the Balkans or sub-Saharan Africa; state policies of forced migration; and the growth in human smuggling as a form of organized crime.[23] At the same time, it is important to remember that, as compared with other indicators of levels of globalization, levels of global migration are still relatively low. Although 1 in 35 people are migrants, 34 of 35 people in the world are not. Similarly, the levels of migration seen in the past decades are not unprecedented in their volume—the late nineteenth and early twentieth centuries, for example, were also characterized by high levels of international migration.[24]

Categories of Migrants and Border Crossers

In examining the relationship between international migration and national security, one of the key issues facing states is which categories of migrants to let in to the state, which to keep out, and how to tell the difference. The question of "who is a migrant?" thus becomes significant. The United Nations defines migrants as those entering a

TABLE 2.1 Top 10 Immigration and Emigration States, 1970–1995

Country	Net Number of Migrants (millions)
Immigration	
1. United States of America	16.7
2. Russian Federation	4.1
3. Saudi Arabia	3.4
4. India	3.3
5. Canada	3.3
6. Germany	2.7
7. France	1.4
8. Australia	1.4
9. Turkey	1.3
10. United Arab Emirates	1.3
Emigration	
1. Mexico	−6.0
2. Bangladesh	−4.1
3. Afghanistan	−4.1
4. Philippines	−2.9
5. Kazakhstan	−2.6
6. Viet Nam	−2.0
7. Rwanda	−1.7
8. Sri Lanka	−1.5
9. Colombia	−1.3
10. Bosnia and Herzegovina	−1.2

Source: United Nations, *The World at 6 Billion* (New York: United Nations Population Division, 1999), 52, as cited in IOM, *World Migration 2003*, 305.

country for 12 months or longer, yet individual states have varying definitions of what constitutes a migrant. Some states measure migration flows based on border crossings and others measure migration by country of birth.[25] In addition, there are broader categories of border crossers who cannot be counted as "migrants" per se, but nevertheless are significant for understanding the political dynamics surrounding migration, security, and border control. Finally, there are also extensive levels of internal migration within countries—particularly significant for many countries' ability to maintain their internal security are the

TABLE 2.2 Countries with Largest International Migrant
Populations, 2000

Country	Net Number of Migrants (millions)
1. United States of America	35.0
2. Russian Federation	13.3
3. Germany	7.3
4. Ukraine	6.9
5. France	6.3
6. India	6.3
7. Canada	5.8
8. Saudi Arabia	5.3
9. Australia	4.7
10. Pakistan	4.2
11. United Kingdom	4.0
12. Kazakhstan	3.0
13. Côte d'Ivoire	2.3
14. Iran	2.3
15. Israel	2.3

Source: United Nations, *Activities of the United Nations Statistics Division on International Migration* (New York: United Nations Statistics Division, 2002), as cited in IOM, *World Migration 2003*, 305.

25 million internally displaced persons (IDPs) around the globe—an issue, however, that is not dealt with in this chapter.[26] In practice, the lines between various categories of border crossers and migrants are difficult to define. Nevertheless, it is useful to think conceptually about who crosses borders and why, as a prelude to thinking about how this impacts on national security.

Voluntary Migration versus Forced Migration   Much of the general literature and political debate on migration has implicitly been concerned with voluntary migration—individuals who have left their home of their own accord, whether it be to pursue economic opportunities, for personal enrichment, to be reunited with their families (family reunification is a standard immigrant category in most industrialized states), or for other reasons. This is to be distinguished from a second category of migration, forced migration. Involuntary or forced migration can stem from a variety of causes ranging from human slavery to ethnic cleansing, forced expulsion, and deportations. Categories of migrants would include refugees and displaced persons. Many of the major migrations throughout history have occurred as a result of forced migration or expulsion. The formation of the Jewish diaspora after the destruction of the Temple of Jerusalem in 586 b.c.; the mass migration flows that occurred during the transatlantic slave trade, in which approximately 15 million Africans were transferred to the Americas prior to 1850; the population exchanges between Greece and Turkey that occurred at the end of World War I; the forced migration of Jews due to Russian pogroms and the Holocaust; the expulsions of Germans from the Sudetenland following World War II; the expulsion of indigenous Arab populations that occurred with the establishment of the Israeli state in 1948; the ethnic cleansing that characterized the Balkan wars in the 1990s; and the coerced trafficking in women in many parts of the world (especially Eastern Europe and East Asia) that has been referred to by many as a contemporary form of slavery are all examples of waves of migration that have been largely involuntary.[27]

The population flows of refugees and exiles that are produced by forced migration have, as often as not, been the product of state action, as opposed to being stateless forces—a useful point to keep in mind when examining the relationship between migration and globalization. Slobodan Milosevic, for example, employed refugee flows during the Kosovo crisis as a weapon of war in what was an asymmetric conflict with the North Atlantic Treaty Organization (NATO).[28] More generally, many instances of forced migration have been intimately bound up with the emergence of new states in the international system—a fact that has been observed by Aristide Zolberg, who has characterized state making as a "refugee-generating process."[29]

Economic versus Political Migration The impetus to migrate can be economic or political or, often, a combination of both. Economic migrants leave their countries in search of economic opportunities, and employment. Refugees and asylum seekers leave their countries to avoid the trauma of war or political persecution. In practice, it is often difficult to disentangle the political and economic factors that contribute to migration flows.[30] Economic migrants can feel compelled to move because of the types of conditions they face in their country of origin; asylum seekers or refugees may be able to exercise a degree of choice in their country of destination, which can be influenced by such factors as available economic opportunities family ties, and existing migration networks.[31] Economic migration can include unskilled or skilled labor, temporary workers, guest workers, or forced migration such as trafficked persons in the sex industry or slave labor. Much of the literature on international migration written primarily from an economic perspective has focused on one particular form of migration—voluntary labor migration. Indeed, it is difficult to analyze the global economy without taking into account global migration patterns and their relationship to the globalization of production.[32] The postwar economic boom in Europe, for example, would have been impossible without massive amounts of labor migration—much of it organized via bilateral agreements between particular states. The economies of some countries would collapse without foreign labor, with particular examples being the Gulf state economies.

As a factor of production in the global economy, however, it is important to remember that, from a comparative perspective, what distinguishes the mobility of labor from other factors of production is its relative *immobility*. Despite the significance of labor migration in terms of sheer numbers and importance, the flow of labor across national borders is generally less liberalized than other factors of production and is subject to more intervention by states. In a global economy, the mobility of labor has not kept pace with the mobility of capital. As Hirst and Thompson note,

> A world market for labour just does not exist in the same way that it does for goods and services. Most labour markets continue to be nationally regulated and only marginally accessible to outsiders, whether legal or illegal migrants or professional recruitment. Moving goods and services is infinitely easier than moving labour.[33]

In general, states still exercise a great degree of control over whom they admit as migrants. It is partly due to the tight restrictions on labor migration that have emerged since the periods of economic boom in the 1960s in Europe that one sees a blurring of the lines between political and economic migration and a corruption of the asylum process. Progress that has been made in liberalizing the global market for labor has been mostly at the high end of the skills continuum, with provisions for increased mobility in the service sector or for highly skilled professionals built into broader economic agreements such as the General Agreement on Tariffs and Trade/World Trade Organization (GATT/WTO) or the North American Free Trade Agreement (NAFTA). However, the flow of labor across borders is still much more restricted than the flow of goods and services in these agreements.[34]

International law distinguishes between economic and political migration by assigning particular categories to individuals who are seeking to cross borders to escape political persecution or violent

TABLE 2.3

Top 10 Refugee-Sending States, 1999–2001 (in Thousands)

1999		2000		2001	
Afghanistan	2,601	Afghanistan	3,586	Afghanistan	3,809
Iraq	641	Burundi	568	Burundi	554
Bosnia-Herzegovina	600	Iraq	525	Iraq	530
Burundi	527	Bosnia-Herzegovina	509	Sudan	489
Somalia	524	Sudan	493	Angola	471
Sierra Leone	490	Somalia	475	Bosnia-Herzegovina	450
Sudan	485	Angola	433	Somalia	439
Vietnam	406	Sierra Leone	402	DR Congo	392
Angola	353	Eritrea	376	Vietnam	370
Croatia	351	DR Congo	371	Occup. Palest. Territ.	349

Top 10 Refugee-Receiving States, 1999–2001 (in Thousands)

1999		2000		2001	
Iran	1,835	Pakistan	2,001	Pakistan	2,198
Pakistan	1,202	Iran	1,868	Iran	1,868
Germany	975	Germany	906	Germany	903
Tanzania	622	Tanzania	680	Tanzania	646
United States	521	United States	508	United States	515
FR Yugoslavia	501	FR Yugoslavia	484	FR Yugoslavia	400
Guinea	501	Guinea	427	DR Congo	362
Sudan	391	Sudan	414	Sudan	349
Armenia	296	DR Congo	332	China	295
China	293	China	294	Zambia	284

Source: UNHCR, *Statistical Yearbook 2001* (Geneva: UNHCR Population Data Unit, 2002) as cited in IOM, *World Migration 2003*, 312–313.

conflict, as opposed to those who cross borders in search of economic opportunities (see Table 2.3). Refugees are defined according to international law as those who have a well-founded fear of persecution due to their race, religion, nationality, or membership in a particular social or political group.[35] In 2001, there were 12.02 million refugees in the world, as compared with 8.8 million in 1980.[36] Of all the refugees,

47.9 percent were concentrated in Asia, 27.3 percent in Africa, and 18.5 percent in Europe.[37]

Similarly, there has been an increase in asylum seekers over the past decades. In 2001, 923,000 people filed asylum requests, up from 180,000 in 1980.[38] Altogether, it is estimated that approximately 6 million asylum applications were filed in advanced industrialized countries during the decade of 1990 to 1999.[39] Of these only a small percentage were eventually deemed to be legitimate asylum seekers. Asylum applications cost advanced industrial states approximately US$10 billion per year. This is ten times the annual budget of the United Nations High Commissioner for Refugees (UNHCR).[40] The number of false asylum seekers, combined with high levels of illegal migration, contributes to the perception that states are losing sovereign control over their borders.

Legal versus Illegal Migration   Illegal migration is also referred to as irregular migration, undocumented migration, or clandestine migration. This distinction is made between those immigrants who enter states through formal and legal channels versus those who enter through illegal channels, including those who are smuggled, trafficked, or enter with forged or no papers. Current estimates are that so-called irregular migrants comprise 30 to 50 percent of all migration to Western industrialized countries—and one must remember that such numbers are not counted in official statistics.[41] The International Organization for Migration (IOM) surmises that approximately 4 million people are smuggled across borders every year; out of those, 700,000 are women or children. In the United States alone, there may be as many as 12 million illegal migrants, with approximately 4,000 illegal border crossings to the United States *per day*.[42] Half of all illegal migrants have some interaction with smuggling or trafficking networks—a global industry that is worth approximately US$10 billion per year.[43]

Permanent versus Temporary Migration   Permanent migration refers to the crossing of national borders leading to permanent resettlement, what many traditionally think of as "immigration." Not all migration can be classified as permanent migration, however. Temporary migration would include so-called guest workers, seasonal labor, or students. In addition, there are the millions of people who cross borders for purposes of travel, and who contribute to the US$3.13 trillion global travel industry.[44] There are also a range of border crossers whose status is less clear—artists on tour, international civil servants working outside their country of origin, military forces abroad, and other such miscellaneous categories.

The complicated dimension with regard to categorization—and of crucial importance for thinking about the general relationship between migration and security—is that categories of border crossers are often not clearly cut. Tourists enter a country and then proceed to stay and look for work; political asylum seekers may leave a country for political reasons, but may then decide to relocate to one particular state and not another due to the existence of economic opportunities or family ties; members of organized criminal networks and international terrorist organizations are unlikely to mention this when they apply for a visa, and may well indeed also have a legitimate pretext to enter a country as, for example, students or businesspeople. Like other dimensions of globalization—whether financial flows or information technology or marketization processes—the important intervening variable for understanding the relationship between migration and security is state policy, and much of migration policy is about designing systems that allow some categories of immigrants in, while attempting to keep other categories out.

MIGRATION AND NATIONAL SECURITY: IMPACTS ON STATE CAPACITY AND AUTONOMY

International migration is often portrayed as a process that overwhelms states' capacities to maintain sovereignty across a number of areas.[45] Increased flows of people across borders, increasingly multicultural populations, and the emergence of informal migration-based transnational networks that circulate capital, goods, and ideas all challenge traditional notions of the territorial state as a bounded entity with a clearly demarcated territory and population. Although migration flows clearly challenge states in these areas, this does not necessarily mean, as some more sensational accounts of how the globalization of migration has impacted on states have claimed, that states are "losing control" due to migration flows.[46] As Gary Freeman has argued, "Anyone who thinks differently should try landing at Sydney airport without an entry visa or go to France and apply for a job without a work permit."[47]

It is states, as opposed to other actors, that still have the primary responsibility both for regulating borders and for conferring citizenship rights and claims to membership in a political community.[48] States have always faced challenges to their sovereignty, and the impact of migration flows across borders is analogous to other instances in history in which states have had to respond to pressures arising from increased transnationalism.[49] All states are not equally able to manage the challenges posed by migration, and clearly states with high levels of institutional capacity are in a much better position to adapt to this new environment as compared with weak or failing states. In this section, I focus on two areas in which migration can be hypothesized to impact on state capacity and autonomy: border control and national identity. The ability of states to maintain control over their borders and to formulate a coherent national identity can be viewed as necessary preconditions for the maintenance of state security in other areas.

State Capacity and Controlling National Borders

The ability to control who has the right to enter the borders of the state is a key dimension of what Krasner refers to as a state's interdependence sovereignty.[50] States have interests in controlling human population movement for a variety of reasons, such as maintaining control over populations, limiting access to public goods, and maintaining internal security. A failure to control and regulate the movement of people across its borders would be an indicator that could precipitate serious security challenges. In weak and failing states, a lack of border control may seriously jeopardize a state's capacity across a number of areas—refugee flows can overwhelm a state's capacity to provide services and can lead to conflicts over resources.

A dramatic example of the relationship between border control and state strength can be seen in how the end of Communism in Eastern Europe was symbolized by the loss of control over state borders. The "beginning of the end" of the Iron Curtain began when thousands of East Germans escaped through Hungary, Poland, and Czechoslovakia in 1989, until the border between East and West Germany was finally declared open by East Germany on November 9, 1989.[51] Similarly, one of the characteristics of states that are weak or failing more generally is the inability to control their territorial borders. The world's poorest states host most of the world's refugees, and the uncontrolled flow of refugees or other migrants across borders produces additional stresses on already weak state institutions, in addition to heightening competition over scarce resources and exacerbating ethnic and sectarian tensions.[52]

Additionally, porous borders in weak states can allow politically organized nonstate actors access to territory and population groups that can be used for political mobilization activities and that lead to the emergence of what Zolberg has referred to as "refugee-warrior communities."[53] Examples include the emergence of the Rwandan Patriotic Front (RPF) in Ugandan refugee camps; the mobilization activities of the

Palestine Liberation Organization (PLO) in refugee camps in Lebanon in the 1960s and 1970s; or the role played by Afghani refugee camps in Pakistan as sites of mobilization for Taliban-related groups.[54] Refugee flows can act as conduits that regionalize and internationalize internal conflicts—the Great Lakes Region of Africa provides just one example of the disastrous consequences such dynamics have on weak states.[55]

For advanced industrial states with very high degrees of internal capacity and control, the concern with maintaining secure borders is also significant. As Torpey has pointed out, the monopolization of the legitimate means of movement of people across borders through the development of the passport and accompanying bureaucracies has been a key feature in the development of modern nation-states.[56] However, the fact that states are authorized to monopolize the legitimate means of movement does not mean that they actually control all movement—just as the fact that states, in actuality, do not always have a monopoly over all means of violence.[57] As the earlier statistics on illegal migration demonstrate, even if states have formal control over migration processes, a number of nonstate actors—in particular organized criminal networks and smugglers—are competing with the state in this area.

The emergence of strong organized criminal networks around illegal migration, beyond the harm that they do to individual migrants, can also pose a significant challenge to state authority and control. As a recent IOM report noted, "Given the vast amounts of money involved, such operations erode normal governance and present real challenges and threats to national sovereignty."[58] Globalization produces a situation that resembles a cat-and-mouse game between migration pressures and state control over borders. If migration pressures on states increase, without the state adapting, then the capacity of states is indeed under threat. However, the record shows that many states are adapting to these pressures quite well, all in all. As Andreas has noted, "Globalization may be about tearing down economic borders, as globalists emphasize, but it is also about creating more border policing work for the state. At the same time as globalization is about mobility and territorial access, states are attempting to selectively reinforce border controls. ..."[59]

Throughout the 1990s, in both the United States and Europe, there have been expansions in the policing of borders, the use of technology to monitor and regulate borders, and a general militarization and securitization of border crossings[60]—the construction of a "Fortress America" and a "Fortress Europe." Since 1993, for example, the budget of the Immigration and Naturalization Service (INS; since 2003, the U.S. Citizenship and Immigration Service) tripled in size, and the number of agents in the Border Control has doubled.[61] The "unintended consequences" of this strengthening has been an increased number of deaths at the U.S.-Mexican border, with approximately 1,700 deaths during the second half of the 1990s, a number that increased 400 percent between 1996 and 2000. Following the reorganization of border control matters into the new Department of Homeland Security in the United States, the control of U.S. borders has become even more securitized.[62] Death tolls have risen, and reportedly, smuggling prices from Mexico into Arizona are now 50 percent lower than what they used to be pre-9/11, because of the higher likelihood that migrants will be interdicted.[63] As a border crosser who was caught trying to enter the United States illegally after 9/11 succinctly put it: "Because of this bearded guy, what's his name, Bin Laden, it is harder now. There are more reinforcements now because America is afraid of terrorism."[64]

As noted by Herrera in this volume, states are learning to employ technology in ways that reinforce their capacity. One sees this in particular in the area of migration and border control. The use of biometric technology to monitor entrants into the United States under the new United States Visitor and Immigrant Status Indicator Technology (US-VISIT) program that commenced in January 2004 is one such example. On both the U.S. border and the external borders of the EU, surveillance technology has been increasingly employed to deter illegal border crossings.[65] The European Union has established a European-wide corps of border guards and a European entry visa linked to a computerized database.[66] Since the Schengen Agreement first came into effect in 1995, and was then incorporated into the EU with the 1999 Amsterdam Treaty, there has been, in effect, the creation of a single external border in the EU, which was accompanied by measures to improve police and judicial cooperation, including the exchange of information through the Schengen Information System (SIS) database.

Thus, it would appear that state capacity, all in all, has been threatened by migration flows to a much lesser degree than many more sensationalist accounts in the globalization literature would have foreseen. Of course, for states with very weak or low capacity to begin with, monitoring borders will continue to be a challenge. However, even here, because of a common interest in the regulation of migration, economic, technical, and development assistance is increasingly being earmarked specifically for border control issues. In Europe during the 1990s, for example, approximately 50 percent of funds spent on technical assistance for the EU Phare programs to Eastern Europe were targeted for issues relating to illegal immigration and border control in candidate states.[67]

What appears to be more plausible, however, is that migration is affecting state autonomy—to effectively implement policy, it is necessary to increase levels of cooperation with other states on issues of border control. What is becoming clear is that states are sharing more information with each other. Europe, of course, is the most prominent example of this, as it has basically managed to harmonize its border control policy, allowing for free movement within the Schengen area. Yet, the trend is more widespread than this: Especially since 9/11, there has been extensive cooperation on border control issues between, for example, the United States and Canada and the United States and European states. In short, it is unclear that migration is posing an insurmountable challenge to states' abilities to regulate their borders, yet states may not be able to meet this challenge without enhancing their cooperation with one another in this area.

State Capacity and Maintaining a National Identity

Migration policy generally focuses on two factors—controlling borders and conferring citizenship or political membership in a community. States may be able to rely on technology to control borders, but what about their ability to respond to more underlying challenges to factors such as their national identity? A state's own definition of its national security is derived from its national interests, which, as social constructivists and others have argued, are derived from a state's national identity.[68] Even rationalist and realist perspectives on security, which focus primarily on material interests rather than identity, acknowledge that an assumption of the model of the state as a unitary rational actor assumes an underlying coherence in its collective identity, which in modern times has generally been provided by an ideology of nationalism.[69]

Given the centrality of nationalism as an ideology that provides legitimacy and cohesion to nation-states, what happens when the cultural basis of a state's identity is called into question through migration processes? States have historically incorporated ethnic and racial criteria in their migration policies, with examples ranging from racial restrictions on immigrants (particularly Asians) to the United States during the nineteenth century, to the favoring of ethnic Germans or *Aussiedler* by Germany in their post-WWII immigration policy, or the automatic right to immigrate that is granted to Jews by Israel in the Law of Return (1950).[70]

Increasing levels of people crossing borders; the rise of civil rights movements and multiculturalism; the economic imperatives that arise due to a changing global structure of production; and the spread of international norms of racial equality and universal human rights have increasingly delegitimized the use of ethnic and national criteria in the formulation of immigration policy.[71] When long-standing patterns of national identity formation are called into question by migration flows of new populations, even highly institutionalized states can suffer from levels of internal instability and incoherence at the societal level—what Ole Waever has referred to as "societal insecurity."[72] The problem is most acute for states whose identity and legitimacy have been derived primarily from an ethnic version of nationalism, rather than a civic nationalism.[73]

However, some would argue that even states whose identity is primarily liberal and constitutional can be threatened by migration, as liberal constitutionalism itself has its origins in a particular culture. Samuel Huntington, for example, has made the argument that recent waves of immigration to the United States threaten to undermine its core identity based on an "Anglo-Protestant" heritage.[74] Whereas language is arguably a symbol of national cohesion in the United States, it is religion, some have argued, that has played that role in many European countries. This would help to explain why, even post-9/11, neither Muslim immigrants nor Islam more generally have been viewed as posing a cultural threat to American identity in ways that have been manifested in France and other European states, who have, for example, outlawed the wearing of headscarves in public schools.[75]

The relationship between migration and national identity provides an example of the many ways in which market forces are challenging the traditional functions of the state. The general trend prior to 9/11 was that states themselves were increasingly using market criteria to make migration policy—with economic skills largely trumping cultural and identity criteria in evaluating potential migration requests. At the same time, however, there is increasingly a "market for identity and political loyalties" of individual migrants and descendants of migrants. In the migration studies literature, for example, old models of "incorporation" or "assimilation" are giving way to a discourse that favors multiculturalism, diasporas, and transnational identities.

Factors such as the ease of travel, new communication technologies, and the emergence of a global mediascape mean that migrants can maintain ties with their homelands, or even take part in wholly new transnational identity communities. Decreasing costs of transportation and new communication technologies such as the Internet, fax machines, and satellite communications mean that networks of relations between migrants in their new homes and those who have either stayed or migrated to yet another locale can be maintained with relative ease and at a relatively reasonable cost. Migrants can maintain dense social networks that stretch across national borders, are rich in social capital, and can be used for a variety of purposes—including political mobilization.[76]

Migrant communities across Europe, for example, are connected by transnational social networks that can be activated by political entrepreneurs. Soysal has observed that migrant communities in Europe increasingly engage in political activities at the supranational level, in addition to the national level.[77] And Basch et al. demonstrate in their work that migrants "live lives ... stretched across national borders."[78] The literature on diasporas points to how the emergence of transnational organizational structures, such as diaspora organizations, create new forms of identities and political loyalties. Sheffer, for example, notes that

> The establishment of diaspora organizations and participation in those organizations can create the potential for dual authority, and consequently also for dual or divided loyalties or ambiguous loyalty vis-à-vis host countries. Development of such fragmented loyalties often results in conflicts between diasporas and their host societies and governments.[79]

Similarly, a number of authors have documented how diaspora organizations are actively involved in the politics of their "home state." Prime examples of this are the political activities of Jews in the diaspora directed toward politics in Israel, or of Armenians vis-à-vis Armenia.[80] Thus, migrants and their descendants, in some respects, form "contested constituencies" in that they are open to political mobilization by a variety of actors for a variety of purposes, ranging from their "host society," their "home state," or nonstate and transnational actors.[81]

The transnationalization of political participation and the existence of diaspora networks can affect, some have argued, a state's ability to formulate a coherent foreign policy based on a unified set of national interests. Huntington and Smith, for example, have both argued that American foreign policy formation has been in danger of being captured by skilled ethnic lobbying groups whose loyalties are to a real or imagined homeland rather than the United States.[82] Interestingly, Huntington makes the comparison between transnational ethnic groups and economic actors, such as multinational corporations. Both, in some sense, illustrate how increased levels of marketization and pluralization can challenge a state's ability to act coherently as a "unitary rational actor" in the area of foreign policy formulation.

Should all this lead one to conclude that migration affects states' capacity and autonomy in the area of maintaining a coherent national identity, which, in turn, is arguably the basis for the formulation of a coherent set of national interests? Many would argue that migration does affect state capacity in this area. As a recent report argued,

> [O]ne thing is beyond doubt: migration is gradually eroding the traditional boundaries between languages, cultures, ethnic groups and nation-states. A transnational flow par excellence, it therefore defies cultural traditions, national identities and political institutions, contributing in the long run to curtailing nation-state autonomy and to shaping a global society.[83]

States are constrained in some areas relating to the maintenance of a particular form of national identity. Whether due to international migration, or the spread of liberal international norms of equality and human rights, many modern industrial states are increasingly identifying themselves according to civic forms of nationalism and defining themselves using liberal criteria. A prime example in this regard is Germany, a state which has traditionally had an ethnic form of nationalism, yet which recently changed its citizenship laws, allowing for a jus soli criterion for citizenship, in addition to the traditional jus sanguinis criterion.[84]

However, these types of shifts are also indicative of the resilience of the state and its ability to adjust to changing circumstances. European states are becoming increasingly multicultural—although France has banned the wearing of the headscarf in public schools, the French state is also working to institutionalize and incorporate Islam as an official religion, on a par with the institutionalized representation given to Christian and Jewish communities—a process that is also taking part in other states. Although cultural conservatives may bemoan the loss of homogenous national identities, many would equally view the global trend toward a convergence in states defining themselves according to nonracial and liberal identities as a positive development. And, the fact that there are ethnic and diaspora lobbies in the United States or Great Britain can easily be viewed as a healthy indicator of the robustness of democracy, and as interest groups operating in a plural society, as opposed to a threat to a unitary national interest.[85]

MIGRATION AND NATIONAL SECURITY: IMPACTS ON THE BALANCE OF POWER

How does immigration affect the balance of power among states? On the most basic level, of course, a country's population is considered as a factor, along with its natural resources, territory, economy, and military strength, when measuring a state's power or "counting poles" in the international system. As Kirshner and Mueller each point out in this volume, the international system may now be unipolar, but as a 2003 report noted, "Migration circuits span the globe like a spider's web, with complex ramifications and countless intersections. The current world map of migration is therefore multipolar."[86]

Migration policy can be a tool for states to exercise their national interests. A country's population is arguably its most important resource; however, it must be effectively mobilized to be an effective instrument of power. Purely on the level of basic demographics, migration can make a difference to a state's power. Many advanced industrialized countries have aging populations and need a younger population if their labor and social security systems are to function and if they are going to be able to compete effectively on the world market. Japan is a key example in this respect, with the government institutionalizing various measures to encourage labor migration in the mid-1990s, as a way of protecting its labor market and social security system.[87]

In this section, I briefly examine how international migration can affect states' abilities to consolidate and project power in the international system, by examining the impact that migration and human mobility can have on three areas of state power: economic, military, and diplomatic. Here, again, the intervening variable between migration and national security is policy: if states have the capacity to design and implement effective policies that "harness the power of migration," international migration flows can enhance state power.

Migration and Economic Power

In an increasingly global economy, some scholars argue that it is inevitable that states will come to see labor migration as a means of maximizing economic gains.[88] In fact, highly industrialized countries have increasingly designed their immigration systems to harness the talent of highly skilled workers, attempting to outdo one another in luring talent in what some have referred to as a "human capital accretion 'sweepstakes.'"[89] This is especially noticeable in the area of information technology and the knowledge economy, which is now an integral component of state power.[90] The United States, for example, encourages this through the H-1B visa, which facilitates temporary work in the information technology and communication sectors, a route that often becomes a fast track for permanent migration.[91] In 2000, Germany instigated a new "Green Card" program, modeled on the U.S. program, as a way of attracting highly skilled labor, especially computer specialists.[92]

Students are another group of "migrants" who are often highly sought after. The United States has been the most significant player in terms of issuing student visas, although other states are increasingly attempting to capture the student "market." Universities in Great Britain, for example, are turning to overseas students as a source of revenue to stem the financial crisis that has hit the education sector in that country, with approximately 50,000 students from China studying in the United Kingdom in 2005.[93] In the wake of 9/11, U.S. leadership in this area has been called into question. Since 9/11, the United States has seen a drop in the number of visas issued to foreign students, delays in the time it takes for students to acquire visas, and an overall drop in foreign graduate student applications to top U.S. universities. There is concern that these post-9/11 measures may have sustained effects on the United States' ability to maintain its leading edge in science and technology, if such restrictions continue.[94]

In the global competition for highly skilled workers, however, there are winners and losers. In particular, many parts of Africa appear to be losing as the entire continent is affected by a brain drain of skilled labor. In 1987, 30 percent of Africa's skilled workforce was living in Europe, and in the 1990s one out of every 18 Africans was estimated to be living outside of his or her country of origin.[95] According to the World Bank, 70,000 professionals or university graduates leave countries in Africa every year with the aim of working in Europe or North America.[96] Over 20,000 Nigerian doctors practice in North America, and in 2003, the IOM estimated that the South African economy had lost approximately US$7.8 billion in human capital due to emigration since 1997.[97] To a lesser extent, there is also a continuing brain drain from Europe to North America for the most highly educated scientists.[98]

Yet, emigration processes from the developing world to the developed world cut both ways. Perhaps the most significant impact of international immigration for developing countries is the capital flows they generate through labor remittances. If states are able to capture remittances, this can contribute substantially to economic growth in ways that have advantages over other types of capital flows. As opposed to other types of external capital flows, which are measured as changes in the assets and liabilities of residents vis-à-vis nonresidents in a state, many labor remittance flows are technically transfers of capital from one set of nationals (living abroad) to another set of nationals. Additionally, analyses have shown that remittances tend to be more stable than other forms of private capital flows across borders.[99]

The impact of remittances on national economies has been rising steadily since the 1970s. Whereas in 1970 global remittances were estimated at just over US$3 billion, by 1988 this had increased tenfold to a figure of US$30.4 billion.[100] A decade ago, global remittances were estimated at US$66 billion, an amount that was greater than the sum of all state-sponsored foreign development aid programs.[101] Current estimates for remittances run as high as US$100 billion annually in transnational flows across national borders.[102]

Labor remittances from migration make up more than half of all total financial inflows in a number of countries. In Morocco, labor remittances total approximately US$3.3 billion a year, accounting for 83 percent of the trade balance deficit.[103] In both Egypt and Tunisia, remittances account for 51 percent of capital inflows into the state.[104] Labor remittances can be put to use for a variety of purposes and, if effectively utilized, can play important roles in stimulating economic development.[105] In 2000, diaspora remittances grew the national economies by more than 10 percent in a number of countries in the developing world, including El Salvador, Eritrea, Jamaica, Jordan, Nicaragua, and Yemen.[106] As such, a number of states are trying to harness the power of labor remittances. Morocco, for example, is prioritizing migration management through the establishment of foundations that encourage temporary return migration and foster a core of elite émigrés who can contribute to the country's development, as well as promote Moroccan culture abroad.[107]

Migration and Military Power

Just as the influx of highly skilled immigrants can boost a state's economic base vis-à-vis other states, so too, by the same logic, can highly skilled immigrants contribute to the military strength of a state. This can range from providing technical expertise to intelligence expertise such as foreign language skills and analysis. A prime example would be the role that émigré scientists played in developing the atomic bomb in the 1930s. Albert Einstein, Edward Teller, and others who fled National Socialism in Europe put their expertise to work in the scientific establishment of their adopted country, thus leading to the development of the bomb in the United States. This is a stark example of the ability of a state to harness the expertise of immigrants for military ends. There are countless other examples, however, including the use of exiles, émigrés, and immigrants to provide intelligence or strategic analysis.

In addition to providing scientific expertise, immigrants can be instrumentalized by the state in the fighting of wars. The use of non-citizens in the American military mirrors, in some respects, the increased use of private contractors in military operations, as detailed in Avant's chapter in this volume.[108] Currently, there are approximately 40,000 noncitizens enrolled in the U.S. army, or 4 percent of all enlistees. Of these, one third are Latino. In fact, joining the military is one way to expedite the naturalization process for noncitizens, as noncitizens serving in the U.S. military can apply for U.S. citizenship after three years of residency (as opposed to the standard five years). Recruiters have even been known to travel to poor communities in Mexico and Canada to engage in recruitment activities. In California, up to half of all enlistees in some areas are noncitizens, and five of the first ten Californians who perished in the war in Iraq were noncitizens.[109] The U.S. military also attempted to mobilize recent immigrants or descendants when they set about to create a separate division of approximately 3,000 Iraqi expatriates and exiles that were known as the Free Iraq Forces in the 2003 war in Iraq.[110]

Migration and Diplomacy

Migration can also enhance a state's ability to engage in diplomacy. In some respects, this is the flip side of the discussion in the section above regarding a state's ability to maintain a coherent national identity. Small states in the international system can involve their diasporas in diplomacy by drawing on emigrants and their descendants within a target country and by sponsoring lobbying and public relations activities. In the United States, for example, NATO enlargement was helped along by the domestic lobbying activities of Americans of Eastern European descent. Armenia has a diaspora desk in its Ministry of Foreign Affairs.[111] The Republic of Cyprus draws on its diaspora in the United Kingdom and elsewhere to represent its interests abroad in the Cyprus conflict. Prominent members of the Cypriot diaspora have acquired the status of very important persons (VIPs) in Cyprus, which has been promoted by specific policies in Cyprus in which, "much like honorary or career consuls, they enjoy a certain number of limited facilities, privileges and immunities."[112]

Powerful states in the international system can project their power abroad by manipulating immigration policy, by drawing on immigrant populations, or even by mobilizing diasporas living within them for foreign policy ends. During the Cold War, for example, the United States used refugee policy as a tool to encourage emigration and defection from the Soviet Union and Eastern Europe, and, in the process, sought to "inflict a psychological blow on communism."[113] As in the economic and military realms, highly skilled immigrants can enhance national strength in the diplomatic realm—in the case of the United States, one need only think of prominent individual examples, such as Henry Kissinger, Zbigniew Brzezinski, and Madeleine Albright—or, in the field of theorizing diplomacy and statecraft, Hans Morgenthau.

In the post–Cold War world, transnational diaspora populations can be a source of national influence abroad. Yossi Shain, for example, has argued, contra Huntington, that, rather than hurting the national interest, migrants and diasporas promote U.S. interests abroad by acting as unofficial ambassadors who propagate American values in their home countries.[114] At the level of official state policy, first and second generation immigrants can be mobilized by states for particular foreign policy projects. Recent examples include the use of Iraqi exiles in the process of postconflict reconstruction and nation building in Iraq, the mobilization of highly skilled Afghani émigrés for nation building in Afghanistan, or the reliance on Palestinian Americans as negotiators in various rounds of Middle East peace talks.

MIGRATION AND NATIONAL SECURITY: IMPACTS ON THE NATURE OF CONFLICT

Having explored the potential impacts of migration on state capacity and the balance of power, it is left to examine the impact of migration on the nature of violent conflict in the international system. This is arguably the area in which migration in particular, and globalization more generally, is most significant in shaping the security environment facing states. Mainstream approaches to security have traditionally assumed that states seek to protect themselves primarily against security threats from other states. What emerges in the context of globalization, however, is the proliferation of a number of security threats to states that emanate from nonstate actors, as opposed to other state entities.

In this section, I focus on three ways in which migration flows can interact with other factors to exacerbate conditions that impact on the nature of violent conflict in the international system: by providing resources that can fuel internal conflicts, by providing an opportunity for networks of organized crime, and by providing conduits for international terrorism. Again, the degree to which each of these factors affects any particular state is highly dependent on the level of a state's capacity—organized crime presents itself as a law enforcement problem to highly institutionalized states; but for weakly institutionalized states, organized crime can lead to much more serious consequences—corrupting, challenging, or even hijacking existing state institutions.[115] Cooley vividly notes the consequences of this for the post-Communist states of the Former Soviet Union (FSU) in his contribution to this volume. All of these conduits somehow imply a change in the balance of power between state and nonstate actors in the international system.

It should be noted that, like many other aspects of the relationship between migration and national security, these factors are not necessarily "new," but rather have been understudied by specialists in international relations and security studies. For example, if we return to the period of pre-WWI globalization in the nineteenth century, which saw similar waves of migration, we see that there was also a plethora of activity by nonstate actors, who mobilized transnationally and, at times, employed political violence. Examples would include nineteenth century networks of anarchists, socialists, and nationalists, who were particularly active in mobilizing within immigrant communities within the United States.[116] Additionally, transnational networks of organized crime are certainly not new. The field of IR has been shaped heavily by the experiences of WWI and WWII—and, in fact, was to some extent an intellectual response to these devastating events. However, to analyze contemporary security challenges, scholars of international security may have to step back and draw on pre-WWI dynamics in the international system to understand some of the post–Cold War challenges facing states.

Migration and Internal Conflict

International migration processes, combined with the availability of new technologies and media markets, allow for migrants and descendants of migrants to remain connected to their home country or their "co-ethnics" through diaspora networks. These transnational diaspora networks, in turn, can be used as a political resource, including a resource in violent conflicts. Studies have shown that diaspora funding played a key role in providing resources for violent conflicts during the 1990s. A World Bank study demonstrated that countries that had experienced violent conflict and had significant diaspora populations outside the country were six times likelier to experience a recurrence of violent conflict than states without a diaspora population abroad. The author of this report, Paul Collier, argued, "diasporas appear to make life for those left behind much more dangerous in post-conflict situations."[117]

This observation has been echoed by a number of qualitative studies of diasporas in internal conflicts.[118] The Independent International Commission on Kosovo, for example, noted that it was Kosovar Albanians in the diaspora who created the Kosovo Liberation Army (KLA), engaged in fundraising activities in the diaspora to support the conflict, and even engaged in the recruiting of fighters.[119] Similar diaspora mobilization activities have characterized other internal conflicts, such as the conflict between the Kurdistan Workers' Party (PKK) and the Turkish state throughout the 1990s, or the conflict between the Tamil Tigers (LTTE) and the Sri Lankan state. Networks of Islamists drew upon migrant workers in Gulf states in the 1980s and 1990s to fund

Islamic fundamentalist networks that were eventually able to take over the state in Sudan.[120] In the Gulf states more generally, and as Lynch notes in his contribution to this volume, there has been a calculated policy shift to recruit labor from Asian as opposed to Arab states—a reaction to the politicization of Arab immigrant communities through mobilization activities by nonstate actors.[121] In many of these cases, diaspora mobilization appears to feed into "transnationalized cycles of political violence," in which displaced populations become part of a cycle of political violence that begins with state policies that lead to displacement, and which is then perpetuated by transnational mobilization around a violent armed conflict or opposition movement that challenges the state.[122]

A similar dynamic exists with regard to refugee populations and violent conflict. Just as political entrepreneurs can mobilize resources and political support for a conflict within diasporas in Western industrial states, refugee populations can also provide a base for political mobilization activities in conflicts. Not all refugee populations are likely to become the targets of political mobilization activities, but when populations are targeted, this creates dilemmas on a number of levels, including the role that humanitarian assistance may play in fueling conflicts by supporting such activities in refugee camps.[123]

Migration and Organized Crime

Perhaps the most obvious link between migration and organized crime is the global industry in human smuggling and trafficking that has emerged to meet the demand of potential migrants who wish to cross national borders. In a sense, this is an instance in which market-based mechanisms take on a role when the demand for opportunities to immigrate clearly outstrips the supply provided by official channels in state migration policies. Smugglers command high prices for their services that range from US$500 for a passage from Morocco to Spain, to prices from some countries in Asia to the United States that can be as high as US$50,000.[124] Although prices are in flux, and information is hard to obtain, Table 2.4 gives some idea of how market mechanisms are at work in the world of human smuggling.

Like other nonstate actors, smuggling networks have also been able to take advantage of new technologies to pursue their interests. Albanian smuggling groups operating in the Czech Republic during the 1990s, for example, were equipped with night vision equipment, cell phones with network cards, and other high-tech gear that could be used to successfully smuggle some 40,000 "clients" across the Czech-German border.[125]

TABLE 2.4 Fees Paid to Smugglers for Travel Assistance to Selected Destinations

Origin	Destination	Price (US$ per Person)
	Europe	
Bulgaria	Europe	4,000
Greece	France, Italy, Germany	800–1,200
Turkey	Greece	1,400
Hungary	Slovenia	1,500
Kurdistan	Germany	3,000
North Africa	Spain	2,000–3,500
Sri Lanka	Turkey	4,000
Pakistan	Turkey	4,000
Dominican Republic	Europe	4,000–10,000
Dominican Republic	Austria	5,000
China	Europe	10,000–15,000
Afghanistan/Lebanon	Germany	5,000–10,000
Iraq	Europe	4,100–5,000
Iran	Europe	5,000
Palestine	Europe	5,000
	North America	
China	New York	35,000
China	USA	30,000
Middle East	USA	1,000–15,000
Pakistan/India	USA	25,000
Mexico	Los Angeles	200–400
Iran/Iraq	Canada	10,000
Venezuela	Canada	1,000–2,500

Source: J. Salt, Current Trends in International Migration in Europe (Strasbourg: Council of Europe, 2001), as cited in IOM 2003, p 315.

The nexus between organized criminal groups, armed rebel organizations, and terrorist networks is often quite difficult to disentangle. Andreas, for example, has pointed out the extent to which transnational criminal networks provided the material basis for the Bosnian conflict.[126] Similar arguments can be made for conflicts in Kosovo and Turkey. The PKK, for example, was heavily involved in human smuggling as a way of raising money for the conflict in Turkey during the 1990s and of smuggling in supporters to engage in political activities in Europe.[127]

Global organized criminal networks may often be defined by a particular ethnicity and are able to operate transnationally by forging networks of solidarity that take advantage of migration-based networks and migration circuits. Again, it is important to reiterate that organized criminal networks are not new. Chinese criminal networks or "Triads," for example, smuggled Chinese into California during the Gold Rush in the 1840s.[128] What is new, however, is the way in which ethnically based criminal networks are now truly global and are able to forge alliances with one another—organizing themselves internationally, just as any legitimate business might do in the global economy. Lupsha details how "Chinese illegals in Naples produced counterfeit French perfume in bottles made in Spain, with faux Chanel perfume made in Mexico, and covered in gold wrappings and labels printed in Belgium."[129] Just as globalization provides opportunities for legal operations to transnationalize production structures, so too does it provide opportunities for criminal operations that operate by relying on networks of individuals that stretch across national borders.

The emergence of transnational criminal networks that strategically use migration networks to pursue their interests can affect the national security interests of states in a number of ways. At the most basic level, it affects the security of the individual victims of its activities—whether those be individuals who die in transit or other circumstances, or who are affected by the violence that accompanies such criminal activities. However, organized crime also is destabilizing at the global level, leading to what Mittelman and Johnston have termed "the corruption of global civil society."[130] Finally, in states that are already weak or failing, the influx of resources provided by international criminal networks can provide resources for mafia-like organizations that actually challenge the ability of states to maintain sovereignty over particular areas or, as Cooley points out, can corrupt the authority of states. When criminal networks take over law enforcement functions and monopolize violence at the local level, as well as engaging in distributive and service-providing activities normally associated with the state, this creates a local dependence on international networks of organized crime and creates serious internal security problems, such as can be seen, for example, in states such as Colombia.[131]

Migration and International Terrorism

Since 9/11, migration and security are increasingly viewed as intertwined in relation to international terrorism. This is not just the case in the United States, but also in Europe and other states. In Spain, for example, the foreign minister argued that "the fight against illegal immigration is also the reinforcement of the fight against terrorism."[132] A recent report by the Nixon Center argued that "immigration and terrorism are linked; not because all immigrants are terrorists but because all, or nearly all, terrorists in the West have been immigrants." The same report went on to cite Rohan Gunaratna's claim that "All major terrorist attacks conducted in the last decade in North America and Western Europe, with the exception of Oklahoma City, have utilized migrants."[133]

This claim is problematic, not the least because it does not take into account attacks by domestic groups in Europe such as Euskadi Ta Askatasuna (ETA; Basque for "Basque Homeland and Freedom"). However, it is certainly the case that migration policies and migration networks provide avenues for terrorist organizations and other nonstate actors to pursue their interests, just as they provide opportunities for states and other actors. Leiken argues that states tend to view immigration from an economic perspective, whereas terrorist organizations view immigration from a strategic perspective—using all aspects of the immigration system as a way of gaining access to target states.[134] He makes the distinction between two different strategies for getting access to the target state: The first is by the use of so-called hit squads, in which a group enters a particular state with the explicit aim of committing a terrorist act—this was the case in the attacks of 9/11. The second strategy is that of sleeper cells, in which groups inside the target state are activated at a particular point to carry out attacks. Although internal surveillance in the United States has focused on the possibility of the latter since 9/11, and has, many would argue, unfairly targeted Muslim Americans living in the United States, all evidence points to the fact that the United States is more at risk from external infiltrators than any form of domestic mobilization around radical Islam—a concern that is much more pronounced in some European states, such as Great Britain, France, and Germany.[135]

U.S. immigration policy and border control has become one of the "front lines" in protecting the United States from further terrorist attacks. In addition to reorganizing the INS and incorporating it into the Department of Homeland Security, the screening of potential border crossers, the use of immigration lists for intelligence purposes, and increased cooperation with other states on such issues as the forgery of passports and other documents have all become tools in the war against terrorism. In this context, striking the balance between border control and intelligence gathering versus facilitating all the benefits of the mobility of people is a delicate task.

One of the dangers in making the link between migration and security with regard to international terrorism would be for states to overreact to this challenge. As Mueller notes in his contribution to this volume, one of the most devastating effects of another major terrorist attack in the United States would be to change the character of U.S. society. As mentioned above, there are already signs that measures taken since 9/11 are deterring students from studying in the United States, which may affect the United States' ability to lead in science and technology over the long run. Just as problematic, if not more so, is the impact that surveillance activities may have had on alienating Muslim and other populations within the United States.[136] The detentions of Muslims and non-Muslim Arabs, the crackdowns on Islamic charities, and the shutting down of money-transfer services that are thought to feed into *hawala* systems have all caused widespread resentment. In addition to raising serious questions with respect to civil liberties and racial profiling, they may contribute to a range of other detrimental and counterproductive outcomes, such as weakening incipient diasporic civil society networks that could support bottom-up processes of political liberalization in the Middle East or negatively impacting efforts of U.S. public diplomacy abroad.

CONCLUSIONS

Similar to the other dimensions of globalization that impact on state security, many of the mechanisms by which migration flows affect national security are not necessarily new, but rather operate cumulatively and in combination with other factors, such as increasing levels of exchange, the emergence of new technologies, and marketization processes. Together, these processes affect the overall security environment facing states under conditions of globalization. As Kirshner notes in his introduction, such pressures "do not present iron laws, but rather they change the cost-benefit calculus of various policy choices."[137] This fits with a perspective on globalization that is relatively consistent with a "transformationalist" perspective.[138]

Based on the analysis in the preceding pages, the overall impact of international migration and human mobility on national security can be summarized as follows. With regard to state capacity and autonomy, there are two broad findings. First, migration flows do impact on both the capacity and autonomy of states; however, the extent varies widely across different states. Migration flows can have serious security impacts on the capacity of states that are already weak or failing. Yet, states with high capacity have generally shown themselves adept at adjusting to the realities of increased human mobility. Second, globalization may bring about a change in the relationship between state autonomy and state capacity. As two components of state sovereignty, autonomy and capacity are often viewed as being complementary and going hand-in-hand. However, one impact of globalization on the state may be an increasing divergence between state capacity and state autonomy as measures of state effectiveness—to effectively manage cross-border challenges, state capacity is enhanced, rather than threatened, by increased cooperation with other states in areas such as the formulation and enforcement of migration policy.

With regard to the impacts of migration on the balance of power among states, the overall conclusion is mixed. On the one hand, current migration regimes, which favor highly skilled workers, tend to exacerbate already existing inequalities in the world by widening the gap between the "winners" and "losers" of globalization and contributing to problems such as brain drain. In addition, global inequalities are reinforced through the greater barriers and obstacles that are placed on the mobility of labor across national boundaries as compared with the mobility of capital. For strong states with the capacity to effectively mobilize the talents of migrant populations, migration generally enhances states' abilities to project power in a number of areas. Economically disadvantaged states, however, can also benefit from the effective mobilization of their overseas populations. Although populations in institutionally weak and economically less developed states suffer disproportionately from current migration regimes, there is also the potential for migration processes to promote development and technology transfer between states that could, over the medium to long term, help to temper levels of global inequality, as well as leading to greater levels of interdependence among states.

Finally, with regard to migration and the nature of violent conflict: My analysis in this chapter echoes the conclusions of others in this volume and elsewhere regarding the security challenges posed by the emergence of nonstate actors, gray economy networks, and networks of political violence. International migration flows provide conduits for the diffusion of network-based forms of political violence and instability, a challenge that affects weak states to a greater degree than strong states, and that requires increased levels of interstate cooperation to meet. However, one danger for states, in the post-9/11 environment, would be an overreaction to these threats in ways that would curtail the many benefits of migration.

In each of these areas, migration flows change the environment in which states formulate policy, including security policy. However, ultimately, it is how states respond to global migration flows through policy formulation and policy implementation that will determine to what extent any particular state's security will be enhanced or diminished by international migration. States that are best able to "harness the power of migration" through well-designed policies in cooperation with other states will also be the best equipped to face the new global security environment.

NOTES

1. As of March 1, 2003, immigration and border control fall within the purview of the new Department of Homeland Security. Since January 2004, the Department of Homeland Security rolled out the new US-VISIT program, which began to introduce biometric technology at all U.S. immigration and border control points. Details are available at the Department of Homeland Security Web site www.dhs.gov.

2. See, for example, Roxanne Lynn Doty, "Immigration and the Politics of Security," *Security Studies* 8(2/3) (1998–1999): 71–93; Keith Krause and Michael C. Williams, eds., *Critical Security Studies* (Minneapolis: University of Minnesota Press, 1997); Myron Weiner, "Security, Stability and International Migration," *International Security* 17(3) (Winter 1992–1993): 91–126; Myron Weiner, ed., *International Migration and Security* (Boulder, CO: Westview Press, 1993); Myron Weiner, ed., *The Global Migration Crisis: Challenges to States and to Human Rights* (New York: HarperCollins, 1995).

3. Fiona B. Adamson, "Globalization, International Migration and Changing Security Interests in Western Europe," paper prepared for presentation at the 95th Annual Meeting of the American Political Science Association, Atlanta, GA, September 2–5, 1999; Sarah Collinson, *Europe and International Migration* (London: Pinter, 1994); Jef Huysmans, "The European Union and the Securitization of Migration," *Journal of Common Market Studies* 38(5) (December 2000): 751–777. Jef Huysmans, "Contested Community: Migration and the Question of the Political in the EU," in *International Relations Theory and the Politics of European Integration: Power, Security and Community,* eds. M. Kelstrup and M. Williams (London: Routledge, 2000): 149–170; Peter J. Katzenstein, "Regional Orders: Security in Europe and Asia," paper prepared for presentation at the 39th Annual International Studies Association Convention, Minneapolis, MN, March 17–21, 1998; Ole Waever et al., eds., *Identity, Migration and the New Security Agenda in Europe* (New York: St. Martins Press, 1993).

4. Malcolm Anderson and Monica den Boer, eds., *Policing Across National Boundaries* (London: Pinter, 1994); Peter Andreas, *Border Games: Policing the US-Mexico Divide* (Ithaca, NY: Cornell University Press, 2000); Peter Andreas and Timothy Snyder, eds., *The Wall Around the West: State Borders and Immigration Controls in North America and Europe* (Lanham, MD: Rowman and Littlefield, 2000); Didier Bigo, *Polices en réseaux: L'Expérience Européene* (Paris: Presses de Sciences Po, 1996); Didier Bigo, "Security, Borders and the State," in *Borders and Border Regions in Europe and North America,* eds. Paul Ganster et al. (San Diego: San Diego University Press, 1997).

5. Aristide R. Zolberg, Astri Suhrke, and Sergio Aguayo, *Escape from Violence: Conflict and the Refugee Crisis in the Developing World* (Oxford: Oxford University Press, 1989); Gil Loescher, *Beyond Charity: International Cooperation and the Global Refugee Crisis* (Oxford: Oxford University Press, 1993); Weiner, *International Migration and Security*; Barry R. Posen, "Military Responses to Refugee Disasters," *International Security* 21(1) (Summer 1996): 72–111; Mary Kaldor, *New and Old Wars: Organized Violence in a Global Era* (Stanford, CA: Stanford University Press, 1999); Paul Collier, "Economic Causes of Civil Conflict and Their Implications for Policy," World Bank working paper, June 15, 2000.
6. Christopher Rudolph, "Security and the Political Economy of Migration," *American Political Science Review* 97(4) (November 2003): 603–620.
7. A prime example of this would be the internment of Japanese Americans during World War II.
8. "National security refers to organized violence that speaks to the vital interests of at least one state." (Kirshner, chap. 1 this volume.)
9. The rise of nonstate actors, the spread of international terrorism or networks of organized crime, the availability of new media and information technology, or the emergence of illicit and informal capital flows in the global economy all dovetail with migration processes and are thus dealt with, but are not the focus of the analysis in this chapter.
10. Saskia Sassen, *The Mobility of Labor and Capital: A Study in International Investment and Labor Flow* (Cambridge: Cambridge University Press, 1988).
11. See, for example, Mary M. Kritz, Lin Lean Lim, and Hania Zlotnik, *International Migration Systems: A Global Approach* (Oxford: Oxford University Press, 1992); James H. Mittelman, *The Globalization Syndrome: Transformation and Resistance* (Princeton, NJ: Princeton University Press, 2000); Thomas Faist, *The Volume and Dynamics of Migration and Transnational Social Spaces* (Oxford: Oxford University Press, 2000). There is, of course, a vast body of literature on the causes of migration, which is not addressed here. For an overview of theoretical approaches and regional applications, see Douglas S. Massey et al., *Worlds in Motion: Understanding International Migration at the End of the Millennium* (Oxford: Clarendon Press, 1998).
12. International Organization for Migration (IOM), *World Migration 2003: Managing Migration: Challenges and Responses for People on the Move* (Geneva: IOM World Migration Report Series, 2003), 4.
13. David Held et al., *Global Transformations: Politics, Economics and Culture* (Cambridge: Polity Press, 1999), 297. See also Stephen Castles and Mark J. Miller, *The Age of Migration: International Population Movements in the Modern World*, 3rd ed. (London: MacMillan, 2003).
14. Examples of the former include Ireland, Italy, and Greece, and the latter, Germany.
15. IOM, *World Migration 2003*, 6.
16. Ibid., 5.
17. Ibid., 17.
18. Ibid., 6.
19. Ibid., 44.
20. Ibid., 224, 231.
21. Seventy percent of the labor force is composed of foreigners in Qatar; 67 percent in the United Arab Emirates; 65 percent in Kuwait. See IOM, *World Migration 2003*, 34.
22. IOM, *World Migration 2003*, 197.
23. Castles and Miller, *The Age of Migration*; Rey Koslowski, *Migrants and Citizens: Demographic Change in the European State System* (Ithaca, NY: Cornell University Press, 2000).

24. During this period, approximately 60 million people emigrated from Europe, 10 million people emigrated from Russia, and 12 million Chinese and 6 million Japanese emigrated to other states in Asia. Aaron Segal, *Atlas of International Migration* (London: Hans Zell, 1993), 16, as cited in Paul Hirst and Grahame Thompson, *Globalization in Question* (Cambridge: Polity Press, 1999), 23. See also Robert Gilpin, *Global Political Economy: Understanding the International Economic Order* (Princeton, NJ: Princeton University Press, 2001), 365–366.
25. IOM, *World Migration 2003*, 8.
26. Global IDP Project, *Internal Displacement: A Global Overview of Trends and Developments in 2003* (Geneva: Norwegian Refugee Council, 2004).
27. Robin Cohen, *Global Diasporas: An Introduction* (London: UCL Press, 1997); Michael R. Marrus, *The Unwanted: European Refugees in the Twentieth Century* (New York: Oxford University Press, 1985); Benny Morris, *The Birth of the Palestinian Refugee Problem, 1947–1949* (Cambridge: Cambridge University Press, 1987); Castles and Miller, *The Age of Migration*; Zolberg et al., *Escape from Violence*.
28. Kelly Greenhill, "The Use of Refugees as Political and Military Weapons in the Kosovo Conflict," in *Yugoslavia Unraveled: Sovereignty, Self-Determination, Intervention*, ed. Raju G. C. Thomas (Lanham, MD: Lexington Books, 2003).
29. Zolberg et al., *Escape from Violence*.
30. Ibid., 30–33.
31. Kritz et al., *International Migration Systems*; Faist, *Volume and Dynamics of Migration*.
32. The literature is vast but see, for example, George J. Borjas, *Heaven's Door: Immigration Policy and the American Economy* (Princeton, NJ: Princeton University Press, 1999); Mittelman, *The Globalization Syndrome*; Leah Haus, "Openings in the Wall: Transnational Migrants, Labor Unions and US Immigration Policy," *International Organization* 49(2) (Spring 1995): 285–333; Lin Lean Lim, "International Labor Movements: A Perspective on Economic Exchanges and Flows," in Kritz et al., *International Migration Systems*; Saskia Sassen, *Mobility of Labor and Capital*.
33. Paul Hirst and Grahame Thompson, *Globalization in Question*, 2nd ed. (Oxford: Polity Press, 2000), 29.
34. Ibid., 29.
35. IOM, *World Migration 2003*, 98.
36. Ibid., 17.
37. Ibid., 29.
38. Ibid., 17, 97.
39. Ibid., 102.
40. Ibid., 102.
41. Ibid., 58.
42. Ibid., 58–59.
43. Ibid., 60–61.
44. World Travel and Tourism Council, "Executive Summary: Travel and Tourism: Forging Ahead," available at www.wttc.org.
45. See, for example, Saskia Sassen, *Globalization and Its Discontents* (New York: The New Press, 1998).
46. Saskia Sassen, Losing Control? Sovereignty in an Age of Globalization (New York: Columbia University Press, 1996); Weiner, *The Global Migration Crisis*.

47. Gary Freeman, "The Decline of Sovereignty? Politics and Immigration Restriction in Liberal States," in *Challenge to the Nation-State: Immigration in Western Europe and the United States,* ed. Christian Joppke (New York: Oxford University Press, 1998), 93, as cited in John Torpey, "States and the Regulation of Migration in the Twentieth-Century North-Atlantic World," in *The Wall Around the West* Andreas and Snyder, 32.

48. Although, some scholars have pointed to how nonstate actors, such as airlines, are taking on some aspects of border control activities. See, for example, Gallya Lahav, "The Rise of Non-State Actors in Migration Regulation in the United States and Europe," in *Immigration Research for a New Century,* ed. Nancy Foner, Ruben Rumbaut, and Steven Gold (New York: Russell Sage, 2000); Gallya Lahav and Virginie Guiraudon, "Comparative Perspectives on Border Control: Away from the Border and Outside the State," in Andreas and Snyder, *The Wall Around the West,* 55–77; Sassen, *Losing Control?*

49. Stephen D. Krasner, Sovereignty: Organized Hypocrisy (Princeton: Princeton University Press, 1999).

50. There are arguably broadly two dimensions of sovereignty that are challenged by international migration: interdependence sovereignty, or the ability of states to control transborder movements, and domestic sovereignty, or the level of effective control exercised by a state within its borders. The other two dimensions of sovereignty enumerated by Krasner, which are less affected by migration flows, are international legal sovereignty and Westphalian sovereignty. Ibid.

51. See Timothy Garton Ash, "The German Revolution," *The New York Times Review of Books,* December 21, 1989, 14–17, as cited in Weiner, "Security, Stability and International Migration," 91.

52. Alan Dowty and Gil Loescher, "Refugee Flows as Grounds for International Action," *International Security* 21(1) (Summer 1996): 43–71; Zolberg et al., *Escape from Violence.*

53. See Zolberg et al., *Escape from Violence.*

54. Sarah K. Lischer, "Collateral Damage: Humanitarian Assistance as a Cause of Conflict," *International Security* 28(1) (Summer 2003): 79–109; Dowty and Loescher, "Refugee Flows as Grounds for International Action," 49; Barnett R. Rubin, "Political Exiles in Search of a State," in *Governments-in-Exile in Contemporary World Politics,* ed. Yossi Shain (New York: Routledge, 1991), 70–91.

55. See Stephen John Stedman, "Conflict and Conciliation in Sub-Saharan Africa," in *The International Dimensions of Internal Conflict,* ed. Michael E. Brown (Cambridge, MA: MIT Press, 1996), 235–265.

56. John Torpey, "Coming and Going: On the State Monopolization of the Legitimate 'Means of Movement,'" *Sociological Theory* 16(3) (November 1998): 239–259; John Torpey, *The Invention of the Passport: Surveillance, Citizenship and the State* (Cambridge: Cambridge University Press, 1999).

57. John Torpey, "States and the Regulation of Migration in the Twentieth-Century North Atlantic World," in Andreas and Snyder, *The Wall Around the West.*

58. IOM, *World Migration 2003,* 60.

59. Peter Andreas, "Redrawing the Line: Borders and Security in the Twenty-First Century," *International Security* 28(2) (Fall 2003): 84.

60. Peter Andreas, *Border Games: Policing the US-Mexico Divide* (Ithaca, NY: Cornell University Press, 2000).

61. Wayne A. Cornelius, "Death at the Border: Efficacy and Unintended Consequences of US Immigration Control Policy," *Population and Development Review* 27(4) (December 2001): 661.

62. Ibid.; Timothy Egan, "Risky Dream and a Rising Toll in Desert at the Mexican Border," *New York Times,* May 23, 2004.

63. IOM, *World Migration 2003*, 60.
64. Ibid., 66.
65. Andreas, *Border Games*.
66. IOM, *World Migration 2003*, 65.
67. Lecture by António Vitirono, European Union Commissioner in Charge of Justice and Home Affairs, Minda de Gunzburg Center for European Studies, Harvard University, March 22, 2001.
68. See Peter J. Katzenstein, ed., *The Culture of National Security: Norms and Identity in World Politics* (Ithaca, NY: Cornell University Press, 1996).
69. See, for example, the discussion of nationalism and states as units in Kenneth Waltz, *Man, the State and War* (New York: Columbia University Press, 1959), 175–176, or the discussion on rationalism and constructivism in James Fearon and Alexander Wendt, "Rationalism v. Constructivism: A Skeptical View," in *Handbook of International Relations,* eds. Walter Carlsnaes, Thomas Risse, and Beth A. Simmons (London: Sage, 2002), 52–72. Representative literature on nationalism, more generally, would include Bendict Anderson, *Imagined Communities: Reflections on the Origins and Spread of Nationalism* (London: Verso, 1983); Ernest Gellner, *Nations and Nationalism* (Ithaca, NY: Cornell University Press, 1983); Anthony D. Smith, *The Ethnic Origins of Nations* (New York: Blackwell, 1989).
70. On discrimination against Asians in U.S. immigration policy, see Sucheng Chan, "European and Asian Immigration into the United States in Comparative Perspective, 1820s to 1920s," in *Immigration Reconsidered: History, Sociology and Politics,* ed. Virginia Yans-McLaughlin (New York: Oxford University Press, 1990); Aristide Zolberg, "Global Movements, Global Walls: Responses to Migration: 1885–1925," in *Global History and Migrations,* ed. Wang Gongwu (Boulder, CO: Westview Press, 1997), 279–302; on the privileging of ethnic Germans, see Rogers Brubaker, *Citizenship and Nationhood in France and Germany* (Cambridge, MA: Harvard University Press, 1992); Israeli policy is codified in the 1950 Law of Return.
71. On international human rights norms and deracialization, more generally, see Neta C. Crawford, *Argument and Change in World Politics: Ethics, Decolonization and Humanitarian Intervention* (Cambridge: Cambridge University Press, 2002); on international human rights norms and citizenship, see Yasemin Nuhoglu Soysal, *Limits of Citizenship: Migrants and Postnational Membership in Europe* (Chicago: University of Chicago Press, 1994).
72. Ole Waever, "Societal Security: The Concept," in Waever et al., *Identity, Migration and the New Security Agenda.*
73. Ethnic and civil nationalism should be viewed as ideal types. Some authors have tried to classify states according to these criteria, with states such as Great Britain, France, and the United States being classified as states deriving their identity from civic nationalism, and states such as Germany deriving their identity from ethnic nationalism. In reality, most states exhibit a mix of ethnic and civic nationalism. For discussions, see Liah Greenfeld, *Nationalism: Five Roads to Modernity* (Cambridge, MA: Harvard University Press, 1992); Brubaker, *Citizenship and Nationhood in France and Germany.*
74. Samuel P. Huntington, *Who Are We? The Challenges to America's National Identity* (New York: Simon and Schuster, 2004).
75. For an interesting discussion, see Aristide Zolberg and Long Litt Woon, "Why Islam Is Like Spanish: Cultural Incorporation in Europe and the United States," *Politics and Society* 27 (1999): 5–38.
76. Faist, *Volume and Dynamics of Migration*, 96–123.
77. Soysal, *Limits of Citizenship.*

78. Linda Basch, Nina Glick Schiller, and Cristina Szanton Blanc, *Nations Unbound: Transnational Projects, Postcolonial Predicaments, and De-territorialized Nation-States* (Langhorne, PA: Gordon and Breach, 1994), 4.
79. Gabriel Sheffer, *Diaspora Politics: At Home Abroad* (Cambridge: Cambridge University Press, 2003), 81.
80. Yossi Shain and Aharon Barth, "Diasporas in International Relations Theory," *International Organization* 57 (3) (Summer 2003): 449–479.
81. Fiona B. Adamson, "Contested Constituencies: Political Entrepreneurs and the Mobilization of Immigrant Communities in France (1954–1962) and Germany (1984–2000)," paper prepared for presentation at the 98th Annual Meeting of the American Political Science Association, Boston, MA, August 29–September 1, 2002.
82. Samuel P. Huntington, "The Erosion of American National Interest," *Foreign Affairs* 76(5) (1997): 28–49; Tony Smith, *Foreign Attachments: The Power of Ethnic Groups in the Making of American Foreign Policy* (Cambridge, MA: Harvard University Press, 2001). See also Eric M. Uslaner, "A Tower of Babel on Foreign Policy?" in *Interest Group Politics*, eds. Allan J. Cigler and Burdett A. Loomis (Washington, DC: Congressional Quarterly, Inc., 1991).
83. IOM, *World Migration 2003*, 4.
84. This challenges some of the claims in Brubaker, *Citizenship and Nationhood in France and Germany.*
85. See, for example, Charles McC. Mathias Jr., "Ethnic Groups and Foreign Policy," *Foreign Affairs* 59 (1981): 975–998; Yossi Shain, "Multicultural Foreign Policy," *Foreign Policy* 100 (1995): 69–97; Robert W. Tucker, Charles B. Keely, and Linda Wrigley, eds., *Immigration and US Foreign Policy* (Boulder, CO: Westview Press, 1990).
86. IOM, *World Migration 2003*, 4.
87. In 2001, for example, over 140,000 economic immigrants entered Japan—a figure that was more than 9 percent higher than in 2000, IOM, *World Migration 2003*, 200. See also Midford, chapter 9 in this volume.
88. Rudolph, "Security and the Political Economy of Migration."
89. IOM, *World Migration 2003*, 149.
90. Rudolph, "Security and the Political Economy of Migration"; Mittelman, *The Globalization Syndrome.*
91. IOM, *World Migration 2003*, 149.
92. For details, see http://www.germany-info.org/relaunch/welcome/work/greencard.html.
93. Nick Mackie, "Chinese Students Drawn to Britain," BBC News, September 7, 2005, available at http://news.bbc.co.uk/2/hi/uk_news/education/4219026.stm [Accessed April 14, 2006].
94. "Science, Visas, and America: On the Turning Away," *The Economist*, May 6, 2004, 76.
95. Mittelman, *The Globalization Syndrome*, 45.
96. IOM, *World Migration 2003*, 6.
97. IOM, *World Migration 2003*, 216–217.
98. Ibid, 6.
99. On these two points, see Claudia M. Buch, Anja Kuckulenz, and Marie-Helene Le Manchec, *Worker Remittances and Capital Flows*, Keil Working Paper No. 1130 (Kiel, Germany: Kiel Institute for World Economics, 2002).
100. Segal, *Atlas of International Migration*, 150, as cited in Hirst and Thompson, *Globalization in Question*, 30.
101. United Nations Population Fund, *The State of World Population 1993* (New York: UNPF, 1993), as cited in Mittelman, *The Globalization Syndrome*, 45.

72 • Fiona B. Adamson

102. Peter Gammeltoft, *Remittances and Other Financial Flows to Developing Countries* (Copenhagen: Danish Institute for International Study, 2002), as cited in IOM, *World Migration 2003*, 310.
103. IOM, *World Migration 2003*, 224.
104. IOM, March 2003.
105. See, for example, Nicholas Van Hear, "Sustaining Societies Under Strain: Remittances as a Form of Transnational Exchange in Sri Lanka and Ghana," in *New Approaches to Migration? Transnational Communities and the Transformation of Home*, eds. Nadje al-Ali and Khalid Koser (London: Routledge, 2002), 202–223.
106. IOM, *World Migration 2003*, 17.
107. IOM, *World Migration 2003*, 225.
108. As in the case of private contractors, this practice is not necessarily new.
109. This information is taken from the American Friends Service Committee (AFSC) Web page, http://www.afsc.org/youthmil/NoncitizensandtheU.S.Military.htm, accessed May 24, 2004.
110. This endeavor was viewed as unsuccessful by many critics. Figures taken from the Department of Defense, available at http://www.defenselink.mil/news/Feb2003/n02242003_200302243.html, accessed May 24, 2004.
111. Shain and Barth, "Diasporas in International Relations Theory."
112. See Madeleine Demetriou and Fiona B. Adamson, "Reshaping the Boundaries of 'State' and 'National Identity': Incorporating Diasporas into IR Theorizing" forthcoming in *European Journal of International Relations*.
113. Aristide Zolberg, "From Invitation to Interdiction: U.S. Foreign Policy and Immigration since 1945," in *Threatened Peoples, Threatened Borders*, ed. Michael S. Teitelbaum and Myron Weiner (New York: W. W. Norton, 1995), 123–124, as cited in Rudolph, "Security and the Political Economy of Migration," 609.
114. Yossi Shain, *Marketing the American Creed Abroad: Diasporas in the United States and Their Homelands* (Cambridge: Cambridge University Press, 1999).
115. For the case of Russia, see Vadim Volkov, *Violent Entrepreneurs: The Use of Force in the Making of Russian Capitalism* (Ithaca, NY: Cornell University Press, 2002).
116. See, for example, David C. Rapoport, "The Four Waves of Rebel Terror and September 11," in *The New Global Terrorism: Characteristics, Causes, Controls*, ed. Charles W. Kegley (Upper Saddle River, NJ: Prentice Hall, 2003), 36–59.
117. Collier, "Economic Causes of Civil Conflict," 6.
118. Kaldor, *New and Old Wars*; Benedict Anderson, "Long-Distance Nationalism," in *The Spectre of Comparisons: Nationalism, Southeast Asia and the World* (London: Verso, 1998), 58–74; Daniel Byman, Peter Chalk, Bruce Hoffman, William Rosenau, and David Brannan, *Trends in Outside Support for Insurgent Movements* (Santa Monica, CA: RAND, 2001).
119. Independent International Commission on Kosovo, *The Kosovo Report: Conflict, International Response, Lessons Learned* (Oxford: Oxford University Press, 2000).
120. Khalid Medani, "Funding Fundamentalism: The Political Economy of an Islamist State," in *Political Islam: Essays from Middle East Report*, eds. Joel Beinin and Joe Stork (Berkeley: University of California Press, 1997).
121. IOM, *World Migration 2003*, 206.
122. Fiona B. Adamson, "Displacement, Diaspora Mobilization and Transnational Cycles of Political Violence," in *Maze of Fear: Migration and Security after 9/11*, ed. John Tirman (New York: New Press, 2004), 45–58.
123. Lischer, "Collateral Damage."
124. IOM, *World Migration 2003*, 60.
125. Rey Koslowski, "The Mobility Money Can Buy: Human Smuggling and Border Control in the European Union," in Andreas and Snyder, *The Wall Around the West*.

126. Peter Andreas, "The Clandestine Political Economy of War and Peace in Bosnia," *International Studies Quarterly* 48 (1) (March 2004): 29–51.
127. Koslowski, "The Mobility Money Can Buy"; Fiona B. Adamson, "Mobilizing at the Margins of the System: The Dynamics and Security Impacts of Transnational Mobilization by Non-State Actors" (Ph.D. dissertation, Columbia University, 2002).
128. Mittelman, *The Globalization Syndrome*, 208.
129. Peter Lupsha, "Transnational Organized Crime versus the Nation-State," in *Transnational Crime*, ed. Nikos Passas (Hants, UK: Dartmouth Publishing Company, 1999). I am indebted to Aymeric Simon for this reference.
130. Mittelman, *The Globalization Syndrome*, 203–222.
131. Louise Shelley, "Transnational Organized Crime: The New Authoritarianism," in *The Illicit Global Economy and State Power*, eds. Richard Friman and Peter Andreas (Lanham, MD: Rowman and Littlefield, 1999).
132. *Migration News*, November 2001, as cited in Rudolph, "Security and the Political Economy of Migration," 616.
133. Robert S. Leiken, *Bearers of Global Jihad? Immigration and National Security after 9/11* (Washington, DC: The Nixon Center, 2004).
134. Ibid., 6.
135. Ibid.
136. For critical overviews of the impact that internal security measures have had on Arab and Muslim populations in the United States, see Louise Cainkar, "Targeting Muslims, at Ashcroft's Discretion," in *Middle East Report* (MERIP), March 14, 2003, available online at http://www.merip.org/mero/mer0031403.html, and Louise Cainkar, "Impact of the September 11 Attacks on Arab and Muslim Communities in the US" in *Maze of Fear* Tirman.
137. Kirshner, chapter 1 of this volume, 5.
138. Held et al., *Global Transformations*.

3

NEW MEDIA FOR A NEW WORLD?

Information Technology and Threats to National Security

Geoffrey L. Herrera

Technology will make it increasing difficult for the state to control the information its people receive…. The Goliath of totalitarianism will be brought down by the David of the microchip.

Ronald Reagan, June 13, 1989[1]

What has steadily, insidiously improved since then, of course, making humanist arguments almost irrelevant, is the technology. We must not be too distracted by the clunkiness of the means of surveillance current in Winston Smith's era. In "our" nineteen eighty-four, after all, the integrated circuit chip was less than a decade old, and almost embarrassingly primitive next to the wonders of computer technology circa 2003, most notably the Internet, a development that promises social control on a scale those quaint old twentieth-century tyrants with their goofy mustaches could only dream about.

**Thomas Pynchon (from the foreword
to the 2003 edition of *1984*, p. xvi)**

We are in the midst of an information revolution.[2] Never mind that the "revolution" has been ongoing for at least one hundred years,[3] new digital technologies for communication, data processing, and storage promise to create a ubiquitous global "infosphere" where every piece of information is available anywhere instantly at little or no cost. The infosphere is (will) transform everything it touches—politics, economics, society, culture. No sphere of human activity will escape its reach. Organizational hierarchies will be flattened; centralized institutions will lose power to smaller, nimbler, more flexible swarms, or networks, or informal groups of like-minded individuals; the massive information processing apparatuses (states, corporations, international organizations) constructed to handle information in its bulky "analog" form will be rendered irrelevant.[4] The information revolution is a historical transformation in human activity on the same scale as the development of agriculture and industrial production techniques.[5]

Of course much of this is hyperbole, pitched either by the overly enthusiastic or those with a financial stake in a particular technological future or both.[6] The reality is likely something far less transformative and far more ambiguous in its salutary effect. But one need not swallow the claims of the enthusiasts wholesale to think that the spread of digital information and communications technologies (ICTs) around the world presages something quite significant. The issues they raise point to the correct question: Who gains the greater political advantage from new information technologies—states (and some states more than others?), individuals, firms, or some novel form of organization?

States function effectively in part because of their ability to accumulate, process, store, use, and monopolize information. The rational-bureaucratic institutions of the modern state are, in essence, vast human-machine information processing devices. As the family firm adapted to the increased information processing demands of an industrial economy by growing vastly in size and bureaucratizing, so too did the state adapt to demands to provide security, welfare and social services, and economic and technological management by increasing the size and complexity of its information capabilities.[7]

State power is dependent on information and systems for gathering, classifying, storing, retrieving, and communicating it.[8] A massive shift in the underlying information infrastructure might, depending on the nature of the transformation, threaten states, or, construing the question more narrowly, threaten national security. Posing the question this way focuses attention on innovation in information technologies as a component in the broader process of globalization—conceived broadly as the rise of stateless forces in competition with nation-states. To what extent does ICT foster or empower stateless forces? To what extent do such forces threaten national security?

This chapter will investigate these information technology-enabled forces and the nature of the threat they pose. As the debate over the meaning of the information revolution indicates, if we cannot be sure of the information future, we will have to proceed with care. I have disaggregated the potential threats to national security into four conceptual categories: specific internal threats to regime survival, specific external threats to regime survival, specific threats to the security of citizens, and the general threat to nation-stateness itself. Each of these threats intersects with a different aspect of new media and generates different political dynamics. A conventional wisdom has built up around each one. Exploring, and debunking where necessary, these conventional wisdoms provides a useful frame for an investigation of the relationship between ICT and national security.

Threats to regime survival are tied to the open flow of information and the quality of that information. Old media such as radio, television, and print and new media such as e-mail and cellular phones are the carriers. Closed regimes are threatened by the organizational capacities ICT may give opposition movements and by the circulation of restricted information that may undermine regime legitimacy. Both of these mechanisms are partial products of globalization—organizational capacity can be supplied from without, as can information flows. In more unstable circumstances, ICT may even undermine the state's claim to a monopoly of violence (for example, in the first Chechen war, cellular phones greatly enhanced information gathering and maneuverability by the Chechen forces). The conventional wisdom here is that as "the Internet interprets censorship as damage and routes around it," efforts to control it are doomed to fail. This view is mostly incorrect. States can control the flow of information to a considerable degree, but to do so, they have to alter their organization and practices—in itself a testament to the shaping power of globalization. The analysis below will focus on censorship efforts to protect the regime from unwanted communication; Internet traffic and satellite television broadcasts are a natural subject for inquiry.

Threats to the conventional military balance of power, the second category of threat, stem mostly from the American near monopoly on the technologies of the ICT-driven "revolution in military affairs" or RMA. If this advantage is extended, or even merely maintained, no country's military will be a match for the conventional capabilities of American forces. Here the principal mechanism maintaining the gap is superior American resources and the willingness to devote them to military technology innovation. This is not a clear-cut case of a threat posed by globalization, but it is so clearly a potential effect of ICT on national security that it cannot be avoided. The conventional wisdom here is that the gap will be maintained for the foreseeable future. The US lead is just too great, and its continued willingness to devote far more research and development resources to military technology than any other state, means no other state has any hope of catching up anytime soon. The consequence is a military monopoly and the transformation of global security provision, with the United States playing a dominant global role not as conventional threat, but as quasi-imperial security guarantor.[9] This view is in some measure correct, but with two significant provisos. First, there are signs of counterbalancing—particularly in the area of space technology—and asymmetric balancing. As the Segal chapter in this volume argues, China is very interested in using ICT to generate some kind of (ill-defined) leapfrog over the United States's RMA lead. Second, the significance of the US lead is undermined by the growth of private sector "RMA-like" activity, from the widespread civilian use of global position systems (GPSs) and satellite imagery to the proliferation of uncoordinated surveillance "networks."[10] What good is the US lead if it cannot enforce its own monopoly over information networks and devices? To focus this discussion, below I will analyze the instruments of American global information dominance: communications and reconnaissance satellites, digital and electronic surveillance, and GPSs.

The third kind of threat comes from rising ICT-enabled stateless actors. Malicious hackers, virus and worm writers, identity thieves, terrorists, and transnational criminal organizations reach easily across state borders to threaten individual citizens, economic infrastructure, firms, and government operations themselves. The principal mechanisms of this threat are global computer networks and a dense global trading system. The global, open character of the Internet, the ubiquity of the arms trade, and the volume and speed of global transportation networks lower the costs and increase the effectiveness of transnational mischief. The conventional wisdom posits an ever-widening gap between the global scale and scope of virtual-world mischief and the political governance institutions (states) available to deal with the problem. As the gap continues to widen, the efficacy and legitimacy of states will be called into question.[11] We may see more robust transnational efforts to deal with the problems posed by insecurity in the digital world. But the claim misunderstands the nature of that world and assumes the architecture itself is somehow beyond the reach of political control. This is clearly not the case, and there are a wide variety of governance techniques, legal changes (both national and global), and infrastructural modifications that would reduce the freedom of "rogue" operators in cyberspace.[12] Therefore, below I focus on anonymity and stealth on the Internet. These make possible the forces of digital disorder: Internet viruses, worms, and targeted attacks, including explicit politically motivated sabotage, economic extortion, and identity theft.

Finally, ICT poses a fourth threat to national security—to state policy efficacy and stateness itself. Historically, there is a relationship between prevailing communications technology and the structure of political authority.[13] In the digital age, the state faces a number of threats to its efficacy and authority. For example, the state's inability to control electronic financial transactions threatens economic policy effectiveness.[14] Or, as ICT can dramatically reduce transaction and organizational costs, it is plausible that new forms of political authority—perhaps in the form of self-organizing entities analogous to markets or in novel forms of global governance—may supplant the state.[15] The common wisdom holds that hierarchical, bureaucratic organizations such as the state are fated to be overwhelmed by newer, more flexible forms better suited to a ubiquitous, global, digital information environment. What is true for economic and social forms is true of political governance forms as well. But just as plausibly, the digital information revolution will only enhance the social control of large, centralized organizations. Digital information and communications technologies will only help do the very statist tasks of information gathering, processing, storing, and communicating more efficiently and effectively. Below, rather than undertake a sweeping overview of global governance and information technology (IT), I focus on efforts by states to control digital financial transactions. If the common wisdom is correct, then as states lose control over such transactions, alternative financial "authorities" should be emerging in their stead.

The conventional wisdoms all suggest that we can know the trajectory of technological, and hence political, change. This is impossible and smacks of determinism—not just because the future is unknowable or uncertain. Rather, prediction is impossible because technology is inherently political, or, better, technology and politics are mutually constitutive.[16] Technology is both a social product and an independent factor because it confronts social actors as a real resource or impediment. ICT is no different. Its political impact will depend how it is constructed by social, economic, political, and even national security forces and how it is buffeted by chance and unintended consequences.[17] So, as the trajectory of the technologies themselves is still open to social and political influence, the kind of national security threat IT becomes will be a consequence of the kind of IT we make.[18]

One conjuncture in particular looms over this entire analysis. The 9/11 terror attacks have—through changes to privacy legislation, wiretap and surveillance authority, and infrastructure—profoundly shaped the state's relationship to the digital world and reshaped our notions of the possible and impossible in Internet regulation. The responses to 9/11 offer, in miniature, my answer to the two original questions: ICT does empower stateless forces, and those forces pose serious threats to national security. However, ICT cuts both ways and offers considerable opportunities to states to respond—but at a cost. States that harness ICT to combat ICT-empowered threats do so by transforming themselves—their organization, the spatial and virtual scale and scope of their activities, their relationships with private actors of all kinds, their relationships with other states, their very definition of security.

THREATS TO REGIME STABILITY

The first kind of threat, to the internal stability of regimes, is the easiest to conceptualize and the easiest to test. Authoritarian regimes in particular that depend on direct and indirect political repression to stay in power also rely on control over the flow of information. They own outright or manage through official and unofficial censorship the print media, television, and even film and popular culture, generally. The goal is to stifle dissent, inhibit opposition organization, and prevent news from the outside that might undermine the regime from circulating within its society. The conventional wisdom on new media (satellite television, the World Wide Web, Internet newsgroups, and listservs, among others) and new communications technologies (cellular and satellite telephones, Internet chat rooms, and e-mail) is that repressive regimes will find it harder to control the news and information their citizens receive. New media, the argument goes, are decentralized and hard or impossible to trace (like newsgroups and chat rooms), harder to tap (like cell phones), or come from outside the state (like CNN and Al Jazeera), or all three. Access to them is cheap or impossible to control. Illegal satellite dishes proliferate throughout the developing world (in democracies and authoritarian regimes alike); Internet access at cybercafes combined with anonymizing remailers and Web browsers make tracing specific Internet activity to a specific person all but impossible. So, if the regimes are right that they are threatened by open flows of information (judging by their willingness to censor and block), then opening those flows should threaten their control.

There is already a fair amount of research into the subject, and perhaps surprisingly, the results are not all positive and the conventional wisdom is most likely wrong.[19] A number of regimes (the examples in Kalathil and Boal's book are Burma, China, Cuba, Egypt, Saudi Arabia, Singapore, the United Arab Emirates, and Vietnam) have been able to control Internet access with varying degrees of success. The news media itself is still quite bound up with state power—despite its apparent state-lessness—and I am not yet sure we can say with confidence that a more global news media necessarily makes authoritarianism harder to sus-tain (Lynch and Segal in this volume, the former more than the latter, disagree with this assessment slightly; I refine this argument below). For every fall of the Berlin Wall, there is a former Yugoslavia, where the regime's mastery of the media was instrumental to encouraging and managing ethnic violence—and to staying in power—or a Rwanda where radio was instrumental in arranging a genocide.[20] (It is worth noting that both of the former regimes were in the end undone—but only by the application of military force.) As far back as the mid-1990s, Rupert Murdoch's Fox Network modified the content of its broadcasts to conform to the Chinese government's restrictions—and to land a large satellite contract.[21]

The Lynch chapter provides an excellent overview of the problems faced by Middle Eastern regimes struggling with global traditional broadcast media (the Al Jazeera effect). Here I discuss many-to-many networks (the Internet), a different (but no less dangerous) kind of threat. If the Internet continues to spread in its current, relatively open[22] form and if the technologies of access continue to drop in price, then authoritarian regimes will be overpowered in the battle for informa-tion supremacy. They will be unable to block, trace, or analyze network activity and so will be unable to control the flow of information domes-tically and between their societies and the outside world. If, on the other hand, the Internet evolves so as to allow more centralized control, then the task of regime survival will be easier to accomplish and the threat will not be as great. For the moment, business interests and consumer inertia keep the Internet relatively open, but nothing inherent in the software and hardware architecture of the Internet mandates that this be so. Any of several developments could push the architecture of the Internet in a less open direction: consumer discontent with unwanted commercial e-mail (or spam), concern with crime—from pedophilia to drug smuggling—or terrorism could all push popular opinion in favor of a more centralized Internet and give policy makers the leverage they need to overcome business opposition.

To give just two examples, it is now a truism that the events of Sep-tember 11 changed the status of privacy in the West—and in the United States in particular.[23] There is now much greater tolerance for changes in the technological environment that make privacy and secrecy much harder to maintain. Recent revelations about the extensive use Al-Qaeda makes of computers and the Internet to plan attacks, build support, and manage the organization may lead to widespread public support for far more draconian controls over the Internet than those mandated by the Patriot Act.[24] Second, the Internet protocol, simple mail transfer protocol (SMTP), has recently come under attack for alleged vulnerabilities to spam.[25] Rewriting the protocol—which governs the sending of almost all Internet e-mail—would almost certainly involve removing the possibility of sending anonymous e-mail. As a global network, changes especially in as important a country as the United States would rapidly spread and become the new standards for Internet data control.

The conventional wisdom persists in spite of a mounting pile of evidence to the contrary.[26] Already studies of Internet censorship in China, Cuba, Malaysia, Saudi Arabia, and Singapore, as well as global surveys conducted by the OpenNet Initiative, show that authoritarian regimes have had considerable success blocking the Internet.[27] Rather than replicate country-specific studies, here I investigate the technological initiatives that go into Internet blocking in general and their relationship to the Internet as a whole. In particular, I am interested in how the efforts states go through to block Internet access for their citizens serve to partially modify the technical nature of the Internet itself. The most interesting implication of this is the potential merging of public and private power. States make use of tools provided by multinational computer software and hardware manufacturers who are pursuing their own vision of a closed, controlled Internet. This possibility is an example of the ways in which states are transforming themselves to meet the threat posed by the emergence of ICT-enabled stateless forces.

The Internet is not a global computer network; it a network of networks. The topology of the Internet reflects its Westphalian underbelly. Local Internet service providers (ISPs) and corporate and public sector networks are connected to national network backbones. Those backbones are connected globally via international gateways. This mode of organization is not a necessary consequence of the technology of computer networks. Private individuals could, if they wished (and could remain undetected), lay fiber-optic lines across international borders. But the Internet, as a sociotechnical system, has developed to reflect its state-centric origins, and the sunk costs associated with its development trajectory makes undoing its topology highly unlikely.[28] It is a simple matter for states to control the information flowing in and out of their territories, especially if, as in most of the developing world, the government owns the backbone.[29]

States control Internet-based information by blocking requests for foreign Web sites; and, as so much of the Internet (in terms of content) is concentrated in the United States and Western Europe, this is suffi-cient to regulate the flow of potentially threatening information. States are thus able to filter content at the backbone or gateway level. They also engage in local level content filtering. This is software installed on a local machine that blocks specified content. Authoritarian governments use local content filtering in some Internet cafes. The latter method excels at filtering specific words or phrases or even logic algorithms to try and determine the meaning of search phrases or e-mail or document contents. The former is better (more efficient) at brute force filtering—blocking access to entire sites or domains based on packet address.[30]

China, for example, has only a handful of national backbones (CHINANet, CERNet, CSTNet, CHINAGBN, and UNINet). Some are private ISPs; others are government-controlled networks. Segal's chapter touches on this, and other studies have shown that content on subjects such as the Falun Gong, Taiwan, Tiananmen Square, Tibet, and human rights, are effectively blocked across the networks.[31] Saudi Arabia has even more control over ISPs and the national backbone than China; although there are a number of local ISPs, the government's Internet Services Unit operates the backbone and links to the global Internet. Unlike most authoritarian regimes, the Saudi government acknowledges that it controls Internet content—filtering in accordance with the Koran to protect the kingdom's Islamic values.[32]

Efforts to circumvent filtering and blocking have tried to keep pace with state capacity. The OpenNet Initiative is busy developing a proxy server tool it calls Psiphon to allow users in censoring countries to temporarily "borrow" another user's Internet connection in another country. This would in principle avoid all efforts at censorship, as the connection would be to an obscure address and would change fre-quently. Other activist (or "hacktivist") groups have developed tools to accomplish the same ends, such as the Peekabooty Project.[33] Yet would-be circumventers need to be careful. Just as on the Internet no one knows you are a dog, no one knows if a piece of circumvention soft-ware is not in fact a monitoring tool for governments. A program called Triangle Boy, developed by Emeryville, California–based SafeWeb and partially financed by the Central Intelligence Agency (CIA), allows states to monitor the users to whom the program is supposedly provid-ing anonymity.[34] More prosaically, the content filtering software and the routers used to detect and filter "bad" packets are eagerly sold to authoritarian regimes by (almost exclusively) American firms includ-ing the router-manufacturing giant Cisco.[35]

From the perspective of national security, these efforts at controlling national Internet space to keep out ideas, arguments, and information considered subversive or dangerous have the effect of creating "virtual borders" as states expand their territoriality beyond the constraints of their physical territory.[36] The United States, as in so many things, leads the world in this expansion and transformation of "border." The most recent effort, the Department of Homeland Security's US-VISIT program,[37] will expand the United States's surveillance of foreign visitors to their own homelands and then will trace, through electronic tracking, their movements into, around, and out of the United States.

Digital border controls are no better than their traditional equivalents, with some intriguing twists. First, the controls are provided by hardware and software vendors from the United States and (in rarer cases) Western Europe—the very cultures that pose the threat of contagion. Triangle Boy opens the possibility of controls with "backdoors" exploitable by other governments or nonstate actors. Second, content filters are notoriously inaccurate and crude tools. They generate large numbers of both false positives (library filter programs in the United States that block search queries for breast cancer, for example) and false negatives. Purchasing governments will not be able to reliably know what is and is not getting through. Third, authoritarian governments in the developing world are forced to depend upon the technical expertise of nonnational private firms, placing them in a position of dependence. Although the conventional wisdom, that censorship on the Internet is impossible, is clearly incorrect, the situation is far from a simple triumph for the forces of state power. To maintain information security against potentially adulterating ideas, states have had to transform their border control regimes and harness the success of their efforts to another global, stateless force—the international computer industry. Returning to the two main questions, there is no doubt the global Internet opens authoritarian regimes up to new sources of information and new means of communication that they do not control. The threat to national security is real, as evidenced by the strenuous efforts to manage it. States have recourse, however, to powerful tools to combat these flows, provided they are willing to transform state practices and enter into new, and potentially troubling, relations of external dependence.

THREATS TO THE CONVENTIONAL MILITARY BALANCE OF POWER

The second threat borrows from traditional international relations theory. If there is an information balance of power, will not those on the

poorer side of the information divide be vulnerable (militarily, politically, culturally) to those states with information dominance? ICT is
creating a permanent gap in conventional military capabilities between
states, or at least the United States military certainly thinks so. The
United States is pursuing an RMA, on two fronts, in the faith that future
military superiority will be based on information superiority. The first
front enhances existing military capabilities: sensors, identification-
friend-or-foe (IFF) and target acquisition technologies, networked
military units, live biometric feedback from soldiers in the field, and
so on.[38] If the future unfolds as the United States hopes, weaker states,
fearing American surgical military action against them, will doubtless
turn to asymmetric strategies of power balancing—including but not
limited to the acquisition of weapons of mass destruction, especially
nuclear weapons (Mueller touches on this in chapter 5). Not only will
this development place individual regimes at greater risk from American military action, but also it does not bode well for the stability of the
international system as a whole.[39]

Second, the United States seeks to maintain or even expand its lead in
so-called soft power.[40] Nye argues that American economic and technological strength, but more importantly the appeal of American ideology
(and public diplomacy to communicate that ideology), give the United
States unprecedented power to control the global agenda—to persuade
instead of coerce. American popular culture, including art, film, music,
and fashion, as well as economic and technological dominance, is
folded into this by Nye and others, but it is far from clear exactly what
mechanism connects the world's fondness for Coca Cola with favorable
views of American foreign policy.[41] Nevertheless, the distinction is useful here. The first kind of soft power is rooted in actions taken (or not
taken) by a state. ICT serves as a conduit for that ideology. The second
is a "stateless force" that may or may not be harnessable by the state.
American IT dominance enhances both forces, though only the former
reliably supports American power and foreign policy objectives.

Even so, the benefits of IT on the battlefield may be overshadowed
by the importance of skill and training; military organizational culture
may prevent the full promise of the RMA from being realized; or the
revolution may be oversold.[42] More spending and additional innovation
may not alter the reality of warfare much and the likely battlefields the
U.S. military will face are impervious to digital rationalization. In the
realm of soft power (in the first sense), control of the conduits will not
necessarily translate into actual influence—as American "communications" missteps in the Iraq War indicate.[43]

Focusing on U.S. dominance in global information networks captures both aspects within a narrow empirical focus. That dominance—in satellites and cables, systems for global positioning, imaging, communications (military and civilian), signals intelligence, broadcasting, and target detection—is if anything greater than Britain's "All-Red-Line" supremacy in undersea telegraph communications at the end of the nineteenth century.[44] That control is in turn crucial to American power, hard and soft (in the first, statist, sense). It provides surveillance and communications capabilities vastly superior to any would-be competitor.

Will this lead last? The available evidence suggests that it will in part, but continued American supremacy will be undermined by increased civilian capabilities (in particular in Western Europe, China, and Japan), and by a complicated and complicating relationship with private sector actors. The American lead in strictly military communications technology will not be directly challenged for some time, but civilian tools (and civilian use of military tools) will undermine the utility of that advantage. Commercialization and privatization of communications technology will weaken the value of the American advantage. This brings the two forms of soft power so close together that they are almost touching, but not in a way necessarily useful for U.S. power. Controlling the conduit of communications may not help if the message is unconvincing while the forces of privatization are undermining that control and rendering it less important.

American global information capabilities are well known. Photoreconnaissance satellites, launched during the Cold War to track Soviet weapons developments, allow the United States to spy, to resolutions of finer than one meter, anywhere on the earth's surface. The U.S.-owned and -operated GPS enables the military to keep track of ships, planes, supplies, and people. The National Security Agency (NSA) is purported to be able to listen in on every satellite-transmitted telephone call. A system of satellites and remote listening posts, called Echelon, expand that capability to many land-based telephone calls.[45] No other state comes close to these capabilities. Russia retains a significant satellite imaging capability and its GPS competitor, global orbiting navigation satellite system (GLONASS), is identical in form to the GPS system (twenty-four satellites; continuous, real-time positioning information) though less reliable. Russia is on the verge of joining the European Union (EU) in their planned navigation system, Galileo. China has a rudimentary satellite imaging capability, a small civilian communications system, and a robust (and rapidly growing) direct broadcast satellite sector. They make use of GPS and GLONASS systems for satellite navigation, but have tentatively agreed to join with the EU in the Galileo system.[46]

Growing Chinese prowess in space launches has made them a competitor with the United States and the EU for low-cost satellite launchings.

Europe, both as the EU and as individual states, has significant communications capabilities, but almost all of it in the civilian sector. The European Space Agency (ESA) oversees communications satellites. The private, mostly French aerospace firm Arianespace dominates the commercial space transport (their Web site claims they launch more than half of all commercial satellites).[47] At the other end of the spectrum, the Pakistani experience shows how great the gap is. As a nuclear power, Pakistan has space aspirations as well. The country received five orbit allocations from the International Telecommunications Union (ITU) in 1984. Four of the five have lapsed, and to avoid losing the fifth, the government "borrowed" a Turkish satellite to fill the slot until it can successfully launch one of its own.[48]

No state is likely to challenge the United States in the military sphere, but developments in the civilian and commercial spheres are altering the importance of the American lead. During the Cold War, satellite imaging was the exclusive domain of the superpowers. Over the past decade, the explosion of commercial satellite launches has led to a widespread diffusion of satellite imagery. Some analysts have argued that this spread marks a wholesale shift in the balance of surveillance power from the state to the private sector and the civic sphere.[49] Others fear this development and see a significant threat to national security.[50] In a fit of whimsy, the June 2004 issue of *Reason Magazine* was able to combine commercial satellite imagery with high-speed, on-the-fly printing technologies to print a satellite image of each subscriber's house on the cover of his or her copy of the magazine.[51] These examples point to an emerging situation: increasingly, the United States, or any other state, has less and less control over the use of highly accurate satellite imagery, thereby weakening its value to the state.

Something similar is happening with global navigation satellite systems. The American GPS system is the global standard, but the European Galileo system, if successfully launched, threatens to do for GPS what private imaging satellites have done for overhead surveillance. Unlike the GPS system, Galileo is intended to be a predominantly civilian enterprise. Military functions have been added only as an afterthought. It is also a multinational undertaking. The EU is the main driver, but cooperation with China, Russia, India, Israel, Canada, and South Korea has already been secured.[52] Galileo will compete directly with GPS, will not have military controls such as selective availability, and will be more reliable (according to the system's designers).[53] But the story of GPS is much the same as satellite imaging. An exclusively military system diffused gradually into the civilian sphere, generating pressures to remove the military-inspired restrictions (such as shutting the system off to nonmilitary users during times of international tension).[54] Now, satellite navigation is as crucial to the global economy as telephone lines and national highway networks. The United States could not shut off GPS (or stop the development of Galileo) even if it wanted to. The open global economy depends on it.

The effect on the traditional balance of power by ICT is complicated and ambiguous. The American lead in information-enabled military capabilities seems secure but only because other states see no point in pursuing competition in that realm. Meanwhile, developments in the commercial sphere hem in, distort, and problematize the American advantage. Stateless forces have grown dependent on state-constructed systems designed for military advantage, and the state driving the systems (the United States) is symbiotically tied to that dependence. Does this pose a national security threat to states other than the United States? Most certainly it does, but interestingly, the response has been not to balance directly and conventionally, or even (militarily) asymmetrically. Instead, the dominant response has been to seek to deepen the extent to which private actors and ICT systems bind the United States.[55]

THREATS FROM NONSTATE ACTORS

The third threat focuses not on states as threats, but on new (or newly empowered) organizations or networks of organizations. The conventional wisdom in this area is that ICT will shift the balance of power from states to stateless actors and make it much harder for states to protect their citizens from these threats. By decreasing the costs of communication and information processing, and increasing the speed and ease of both, ICT is thought to enable new kinds of organizations: smaller, less hierarchical, decentralized or barely organized at all, nimbler, nonterritorial. As the scale and density of the infosphere increases, networked organizations can rely on it to perform the functions that older firms and states built huge bureaucracies to accomplish. Some of these networks will be firms and legitimate political organizations. But some will be transnational terrorist and criminal organizations, or clandestine transnational actors (CTAs) as Peter Andreas terms them (the Adamson chapter addresses the role of communications technology in maintaining connections between diaspora populations and their home communities).[56] The infosphere provides communication, coordination, anonymity, and access to financial, material, and knowledge resources. It should be the ideal organizing tool for those who wish to plan and execute in secret with the minimum amount of human and material resources.[57]

To investigate the broad realm of CTA threats, this analysis focuses on the key enabler of their infosphere activities: anonymity on the Internet. Anonymity allows for clandestine communication, propagandizing, and financial transactions. It also allows the Internet to be used as a low-risk launching point for criminal activities ranging from traditional theft and extortion to espionage and sabotage. As an empirical plausibility probe, it has the advantage of being both narrow and broad. It is narrow as it concerns only one specific feature of the Internet; but it is also broad because that feature figures so prominently in so many of the security concerns the Internet generates: hacking, denial-of-service attacks, identity theft, credit card fraud, secret communication, and infrastructure vulnerability, to name just a few.

Since 9/11, Al-Qaeda's use of encrypted chat rooms, illicit electronic financial transactions, and steganography (the hiding of secret messages within a digital image) has been widely reported.[58] If the hypotheses and evidence are true, then the development of an infosphere should prove a tremendous boon to groups and individuals who wish to operate illegally and beneath the scrutiny of legitimate authority. The threat to national security will then depend upon two things—the degree to which they are enabled by the technology and by their goals. Assuming capabilities scale with goals (not unproblematic as an assumption, but a place to start), then the scarier the goals of the organization, the bigger the threat to both national and individual security.

Terror and crime are symbiotic, and both benefit from the same global ICT infrastructure. Terror groups around the world engage in all manner of illegal activity, from credit card fraud, to drug smuggling, to trafficking in illicit diamonds, so terror groups are also transnational criminal organizations.[59] The information technologies relevant to the disruptions caused by CTAs are those that contribute to the financial, human, and knowledge "sea" of the infosphere—the Internet, physical global networks (transatlantic cable, satellites, etc.), as well as the rules, protocols, standards, and regulations that make anonymity and stealth possible and even easy. The rules (both in terms of law and also in how legal, economic, and political constraints affect the trajectories of the relevant technologies) are critical to the nature of the threat, as the rules determine just how easy it is for terrorist and criminal organizations to continue to operate in the digital sea.

If global crime and terrorism flourish because the international financial system is too open and insufficiently regulated—making it easy to hide, move, and launder money—then the development of better tools for data mining and better cooperation across the global financial system can reduce this vulnerability.[60] From cryptography and universal digital communication, to biometrics and satellite surveillance, at a general level, the abilities of nonstate actors to threaten national and individual security can be checked or even rolled back by expanded state capabilities. Greater state power can be legislated—both at the national and international levels—pushed through at historical conjunctures such as 9/11 where societal resistance to greater state penetration is weakened by a perceived increase in vulnerability to stateless forces from within and without. The state lacks an obvious response to increased nonstate actor illicit activity in only one respect: to the extent that this activity benefits from the sheer volume of international transactions—the small-fish-in-the-big-pond effect—continued globalization will continue to challenge states to control "illegal" activity in the international sphere. This, however, is only a second-order effect of technology.[61]

The conventional wisdom on anonymity and all that it allows is that there is little the state can do. It is literally written into the structure of the Internet itself and cannot be dislodged without destroying the networks themselves. But the conventional wisdom is only partially correct; states retain considerable ability to bite back. The same features that enable terrorists, malicious hackers, and criminals can also, in modified form, strengthen state surveillance and law enforcement capability. The situation is somewhat analogous to an arms race (those in global law enforcement are amazed at the speed with which transnational criminal organizations stay one step ahead in the technology race[62]), though the state has the advantage of law—and the ability to modify the technological environment by fiat. If nonstate actors make use of digital communications technologies to plan and coordinate illicit activities, then the state can modify the architectures of these networks to make tracking and surveillance easier. For example, in the United States, the creation of a national 911 system for cell phones in principle would give the physical position of every activated cell phone in the system with great precision—imperative for rescue operations, but also useful for law enforcement.[63] In the end, the future of anonymity on the Internet will be written through the interaction of three distinct forces: efforts by states to secure their cyberinfrastructure, private sector efforts to create a secure (or "trusted") computing environment, and the forces of "anarchy"—stateless forces.

Anonymity and clandestine communications are rooted in the technological character or "nature" of the Internet itself. Anonymity is a "feature" of the network because of the way digital information moves through it and the way the Internet is governed. The Internet is distributed and packet switched. The underlying architecture, devised in the mid-1960s in a collaboration between the U.S. government, academic researchers, and the RAND Corporation, was intended to be robust and survivable. The solution to this problem was multiple nodes, or pathways, through the network for any given piece of information (a distributed network), and the division of each piece of information into a group of standard length chunks, or packets. Each packet could find its way to its destination via any available route and arrive in any order. The result was (and is) a network more or less immune to disruption.[64] The Internet was also designed "stupid," in that the intelligence was at the ends of the network, not in the network itself.[65] Routing tools, software applications, and information requests come from the ends. This is in contrast to a traditional telephone network in which the switches, routing protocols, and so forth are in the network itself. This difference makes a distributed, packet-switched network more robust, but it also makes it simpler to use and much harder to trace individual bits of information once they are in the network. Lastly, the Internet has a governance structure that reflects its design. The Internet Engineering Task Force (IETF) is open, democratic, and nonhierarchical. Decision making is carried out via electronic request-for-comments (RFCs). IETF members (who could be any interested person) read RFCs, comment and critique, and eventually a collaborative decision is made.[66] Because of these three features, it is very hard to control who moves what information over the Internet.

Two distinct, though overlapping, efforts at control may have some success in spite of the supposed technical "nature" of the Internet. This is how the state may combat clandestine Internet users and shift the "balance of power" between states and stateless actors. The first emerges from government, the second from the private sector. Concern with the security of the "national information infrastructure" has preoccupied government policy makers in the United States since the Clinton administration, but the 9/11 attacks have served to focus the attention even more. The vulnerability of the national information infrastructure to terrorist attacks generated an extensive 2003 report full of recommendations and policy initiatives. The report acknowledges that, as the Internet is almost completely held in private hands, a public-private partnership is necessary to secure the infrastructure. Nevertheless, federal initiative is necessary for "forensics and attack attribution, protection of networks and systems critical to national security, indications and warnings, and protection against organized attacks capable of inflicting debilitating damage to the economy."[67] The report goes on to recommend a wide range of proposals for detecting attacks before they take place, developing plans for coordinated response to attacks, and even changing the routers and protocols of the Internet itself to make it more secure.[68] Finally, the report recommends supporting private sector initiatives to construct trusted digital control systems, more on which below.

In the wake of the Patriot Act, the U.S. government has taken another strategy toward securing (and deanonymizing) the Internet. The Department of Justice has sought to increase its wiretap capacities in the law and its technical capabilities in relations with ISPs. The Patriot Act has made it easier for digital wiretaps to be established and expanded their scope.[69] The FBI is also seeking to expand its telephone wiretap capacity to include voice-over-Internet protocol (VoIP).[70] Any one or combination of these initiatives would erode the distributed and "stupid" character of the Internet and imbed physical controls within the network itself. However, such efforts are likely to fail, in part because the global nature of the Internet makes national-level initiatives insufficient.[71] Changing the global nature of the networked computing experience, however, would achieve the government's objectives. This is the goal of trusted computing architecture and is indicative of the power of the private sector.

In September of 2003, the software engineer John Walker published on his Web site a jeremiad against what he sees as the increasing threat to free expression on the Internet and the possibility of the reimposition of "the producer/consumer information dissemination model on the Internet, restoring the central points of control which traditional media and governments see threatened by its advent."[72] The chief targets of his ire are firewalls, digital certificates, digital rights management, and trusted computing, which together would turn the Internet into a tightly controlled and surveilled space *not* by altering the physical characteristics of the Internet or by changing the legal environment in which it is embedded, but instead by altering the "intelligence" at the ends of the network and turning every piece of information traversing the network into a self-surveilling entity. Distributed computing platforms are intended to solve multiple security problems found on the Internet—including unwanted e-mail (spam), intellectual property theft, identity fraud, and so forth—by requiring authentication for activities such as sending e-mail, distributing files, and engaging in e-commerce. Documents, publications, images, audio and video files, and software itself would be coded to report who created them, who has rights to use them, and where they have been. Microsoft's long-delayed update to its market-dominating system software Windows XP, code-named Vista, is the most important piece of the push for trusted computing by the computer software industry. Given the global dominance of the Microsoft Windows platform, if Vista were to be developed along the lines the company's press releases suggest, then Walker's world would be very real indeed.[73] Anonymity on the Internet would end; it would turn into a tightly controlled and monitored space where none of the illegalities that bedevil the networks today could exist. This would cripple the activities of CTAs that depend upon the cloaking power of the Internet to mask their activities.

There are reasons for skepticism. Vista is much delayed, and some of the more robust trusted computing features have been dropped for the time being.[74] However, as a trusted computing platform promises solutions to so many of the security problems that afflict the industry, the goal will continue to tantalize. Others find Walker's position too extreme and argue that the threats he sees to the open, distributed nature of the Internet are overstated.[75] The critics are doubtless right; the Vista that finally gets released will be a compromise version of that first sketched out by Microsoft, gaps in the trusted infrastructure will exist, and some of the original, "anarchic" nature of the Internet will remain. However, the most important thing for this analysis is that both the U.S. government's wishes and Walker's fears are possible, maybe even probable, developments even if in slightly diminished form. Anonymity is not an inherent characteristic of the Internet. Its status as an uncontrolled space free from the control of formal political authorities is questionable. There is no question, then, that ICT empowers CTAs and other more benign forms of stateless forces (see the Adamson chapter). Nevertheless, the state is far from toothless. Legal authority gives states power over the architecture of the infosphere and with that the ability to reduce the scope and anonymity and turn the infosphere into a surveilled space. However, this analysis points to a fundamental tension between the interests of the state to control this version of the security threat posed by IT and the interests of private capital.

THREATS TO THE EFFICACY
OF THE WESTPHALIAN STATE

Lastly, ICT can threaten the entire edifice of the Westphalian territorial state. Harold Innis, the great Canadian economist, historian, and communications theorist, argued that there was a link between the prevailing communications technology and the architecture of political authority.[76] For Innis, technologies were either space-binding (allowing for the effective spatial extension of political authority) or time-binding (allowing for the temporal extension of political authority).

Thus, a society with oral language only would be able to perpetuate itself in time quite effectively, but would not be very spatially extensive. For Innis, the modern communications technologies—the book, the printing press, the newspaper, the telegraph, the telephone, and even television and radio—added progressively to the capacity of territorial political authorities to extend their control (both in scope and in scale—how widely they were able to extend territorial control and how intensively they were able to control the populations). But, some argue, the computer and digital communications technologies are different. All the industrial-age communications media were either one-to-many (the broadcast model) or many-to-many (the telephone, the telegraph), which must exist within tightly controlled, monopolistic hierarchies that reinforce centralized, territorial modes of organization. ICT, on the other hand, is in the process of creating a different form of political authority—one less territorial and more functional in its architecture—where individuals and organizations receive rights and owe duties to a variety of overlapping authorities, not to a single one above all others (the nation-state).[77]

Assessing this hypothesis involves a functional analysis of state practices—to what extent is the architecture of political authority being reconfigured by information-enabled individuals and institutions; to what extent are they prizing bits and pieces of sovereignty from territorial states and reassembling them in loosely coordinated networks of authorities? The evolving nature of code (legal and software, to borrow the pun from Lawrence Lessig)[78] will determine just how robust stateless authority will be. The relevant places to look are those areas where ICT appears to be stressing state authority—for example, in global financial transactions or with global governance organizations.

Testing this hypothesis against empirical evidence will be harder than any of the other three. There is the additional conceptual difficulty that we cannot even be sure what the alternative organizational form looks like, what its capabilities might be, and how it might supplant the nation-state. The literature on networked organizations is highly suggestive and fascinating, but it is far from offering answers to these basic questions.[79] Yet already some observers see ICT driving the growth of international institutions and global governance.[80] Perhaps a network of governance organizations with overlapping authority is the future.

To see whether the hypothesis has initial plausibility, I have only a suggestive probe into an area of decaying state capacity. Money is a natural place to turn. National currency is a powerful symbol of state autonomy and a true measure of the power of the state against global market forces. Money is also an expression of pure information. Its physical form in coins, bills, and checks is purely incidental; its "natural" condition is as the ones and zeros of the digital world. Here the conventional wisdom involves two, separate assertions. First, deterritorialized "super" currencies such as the dollar will crowd out local, national currencies. Money will still be issued by the state, but as several currencies will circulate without impediments in most territories, conventional monetary controls will no longer work as intended.[81] Second, private currencies, in digital form, will oust state-sponsored currencies. ICTs are a crucial part of both scenarios because they allow for tremendous savings on transactions costs associated with creating and maintaining a currency. Were supranational or private currencies to become widespread, this would be a major blow to the efficacy of the state, though the latter is the greater threat to Westphalian autonomy.

The early literature in international political economy is divided on the question. When the issue of purely digital money emerged in the mid-1990s, Stephen Kobrin argued that electronic cash represented a fundamental challenge to the territorial state. There would be no stopping the rush past supercurrencies to private sector "cash."[82] Because the coming deluge was digital, authenticated (and authenticatable) by nonstate entities, anonymous, distanciated,[83] and swappable in an infinite number of ways, there was little states could do to control it. Eric Helleiner, on the other hand, saw no significant threat from electronic money.[84] Although true digital networks had reduced the transaction costs associated with moving money around the globe, Helleiner thought its digital nature might even enhance state power, as digital money would be that much easier to trace.

Both Kobrin and Helleiner were responding to a rush of enthusiasm in the Internet community and the popular press in the mid-1990s for e-cash. In particular, the press was enamored with a Berkeley-trained mathematician and ardent libertarian named David Chaum who had developed a system for completely secure (encrypted), totally anonymous, privately issued e-cash.[85] Chaum was responding to what many felt was an inherent shortcoming with the existing electronic-commerce infrastructure. Existing methods for conducting transactions at a distance were either ill-suited to the digital medium (bank drafts) or too expensive (credit cards, bank transfers). Some system was needed to enable the trillions of small, even tiny, Internet transactions that were just waiting to be consummated. This system needed to be inexpensive and anonymous, or most users would shy away from having their reading, listening, and watching habits available in fine-grained detail to whom- or whatever wished to peer at them.[86]

Yet an odd thing happened to the inevitable emergence of digital money. It did not emerge. Credit cards are the overwhelming choice for online transactions. Consumers around the world appear to be comfortable with the tradeoff of privacy for security[87] and convenience. Some quasi-cash modes have emerged for smaller transactions or for vendors who lack the infrastructure to accept credit cards, most notably PayPal. But PayPal is far from anonymous and, in its cooperation with regulatory authorities, operates more like a traditional bank. The initial enthusiasm for a free and unregulated digital realm for economic transactions has faded as the Internet has matured. The debate in international political economy has reflected this. Ronan Palan argues that the great financial powers intentionally allowed the offshore banking industry to emerge in order to establish a separate juridical space for certain parts of the global economy; offshore is not something that has sprung up in spite of state efforts.[88] Roland Paris argues that the rise of electronic commerce is complicating the fiscal activities of states considerably, but he claims that they will respond by trasnsnationalizing taxation schemes.[89] Finally, as Benjamin Cohen points out, supranational currencies are nothing new. What he calls "Westphalian money" is really only an innovation of the past two hundred years. There is no necessary incompatibility between multiple currencies and territoriality, and several state strategies have emerged to bridge the gap. Some states subordinate their currency to a supercurrency (either by pegging their currency to the dominant one or by allowing its free circulation) or pool their currencies (for example, the euro).[90] The first reinforces hierarchy in the international political economy; the second aggregates traditional sovereignty, but does not challenge it.

All these arguments suggest that the state has adapted quite well to the challenge posed by electronic money—not by reasserting its authority in traditional ways, but by adapting its monetary regime to a changed environment. Two recent, apparently opposing, developments make the point in another way. First, the European Union has begun experiments with radio-frequency identification tags (RFID) in bank notes.[91] The measure is claimed to help prevent counterfeiting, but it would also enable tracking of cash transactions in some settings—heretofore an impossible task for states. This is a wonderful illustration of the double-edged nature of digital information technologies; they give unprecedented power to private citizens and to states depending on the precise form they take. Second, there is widespread agreement among money-laundering experts that although efforts at disrupting Al-Qaeda's financial networks post-9/11 have been successful, they have not succeeded in stopping the flow of money from supporters to organizers to operatives in the field.[92] This paradoxical result has come about because Al-Qaeda has largely abandoned conventional methods of storing and moving money and instead is depending more and more on cash, diamonds, drug smuggling, and other illicit business, and the *hawala*[93] method for money transfer.[94] To escape detection from state-based international financial surveillance mechanisms, Al-Qaeda has gone low tech (including barter), not high tech. The Adamson and Lynch chapters touch on the importance of remittances for diaspora populations. Digital methods are likely to continue to be subject to surveillance by state authorities. If migrants should wish (and there are many reasons) for their transactions to remain hidden, these sorts of low-tech methods will remain popular. There is even evidence, as the Avant chapter suggests, of private military concerns accepting cash, drugs, precious stones, and other valuable natural resources (or even rights to exploit their markets) as payment.[95] But these methods do not leverage the power of ICT for organizational transformation. They remain—as clandestine methods for skirting state authority have for centuries—expensive, time-consuming, and burdensome. In short, they only appeal to a small minority with a great interest in secrecy. The state retains, albeit in altered form, considerable control over electronic commerce. ICT does represent a security threat to the Westphalian character of states. But states are able to fashion responses that promise success meeting those threats. New state practices do not come without a cost, however. States have to expand their activities (technological innovation and new laws to better trace digital financial transactions) or extend them in time and space (supercurrencies, currency pooling). This represents a kind of transformation of sovereignty, but in no way the end of territorial statehood.

CONCLUSION

This chapter points toward two conclusions. First, ICT does indeed represent a serious threat to national security. New media weakens the communications monopoly of authoritarian regimes; the American RMA threatens less technologically adept and more resource-poor states; anonymity on the Internet poses a new, transnational, criminal threat to citizens; and digital financial transactions threaten the monetary autonomy of states. Second, an assessment of the threats does not show either a clear victory for stateless forces or for the state as traditionally understood. Instead, the state is in the process of transforming itself to cope with the threats posed by ICT. It is altering the definition of border, empowering private actors to asymmetrically balance against

98 • Geoffrey L. Herrera

the global hegemon, cooperating with corporate actors to create a pan-optic infosphere, and changing how it manages money—and responding to all of the threats by using and reshaping the very nature of ICT in the process. This is possible because the infosphere has not been fully developed just as the range of possible state policy responses to threats has not been exhausted. This is a political question, not a technological one. I expect that the infosphere will be shaped in the directions traced above, but as 9/11 showed, conjunctural moments in history have a way of disturbing settled trajectories. Finally, this analysis suggests a way beyond the rather sterile, ping-pong debate over the effects of globalization on states. It is not an either-or question: either the state is in retreat, or it is just the same as it always was. ICT, and globalization with it, is profoundly reshaping the environment in which states operate. States have responded to these shifts by changing their practices, sometimes in radical, even revolutionary ways. This has happened before (in the mid-to-late nineteenth century, to pick just one example[96]), so we should not be surprised. But this means we should not be focusing on whether sovereignty is disappearing, but on the ways in which globalization is transforming it.

NOTES

1. David S. Broder, "Reagan: Spread of Ideas Can Outdate NATO," *Washington Post,* June 14, 1989.
2. Ithiel de Sola Pool, *Technologies of Freedom* (Cambridge, MA: Belknap Press, 1983); Tom Forester, ed., *The Information Technology Revolution* (Cambridge, MA: MIT Press, 1985).
3. James R. Beniger, *The Control Revolution: Technological and Economic Origins of the Information Society* (Cambridge, MA: Harvard University Press, 1986).
4. John Arquilla and David Ronfeldt, *Swarming and the Future of Conflict* (Santa Monica, CA: RAND, 2000); Manuel Castells, *The Rise of the Network Society* (Cambridge, MA: Blackwell Publishers, 1996); Margaret E. Keck and Kathryn Sikkink, *Activists Beyond Borders: Advocacy Networks in International Politics* (Ithaca, NY: Cornell University Press, 1998).
5. Daniel Bell, "The Third Technological Revolution: And Its Possible Socioeconomic Consequences," *Dissent,* 36(2) (1989): 164–176.
6. Ithiel de Sola Pool, *Technologies Without Boundaries: On Telecommunications in a Global Age* (Cambridge, MA: Harvard University Press, 1990); Nicholas Negroponte, *Being Digital* (New York: Knopf, 1995); George F. Gilder, *Telecosm: How Infinite Bandwidth Will Revolutionize Our World* (New York: Free Press, 2000).
7. Alfred D. Chandler, *The Visible Hand: The Managerial Revolution in American Business* (Cambridge, MA: Belknap Press, 1977); Charles Tilly, *Coercion, Capital, and European States, AD 990–1990* (Cambridge, MA: Blackwell, 1992); Martin Van Creveld, *The Rise and Decline of the State* (Cambridge, New York: Cambridge University Press, 1999); R. Rudy Higgens-Evenson, *The Price of Progress: Public Services, Taxation, and the American Corporate State, 1877 to 1929* (Baltimore, MD: Johns Hopkins University Press, 2003).

8. Daniel R. Headrick, *When Information Came of Age: Technologies of Knowledge in the Age of Reason and Revolution, 1700–1850* (Oxford, New York: Oxford University Press, 2000).

9. Stephen Peter Rosen, "An Empire, If You Can Keep It," *The National Interest* 71 (2003): 251–261.

10. For example, cell phone cameras and Web cams.

11. This is the argument made for the effects of globalization generally. Philip G. Cerny, "Globalization and the Changing Logic of Collective Action," *International Organization* 49(4) (1995): 595–626; Ann M. Florini, "Who Does What? Collective Action and the Changing Nature of Authority," in *Non-State Actors and Authority in the Global System*, eds. Richard A. Higgott, Geoffrey R. D. Underhill, and Andreas Bieler (London: Routledge, 2000), 15–31.

12. Lawrence Lessig, *Code: And Other Laws of Cyberspace* (New York: Basic Books, 1999); Geoffrey L. Herrera, "The Politics of Bandwidth: International Political Implications of a Digital Information Infrastructure," *Review of International Studies* 28(1) (2002): 93–122.

13. Harold A. Innis, *The Bias of Communication* (Toronto: University of Toronto Press, 1991); Ronald J. Deibert, *Parchment, Printing, and Hypermedia: Communication in World Order Transformation* (New York: Columbia University Press, 1997).

14. Stephen J. Kobrin, "Safe Harbours Are Hard to Find: The Trans-Atlantic Data Privacy Dispute, Territorial Jurisdiction and Global Governance," *Review of International Studies* 30(1) (2004): 111–131.

15. Howard Rheingold, *Smart Mobs: The Next Social Revolution* (Cambridge, MA: Perseus Publishing, 2002); Richard A. Higgott, Geoffrey R. D. Underhill, and Andreas Bieler, eds., *Non-State Actors and Authority in the Global System* (London, New York: Routledge, 2000).

16. As historians and sociologists of technology have long understood: Wiebe E. Bijker, Thomas P. Hughes, and Trevor J. Pinch, eds., *Social Construction of Technological Systems: New Directions in the Sociology and History of Technology* (Cambridge, MA: MIT Press, 1987); Donald A. MacKenzie and Judy Wajcman, eds., *The Social Shaping of Technology* (Milton Keynes, Philadelphia: Open University Press, 1999); John M. Staudenmaier, "The Politics of Successful Technologies," in *In Context: History and the History of Technology: Essays in Honor of Melvin Kranzberg*, eds. Stephen H. Cutcliffe and Robert C. Post (Bethlehem, PA: Lehigh University Press, 1989), 150–171; Trevor J. Pinch and Wiebe E. Bijker, "The Social Construction of Facts and Artefacts: Or How the Sociology of Science and the Sociology of Technology Might Benefit Each Other," *Social Studies of Science* 14(3) (1984): 399–441; Langdon Winner, *Autonomous Technology: Technics-Out-of-Control as a Theme in Political Thought* (Cambridge, MA: MIT Press, 1977).

17. Edward Tenner, *Why Things Bite Back: Technology and the Revenge of Unintended Consequences* (New York: Knopf, 1996).

18. Lessig, *Code;* Herrera, "The Politics of Bandwidth."

19. See in particular Shanthi Kalathil and Taylor C. Boas, *Open Networks, Closed Regimes: The Impact of the Internet on Authoritarian Rule* (Washington, DC: Carnegie Endowment for International Peace, 2003) and http://www.citizenlab.org.

20. V. P. Gagnon, "Ethnic Nationalism and International Conflict: The Case of Serbia," *International Security* 19(3) (1994): 130–166; Philip Gourevitch, *We Wish to Inform You That Tomorrow We Will Be Killed with Our Families: Stories from Rwanda* (New York: Farrar Straus and Giroux, 1998); Samantha Power, *A Problem from Hell: America and the Age of Genocide* (New York: Basic Books, 2002).

21. Ken Auletta, "The Pirate," *The New Yorker* 71 (November 13, 1995): 80–93.

22. By open I mean network topology is relatively decentralized, the network itself is "dumb" (information processing happens at the network ends, not in the middle— the telephone network, with its centralized switches, is a "smart" network), and the software protocols that route Internet traffic allow anonymity. David Isenberg, "Rise of the Stupid Network," isen.com, http://www.hyperorg.com/misc/stupidnet.html (accessed October 19, 1998). The Internet is not a truly open network, however (at least not any more). Virtual private networks (VPNs), digital rights management (DRM) to protect intellectual property rights, network address translation (NAT) firewalls, and other developments have all served to introduce some measure of centralization and control over the Internet. This issue is taken up explicitly in the discussion of the third threat below.

23. Marc Rotenberg, "Privacy and Secrecy after September 11," in *Bombs and Bandwidth: The Emerging Relationship Between Information Technology and Security*, ed. Robert Latham (New York: The New Press, 2003), 132–142.

24. Lawrence Wright, "The Terror Web," *The New Yorker*, August 2, 2004, 40–53; Alan Cullison, "Inside Al-Qaeda's Hard Drive," *The Atlantic Monthly* 294 (September 2004): 55–70; Dan Eggen and Dana Priest, "Pre-9/11 Acts Led to Alerts," *Washington Post*, August 3, 2004.

25. Paul Festa, "End of the Road for SMTP?" *CNET News.com*, August 1, 2003, http://news.com.com/2100-1038-5058610.html (accessed August 1, 2003).

26. Michael Chase and James Mulvenon, *You've Got Dissent! Chinese Dissident Use of the Internet and Beijing's Counter-Strategies* (Santa Monica, CA: RAND, 2002); David Post and Bradford C. Brown, "The Slingshot of Information Freedom," *InformationWeek*, September 9, 2003, 76; Leslie David Simon, Javier Corrales, and Donald R. Wolfensberger, *Democracy and the Internet: Allies or Adversaries?* (Baltimore, MD: The John Hopkins University Press, 2002).

27. For China see: Jason P. Abbot, "Democracy@internet.asia? The Challenges to the Emancipatory Potential of the Net: Lessons from China and Malaysia," *Third World Quarterly* 22(1) (2001): 99–114; Kalathil and Boas, *Open Networks, Closed Regimes;* Joshua Kurlantzick, "The Dragon Still Has Teeth," *World Policy Journal* 20(1) (2003): 49–58. For Cuba: Jeremy Hildreth, "YAHOO O MUERTE!," *American Spectator* 34 (September/October 2001): 90–91; Kalathil and Boas, *Open Networks, Closed Regimes.* For Malaysia: Abbot, "Democracy@internet.asia?" For Saudi Arabia: Kalathil and Boas, *Open Networks, Closed Regimes.* For Singapore: Garry Rodan, "The Internet and Political Control in Singapore," *Political Science Quarterly* 113(1) (1998): 63–90; Garry Rodan, "Embracing Electronic Media but Suppressing Civil Society: Authoritarian Consolidation in Singapore," *Pacific Review* 16(4) (2003): 503–524. The OpenNet Initiative is at http://opennetinitiative.net.

28. A global low-earth-orbiting (LEO) satellite network for high-speed Internet access would upend the territorial basis of Internet topology. A number of ambitious plans to build such a network emerged in the early-to-mid 1990s, but none have achieved anything like comprehensive global reach. Herrera, "The Politics of Bandwidth," 110–112.

29. Even in the United States this was the case. Until 1993, when it was privatized, the Internet backbone in the United States was owned by the National Science Foundation. National Science Foundation, "A Brief History of NSF and the Internet," 2003, http://www.nsf.gov/od/lpa/news/03/fsnsf_internet.htm (accessed May 24, 2004).

30. Nart Villeneuve, "Project C: Tracking Internet Censorship in China," http://www.chass.utoronto.ca/~citizenl/assets/articles/ProjectC-rl.pdf (accessed May 24, 2004).

31. Ibid.; Jonathan Zittrain and Benjamin Edelman, "Empirical Analysis of Internet Filtering in China," Open Net Initiative, 2002a, http://cyber.law.harvard.edu/filtering/china (accessed May 24, 2004).

32. Jonathan Zittrain and Benjamin Edelman, "Documentation of Internet Filtering in Saudi Arabia," Open Net Initiative, 2002b, http://cyber.law.harvard.edu/filtering/saudiarabia/ (accessed May 24, 2004).

33. http://www.peek-a-booty.org.

34. Oxblood Ruffin, "Great Firewall of China," *New Scientist* 176 (November 9, 2002): 27.

35. Jennifer 8. Lee, "Companies Compete to Provide Internet Veil for the Saudis," *New York Times*, September 19, 2001.

36. Peter Andreas, "Redrawing the Line: Borders and Security in the Twenty-First Century," *International Security* 28(2) (2003): 78–111.

37. Information is available at http://www.dhs.gov/dhspublic/interapp/content_multi_image/content_multi_image_0006.xml.

38. This is a huge amount of literature. The following list mixes military assessments, scholarly analyses, and policy advocacy: John Arquilla and David F. Ronfeldt, eds., *In Athena's Camp: Preparing for Conflict in the Information Age* (Santa Monica, CA: RAND, 1997); Bruce D. Berkowitz, *The New Face of War: Lethal Networks in the Information Age* (New York: Simon and Schuster, 2003); Eliot A. Cohen, "A Revolution in Warfare," *Foreign Affairs* 75(2) (1996): 37–54; Dale R. Herspring, "Nikolay Ogarkov and the Scientific-Technical Revolution in Military Affairs," *Comparative Strategy* 6(1) (1987): 29–59; Stephen Biddle, "Victory Misunderstood: What the Gulf War Tells Us about the Future of Conflict," *International Security* 21(2) (1996): 139–179; Andrew F. Krepinevich, Jr., "Cavalry to Computer: The Pattern of Military Revolutions," *National Interest* 37 (1994): 30–42; Andrew A Latham, "Warfare Transformed: A Braudelian Perspective on the 'Revolution in Military Affairs,'" *European Journal of International Relations* 8(2) (2002): 231–266; John Orme, "The Utility of Force in a World of Scarcity," *International Security* 22(3) (1997): 138–167; William A. Owens, "The Emerging System of Systems," *U.S. Naval Institute Proceedings* 121(5) (1995): 35–39; William A. Owens and Edward Offley, *Lifting the Fog of War* (Baltimore, MD: Johns Hopkins University Press, 2001); Alvin Toffler and Heidi Toffler, *War and Anti-War: Survival at the Dawn of the 21st Century* (Boston: Little, Brown, 1993); Michael Vickers, "Kosovo and the Revolution in Military Affairs," in *War Over Kosovo: Politics and Strategy in a Global Age,* eds. A. J. Bacevich and Eliot A. Cohen (New York: Columbia University Press, 2001), 189–210.

39. Bradley A. Thayer, "The Political Effects of Information Warfare: Why New Military Capabilities Cause Old Political Dangers," *Security Studies* 10(1) (2000): 43–85.

40. Joseph S. Nye, *Bound to Lead: The Changing Nature of American Power* (New York: Basic Books, 1990); Joseph S. Nye, *Soft Power: The Means to Success in World Politics* (New York: Public Affairs, 2004).

41. The post-9/11 collaboration between the White House and Hollywood suggests one possible mechanism (as do, for that matter, the propaganda films made for the war effort by Hollywood during WWII). Howard Rosenberg, "Propaganda Machine Signs Media Enlistees," *Los Angeles Times*, November 12, 2001, http://www.latimes.com/news/nationworld/nation/la-111201howard,1,3446071.column (accessed August 6, 2004).

42. Biddle "Victory Misunderstood"; Stephen Biddle, "Afghanistan and the Future of Warfare," *Foreign Affairs* 82(2) (2003): 31–46; Vickers, "Kosovo and the Revolution in Military Affairs," in *War Over Kosovo.*

43. Robert A. Pape, "The World Pushes Back," *Boston Globe*, March 23, 2003.

44. Daniel R. Headrick, *The Invisible Weapon: Telecommunications and International Politics 1851–1945* (New York: Oxford University Press, 1991); Paul M. Kennedy, "Imperial Cable Communications and Strategy, 1870–1914," *English Historical Review* 86(341) (1971): 728–752.

45. Steve Wright, "An Appraisal of Technologies of Political Control," Luxembourg: European Parliament Directorate General for Research Directorate B The STOA Programme, 1998.
46. Galileo's World, "Galileo Progress: New Alliances, ITTs," 2003, http://www.galileosworld.com/galileosworld/article/articleDetail.jsp?id=75613 (accessed May 25, 2004).
47. http://www.arianespace.com/.
48. Nadeem Iqbal, "Pakistan Scrambles to Launch Satellite, Eyes Bigger Plans," Islamabad: IPS-Inter Press Service, 2002, http://www.spacedaily.com/news/nuclear-india-pakistan-02za.html (accessed May 25, 2004).
49. Karen Litfin, "Public Eyes: Satellite Imagery, The Globalization of Transparency, and New Networks of Surveillance," in *Information Technologies and Global Politics: The Changing Scope of Power and Governance,* eds. James N. Rosenau and J. P. Singh (Albany: State University of New York Press, 2002), 65–89; David Brin, *The Transparent Society: Will Technology Force Us to Choose Between Privacy and Freedom?* (Reading, MA: Addison-Wesley, 1998).
50. Steve Livingston and Lucas Robinson, "Mapping Fears: The Use of Commercial High-Resolution Satellite Imagery in International Affairs," *Astropolitics* 1(2) (2003): 3–25.
51. http://www.reason.com/0406/fe.dm.database.shtml.
52. Galileo's World, "Galileo Progress."
53. David Last, "GPS and Galileo: Where Are We Headed?," Paper presented at The European Navigation Conference GNSS2004, Rotterdam, May 17–19, 2004.
54. Irving Lachow, "The GPS Dilemma: Balancing Military Risks and Economic Benefits," *International Security* 20(1) (1995): 126–148.
55. I cannot claim that this is the actual intent of states. It may be, but it is the effect.
56. Andreas, "Redrawing the Line."
57. Kevin Soo Hoo, Seymour Goodman, and Lawrence Greenberg, "Information Technology and the Terrorist Threat," *Survival* 39(3) (1997): 135–155.
58. Andrew Higgins, Karby Leggett, and Alan Cullison, "How al Qaeda Put Internet in Service of Global Jihad," *Wall Street Journal,* November 11, 2002; Wright, "The Terror Web."
59. Douglas Farah, *Blood from Stones: The Secret Financial Network of Terror* (New York: Broadway Books, 2004).
60. United States General Accounting Office, *Extent of Money Laundering through Credit Cards Is Unknown* (Washington, DC: Government Printing Office, 2002); Ronen Palan, "Trying to Have Your Cake and Eating It: How and Why the State System Has Created Offshore," *International Studies Quarterly* 42(4) (1998): 625–644; Sidney Weintraub, "Disrupting the Financing of Terrorism," *The Washington Quarterly* 25(1) (2002): 53–60.
61. To the extent that the increased density of transactions (interactions) is enabled by ICT, then ICT can be seen as creating the environment in which illicit actors flourish.
62. Douglas Farah, "Colombian Drug Cartels Exploit Tech Advantage," *Washington Post,* November 15, 1999.
63. Peter Wayner, "Technology That Tracks Cell Phones Draws Fire," *New York Times,* February 23, 1998.
64. Janet Abbate, *Inventing the Internet* (Cambridge, MA: MIT Press, 1999); Paul Baran, "On Distributed Communications: IX. Security, Secrecy, and Tamper-Free Considerations," *RAND Memorandum, no. 3765* (Santa Monica, CA: RAND, 1964).
65. Isenberg, "Rise of the Stupid Network."

66. Abbate, *Inventing the Internet*, 207–208; Paulina Borsook, "How Anarchy Works," *Wired* 3 (October 1995): 110, http://www.wired.com/wired/archive/3.10/ietf.html (accessed April 26, 2006); Michael T. Zimmer, "The Tensions of Securing Cyberspace: The Internet, State Power and the National Strategy to Secure Cyberspace," *First Monday* 9(3) (2004): http://firstmonday.org/issues/issue9_3/zimmer/index.html (accessed May 1, 2004).

67. Department of Homeland Security, *The National Strategy to Secure Cyberspace* (Washington, DC: Government Printing Office, 2003), ix.

68. For example, the report recommends improving the Internet protocol by securing the domain name system (DNS) and improving the reliability of the connections between networks and improving routing via address verification. Ibid., pp. 30–31.

69. http://www.epic.org/privacy/terrorism/usapatriot/.

70. Stephen Labaton, "Easing of Internet Regulations Challenges Surveillance Efforts," *New York Times,* January 22, 2004, http://www.nytimes.com/2004/01/22/technology/22VOIC.html (accessed January 26, 2004); Declan McCullagh, "FBI Pushes for Broadband Wiretap Powers," *CNET News.com,* March 12, 2004, http://news.com.com/2100-1028-5172719.html (accessed March 14, 2004). The Federal Communications Commission (FCC) seems to agree. Federal Communications Commission, *FCC Adopts Notice of Proposed Rulemaking and Declaratory Ruling Regarding Communications Assistance for Law Enforcement Act* (Washington, DC: Government Printing Office, 2004).

71. Stephen J. Lukasik, Seymour E. Goodman, and David W. Longhurst, "Protecting Critical Infrastructures Against Cyber-Attack," *Adelphi Papers* (2003): 359; Zimmer, "The Tensions of Securing Cyberspace."

72. John Walker, "The Digital Imprimatur," 2004, http://www.fourmilab.ch/documents/digital-imprimatur (accessed May 7, 2004).

73. Richard Forno, "MS to Micro-Manage Your Computer," *The Register,* June 24, 2002, http://www.theregister.co.uk/2002/06/24/ms_to_micromanage_your_computer/ (accessed May 11, 2004).

74. Andrew Orlowski, "MS Trusted Computing Back to Drawing Board," *The Register,* May 6, 2004, http://www.theregister.co.uk/2004/05/06/microsoft_managed_code_rethink (accessed May 11, 2004); Mike Ricciuti and Martin LaMonica, "Longhorn Goes to Pieces," *CNET News.com,* May 13, 2004, http://news.com.com/2100-1016-5212077.html (accessed May 11, 2004).

75. Jeroen Meijer, "Lights Going Out on the Internet? Not Just Yet," *CircleID,* May 21, 2004.

76. Innis, *Bias of Communication.*

77. For a contemporary example of Innis-inspired work see: Deibert, *Parchment, Printing, and Hypermedia;* Castells, *The Rise of the Network Society.*

78. Lessig, *Code.*

79. Albert-László Barabási, *Linked: The New Science of Networks* (Cambridge, MA: Perseus, 2002); Carl Shapiro and Hal R. Varian, *Information Rules: A Strategic Guide to the Network Economy* (Cambridge, MA: Harvard Business School Press, 1998); Felix Stalder, "The Network Paradigm: Social Formations in the Age of Information," *Information Society* 14(4) (1998): 301–308; Grahame Thompson, Jennifer Frances, Rosalind Levacíc, and Jeremy Mitchell, eds., *Markets, Hierarchies, and Networks: The Coordination of Social Life* (London, Newbury Park: Sage Publications, 1991); Barry Wellman and Stephen D. Berkowitz, eds., *Social Structures: A Network Approach* (Cambridge, New York: Cambridge University Press, 1988).

80. James N. Rosenau and J. P. Singh, eds., *Information Technologies and Global Politics: The Changing Scope of Power and Governance* (Albany: State University of New York Press, 2002); Roland Paris, "The Globalization of Taxation? Electronic Commerce and the Transformation of the State," *International Studies Quarterly* 47(2) (2003): 153–182.

81. Benjamin J. Cohen, *The Future of Money* (Princeton, NJ: Princeton University Press, 2003).

82. Stephen J. Kobrin, "Electronic Cash and the End of National Markets," *Foreign Policy* 107 (1997): 65–77.

83. A term coined by Anthony Giddens to describe the manner in which modernity takes interactions that formerly required a physical meeting and separates them in time or space. Anthony Giddens, *The Consequences of Modernity* (Palo Alto, CA: Stanford University Press, 1990).

84. Eric Helleiner, "Electronic Money: A Challenge to the Sovereign State?" *Journal of International Affairs* 51(2) (1998): 387–409.

85. Steven Levy, "E-Money (That's What I Want)," *Wired* 2 (December 1994): 174–179, 213–219; David Chaum, "Achieving Electronic Privacy," *Scientific American* 267 (August 1992): 96–101.

86. Herrera, "The Politics of Bandwidth," 117–119.

87. Credit cards are of course far from secure, but as the burden of risk is largely on the card issuer, they are from the consumer's point of view secure.

88. Palan, "Trying to Have Your Cake."

89. Roland Paris, "The Globalization of Taxation? Electronic Commerce and the Transformation of the State," *International Studies Quarterly* 47(2) (2003): 153–182.

90. Cohen, *The Future of Money*, 3–10.

91. Janis Mara, "Euro Scheme Makes Money Talk," *Wired News*, July 9, 2003, http://www.wired.com/news/privacy/0,1848,59565,00.html (accessed July 15, 2003).

92. Don Van Natta, Jr., "Terrorists Blaze a New Money Trail," *New York Times*, September 28, 2003, http://www.nytimes.com/2003/09/28/weekinreview/28VANN.html (accessed September 30, 2003); Mark Basile, "Going to the Source: Why Al Qaeda's Financial Network Is Likely to Withstand the Current War on Terrorist Financing," *Studies in Conflict and Terrorism*, 27(3) (2004): 169–185.

93. http://www.interpol.int/Public/FinancialCrime/MoneyLaundering/hawala/default.asp.

94. Farah, *Blood from Stones*.

95. Ibid.

96. On military practices, see: Geoffrey L. Herrera, "Inventing the Railroad and Rifle Revolution: Information, Military Innovation and the Rise of Germany," *Journal of Strategic Studies* 27(2) (2004): 243–271. For monetary policy: Cohen, *The Future of Money*. This is Krasner's argument, though to my mind the connotation of his argument is that transformations to the nature of sovereignty are not important. Stephen D. Krasner, *Sovereignty: Organized Hypocrisy* (Princeton, NJ: Princeton University Press, 1999).

4

THE MARKETIZATION OF SECURITY
Adventurous Defense, Institutional Malformation, and Conflict

Deborah Avant

WHEN THE UNITED STATES DEFEATED the Iraqi Army in 2003, one out of every ten people deployed to the theater in the conflict were civilian personnel employed by private security companies (PSCs) performing the work (logistics; operational support of equipment, weapons, and information systems; and training) that used to be done by soldiers. As lawlessness followed the fall of Saddam Hussein and US forces were stretched thin, an "army" of PSCs surged into the country—to train the Iraqi police force, the Iraqi army, a private Iraqi force to guard government facilities and oil fields, and simply to protect expatriates working in the country. It was estimated that in excess of 20,000 private security personnel, mostly retired military or police from countries as varied as Fiji, Israel, Nepal, South Africa, the United Kingdom, and the United States, employed by some 25 different PSCs worked for the US government, the British government, the Coalition Provisional Authority (CPA), private firms, and international nongovernmental organizations (INGOs) in that country.[1] This little known feature of the Iraqi occupation was thrust into the public eye when four private security personnel working for the US PSC, Blackwater USA, were killed and mutilated on March 31, 2004, and amplified when contracted interrogators were implicated in the abuses of prisoners at Abu Ghraib.[2]

The role of PSCs in Iraq is not an aberration, but represents a global trend toward the use of markets to allocate security. The marketization (private financing for and delivery of) security is partly a result of marketization in other spheres. It is also intertwined with advances in information technology and the ease with which people cross borders. This chapter examines marketization as a process of globalization by focusing on the security sector and particularly on services. In the first three sections, I briefly describe the market for force, compare it with past markets, and explain how the processes of globalization contributed to its present form. I then examine how the marketization of force matters for national security.

My argument relies on institutional logic, which leads me to expect changes in the institutions available for using violence to change the mechanisms through which it is controlled and thereby redistribute power over the control of force. In the current context, the redistribution has consequences for both the autonomy and capacity of states and the balance of power, though the consequences are different for strong states than they are for weak states. Particularly, strong states can choose to either eschew market options, and thereby avoid the redistribution of power associated with the market (maintaining domestic political processes and thus state autonomy from commercial forces but potentially giving up new capacities), or to embrace market options (and change domestic political processes eroding their autonomy from commercial forces but potentially gaining new capacities). Those that give up autonomy may gain capacity and thus maximize their relative power vis-à-vis other states—those that choose to maximize autonomy may lose relative power. The embrace of the market by strong states also, though, tends to erode the democratic practices associated with restraint in defense policy, which may increase security dilemmas and reduce military effectiveness. In weak states, the market often diffuses control of violence in ways that reinforce institutional malformation—reducing state autonomy and capacity and weakening relative power. Finally, as more actors (strong states, weak states, and nonstate actors) take advantage of market options for security, we should expect to see changes in the nature of conflict. Particularly, the diffusion of control associated with the market for security services often generates uncertainty that increases the potential for conflict, as well as changing its nature—leading to more poorly governed conflict and more uses of violence to achieve individual rather than collective purposes.

THE MARKETIZATION OF SECURITY AT THE TURN OF THE TWENTY-FIRST CENTURY

The market for security services manifests itself in several ways—all of which are apparent in the Iraqi conflict. First, private military and security companies now sell more services, some of which are core military capabilities.[3] A small number of firms have provided armed troops that operate with troops on the battlefield. Executive Outcomes (EO) provided armed personnel that worked on the battlefield with troops in Sierra Leone and Angola. Sandline International did the same in Sierra Leone and Papua New Guinea. United States–based Blackwater USA also provides armed personnel and has its own aircraft and lift capacity that can more or less replace US troops in some circumstances.[4] More common are PSCs that support weapons systems, provide logistics, and provide advice and training to state militaries. The US Army's Task Force XXI Army Warfare Experiment (AWE) in March 1997 relied upon 1,200 civilian contractors from 48 different vendors. All of these people were in the field at the National Training Center providing advice, maintenance, and technical support.[5] As these systems have been integrated into US operations, along with them has come the deployment of private personnel to the battlefield. In Operation Iraqi Freedom, contractors supplied operational support for the B-2 stealth bomber, the F-117 stealth fighter, Global Hawk UAV (unmanned aerial vehicle), and U-2 reconnaissance aircraft, among others. Halliburton's Kellogg, Brown, and Root (KBR) built bases, provided food, water, laundry services, and much more for American troops, all part of a multiyear Logistics Civil Augmentation Program (LOGCAP) contract to support US forces.[6] Though the United States is the largest consumer of these kinds of services, it is not the only one; the United Kingdom and Australia have also increased their reliance on PSCs to provide logistics and operational support.[7] Every U.N. peace operation in the 1990s was conducted with support from the private sector in logistics. PSCs draw personnel from all over the world and offer their services both to strong and weak states.

Second, changes in the nature of conflicts have led tasks less central to the core of modern militaries (such as technical support and policing) to become more important, and private security companies provide these services readily. Advances in technology, though mentioned above, deserve greater emphasis. For instance, one of the key advances has been in the use of unmanned aircraft, such as the Predator. This tool has not only been useful on the battlefield, but has also proved its worth in the US fight against terrorism. This system is not only supported by PSCs, contractor personnel essentially fly the plane until it is in the position to launch its missile, which is when military personnel take over to push the button that launches the missile. As conflicts have become more technology-dependent, private provision of operational support has moved closer to the core. Similarly, many of the conflicts in the 1990s were civil wars and their resolution required the provision of order and stability. In pursuing the Global War on Terrorism, the importance of providing order and stability to particular territories has only grown. One key tool for creating order is international civilian police. The United States does not have an international civilian police force, so it turned to a PSC, DynCorp, to recruit and deploy one. In Iraq, DynCorp continued this mission and also developed a prison and justice system and trained the Iraqi police force. As the successful resolution of conflicts has come to depend on rebuilding governance, the role of PSCs has moved closer to the core.

Finally, states are no longer the only organizations that purchase security services. Increasingly, nongovernmental actors finance their own security. For instance, multinational corporations that work in the extractive sector often pay for security—either by financing a portion of the state's forces or hiring PSCs—to accomplish their goals. Both Shell and Chevron have paid portions of the Nigerian military and police to secure their facilities in Nigeria. British Petroleum hired Defense Systems Limited, DSL (now ArmorGroup), a British PSC, to train local forces to protect their pipelines in Colombia. Not only commercial firms finance security, however. Since the 1970s, conservation INGOs have routinely paid portions of states' security apparatuses to help protect endangered species. In some recent cases, they have supplied their own personnel or hired PSCs to do the same.[8] Relief INGOs have also financed security, sometimes inadvertently and indirectly as the resources they provide are skimmed off, but other times more directly as they have hired PSCs to provide armed escort, site security for their facilities, and security planning. Again, this is a feature in postwar Iraq. INGOs must hire security to operate in the country. Even the United Nations (UN), whose security strategy was questioned in the wake of the August bombing of UN headquarters in Baghdad, has entertained the possibility of hiring a high-end PSC to help it generate and implement security—in Iraq and more generally. As nongovernmental entities move to generate their own security, the demand for security is deepened and broadened, and opens additional avenues for PSC activity.

The market for force is global. States, international organizations, INGOs, and commercial firms purchase security services all over the world. PSCs recruit personnel from many different countries and frequently not only deploy expatriate personnel but also work with, train, and employ local personnel. Virtually every continent is a part of this market. Private industry projections in 1997 suggested that revenues from the global international security market were about $55.6 billion in 1990 and were expected to rise to $202 billion in 2010.[9] Recent estimates suggest that the revenues may be as much as $100 billion already.[10] Private security companies with publicly traded stocks grew at twice the rate of the Dow Jones Industrial Average in the 1990s.[11]

THE CURRENT MARKET COMPARED

This is not the first market for force. Markets for allocating violence were common before the systems of states came to dominate world politics. Feudal lords supplemented their forces with contracted labor from the beginning of the twelfth century, and from the end of the thirteenth century through the Peace of Westphalia in 1648, virtually all force was allocated through the market. Even early modern states used the market—delegating control over force to commercial entities and supplying or purchasing troops from other states. Finally, smaller, national markets for particular services have remained in some countries throughout the modern period.

In the era before the rise of the state, market allocation of force prevailed—virtually all force was contracted.[12] Stretching from the twelfth century through the peace of Westphalia, military contractors employed forces that had been trained within the feudal structure and then contracted with whoever could pay—Italian city-states, the pope, emerging states, other feudal lords, and more.[13] In this period, military enterprisers would put together forces to meet the diverse needs of a variety of different political forms. Their services ranged from war fighting to maintaining order to providing administration.[14]

Chartered companies, prominent in the seventeenth and eighteenth centuries, were an instance of state-delegated commercial control over violence.[15] The Dutch, English, French, and Portuguese all chartered companies either as private wealth seeking enterprises to enhance the mother economy's profit (as in the Dutch and English cases) relative to others or as state enterprises forged by the king to increase state power later in the game (as in the French case).[16] Chartered companies had forces that established order and then protected both trade routes and new territory.

Also during the early period of state dominance, states rented out their forces to other friendly states. Britain rented German troops during the American Revolution.[17] German states supplied troops to a number of other countries including the Netherlands, Venice, and France, in addition to Britain. The Dutch provided regiments to German princelings during the Seven Years War and to Britain in both the 1701 war with France and the 1745 Jacobite Rebellion within Britain.[18] These troops would arrive equipped and ready to fight under the command of the foreign government.

Even in the modern system, some elements of the market have remained. The US government has long used markets for military purposes.[19] Up until the beginning of World War II, most of these were in logistics and weapons. During the Cold War, however, the United States hired firms to perform military training missions as well and in Vietnam contractors provided logistics support for American troops (food, laundry, sanitation, etc.) and were involved in large construction projects.[20] Also, states still do "rent out" their forces—to UN peacekeeping units or to other states. In the first Gulf War, for instance, US forces were subsidized by Japan. In the 2003 war with Iraq, the United States paid forces from other countries to participate in the coalition.

The extent of recent private security activity, though, is a significant shift away from the practice common in the nation-state system since the French Revolution where citizen armies have been touted as the most appropriate (and effective) vehicles for generating security.[21] Although market allocation of security was never completely eliminated, it was frowned upon and thus informally organized, secretive, and directed to a specific customer base. Contrast this with the current market where PSCs have a corporate structure, post job listings on their Web sites, and write papers mulling over the costs and benefits of private security. PSCs have sought, and received, some international acceptance. In addition, PSCs operate in a global market—not only does the United States hire American PSCs, but so do foreign governments and nongovernmental actors, and the United States hires foreign PSCs as well. Although some PSCs certainly operate with an eye toward their home government, they also attend to the character of demand from the wider consumer base.

The corporate form, relative openness, acceptance, and transnational spread of today's security industry bear many similarities to the late Middle Ages and early Modern period. There are some features of today's market, though, that are unique. First, unlike the military enterprisers of the late Middle Ages, today's PSCs do not only provide the foot soldiers, but act as supporters, trainers, and force multipliers for local forces. PSCs, then, operate differently from private armies—when they leave, they leave behind whatever expertise they have imparted—subject to whatever local political controls (or lack thereof) exist. Second, unlike the period of the chartered companies, states do not authorize private takeover of other territories, even though transnational corporations (TNCs) and INGOs finance security on their own—either by subsidizing weak states or by hiring PSCs. The state charter of companies provided a more specific administrative and legal framework for the private use of force than is the case with private financiers today.

GLOBALIZATION AND THE MARKETIZATION OF SECURITY

The pressures and challenges associated with globalization—both material and social—have been important components in the growing demand for and supply of security in the marketplace, and the resulting market for force is itself a global force. Though many analysts focus on globalization's economic effects, the increased intensity of information, exchange, and marketization have come along with revised interests and values that have led to security as well as economic concerns.[22] Common conceptions of globalization refer to a "shift in the spatial reach of social action and organization toward the interregional or intercontinental scale."[23] This shift's impact on material well-being and social identification suggests many ways that globalization might affect the security goals and worries of a population. The variety of "new" security issues bandied about in recent years—including environmental, economic, and social well-being—may be attributable to the increased social connectedness among peoples in different parts of the world.[24] This connectedness—made possible by new communications technology that Herrera discusses, as well as the ease with which people can move from place to place that Adamson points out—has also brought new worries. As disorder in one part of the world has combined with information technology and the speed to travel to feed threats to life and property in another, security has become increasingly diffuse, transforming the meaning of borders as well as their defense.[25]

The new threat environment has been heralded (from the right and the left) as bringing with it new forms of warfare and the merging of security with a variety of other economic and political forms.[26] Thus, "national" security has become difficult to distinguish from international or global security and the lines between internal and external security have blurred. This is true for moralists who feel responsible to intervene in order to help quell violence, pragmatists who worry about economic disruptions, and realists who worry about breeding grounds for terrorists. When illicit criminal networks not only produce social "bads" such as drugs and prostitution, but also funding for terror, the internal governance of far-flung territories become a national security concern.

Ideational shifts—particularly belief in the superiority of market-based solutions to collective problems—have led even states to view the market and private actors as one obvious response to new security demands.[27] In the United States and Britain, a privatization movement led governments to look increasingly to markets for solutions to government problems.[28] Arguing that social programs generated inefficiencies and financing them required incentive-sapping levels of taxation and inflationary budget deficits, conservatives "viewed retrenchment not as a necessary evil but as a necessary good."[29] Initially associated with the powerful conservative coalitions in the United States and the United Kingdom in the 1980s, the endorsement of privatization widened with the Soviet bloc collapse, the ensuing privatization of state-owned industries across Europe, and the endorsement of these principles by international financial institutions such as the IMF and the World Bank. Private has come to denote competition, efficiency, and effectiveness; public stands for bureaucratic, staid, expensive, and backward.[30] This has led governments to turn over functions to private entities and to insert market-type mechanisms such as competition over authority to do certain jobs into bureaucracies, both of which have enhanced marketization. Though I am focusing on security in this chapter, marketization has exerted widespread pressure on foreign and domestic governance.

Arguments about the future of defense in the United States demonstrate how these pressures have led to the embrace of market options for security in one country.[31] The United States, as the sole remaining superpower, it is argued, must accomplish a variety of ends. It must leap ahead technologically, search for the next peer competitor, and maintain the capacity to keep order in important, but less than vital, arenas.[32] Maintaining stability includes combating illicit by-products of globalization such as organized crime, drugs, and terrorism as well as enforcing emerging global norms about human rights and encouraging the democratic institutions (seen as supporting such norms).[33] In response to these imperatives, Cohen argues that it makes good sense to privatize. This way the United States can make the most of information "spin on," take advantage of capitalist economies, and manage in a complex world with fewer troops.[34] Privatization will also connect the military with the civilian sector, which is driving technological change in the information age and will produce the most cost-efficient solutions.[35]

The purchase of security by nonstate actors is also connected to global pressures—either the desire to exploit global markets or the wish to protect global common goods such as conservation or human rights. Whether due to economic interests, human concerns, or concern with the global environment, many Western states and peoples feel compelled to respond to issues not specifically tied to their national territory. When responses to these issues require a physical presence in a poorly governed territory, security becomes important—and increasingly actors are looking for solutions outside of state bureaucracies.

Global forces have also made it easier for the private sector to *supply* security services through the market. Internet technology allows PSCs to document their capacities on Web pages. Many exist as almost virtual companies, with a small full-time contingent and a very large database with which to staff contracts—the Internet also allows easy maintenance of ties between retired military personnel. The speed of air travel and availability of global communications makes it possible for firms to bring together quickly teams to serve a contract and deploy them. Moreover, the diffusion of professional information allows retired troops from different countries to work together.

Most importantly, this increased supply of and demand for private security has led to a market for force that operates outside the control of any one state and is a precipitating global force itself. The market for force does not replace state militaries, but exists alongside the state system even as it operates on a global scale. The supply of force on a global scale feeds back into processes that further enhance globalization by offering tools to meet a variety of goals not attached to states—promising to enhance the market further.

HOW IS MARKETIZATION LIKELY TO AFFECT NATIONAL SECURITY?

Conventional wisdom has it that globalization processes erode state power.[36] As Cerny puts it,

> the more that the scale of goods and assets produced, exchanged, and/or used in a particular economic sector or activity diverges from the structural scale of the national state—both from above (the global scale) and from below (the local scale)—and the more these divergences feed back into each other in complex ways, then the more that the authority, legitimacy, policymaking capacity, and policy-implementing effectiveness of states will be challenged from both without and within.[37]

Relying on functionalist logic, Cerny assumes that as the efficiency of the state erodes, so will state power.

Signs that the market has challenged states have appeared already. Global demand has made it difficult for states seeking to outlaw market supply of security to be successful.[38] South Africa sought to reign in its vibrant security industry with the 1998 Regulation of Foreign Military Assistance Act, but the continued demand for security services encouraged South African PSCs to simply shift their operations to avoid government scrutiny. In addition, the nature of the industry (service unattached to particular territory) made it difficult for the South African government to prosecute offenders.[39] Indeed, some claim that the act simply pushed PSCs under cover and further from government control.[40] Though government officials and academics hold that delegitimizing the industry was worth the loss of control—the act preserved the South African government's rightful claim to monopoly over the legitimate use of violence and made it clear that PSCs were illegitimate mercenaries—South Africa alone has not been able to delegitimate the industry.[41] Because other legitimate actors continued to purchase services from South African PSCs, the industry continued and even grew. In 2004, private soldiers from South Africa flooded into Iraq under contract with the US government, the CPA, and private industry.[42]

The market has also furthered connections among professional networks of security experts that span borders and trade information about best practices in ways that affect the options available to states. This was apparent in the late 1990s as representatives from PSCs such as DSL, Sandline, Military Professional Resources Incorporated (MPRI), KBR, and others were frequent participants in conferences about how to deal with low-level conflicts, proper behavior in conflict zones, and even US Army professionalism. PSCs are also increasingly intertwined with global firms involved in the production of systems, weapons, and equipment, making governments increasingly dependent on interconnected firms.[43] This complicates state control of force. As Rachel Epstein argues, the increasing cross-national defense industry integration has widened the gap between foreign policy ambitions and defense needs in Europe because without integrated *political* processes and goals, European governments cannot take advantage of the industry's integration but also do not have domestic alternatives.[44]

There are also signs, however, that PSCs enhance the power of states. States that embrace the market claim to have flexible new tools with which to pursue foreign policy. The United States affected events on the battlefield in Croatia without either deploying its forces or paying the bill simply by licensing a PSC to give advice and training to the Croatian Army.[45] The United States also managed the chaos in Iraq with fewer troops than many argued were necessary by hiring PSCs. Also, PSCs, in effect, substituted for UN peacekeepers in Iraq not only with security forces, but international forces. As one American Army staff sergeant claimed, "we're trying to get more international participation here and the contractors can hire internationally."[46] Similarly, the Hungarian government upgraded its military to NATO standards more quickly by employing Cubic. The Saudi government trained a national guard to protect the regime with the help of Vinnell Corporation and dramatically enhanced the functioning of its army, air force, and navy with help from a range of different firms including BDM, Booz Allen Hamilton, and Science Applications International Corporation (SAIC).[47]

An alternative use of the institutionalist logic Cerny employs abandons the functionalist assumption and focuses instead on how environmental changes, such as marketization, alter the playing field on which states and other actors compete and thus the nature of the political game.[48] This need not erode the power of individual states per se, but may lead to different patterns of competition and cooperation—both within states and between them. Markets work differently than hierarchies and thus should advantage different actors and strategies. Reactions to marketization may vary—leading to different policies, with various consequences for the autonomy and capacity of states and their relative power. Drawing on this logic, I argue that the market poses dilemmas for strong states—offering potential gains in capacity and the balance of power, but at a risk of autonomy and increased conflict. For weak states, the market often exacerbates already present institutional malformation in a way that decreases capacity and relative power in addition to increasing the risks of conflict. Finally, the increasing use of markets to allocate force (though partially a product of state decisions) is likely to change the nature of conflict as well as its frequency in ways that individual states have little control over.

The Market for Force, Redistribution of Power in Strong States and Adventurous Defense: Trade-Offs between Autonomy and Capacity

Market alternatives for military services increase the options with which states conduct defense. The use of the market, however, operates differently from military organizations and advantages some actors more than others. Generally, using market alternatives advantages executives relative to legislatures, reduces governmental transparency, erodes the connection between citizenship and military service, and allows PSCs a role in shaping or interpreting policy. The first three change the operation of institutional checks and balances and democratic practices that have been connected to restraint in military policy.[49] The fourth assigns influence to actors who may have a commercial interest in a lack of restraint. Altogether, these changes suggest that the embrace of market alternatives open the way for greater adventurousness in defense policy. Below, I illustrate this argument with examples from the United States.

Market Options Redistribute Power within Government—Increased Capacity Executives are advantaged in military decision making to begin with, but contracting with PSCs enhances this advantage.[50] The executive branch hires contractors, not Congress. Though Congress approves the military budget, it does not approve individual decisions for contracts. It is also harder for Congress to oversee PSC behavior in contract with the US government. Although Congress has access to the ins and outs of the process and behavior of military institutions—indeed, Congress often has created these processes at a previous time—its access to information about contracts is more circumscribed.[51] The executive branch can use its advantage to evade congressional restriction on US actions—effectively limiting the influence of Congress as a veto player. For instance, Congress often limits US involvement in a conflict by stipulating a ceiling on the numbers of US troops. By employing contractors, the executive branch can increase de facto US involvement—if Congress stipulates a limit on the number of contractors, PSCs can hire more local personnel.[52] PSCs concentrate power with those in charge of hiring dispersing funds to and overseeing the contractor—generally the executive branch. Furthermore, the market can allow governments to conduct foreign policy "by proxy" in authorizing direct contracts between foreign governments and PSCs. The United States licensed MPRI to provide advice and training to the Croatian government in 1994. President Tudjman received many of the advantages of US military assistance, but through a private entity. Indeed, he touted the contract as evidence of the alliance between the United States and Croatia.[53] The British government encouraged similar contracts between PSCs and states in which British firms have an interest—for instance, it encouraged Mozambique to hire DSL to facilitate security for rail lines on which British firms transported goods. Though the processes within individual states differ at the margins (exports of military services are regulated in the United States, for instance, and not in the United Kingdom), contracts between foreign governments and PSCs reduce the veto power of some players.[54]

Using PSCs also reduces transparency. By avoiding the mobilization of military machinery, deploying private force avoids institutionalized mechanisms by which people become aware of force deployments. When private forces are sent abroad, the deployment itself gets less publicity—as do any mishaps. Consider the experience of the three contractors working for the United States in the Colombian drug war who were shot down by the Fuerzas Armadas Revolucionarias de Colombia (FARC; Revolutionary Armed Forces of Colombia). Keith Stansell, Marc Gonsalves, and Thomas Howes have been held by the FARC in Colombia since February 2003.[55] A scan of Lexus/Nexus reveals that only 76 articles have mentioned "hostage," "Colombia," and "contractor" in full text during the last two years.[56] Even fewer (21) have mentioned these terms within the articles' titles or lead paragraphs. Thirty articles total mentioned the hostages' names. Contrast this with American hostages Shoshana Johnson and Jessica Lynch, captured in Operation Iraqi Freedom. During her 22 days of her captivity, Shoshana Johnson was mentioned in 98 articles (excluding articles about the rescue itself). The terms "Shoshana," "Johnson," and "Iraq" in the full text over the last 2 years yielded 360 hits. During Jessica Lynch's seven days of captivity, 36 articles contained her name (excluding news of the rescue itself) and the terms "Jessica," "Lynch," and "Iraq" in full text over the past two years yielded more than 1,000 documents.[57]

When PSCs contract directly with foreign governments, Congress has even less opportunity to weigh in and the public less opportunity to find out. The State Department's Office of Export Controls does regulate direct contracts for military services between a PSC and a foreign government, but the executive branch is not required to notify Congress of such contracts ahead of time unless they are for more than $50 million. Recently countries as varied as the United Kingdom, Hungary, Colombia, Nigeria, Equatorial Guinea, and Croatia have contracted directly with US PSCs for security services—with little attention from Congress or the public.

Moreover, one of the cornerstones of democratic restraint is taken to be the relationship between citizenship and military service. This is tied to the idea that in democracies those with influence over foreign policy are also those called upon to sacrifice for that policy in a way that raises the bar for the use of force.[58] PSCs may evade this dilemma, eliciting less response from a democratic public, not only because of reduced transparency but also because they are not serving, simply working. Though empirical validation of this logic is yet to be completed, there is a difference between the news coverage of private forces and soldiers in Iraq. Articles about soldiers usually assume a patriotic motivation for serving, but articles about private security contractors generally explain their behavior as commercially motivated.[59] Even in the coverage of the Blackwater employees killed in Falluja, more generous to the contractors given the gruesome details of their deaths, there were many references to the men's monetary rather that service motivations.[60]

Private tools allow American leaders to use force when they otherwise might not. During the 1990s, market alternatives gave the Clinton administration means with which to affect outcomes in the Balkans without mobilizing the population around the importance of the "engagement" policy. When Croatia and MPRI signed a contract in September of 1994 and the State Department licensed the project, the United States wanted to change the Balkan game. Senior State Department officials admitted that Croatia became our de facto ally—that arms flowed in despite the embargo and that top retired American generals were allowed to advise the Croatian Army.[61] Richard Holbrook recounts the contents of a note passed to him by Bob Frasure before his death that said, "We 'hired' these guys to be our junkyard dogs because we were desperate. Now we need to control them...."[62] MPRI's mere presence was evidence of this "alliance." It changed the strategic environment in Croatia, provided benefits to Tudjman personally in his effort to consolidate political power,[63] and boosted Croatian Army morale.[64] Also, MPRI presence provided to Milosevic a signal of American commitment to Tudjman—some have argued that Serbs in the Krajina put up less resistance once they realized that Milosevic was not going to back them up with Jugoslavenska Narodna Armija (JNA; Yugoslav People's Army) forces.[65] Croatian military successes that followed changed the balance of power in the region such that strategic bombing by NATO could push the Serbs to the negotiating table—the results of which were the Dayton Accords.[66] By licensing MPRI, the United States retained its official neutral status while changing events on the ground in the direction it favored.[67]

Private support also reduced the numbers of US troops deployed to the Balkans. KBR (then Brown and Root Services) first provided support services to US troops operating out of Aviano air base in Italy as they participated in patrols of the no-fly zone over Bosnia (Operation Deny Flight) in early 1995. Then, in 1995, the US Army paid KBR $546 million to provide logistical support for US soldiers deployed to the region as part of NATO's implementation force (IFOR) peacekeeping mission.[68] It is estimated that one out of every ten people deployed to the region were contractors—cutting requisite US troops by at least one-tenth.

PSCs played a large role in the US intervention in Somalia, Haiti, the Colombian drug war, and more. Common to all of these interventions were questionable levels of public support and civilian disagreement over either their importance to US security or the best way to affect outcomes or both. In the wake of low levels of public support and civilian disagreement, it should be hard for the United States to move forward on policy—particularly policy that requires the deployment of forces.[69] Private options eased some of these difficulties.

Since the September 11, 2001, attacks on the United States, private capacities have enhanced the options available to the Bush administration. The level of contractor support for American troops reduced the number of troops necessary to take offensive action in both Afghanistan and Iraq. In Operation Iraqi Freedom, particularly, the government made decisions and made arguments that led the war to be authorized based on the number of troops they would need. There were heated disputes over these numbers, particularly the numbers of US troops that would be needed to stabilize the country after the war. General Shinseki claimed that it would take 200,000 plus troops, a number that was politically unacceptable. Secretary of Defense Donald Rumsfeld claimed that the stabilization of Iraq could be done with many fewer troops. After the overthrow of Hussein's government, stabilization proved to be more difficult than Rumsfeld had anticipated and, with international support for the United States not immediately forthcoming, PSCs provided surge capacity that filled in for the lack of adequate numbers of troops.

Market Options Redistribute Power to Commercial Actors—Decreased Autonomy   Using PSCs opens the way for commercially interested PSCs to affect policy implementation and goals. Private impact on implementation manifests itself most clearly where outcomes are hard to measure. When PSCs provide foreign military training missions, the information the US government receives about their progress generally comes from either the PSC or the host government—both of whom have an interest in reporting progress, even when none has been made, to ensure the continuation of funding. Rosy reporting may encourage investment that increases PSC revenues and host government military assistance. Pentagon employees complained that in Bosnia the information on progress in military training came from either the PSC conducting the training or the host government in ways that kept the gravy train going even though the effects were questionable.[70] PSCs also advise governments on future programs, laying the groundwork for future contracts. KBR, for instance, was awarded a contract to repair Iraqi oil fields without competition in anticipation of their destruction during Operation Iraqi Freedom because, "according to the Army's classified contingency plan for repairing Iraq's infrastructure, KBR was the only company with the skills, resources and security clearances to do the job on short notice. Who wrote the Army's contingency plan? KBR."[71] PSCs are also able to affect policy goals. They can make arguments that interpret policy, or reinterpret it through different frames, opening the way for changes that enhance their commercial interests. Consider MPRI's contract with Equatorial Guinea. When MPRI first requested a license to evaluate Equatorial Guinea's defense department in 1998, the regional affairs office for Africa at the State Department rejected the request immediately because of Equatorial Guinea's poor human rights record.[72] Officials from MPRI then visited the assistant secretary for African affairs and congressional members to suggest looking at the license from a different perspective.[73] There are benefits, MPRI argued, to "engaging" with a country rather than punishing it. Engagement might foster better behavior (fewer human rights abuses) in the future and enhance US (as opposed to French) oil interests, especially given that Equatorial Guinea was going to hire someone (if not MPRI, it could be a less savory company or one less interested in the interest of American companies abroad).[74] These arguments, coming from esteemed, high level (retired) military officers and reflecting a deep understanding of the ins and outs of American defense policy, had an impact.[75] When the application was submitted again, it was approved by the regional office but held up in the Office of Democracy, Human Rights, and Labor. Again, MPRI went to visit and explain their case, to the assistant secretary, to more members of Congress, and officials at Democracy, Human Rights, and Labor.[76] In the spring of 2000, the contract was approved—based on a different set of guidelines than when it was originally rejected.[77] One may find MPRI's logic persuasive or not, but the standard for licensing a contract shifted with no new information about the impact of such a contract on Equatorial Guinea's human rights processes and no change in MPRI's contract with them. Some argue that MPRI simply gave more power to those in government that were arguing for this approach to begin with. This is true, but beside the point. These people were losing the argument before MPRI joined forces.[78]

That an agent might exploit information asymmetry to its advantage is hardly new. Delegation always leads to a degree of information asymmetry and some degree of slack.[79] This is at work when governments delegate to military organizations as well. However, delegating to a private entity brings a commercial interest to the policy decisions. This not only increases the potential for policy that does not match the goals of leaders, it biases policy in a particular way. This influence can enhance what Gowa calls "political market failures" or the tendency for resource endowments to benefit special rather than general interests.[80] This can happen in a variety of ways—PSCs can report information that encourages training programs that are not worth their cost, encourage relationships with governments that do not support US interests, encourage investment in areas that do not serve US interests, and more.

Reduced state autonomy (via greater influence for commercially interested actors) combined with the change in the processes of decision making (fewer veto points and less transparency) give political officials more leeway to make decisions that enhance their welfare or that of PSCs rather than the polity as a whole. These procedural changes offer a way around what is often termed "democratic restraint" in military policy. If a leader can deploy military services or otherwise use force in a way that reduces or eliminates mobilizing troops, the visibility, sacrifice, and political cost of using force go down. Though this logic applies most clearly to democracies, where checks and balances are frequently assumed to exact higher costs on executives who choose to deploy forces, the logic should hold for other kinds of polities as well. As Gowa points out, no leader can "jeopardize the cohesion of the coalition of forces that maintain them in office."[81] If the costs of using force go down, all things being equal, force is more likely to be used.[82]

This is not to suggest that PSCs *cause* adventurous policies. The causal arrow may go the other way. Interest in adventurous policies may lead governments to seek out private actors to implement their policies. The ready availability of private options, though, may affect the perception of threats by reducing the costs associated with using military tools and the depth of the market for force make the use of private options easier.[83] Nor is it to suggest that only PSCs allow governments to be less restrained in their use of violence. Other tools, such as covert action and joining with foreign forces, similarly skirt democratic processes.[84] The presence of a market option for the use of force, though, is an additional permissive factor for adventurous policies. Intriguingly, arguments about the usefulness of contracted forces in the early Modern period also associate market allocation with adventurous goals. According to Thomson, "it appears that the European market for mercenaries was largely a creation of war-makers seeking to escape the constraints of feudal military obligations."[85]

The Restraint Trade-Off: Democratic Practices and Autonomy versus Increased Capacity and Relative Power Less restraint may allow polities that avail themselves of PSCs more tools for using force in ways that enhance their power relative to other states. Some analysts argue that democracies have too many hoops to jump through in defense policy making.[86] The need to build consensus and design policy transparently reduces the capacity to respond effectively to the international system—and may produce perverse or ineffective policy that reduces national security.[87] These analysts may view PSCs as a mechanism for generating better security in the face of difficulties posed by democratic processes. For instance, Barnett claims that the United States secures its interests around the globe and has expressed concern that the United States lacks the will to undertake the tough ground actions necessary to solidify its hegemonic position.[88] From a different political perspective, the Carnegie Commission on the Prevention of Deadly Conflict argued that the international community needed to find a way to intervene where conflict was likely.[89] Moreover, Shearer argued that PSCs could be the answer—a means to quell civil wars in the face of reluctant Western states.[90] The use of private alternatives, however, simultaneously erodes democratic processes. As the previous section made clear, using PSCs reduces both the institutional checks on foreign policy and the amount of transparency in the process. Although one could still argue that the process would be accountable in that citizens have a chance to vote leaders out of office if they do not like the results, the erosion of democratic processes is likely to have an impact on citizen involvement. This has some obvious political consequences. There are many benefits that come along with democratic processes that may be lost or reduced if these processes are abandoned.[91] The benefits of democratic processes also extend to important dimensions of national security. Particularly, democracies are said to ameliorate security dilemmas and generate more effective military action.

A variety of arguments have linked the need for domestic coalitions and transparent processes to the development of trust that reduces security dilemmas and enhances the credibility of threats. Lipson argues, for instance, that democratic processes generate contracting advantages, making it easier for democratic states to keep commitments.[92] Military threats are different among democracies, Lipson argues, because these states are less likely to bluff and thus their threats (and promises) are more credible. The transparency of processes reduces misperceptions that can lead to war. The need to build coalitions and the openness of the policy process sometimes leads democratic states to expand the range of potential options in ways that reduce the chance of conflict. Over time, democracies develop expectations about each other based on learning.[93]

The restraint that makes democratic states less likely to initiate wars also makes these states more effective in the wars they do fight.[94] Lake claims that the lower levels of rent seeking that is common in democracies provide more services to the state's citizens at less cost. This leads both to better economic growth and thus easier mobilization for war, but also encourages loyalty among citizens that lead them to fight harder to preserve the benefits they enjoy. Moreover, democracies will join together to prevent mutual exploitation by autocracies. These factors make democracies more effective militarily.[95] Reiter and Stam contend that democratic leaders are wary of the cost of war and thus more discriminating: they choose wars they are likely to win. Furthermore, because democracies are consent-based systems, soldiers have greater morale, fight harder, and exhibit superior leadership on the battlefield.[96]

The use of private options for security may eat away at these democratic benefits. If leaders can choose to use private forces, they may have less incentive to mobilize the public behind foreign policy and may make security decisions through processes less open to public view, less subject to challenges from opposition parties, and less scrutinized by the press. Options that reduce transparency may simultaneously increase the chance of misperception. Solutions that do not require the mobilization of domestic coalitions may lead nonconflictual alternatives to appear less beneficial. States that systematically evade these processes may erode trust and increase tensions among democracies.

The ability to hire an international force may curb the willingness of American leaders to bargain with other governments to build effective international coalitions. Furthermore, private recruiting may infringe on the security resources of other states. For instance, recent recruiting activity by United States–based Blackwater, USA has caused Chilean defense officials to worry that Chilean military personnel will be lured away from national service by the lucrative pay in the private security market. The increased influence of PSCs in the policy process may generate rent, as collective resources are deployed to accomplish subgroup goals. Just this concern arose in the recent Iraqi conflict. Ultimately, when private soldiers work side by side with regular military forces—but under different rules—it may erode the loyalty, initiative, and fighting power of soldiers.

Others argue that the democratic peace and military effectiveness of democracies are overstated.[97] Even those who do not buy the "democratic goods" argument should agree that encouraging leaders to engage in foreign policies that do not have widespread support should remove restraint and enhance the potential for the use of force. This may lead to some national security goods–enhanced capability (at least in the short term) and an increase in power relative to other states (particularly other states that do not embrace market alternatives). It also, however, leads to some national security risks. States that rely on market alternatives may exacerbate security dilemmas. This has obvious ramifications for the national security of individual states.

Strong states can choose to eschew market alternatives. South Africa has both refused to purchase services from PSCs and acted to make the export of such services illegal. This strategy maintains state autonomy from commercial forces and the democratic processes that the state enjoys. It also, however, reduces the state's relative power. Indeed, South African PSCs and personnel are working for the United States in Iraq—a war that the South African government did not support. South Africa could (and may yet) choose to prosecute these individuals—but the costs of halting their activities in Iraq would be high.

The Market for Force, Redistribution of Power in Weak States and the Diffusion of Control over Violence: Institutional Malformation   In weak states, the market's redistribution of power has a greater impact on state autonomy—empowering actors outside the state. Also, the market often generates long-term institutional malformation that reduces state capacity. As Cooley suggests in his analysis of postimperial states, the market frequently leads to rent seeking, the institutionalization of illicit markets, the erosion of authority and accountability, and weakened capacity to cope with transnational threats.[98] This argument can be extended to a variety of weak states where the market works to diffuse control over violence. When nonstate actors finance violence, they gain influence over security decisions that can affect state policy.[99] Their purchases, though, also create alternative revenue streams that diffuse control over violence. Although some might imagine that nonstate financing could bolster or shore up a weak state, nonstate financing frequently either leads to an extreme form of "political market failure" where the state works to guarantee private rather than public interest, or disperses power over the control of force, which decreases the performance and effectiveness of forces—or both. The former frequently accompanies states rich in natural resources—and has been labeled the "resource curse." The latter is likely when transnational actors (whether financing the state's security apparatus, financing rebels, or hiring private security) become additional principals in the control of violence. When multiple principals with different aims have a say over forces, they often issue competing instructions—resulting in forces that can shirk and follow neither. Even if principals share goals, if they do not coordinate their actions, they can still issue competing instructions that reduce the capacity of forces to carry out basic missions.[100] Increasingly, these two effects work together to create forces that are not only repressive and corrupt but also incompetent.[101]

Examples of the resource curse abound. Case study research has suggested a relationship between foreign investment in oil, diamonds, and other minerals and a repressive state security apparatus that is perceived to work primarily on behalf of the property rights of foreign investors in Latin America, Africa, the Middle East, and Asia.[102] The logic of the argument is that foreign direct investors supply the state with needed revenue, eclipsing the state's need to build support among its populace in return for taxes. The resulting "rentier" state is beholden to external investors rather than internal support. This is said to erode the potential for democracy and harness coercive forces for the protection of foreign property.[103]

In a twist on this logic, Will Reno has pointed out that foreign investment can lead in more perverse directions—instead of building effective state instruments of coercion, rulers may opt to guarantee foreign property with a variety of nonstate coercive instruments. Though the enhanced influence of external investors on security decisions is similar, worries about internal threats may lead rulers of weak states to funnel foreign funds into privately controlled security rather than into state bureaucracies. In these instances, the effect of foreign financing leads not only to repressive forces, but also to the erosion of the state's forces altogether, leading to "quasi-states," "shadow states," and "warlords."[104]

For instance, in Nigeria, the huge sums of money paid by oil companies for security have been a magnet for corruption. The corruption also extends down into the forces.[105] Both the police and military in Nigeria have been distracted by money-making potential in a way that decreases their capacity. Though there are many examples of the way corruption has impinged on the capacity of the Nigerian police,[106] some of the most obvious problems come up in the military's behavior abroad. Both officers and common soldiers subsidize their salaries with private activities. In the officer corps, this takes the form of administrative assignments, payoffs, and involvement in illicit trade; in the force at large, it takes the form of looting.[107] Nigerian troops' peacekeeping capacities are diminished by these activities. Leading the Economic Community of West African States Monitoring Group (ECOMOG) regional peacekeeping force in Liberia in 1997, the Nigerians reportedly engaged in systematic looting—including shipping entire buildings to be sold for scrap abroad, trafficking in heroin, and child prostitution.[108] The dynamics of the Nigerian case bear much resemblance to those Cooley points out in the postimperial states of the Former Soviet Union.

Multinational corporations do not have a corner on perverse private financing efforts, though. INGOs seeking to "do good" can also contribute to institutional malformation. For instance, the transnational conservation community's efforts to protect species have also been prone to multiple principal problems that have similarly led to repressive or ineffective forces. During the Cold War, some conservation INGOs provided financing to repressive governments, who, in turn, used the money to build up military forces contrary to what the INGOs may have intended.[109] More recently, conservation INGOs have often worked in failed states, where their financing efforts have simply led to ineffective forces. In one case, the conservation community working to save the last few Northern White Rhinos in the wild poured millions of dollars into a park for little or no gain.[110]

In this case, the INGO did not negotiate a clear legal status in the park. Though INGO staff financed and oversaw the guard force, they did not have control over personnel.[111] With the government in charge of personnel and the INGO controlling resources, neither set nor enforced basic operating objectives and performance standards. Despite the vast infusion of resources over more than ten years, the guard force was no larger or better able to perform its duties in 1996 than it had been in the mid-1980s.[112] A good portion of the forces was unable to field strip or clean their weapons and many were too old to patrol.[113] More importantly, the chain of command was unclear. The management committee, through which the park was run, allowed debate over the daily routine but did not chart lines of responsibility or accountability.[114] Without basic professional procedures, the money dedicated to antipoaching in the park did not build a solid and professional force but allowed the project to operate in a constant state of "crisis-management."

As the Democratic Republic of Congo (DRC) descended into civil war, some guards joined in looting the park's supplies and weapons; but the INGO had no authority to fire them. In a twist on the imperative for organizations to compete over functional jurisdiction that Cooley talks about, as the civil war dragged on, NGO staff allied themselves with whatever forces were willing to do patrols in the park—inadvertently exacerbating competition over jurisdiction to carry out violent activities in the park. This was arguably problematic for conservation but even more so for the performance of security forces. Poorly paid troops found the park—either through INGO support or poaching—to be a source of rent. However, patrolling for poachers or poaching reduced their focus and capacity to defend against the variety of incursions from other forces.

The availability of transnational capital to finance violence in weak states is not only tied to the rentier state phenomenon that others have analyzed at length. When the state controls one lever of control and transnational financiers another, it can also reduce the effectiveness of forces. Furthermore, the marketization of security offers opportunities for security forces to participate in commercial or other activities that increase their revenue but distract from developing competence. The diffuse web of multiple controls over violence impedes weak state power and authority even further—often leading to habitually malformed security institutions where the organizational imperatives lead to individual incentives that reduce the potential for developing functional capacity. Though this tendency is not impossible to overcome, moving toward functional and legitimate security institutions requires coordinated action that is hard to engender with market mechanisms alone.[115]

The Marketization of Security, Increased Conflict, and Changes in the Purpose of Violence

Features of marketization in both strong and weak states also promise changes in the frequency and nature of conflict. Among strong states, increased opportunities for adventure should lead to more intervention. As the previous section suggested, the use of PSCs makes it easier for the United States to launch both "humanitarian" and "imperial wars." Once involved, it is conceivable that in the course of operating to secure oil fields or other private facilities in Iraq (or Afghanistan), PSCs could take action that could bring retribution on US forces and cause an escalation of the conflict. Furthermore, PSC recruitment could encourage tensions between strong states—as PSCs recruit internationally they infringe upon the military capacities of other states as well as the ability of these states to control the violent activities of their citizens abroad—as the earlier mention of PSC recruiting in Chile and South African PSC activity in Iraq demonstrate. Even the United States and the United Kingdom have suffered a larger than usual separation from special forces that they attribute to PSC recruiting.

The impact on conflict should be even greater in weak states. The market for force allows actors with different constituents, roles, and authority claims to wield violence—potentially leading to overlapping claims that exacerbate conflict. In many territories of the developing world, weak states, warlords, PSCs, INGOs, TNCs, rebels, criminals, terrorists, and sometimes strong state forces as well—each with some claim to the use of force—operate within the same territory. Even a neorealistic analysis might predict that the growing numbers of actors alone would increase the potential for misperception and thus the chance for conflict.[116] More classical realistic analyses are on record envisaging that the range of actors will exacerbate conflict.[117] Institutionalist insights about the logic of incomplete contracts focus on an entirely different logic—suggesting that market solutions are unlikely to generate enduring efficient solutions to governance problems—but also expect tumultuous outcomes.[118]

These expectations ring true historically. In the thirteenth and four-teenth centuries, Europe was characterized by a fragmentation of polit-ical authority, public power in private hands, and a military system in which an essential part of the armed forces was secured through private contracts.[119] Military enterprisers allowed merchants, princes, kings, popes, and even themselves to garner political power. According to many, until the dawn of the modern state, the complex array of overlap-ping claims and power led to conflicting demands, rampant tensions, and frequent war.[120] Systematic examination of the number of histori-cal conflicts lends support to this expectation. Even using Jack Levy's list of wars from 1495 to 1975 (which excludes civil wars, imperial and colonial wars, and wars that do not involve a great power, and thus may dramatically undercount the degree of actual conflict) demonstrates a strong association between the prevalence of competing authorities, contracted forces, and war.[121] In the period from 1495 to 1688, when jurisdiction over territory often overlapped and markets allocated vir-tually all force, there were, on average, 2.23 wars per year. In the period from 1689 to 1813, as the nation-state system began to consolidate, the rate of war was cut almost in half to 1.40 per year. In the period from 1814 to 1975 when the nation-state system was fully consolidated, the rate of war fell more than one-half again to 0.49 per year.[122]

As Levy argues, the modern nation-state has been associated with a decrease in the rate of conflict, but an increase in its deadliness. Indeed, the average annual battle fatalities from 1495 to 1975 were greatest in two periods: from 1790 to 1813 (encompassing the Napoleonic Wars at the end of the period of nation-state consolidation) and from 1917 to 1939 (encompassing World Wars I and II when the nation-state system was consolidated).[123] One interpretation is that the nation-state system has harnessed violence to be deployed in a particular way—against other nation-states and for collective purposes in a way that simultaneously increases the relentless pursuit of goals even in the wake of battle deaths.

Competing authorities with control over force may cause violence to be used for a greater variety of ends, but also may make it harder to harness violence for large collective purposes. This may lead us to expect different kinds of conflict between different kinds of entities, more civil wars, more frequent uses of violence for individual or small group gain, greater use of violence for purposes that do not entail collective justifications, and perhaps more random violence. Furthermore, the laws of war, institutionalized among states and state-based military organizations, may become less frequently observed—potentially leading to greater use of violence against civilians. In other words, the diffusion of control over violence may lead not only to increased conflict but also to different kinds of conflict.[124]

There is some macro evidence supporting the plausibility of these trends in recent years—particularly in Africa. After spiking at the beginning of the decade, the number of armed conflicts in all regions of the world declined in the 1990s (armed conflict defined as a contested incompatibility that concerns government or territory or both where the use of armed force between two parties—one of them a government—results in at least 25 battle-related deaths).[125] The rate of armed conflict during the decade, however, remained the same in Africa. Moreover, the number of civil wars in Africa (a conflict that produces at least 1,000 battle deaths) almost doubled in the 1990s.[126]

There is also anecdotal evidence that the market's forces, even the more legitimate portions, have aggravated many of these internal conflicts.[127] PSCs and transnational financiers have played a large role in internal conflicts. Though they have sometimes enhanced the short-run capacity of state forces, their focus on short-run goals, as well as their frequent allegiance to the private interests that finance their work have often exacerbated conflict over the long term. EO's work in Sierra Leone, for instance, saved the capital from imminent defeat in 1995. However, EO's decision to remain working during a coup to oust the very leader that had hired them (to suit the wishes of the diamond industry keenly interested in maintaining control of the mines) and to work with the local militias as they moved to the countryside exacerbated instability.[128] Similarly, in the DRC, mining companies, PSCs, and smuggling networks are integrally networked with the military forces of Rwanda, Uganda, and Zimbabwe, perpetuating a conflict based on competing claims to the resources of the country.[129] Also in Colombia, the combination of paramilitaries, PSCs, government forces, and a rebel movement, all interspersed with criminal networks in the export of coca has been tied to endemic conflict in that country.[130] Some multinational firms, particularly oil companies, have turned to PSCs to help train local forces out of exasperation with the inability of government forces, but neither the oil companies nor the PSCs can exercise control over these forces once they are trained. Some forces have allegedly used their new skills to extort the local population or sold them to the FARC or paramilitaries. The violent capacities of these different groups allow them to turn to violence more easily to solve jurisdictional problems—over coca fields, transportation routes, or revenues from the local population. In all of these conflicts, violence is used to meet many different goals, operates without attention to international law, and often affects civilians.[131]

CONCLUSION

The market for force presents both opportunities and challenges to states and its impact depends, in part, on the choices states make. Continued marketization, with the associated increase in adventurous foreign policy and diffusion of control, may feed back into increased pressures for market solutions to security. If the United States intervenes more quickly—for humanitarian or imperialistic reasons—it is both more likely to need forces to accomplish postconflict stability operations and may be less likely to get its friends and allies to go along via multilateral institutions. Postconflict scenarios without UN peacekeepers, however, pose additional opportunities to PSCs. Also, the increased number of civil wars in Africa has led to increased financing for security by the private sector—extractive industries that want to retain access to natural resources, conservation organizations that want to preserve species, and humanitarian organizations that want to ease suffering—further deepening the diffusion of control over violence on that continent. Even increased tensions among the Western powers may make multilateral negotiations more difficult and enhance the appeal of market solutions to deal with perceived threats. Efforts to tame the market for force, though, either by slowing its growth or cooperating to regulate its operation, are likely to engender a different future. The political reaction to the more visible use of PSC in Iraq will be important for influencing US choices and what the United States, with a defense budget near 1 percent of gross world product, chooses will carry particular importance—an example of the "mock systemic" forces to which Kirshner refers.[132]

NOTES

1. In a letter to Ike Skelton (ranking Democrat on the House of Representatives Committee on Armed Services) dated May 4, 2004, Secretary of Defense Donald Rumsfeld estimated that some 20,000 private security personnel were working in Iraq and attached a list of 60 PSCs. The letter and list are available at http://www.house.gov/skelton/pr040504a.htm. This list, however, does not include companies such as Vinnell and MPRI, who were known to have personnel in the country training the Iraqi Army. It also does not include CACI, known to have personnel in the country working as interrogators at military prisons. This estimate came in the wake of a variety of estimates from a variety of sources, but several former members of the CPA as well as military personnel that worked in Iraq claim that no one really knows how many private security personnel are in the country. Interviews in Washington, DC, with former CPA officials, March 2004, May 2004, and July 2004. Interviews in Washington, DC, with military officers returned from Iraq, May 2004, June 2004, and July 2004.
2. Seymour M. Hersh, "Torture at Abu Ghraib," *New Yorker*, May 6, 2004; Major General Antonio M. Taguba, "Article 15-6 Investigation of the 800th Military Police Brigade," report to U.S. Central Command, March 2004.
3. There is a debate over how to identify these companies—private military company (PMC), private security provider (PSP), and privatized military firm (PMF) have all been suggested in addition to PSC. I use PSC because it refers to the broader range of security more pertinent to conflicts today.
4. Interview with Erik Prince, owner, and Gary Jackson, president, of Blackwater, USA, Washington, DC, July 2004.
5. See Mark Hanna, "Task Force XXI: The Army's Digital Experiment," *Strategic Studies* 119 (July 1997).
6. Colonel Donald Wynn, "Managing the Logistics-Support Contract in the Balkans Theater," http://call.army/call/trngqtr/tq4-00/wynn.htm; "GAO Report: Balkans Contracts Too Costly," *European Stars and Stripes*, November 14, 2000; Jane Nelson, *The Business of Peace*, London: Prince of Wales Business Leaders' Forum (2000), 91. See also Dan Baum, "Nation Builders for Hire," *New York Times Magazine*, June 22, 2003, 32–37.
7. See, "Public/Private Partnerships in the MOD: The Private Finance Initiative in Government," http://www.mod.uk/commercial/pfi/intro.htm.
8. See Deborah Avant, "Conserving Nature in the State of Nature: The Politics of INGO Implementation," *Review of International Studies* 30 (July 2004): 361–382.
9. Equitable Securities Corporation, *Equitable Securities Research* 27 (August), 97. Cited in Alex Vines, "Mercenaries and the Privatization of Security in Africa in the 1990s," in *The Privatization of Security in Africa* (Johannesburg: SAIIA Press, 1999), 47.
10. Peter Singer, *Corporate Warriors: The Rise of the Privatized Military Industry* (Ithaca, NY: Cornell University Press, 2003).
11. Jack Kelly, "Safety at a Price: Security is a Booming, Sophisticated, Global Business," *Pittsburgh Post Gazette*, February 13, 2000.

12. For examinations of pre-Modern contractors, see Fritz Redlich, *The German Military Enterpriser and His Workforce: A Study in European Economic and Social History* (Wiesbaden, Germany: Franz Steiner Verlag, 1964); Geoffrey Trease, *The Condottieri* (New York: Holt, Rinehart and Winston, 1971); Charles Oman, *History of the Art of War in the Middle Ages*, 2nd ed. (London: Greenhill Books, 1924); Geoffrey Parker, *The Thirty Years War* (London: Routledge, 1984); B. Guenee, *States and Rulers in Later Medieval Europe* (Oxford: Oxford University Press, 1985); Frederick H. Russell, *The Just War in the Middle Ages* (London: Cambridge University Press, 1975); Johan Huizinga, "The Political and Military Significance of Chivalric Ideas in the Late Middle Ages," in *Men and Ideas* (New York: Meridian Books, 1959); Richard Barber, *The Knight and Chivalry*, rev. ed. (Woodbridge: Boydell Press, 1995); Richard W. Kaeuper, *War, Justice and the Public Order* (Oxford: Clarendon Press, 1988); and, of course, Niccolo Machiavelli, *The Prince*, eds. Quentin Skinner and Russell Price (New York: Cambridge University Press, 1988), chap. 12.
13. Redlich, *The German Military Enterpriser*; Anthony Mockler, *The New Mercenaries* (London: Garden City Press, 1985); Oman, *History of the Art of War*.
14. Martin Van Creveld, *The Transformation of War* (New York: Free Press, 1991).
15. S. P. Sen, *The French in India, 1763–1816* (Calcutta: Frima K. L. Mukhopadhyay, 1958); Holden Furber, *Rival Empires of Trade in the Orient, 1600–1800* (Minnesota: University of Minnesota Press, 1976); R. Mukherjee, *The Rise and Fall of the East India Company* (New York: Monthly Review Press, 1974); Bernard H. M. Velkke, *Evolution of the Dutch Nation* (New York: Roy Publishers, 1945); Gary Anderson and Robert Tollison, "Apologiae for Chartered Monopolies in Foreign Trade, 1600–1800," *History of Political Economy* 14(4) (1983): 549–566; C. R. Boxer, *Jan Compagnie in War and Peace, 1602–1799* (Hong Kong: Heinemann Asia, 1979).
16. The idea of a charter was proposed by a commission recommended by Johan van Oldenbarnevelt, the most prominent political figure of the time in Holland in the wake of news of dramatic profits had by Admiral Jacob Corneliszoon van Neck's ship in July 1599 (the haul of spices yielded a 400 percent profit) and similar English efforts. The United Netherlands Chartered East India Company was established in 1602. See Furber, *Rival Empires of Trade*, 31–33. The English East India Company (incorporating the English Levant Company) was established in December 1600. The charter was renewed and altered in 1661. See Furber, *Rival Empires of Trade*, 32. See also the discussion in Janice Thomson, *Mercenaries, Pirates and Sovereigns: State Building and Extraterritorial Violence in Early Modern Europe* (Princeton, NJ: Princeton University Press, 1994), 33–35; Sen, *The French in India*; Mukherjee, *The Rise and Fall of the East India Company*; Velkke, *Evolution of the Dutch Nation*.
17. German rulers who supplied troops in the American Revolution included, His Most Sincere Highness of the Heriditory Court of Hanau offered a few hundred infantry, His Most Sincere Highness the Duke of Brunswick offered 4,000 foot and 300 dragoons, and His Most Sincere Highness the Landgrave of Hesse Cassel offered 12,000 foot, 400 Jagers armed with rifles, 300 dismounted dragoons, 3 corps of artillery, and f4 major-generals. See Mockler, *The New Mercenaries*, 3.
18. Thomson, *Mercenaries, Pirates and Sovereigns*, 28–29; C. C. Bayley, *Mercenaries for the Crimea* (London: McGill-Queens University Press, 1977), 4.
19. However, the first official statement on contracting did not come out until 1954. It is the Budget Bureau Bulletin 55-4 (revised in 1959 and 1966 and eventually renamed OMB Circular A-76) and is still in effect. The thrust of this directive is that government agencies should seek to obtain products and services through the private sector except in cases of national interest. See James Althouse, "Contractors on the Battlefield," *Army Logistician* 14 (November/December 1998).

20. The British government hired from the market for military services less frequently in the Modern period than the United States, but allowed its citizens to sell their services abroad. The commercial sale of security services by British citizens abroad can be traced back through the centuries. See Thomson, *Mercenaries, Pirates and Sovereigns*, 22. More recently, UK Special Air Services (SAS) personnel formed firms to sell military and security services during the Cold War. For instance, in 1967, Colonel Sir David Stirling founded WatchGuard International. See, Kevin O'Brien, "PSCs, Myths, and Mercenaries," *Royal United Service Institute Journal* (February 2000). In addition, individuals acting on their own sold a variety of services in Africa during the Cold War. See, S. J. G. Clarke, *The Congo Mercenary* (Johannesburg: SAIIA Press, 1968); Mockler, *The New Mercenaries*.

21. Eliot Cohen, *Citizens and Soldiers* (Ithaca, NY: Cornell University Press, 1985); Thomson, *Mercenaries, Pirates and Sovereigns*; Deborah Avant, "From Mercenary to Citizen Armies: Explaining Change in the Practice of War," *International Organization* 54 (1) (Winter 2000): 41–72.

22. David Held, Anthony McGrew, David Goldblatt, and Jonathan Perraton, *Global Transformations: Politics, Economics and Culture* (Palo Alto, CA: Stanford University Press, 1999), introduction, chap. 2; Jean-Marie Guehenno, "The Impact of Globalization on Strategy," *Survival* 40 (4) (Winter 1998–99): 5–19.

23. David Held and Anthony McGrew, "The Great Globalization Debate," in David Held and Anthony McGrew, *Global Transformation Reader: An Introduction to the Globalization Debate* (Cambridge: Polity Press, 2003), 3.

24. For the debate about how to define security, see Joseph Nye and Sean Lynn Jones, "International Security Studies: Report of a Conference on the State of the Field," *International Security* 12 (4) (Spring 1988); Jessica Tuchman Mathews, "Redefining Security," *Foreign Affairs* 68 (2) (Spring 1989): 162–177; Barry Buzan, "New Patterns of Global Security in the 21st Century," *International Affairs* 67 (3) (1991); Stephen Walt, "The Renaissance of Security Studies," *International Studies Quarterly* 35(2) (June 1991): 211–240; Edward Kolodziej, "Renaissance of Security Studies? Caveat Lector!" *ISQ* 36 (December 1992): 421–438; David Baldwin, "Security Studies and the End of the Cold War," *World Politics* 48(1) (October 1995): 117–141; Roland Paris, "Human Security: Paradigm Shift or Hot Air?" *International Security* 26(2) (Fall 2001).

25. Peter Andreas, "Redrawing Borders and Security in the Twenty-first Century," *International Security* 28(2) (Fall 2003): 78–111.

26. See Van Creveld, *The Transformation of War*; Mary Kaldor, *New and Old Wars: Organized Violence in a Global Era* (Palo Alto, CA: Stanford University Press, 1999); Mark Duffield, *Global Governance and the New Wars: The Merging of Security and Development* (New York: Zed, 2002).

27. Another "obvious" solution, at least in the 1990s, was multilateral institutions. Why markets and not multilateral solutions have taken hold is an interesting question.

28. This movement began to take hold as Margaret Thatcher took office in 1979. See Madsen Pirie, *Dismantling the State* (Dallas: National Center for Policy Analysis, 1985); John Donahue, *The Privatization Decision: Public Ends, Private Means* (New York: Basic Books, 1989).

29. Paul Pierson, *Dismantling the Welfare State* (Cambridge: Cambridge University Press, 1994), 1.

30. Harvey Feigenbaum, Jeffrey Henig, and Chris Hamnett, *Shrinking the State: The Political Underpinnings of Privatization* (Cambridge: Cambridge University Press, 1998), chap. 1.

31. Not all states feel exactly the same global pressures and not all are so eager to choose private solutions. Indeed, there is much evidence that politics (particularly the military reaction to PSCs and the strength of coalitions associated with privatization more generally) within countries has a significant impact on the degree to which governments respond to these challenges with privatization—but the challenges posed by making the most of technology and reacting to a variety of disorders—and the increasing use of PSCs to meet these challenges—are associated with globalization.

32. It is assumed that those countries most able to leap ahead in the technology necessary to integrate complex information systems will be advantaged in the next conflict as the information revolution and the unbridled flow of capitalism make the most successful military one that can take advantage of these developments. See Joseph Nye and William Owens, "America's Information Edge," *Foreign Affairs* 75 (March/April 1996): 20–36; Andrew Krepinevich, "Cavalry to Computer," *The National Interest* (Fall 1994): 30–42; Eliot Cohen, "A Revolution in Warfare," *Foreign Affairs* 75 (March/April 1996): 37–54; Eliot Cohen, "Defending America's Interest in the Twenty-first Century," *Foreign Affairs* 79(6) (November/December 2000): 40–56.

33. Thomas P. M. Barnett, "The Pentagon's New Map of the World," *Esquire*, March 2003; Robert Kaplan, "The Coming Anarchy," *The Atlantic Monthly*, February 1994. For the illicit side of globalization, see H. Richard Friman and Peter Andreas, *The Illicit Global Economy and State Power* (Lanham, MD: Rowman and Littlefield, 1999). For the trend toward enforcing norms of human rights, see Anthony Clarke Arend and Robert J. Beck, *International Law and the Use of Force: Beyond the UN Charter Paradigm* (New York: Routledge, 1993); Martha Finnemore, "Constructing Norms of Humanitarian Intervention," in *The Culture of National Security: Norms and Identity in World Politics,* ed. Peter Katzenstein (Ithaca, NY: Cornell University Press, 1996); Laura Reed and Carl Kayson, *Emerging Norms of Justified Intervention* (Cambridge, MA: Committee on International Security Studies, American Academy of Arts and Sciences, 1993); Fernando Teson, *Humanitarian Intervention: An Inquiry into Law and Morality* (Dobbs Ferry, NY: Transaction Publishers, 1988).

34. Van Creveld builds this notion when he argues that the nature of war as we have known it because the peace of Westphalia is changing. Unless the state can muster its capacity to confront low intensity conflict, it will destroy the basis of state authority and break down the divisions between public and private, crime and war, and so forth. Pretending that war against other states is the only real war and that past conventions will dictate the future, fallacies he attributes to Clausewitz, will cause the demise of the state. Van Creveld, *The Transformation of War.*

35. Though proponents of the above argument claim the US reaction is a natural response to unipolarity more than globalization, unipolarity alone should not lead the US to be concerned with such a range of issues. Furthermore, it is not at all clear that privatizing military services always, or even most of the time, generate cost efficiencies. Moreover, the United States is not the only country experiencing these pressures. Similar arguments for privatization are made in the United Kingdom, Canada, and other European states that also feel themselves pulled in many different directions to manage security. See, for instance, *Private Military Companies: Options for Regulation,* Foreign and Commonwealth Office, British Green Paper, February 12, 2002, HC 577 (London: Stationary Office, 2002).

36. Philip Cerny, "Globalization and the Changing Nature of Collective Action," *International Organization* 49(4) (Autumn 1995): 595–625; Susan Strange, *Retreat of the State: The Diffusion of Power in the World Economy* (Cambridge: Cambridge University Press, 1996); Held et. al. *Global Transformations*, 137–143; E. Skons, "The Internationalization of the Arms Industry," *Annals of the American Academy of Political and Social Sciences* 593 (1994); D. Silverberg, "Global Trends in Military Production and Conversion," *Annals of the American Academy of Political and Social Sciences* 593 (1994).

37. Cerny, "Globalization and the Changing Nature of Collective Action," 597.

38. See particularly, the example of South Africa in Deborah Avant, *The Market for Force: the Consequences of Privatizing Security* (Cambridge: Cambridge University Press, 2005), chap. 4.

39. Republic of South Africa, *Regulation of Foreign Military Assistance Act*, No. 18912, May 20, 1998, available at http://www.gov.za/acts/98index.html.

40. Kevin O'Brien, "PSCs, Myths, and Mercenaries."

41. This claim was voiced in over fifteen interviews with academics, members of parliament, and defense officials.

42. Beauregard Tromp, "Hired Guns from SA Flood Iraq," *Cape Times*, February 4, 2004, and "Are We Fighting Foreign Wars?" *The Star*, February 10, 2004.

43. Armor Holdings, for instance, purchased DSL, L-3 Communications purchased MPRI, CSC purchased DynCorp, just to name a few. For analyses of the way the transnational defense industry might impede state control, see Ann Markusen and Sean Costigan, eds., *Arming the Future: a Defense Industry for the Twenty-First Century* (Washington, DC: Council on Foreign Relations Press, 1999).

44. Rachel Epstein, "Divided Continent: Globalization and Europe's Fragmented Security Response," chapter 8 of this volume.

45. The primary effect was not the training itself but the communication of US support for the Tudjman government, which had effects on Tudjman's power vis-à-vis his rivals both domestically and within the greater Balkans region. See Avant, *The Market for Force*, chap. 3.

46. Borzou Daragahi, "For Profit, Private Firms Train Iraqi Soldiers, Provide Security, and Much More," *Post-Gazette*, September 28, 2003, http://www.post-gazette.com/pg/03271/226368.stm.

47. Ken Silverstein, "Mercenary Inc?" *Washington Business Forward*, April 26, 2001; Ken Silverstein, "Privatizing War," *The Nation*, July 7, 1998; Jonathan Wells, "US Ties to Saudi Elite May be Hurting the War on Terrorism," *Boston Herald*, December 10, 2001; William Hartung, "Mercenaries, Inc: How a US Company Props up the House of Saud," *The Progressive* 60 (April 1996): 26.

48. Other institutional economists, such as Douglass North, have noted that seemingly inefficient institutional solutions, nonetheless, persist in many environments. North's micro level, process-oriented approach can explain not only change in response to global pressures, but also how the variation in responses to new pressures can lead to different outcomes. See Douglass North, *Institutions, Institutional Change and Economic Performance* (Cambridge: Cambridge University Press, 1990).

49. This logic is most clearly stated in the literature on foreign policy in democratic states. It is frequently argued that the checks and balances created by "veto players" make it more difficult for democracies to change the status quo. This means it is harder to build consensus for action—but once a consensus exists also harder to change it—and thus is argued to lead to both restraint and effective action. For a clear discussion of the notion of veto players, see George Tsebelis, "Veto Players and Law Production in Parliamentary Democracies," *American Political Science Review* 93(3) (September 1999: 591–608). See also Kurt Gaubatz, "Democratic States and Commitment in International Relations," *International Organization* 50(1) (Winter 1996): 109–139. For applications to military effectiveness, see David Lake, "Powerful Pacifists: Democratic States and War," *American Political Science Review* 86(1) (March 1992: 24–37); Dan Reiter and Allan Stam, "Democracy, War Initiation, and Victory," *American Political Science Review* 92(2) (June 1998: 377–389).
50. Stephen Krasner, "Policy Making in a Weak State," in *American Foreign Policy: Theoretical Essays*, ed. G. John Ikenberry (New York: Harper Collins, 1996), 293.
51. Lora Lumpe, "US Foreign Military Training: Global Reach, Global Power, and Oversight Issues," special report, *Foreign Policy in Focus* (May 2002).
52. Lumpe, "US Foreign Military Training"; Baum, "Nation Builders for Hire," 36.
53. Deborah Avant, *The Market for Force*, chap. 4.
54. In the United Kingdom, the lack of regulation also advantages executive personnel closer to the action—for instance, the high commissioner in Sierra Leone, Peter Penfold, exercised much discretion in his interactions with Sandline that was not well coordinated with either Parliament or the Cabinet. See "Sierra Leone: Second Report," Foreign Affairs Committee, House of Commons, Session 1998–1999.
55. John McQuaid, "US hostages in Colombia mark 1 year," *New Orleans Times-Picayune*, February 13, 2004.
56. Of the 76 articles mentioning the hostages, 65 were from American papers.
57. Thanks to Katie Tobin for running these figures.
58. Cohen, *Citizens and Soldiers*.
59. See Deborah Avant and Lee Sigelman, "Private Soldiers: A Challenge to Democratic Practices and the Democratic Peace?" (unpublished manuscript).
60. See Allison Connolly and Melissa Scott Sinclair, "N.C.-Based Blackwater Known as Leader in Security Business," *The Virginian-Pilot,* April 1, 2004; "Private Armies for Hire," ABC News, April 1, 2004; "High Risks and Pay for Contractors in Iraq," CNN, April 1, 2004; James Dao, "Corporate Security Goes to the Front Line," *New York Times*, April 2, 2004; Allissa Rubin and Esther Shrader, "A Secret World of Security in Iraq," *Los Angeles Times,* April 2, 2004; Barry Yeoman, "Need An Army? Just Pick Up the Phone," *New York Times*, April 2, 2004; Ann Scott Tyson, "Private Firms Take on More Military Tasks," *Christian Science Monitor*, April 2, 2004; James Dao, "Private US Guards Take Big Risks for Right Price," *New York Times*, April 2, 2004; Kenneth Bazinet, "Three Victims of Brutality in Iraq Were Veterans," *New York Daily News*, April 2, 2004; "15,000 Private Security Guards in Iraq Now Targets," special section, *World Tribune*, April 2, 2004; Carol Rosberg, "Rumors of Spies Spread as Mob Raged," *Miami Herald*, April 2, 2004. For an exception, see Manuel Roig-Franzia, "Ohioan Gung-Ho, Despite Dangers," *Washington Post*, April 2, 2004.
61. Roger Cohen, "US Cooling Ties with Croatia after Winking at its Buildup" *New York Times*, October 28, 1995, A1.
62. See Richard Holbrooke, *To End a War* (New York: Modern Library, 1999), 73.
63. Biljana Vankovska, "Privatization of Security and Security Sector Reform in Croatia," (unpublished manuscript).

64. Carlos Zarate, "The Emergence of a New Dog of War: Private International Security Companies, International Law, and the New World Disorder." *Stanford Journal of International Law* 34 (1998): 75–162; interview with Pentagon official January 2000, April 2002.

65. Some have suggested that Tudjman and Milosevic made a deal: little Serb resistance in Krajina in return for Tudjman's support for Milosevic in Bosnia. See Vankovska, "Privatization of Security," 20. Vankovska cites interview with General Martin Spegelj, "HVO I dejelovi Hrvatske vojske su izvrsili agresiju na BiH," and Martin Spegelj, *Sijecanja vojnika* [Memories of a Soldier] (Zagreb: Znanje, 2001).

66. Vankovska, 72–73.

67. Even those who refuse to admit any MPRI influence on the Croatian Army during Operation Storm nonetheless state that MPRI allowed the United States to influence events on the ground when it would have been politically untenable to use US troops for such a task. Interview with Pentagon official June 1999, January 2000, April 2002.

68. Government Accounting Office, *Contingency Operations: Army Should Do More to Control Contract Cost in the Balkans*, GAO/NSIAD-00-225 (Washington, DC: Government Printing Office, 2000). See also Singer, *Corporate Warriors*, 143.

69. Deborah Avant, "Are the Reluctant Warriors Out of Control?" *Security Studies* 6(2) (Winter 1996/97): 51–90.

70. Interviews with Pentagon officials serving on the Joint Staff, May 2002.

71. Baum, "Nation Builders for Hire," 34.

72. Interview with Ed Soyster, MPRI, December 1, 1998.

73. Ibid.

74. Several U.S. oil companies, including Exxon and Chevron, have discovered significant petroleum reserves off the coast of Equatorial Guinea. See Ken Silverstein, "US Oil Politics in the 'Kuwait of Africa,'" *The Nation*, April 22, 2002.

75. Interview with State Department official, January 1999.

76. Ibid.

77. Interview with Ed Soyster, MPRI, April 2000; interview with Bennett Freeman, Department of State, Office of Democracy, Human Rights, and Labor, April 24, 2000.

78. The story did not end here. Once MPRI did its assessment for Equatorial Guinea, the State Department approved only a portion of what the Equatorial Guinea government wanted to purchase from MPRI. MPRI was lobbying not only the State Department and Congress, but also the Pentagon for help in moving the approval forward. An April 2001 memo suggests the result of the lobbying, "[MPRI] may need our help or moral support...." "The Curious Bonds of Oil Diplomacy," in *The Business of War*, International Consortium of Investigative Journalists report, available at http://icij.org/dtaweb/icij_bow.asp.

79. See Jonathan Bendor, Serge Taylor, and Roland van Gaalen, "Stacking the Deck: Bureaucratic Missions and Policy Design," *American Political Science Review* 81(3) (September 1987): 873–896; Gary Miller, *Managerial Dilemmas: The Political Economy of Hierarchy* (Cambridge: Cambridge University Press, 1992). For application to defense bureaucracies and civil-military relations, see Deborah Avant, *Political Institutions and Military Change: Lessons from Peripheral Wars* (Ithaca, NY: Cornell University Press, 1994); Peter Feaver, *Armed Servants* (Cambridge, MA: Harvard University Press, 2003).

80. Joanne Gowa, "Democratic States and International Disputes," *International Organization* 49(3) (Summer 1995): 517.

81. Gowa, "Democratic States and International Disputes," 518.

82. Exactly this logic is used in a recent Refugees International report. See Clifford H. Bernath and David C. Gompert, *The Power to Protect: Using New Military Capabilities to Stop Mass Killing*, Refugees International, July 2003, http://www.refugeesinternational.org/content/publication/detail/3026/. The report claims that reducing the cost of intervention with the use of new military technology can increase the potential for intervention.

83. Ben Fordham links threat perception to domestic factors that affect the cost of using force. See Benjamin Fordham, "The Politics of Threat Perception and the Use of Force," *International Studies Quarterly* 42 (1998): 567–590.

84. David Forsythe, "Democracy, War and Covert Action," *Journal of Peace Research* 29(4) (1992): 385–395.

85. Thomson, *Mercenaries, Pirates and Sovereigns*, 27.

86. Theodore Lowi, "Making Democracy Safe for the World: On Fighting the Next War," in G. John Ikenberry, *American Foreign Policy: Theoretical Essays* (New York: HarperCollins, 1989), 258–292. See also Samuel Huntington, "American Ideals Versus American Institutions," in G. John Ikenberry, *American Foreign Policy: Theoretical Essays* (New York: HarperCollins, 1989), 223–257. See also Cohen's discussion of the dilemma in American manpower policy. Cohen, *Citizens and Soldiers*, chap. 9.

87. There is a variety of additional logics. Edward Luttwak, for instance, looks particularly at casualty aversion—tying it to small families common among industrial democracies. Edward N. Luttwak, "Toward Post-Heroic Warfare," *Foreign Affairs* 74(3) (May/June 1995): 109–122.

88. See Barnett, "The Pentagon's New Map of the World." Posen argues that given the expense of ground force, the United States should pursue a more modest policy of selective engagement rather than dominance and rely on allies in its efforts to contain contested areas. Barry Posen, "Command of the Commons: The Military Foundations of US Hegemony," *International Security* 28(1) (Summer 2003): 5–46.

89. Carnegie Commission on Preventing Deadly Conflict, *Preventing Deadly Conflict: Final Report* (Washington, DC: Carnegie Corporation, 1997).

90. David Shearer, "Private Armies and Military Intervention," *Adelphi Paper* 316 (1998).

91. See Lisa Anderson, "Shock and Awe: Interpretations of the Events of September 11," *World Politics* 56(2) (January 2004): 303–325.

92. Charles Lipson, *Reliable Partners* (Princeton, NJ: Princeton University Press, 2003).

93. Ibid., 53–55.

94. David Lake, "Powerful Pacifists: Democratic States and War," *American Political Science Review* 86(1) (March 1992): 24–37; James D. Fearon, "Domestic Political Audiences and the Escalation of International Disputes," *American Political Science Review* 88(3) (September 1994): 577–592; Charles Lipson, *Reliably Partners: How Democracies Have Made a Separate Peace* (Princeton, NJ: Princeton University Press, 2003); Dan Reiter and Allan Stam, *Democracies at War* (Princeton, NJ: Princeton University Press, 2002); see also Dan Reiter and Allan Stam, "Understanding Victory: Why Political Institutions Matter," *International Security* 28(1) (Summer 2003): 168–179. See also Michael Doyle, "Liberalism and World Politics," *American Political Science Review* 80(4) (December 1986): 1151–1169; Carol R. Ember, Melvin Ember, and Bruce Russett, "Peace between Participatory Polities: A Cross-Cultural Test of the 'Democracies Rarely Fight Each Other' Hypothesis," *World Politics* 44(4) (July 1992): 573–599.

95. Lake, "Powerful Pacifists"; David Lake, "Fair Fights: Evaluating Theories of Democracy and Victory," *International Security* 28(1) (Summer 2003): 154–167.

96. Reiter and Stam, *Democracies at War*, chap. 6.

97. See Gowa, "Democratic States and International Disputes"; Michael Desch, "Democracy and War: Why Regime Type Hardly Matters," *International Security* 28(1) (Summer 2003): 154–167.

98. Alexander Cooley, chapter 7 of this volume.

99. Transnational nonstate actors finance security in a variety of ways: subsidizing state forces (for instance, corporations subsidize state protection of their property), paying for protection by noncorporate forces such as paramilitaries or rebel groups that offer protection, or hiring private forces (either to provide security themselves or to train elements of state or other local forces), and in a variety of guises—as contractors for powerful states, as representatives of transnational concerns, or as commercial enterprises.

100. Andrew Natsios, "NGOs and the UN System in Complex Humanitarian Emergencies," *Third World Quarterly* 16(3) (1995): 405–419; Alexander Cooley and James Ron, "The NGO Scramble: Organizational Insecurity and the Political Economy of Transnational Action," *International Security* 27(1) (Summer 2002), 5–39. These expectations are based on a larger literature focused on the effects of multiple principals. See Bendor et al., "Stacking the Deck," and the review of this literature in Jonathan Bender, Ami Glazer, and Thomas Hammond, "Theories of Delegation," *Annual Review of Political Science* 4 (2001): 235–269. For an application to military forces, see Avant, *Political Institutions and Military Change*.

101. Terry Karl, "The Perils of the Petro-state: Reflections on the Politics of Plenty," *Journal of International Affairs* 53(1) (Fall 1999): 34; Jedrzej George Frynas, "Political Instability and Business: Focus on Shell in Nigeria," *Third World Quarterly* 19(3) (1998): 457–478; Global Witness, *A Crude Awakening: The Role of Oil and Banking Industries in Angolan Civil War* (London: Global Witness, 1999); Scott Pegg, "The Costs of Doing Business: Transnational Corporations and Violence in Nigeria," *Security Dialogue* 30(4) (1999): 473–484.

102. See Olle Tornquist, "Rent Capitalism, State and Democracy: A Theoretical Proposition," in *State and Civil Society in Indonesia*, ed. Arief Budiman, Monash Papers on Southeast Asia 22 (1990); Terry Karl, *The Paradox of Plenty: Oil Booms and Petro States* (Berkeley: University of California Press, 1997); Clark, "Petro-Politics in Congo," *Journal of Democracy* 8 (July 1997): 62–76; Theda Skocpol, "Rentier State and Shi'a Islam in the Iranian Revolution," *Theory and Society* 11 (April 1982): 265–283. Quantitative analysis of these relationships has been more guarded. Michael Ross finds that oil exporters demonstrate greater military spending, but that other mineral exports are negatively associated with military spending. See Michael Ross, "Does Oil Hinder Democracy?" *World Politics* 53 (3) (April 2001): 350–351.

103. Ross, "Does Oil Hinder Democracy"; Skocpol, "Rentier State"; Tornquist, "Rent Capitalism."

104. See Robert Jackson, *Quasi-States: Sovereignty, International Relations and the Third World* (New York: Cambridge University Press, 1990); William Reno, *Warlord Politics and African States* (Boulder, CO: Lynne Rienner, 1998); William Reno, "Shadow States and the Political Economy of Civil War," in *Greed and Grievance*, eds. Mats Berdal and David Malone (Boulder, CO: Lynne Rienner, 2000).

105. Sayre P. Schatz, "Pirate Capitalism and the Inert Economy of Nigeria," *Journal of Modern African Studies* 22(1) (1984): 45–57. See also Claude Welch, "Civil-Military Agonies in Nigeria," *Armed Forces and Society* 21(4) (Summer 1995): 608.

106. See Amnesty International, "Security Forces: Serving to Protect and Respect Human Rights?" December 19, 2002; Human Rights Watch Report, "THE BAKASSI BOYS: The Legitimation of Murder and Torture," May 2002; Department of Justice, "International Criminal Investigative training Assistance Program (ICITAP): Nigeria," http://www.usdoj.gov/criminal/icitap/nigeria.html.

107. Reno, *Warlord Politics and African States*, chap. 6 (particularly, 196–197, 199–200, 204–208), Kenneth Cain, "Send in the Marines," *New York Times*, August 8, 2003.
108. Cain, "Send in the Marines."
109. See Nancy Peluso, "Coercing Conservation," in *The State and Social Power in Global Environmental Politics*, eds. Ronnie D. Lipschutz and Ken Conca (New York: Columbia University Press, 1993).
110. Avant, "Conserving Nature in the State of Nature."
111. The issues in Garamba were also complicated by the INGO's lack of expertise on security issues.
112. Confidential correspondence with World Wildlife Fund (WWF) staff member, February 18, 2001.
113. Mike Buser, "Law Enforcement Field Inspection Report," Garamba National Park, Democratic Republic of Congo, submitted to World Wildlife Fund, June 1998.
114. Correspondence with Mike Buser, February 2001.
115. Weak states have developed more functional and legitimate security institutions with the help of PSCs. See the discussion of Croatia, for instance, in Avant, *The Market for Force*, chap. 3. In this case, the conditionality imposed by NATO, the particular training programs sold by the PSC, and some lucky breaks all played a role.
116. Kenneth Waltz, *The Theory of International Politics* (New York: Random House, 1979), chaps. 7–8.
117. For instance, see Kaplan, "The Coming Anarchy." See also Van Creveld, *The Transformation of War*. Though this was not his purpose, the description of feudal Europe in Markus Fisher's "Feudal Europe, 800–1300: Communal Discourse and Conflictual Practices," *International Organization* 46(2) (Spring 1992) also supports this argument.
118. Oliver Williamson, *Markets and Hierarchies: Analysis and Anti-trust Implications* (New York: Free Press, 1975); Donahue, *The Privatization Decision*; and others. Samuel Bowles even describes the way market forces can transform preferences in such a way as to undermine the potential for future trust. See Samuel Bowles, "Endogenous Preferences: The Cultural Consequences of Markets and other Economic Institutions," *Journal of Economic Literature* 36 (March 1998): 75–111; Philip Cerny, "Neomedievalism, Civil War and the New Security Dilemma: Globalization as Durable Disorder," *Civil Wars* 1(1) (Spring 1998): 36–64.
119. Joseph Strayer, *Feudalism* (New York: Van Nostrand Reinhold, 1964), 13.
120. Held et al., *Global Transformations*, 35.
121. Jack Levy, *War in the Modern Great Power System* (Lexington: University of Kentucky Press, 1983), table 3.1, 70–73.
122. My calculations are based on Levy's list.
123. Joshua Goldstein, "Kondratieff Waves as War Cycles," *International Studies Quarterly* 29 (1985): 411–444, particularly figure 1, 422 and table 5, 423.
124. This echoes a variety of claims that the world faces new kinds of conflict. Mary Kaldor warns of the "new wars" of the 1990s, William Reno writes about the conflicts endemic to warlord politics, and Mark Duffield notes the nonterritorial network war. And Martin van Creveld warned of the transformation of war just as the Cold War was ending. Kaldor, *New and Old Wars*; Reno, *Warlord Politics in African States*; William Reno, "Privatizing War in Sierra Leone," *Current History* 96 (May 1997): 227–231; Duffield, *Global Governance and the New Wars*.
125. See Nils Getter Gleditsch, Havard Strand, Mikael Eriksson, Margareta Sollenberg, and Peter Wallensteen, "Armed Conflict 1946–99: A New Dataset," *Journal for Peace Research* 38(5) (2002): 615–637.

126. The fact that other regions of the world do not show the same steadily upward trend in armed conflicts may partly be the result of what data collectors are paying attention to. As Nils Gledisch et al. discuss, their data set does not include conflicts where one side in the conflict is not an organized actor. Furthermore, battle-related deaths do not extend to all deaths directly caused by the conflict—thus Rwanda in 1994 is listed as only having an intermediate level of conflict. With more sophisticated measures of internal conflict and internal violence, we may see a stronger relationship between the diffusion of control over violence and increases in particular types of conflict. Gleditsch et al., "Armed Conflict."

127. As have a variety of other forces, see Paul Collier, "Doing Well Out of War: An Economic Perspective," in Berdal and Malone, *Greed and Grievance.*

128. See Reno, "Privatizing War in Sierra Leone"; Will Reno, "Shadow States and the Political Economy of Civil-War," in Berdal and Malone, *Greed and Grievance.* See also Avant, *The Market for Force,* chap. 3.

129. Chris Dietrich, *The Commercialisation of Military Deployment in Africa* (Pretoria: ISS, 2001), available at http://www.iss.co.za/Pubs?ASR/9.1/Commerciallisation.html.

130. Alexandra Guaqueta, "The Colombian Conflict: Political and Economic Dimensions," in *The Political Economy of Armed Conflict,* eds. Karen Ballentine and Jake Sherman (Boulder, CO: Lynne Rienner, 2003), 73–106.

131. Kaldor, *New and Old Wars.*

132. Posen, "Command of the Commons," 10. See footnote 14 for his method of calculation. See Kirshner, chapter 1 this volume for discussion of mock systemic forces.

5

THE PARADOX OF LIBERAL HEGEMONY
Globalization and U.S. National Security

Karl P. Mueller

ALTHOUGH THE FORCES OF GLOBALIZATION are by definition state-less, the government, economy, and society of the United States have been powerful drivers of many of them, sometimes deliberately, often inadvertently. As most of the regionally oriented chapters in this project describe, the belief that the United States benefits more from globalization than any other major power is widespread—and is fundamentally correct. Yet even for the United States, the national security implications of globalization are a mixed bag. Thanks to the economic size, technological preeminence, and political characteristics of the United States, globalization tends to reinforce American hegemony and the unipolarity of the international system (and vice versa). However, it also contributes to the most prominent threats to U.S. national security in the early twenty-first century, and it significantly constrains the ability of the United States to deal with them.[1]

To describe and analyze all of the connections between globalization and U.S. security in even a superficial way would require an entire volume at least as large as this one. Therefore, this chapter focuses on the narrower question of considering what impact the forces of globalization have upon the nature and magnitude of security threats to the United States and some resulting implications for American foreign and defense policy. This is only one aspect of understanding the evolving security environment facing the United States, however. Most of the factors that affect U.S. national security fall largely outside the realm of globalization, though many of these are related to it in some way. For example, the extent to which nuclear weapons proliferate to states that do not yet possess them has important implications for the security landscape, but insofar as nuclear proliferation is the result of state policy choices, its pace and direction has been affected only marginally by globalization, and this is likely to continue to be true for the foreseeable future.[2] Yet even in this very state-centered issue area, globalization leaves its mark, for example, by contributing to the incentives for Russia and especially North Korea to treat nuclear weapons technology as a marketized export commodity.[3] However, even if globalization were purely beneficial for U.S. national security, it would not necessarily follow that the United States will become more secure as globalization proceeds (because its favorable effects could be more than offset by other forces), only that it will be more secure than it would be without globalization. In short, the subject here is not how secure the United States will be in an increasingly globalized world, but the differences in that picture that are created by globalization.

The discussion that follows deals in turn with the consequences of globalization for two principal categories of security threats to the United States. The first is those from other states, the traditional focus of defense policy, for which globalization's impact on the distribution of power is key. The second is threats posed by violent nonstate actors, particularly transnational terrorist groups, for which globalization's effects on state capacity and axes of conflict loom large. The final sections of the chapter then consider how these shifts in the threat constellation and in state capabilities affect the objectives and the instruments of U.S. national security policy.

Two central arguments lie at the core of this essay. First, globalization both reinforces and weakens American hegemony in the international system: it shifts the distribution of relative power in favor of the United States and its allies, but it constrains the autonomy and increasingly limits the absolute capacities of states, including the hegemon. Second, globalization is helping to shift the axes of conflict that face the United States in the relatively near term, and is feeding the principal dangers to the United States, although there is reason to expect that over the much longer run it will tend to diminish them. Therefore, insofar as American liberal hegemony facilitates globalization, it contributes both to the leading security threats against the United States and to its own gradual erosion. What separates the creative self-destruction of liberal hegemony from the usual course of imperial rise and decline, and makes it genuinely paradoxical, is that this pattern is a logical consequence of the spread and entrenchment of a liberal order, the result of success rather than of failure.[4] This is not to say that American foreign policy success is predestined, however, for if the United States fails to adapt well to the demands of the globalizing world system, the potential for a slow and graceful obsolescing of American hegemony could easily give way to a far less comfortable future.

THE REDISTRIBUTION OF POWER

As the unchallenged global hegemon, the United States would seem to be the state with the most to lose from fundamental changes in the existing international political order. Indeed, as globalization is the growth of forces beyond the control of states, its advance must necessarily imply some measure of erosion of U.S. hegemony, assuming that by hegemony, we mean the ability to shape the world as it desires and not merely being the most powerful state. Yet there are three reasons why U.S. leaders should be relatively sanguine about the consequences of globalization for the balance of power, all of which relate to the basic fact that globalization does not affect all states equally. First, the size, power, and wealth of the United States tend to moderate the effects of globalization, so that the process threatens U.S. security less than that of most other states. Second, globalization is generally less beneficial—or more toxic—for the states that pose the most significant security threats to the United States than it is for modern Western powers, thus strengthening the latter relative to the former. Finally, at least over the long run, globalization should tend to drive the international system in directions that are relatively compatible with the goals and principles of the United States and the West, so that not being able to control these forces is a problem that Americans should be able to tolerate. However, in diminishing the power of illiberal states, globalization may also make them more dangerous to their neighbors, by increasing domestic political incentives for the pursuit of aggressive foreign policies or by contributing to internal conflicts that can spill over national borders.

Big Fish in a Big Pond

The scale of U.S. population, economy, and resources is the most basic factor shaping the differential effects of globalization upon it and other states. Continental size provides a significant degree of insulation from the disruptive forces of globalizing exchange, information, and marketization. It not only cushions the effects of international economic crises but also makes migratory population flows proportionally smaller than they are for most other states, dilutes the political impact of external media, and in general diminishes the extent to which stateless forces penetrate and affect the United States.[5] In short, if the sea gets rough, larger ships are tossed about less violently than smaller ones.

This is essentially parallel to, though somewhat broader than, the traditional international political economy argument that economic interdependence affects small states more than large ones. Because the United States is not an insular state like the Soviet Union, it is sheltered less from the turbulent effects of globalization than another superpower of its size might be, and it is not isolated from enjoying the benefits of participation in the globalizing world economy (one of the factors that helped to bring the Soviet economy, and thus the state, to its knees in the 1980s).[6] Yet its size still provides a considerable measure of security, so that other things being equal, the rising tide of globalization imperils other states more than the United States, making generalized instability potentially attractive for the United States from a relative gains perspective. Moreover, relatively stable growth over the long run offers advantages for a state concerned with building and maintaining large, high quality armed forces that are less significant for states that are not. Finally, its role as the hegemon brings the United States a disproportionate share of the benefits of the economic pie that globalization is helping to expand.[7]

The Relativity of Power

The second respect in which globalization provides relative security advantages to the United States is that the countries posing the greatest security threats to it tend to be poorly suited by their political and economic systems to reap the full benefits of globalization. Conversely, many natural or historical U.S. allies are greatly enriched by globalization, even more than the United States in some cases, but few threats to U.S. security interests are likely to emerge from their ranks.[8] As Alexander Cooley notes, globalization did much to destroy the Soviet Union and create a world in which the United States faces only comparatively minor threats to its security.[9] Today the countries about which the United States worries tend not to be as economically self-destructive as the Soviet Union, but happily for the United States's position in the distribution of power, globalization still presents problems for them. The states that currently trouble U.S. grand strategy fall into two basic categories: one can be labeled reasonably as "rogue states," and the other has a single member, China.[10] (Failing states represent a third important class, but they matter to the United States primarily because of their potential contribution to threats from nonstate actors, addressed in the next section of this chapter.)

The term *rogue state* has often been ill used, but it arguably merits rehabilitation. If we take the label literally, a rogue state can be conceived as one that opposes the dominant international order and is willing to defy it, usually in part because it has either withdrawn or been excluded from membership in the system to the point that the opportunity costs of lashing out against it are relatively low. By this definition rogue states are not distinguished primarily by being anti-American, they need not be (and usually are not) undeterrable, and they do not have to be minor powers—Stalin's Soviet Union and Hitler's Germany were rogue states by any sensible definition. Fortunately for Washington—and partly because of globalization, it should be noted—today's remaining rogue states are a comparatively anemic lot: Iran and North Korea seem to be its most prominent members, although Pakistan could perhaps be only one assassination away from taking over that distinction.[11] In general, such states are potentially dangerous to the United States not because of their ability to attack it directly, but because of the threats they can pose to the security of states or the stability of regions that are important to the United States.[12]

Globalization may well make these states, and others that share important domestic characteristics with them, more roguish, but it does not do very much to make them more powerful. Police states, theocracies, and countries that pursue economic or political isolation are ill-suited to prosper in a world where economic success depends on reasonably unfettered commerce, communication, and education. Such inefficiencies are compounded in cases where important human potential is squandered because the subjugation of women or ethnic minority groups is intrinsic to the state's political culture,[13] practices that globalization should help to weaken through competitive market pressures and the transnational spread of emancipatory ideas, a trend that is further reinforced by the net migration of their best and brightest citizens to more prosperous and progressive states.[14] Globalization should cause significant internal disruption for some of these states as well, in extreme cases, even placing the survival of their regimes or their political systems at risk and forcing governments to concentrate their resources on dealing with these threats.[15] As Marc Lynch explains, globalization presents such problems for even the most progressive and stable Arab countries.[16] However, even where it is not actually desta-bilizing, globalization should tend to shift the international distribu-tion of power in favor of relatively liberal (mostly but not only Western) states or others better able to adapt to its demands and for whom mar-ketization is more natural.[17]

China, on the other hand, is rapidly increasing in potential military and economic power; the security threat it poses to the United States is not so much that it will seek to replace America as the global hegemon, at least not soon enough to matter for contemporary strategists, but that it will become a regional aggressor.[18] China has met with considerable economic success in the globalizing world by relaxing central control of its economy, even though its ability to take full advantage of the opportunities presented by globalization remains constrained by many factors, particularly its illiberal political system,[19] and thus poses a serious challenge to the claim that globalization will tend to weaken less liberal countries more than the United States. Adam Segal describes in detail the role of globalization in improving China's access to the information technology (IT) and human expertise it needs to modernize its armed forces, as well as its contribution to the economic boom that makes rapidly rising defense spending possible for Beijing (although he also notes that both the pursuit and the effects of globalization-based prosperity pose obstacles to the enhancement of Chinese military power).[20] Yet the proliferation of information and other technology has also been exploited by the United States, whose military capabilities have increased enormously in recent years, though the physical dimension of these advances is often deceptively inconspicuous: hardware associated with intelligence collection, military command and control, training simulators, and the like.[21] In many of these areas, even close American allies are unable to keep pace. For China to plausibly try to do so will require political and cultural reforms that will increase its compatibility with the globalizing economy but are also likely to reduce the potential of conflict with the United States even as they increase China's power potential.[22]

This is not to deny that China has grown more economically and militarily powerful in recent decades, for of course it has, and indeed this growth has been considerably greater as a result of globalization than it would have been otherwise. However, Chinese power must be considered in context, and although globalization has contributed to China's development, it has also helped fuel booms in many of China's neighbors. In particular, Taiwan's involvement in the globalizing economy has greatly increased its wealth and power, and after decades of investment preparing for the contingency, China still lacks the military capabilities that would be required for a cross-strait invasion to have good hope of success.[23] Globalization has similarly helped make many of China's other neighbors into significantly capable players in the East Asian security arena, and as China's armed forces modernize, these states will have ever greater incentives to balance against Beijing, limiting China's prospects for regional hegemony and bolstering the defense of U.S. interests in the region. Whether they will in fact do so is uncertain, for states often fail to balance against rising powers, especially if their conduct is less than unmistakably threatening.[24] However, although China's power is growing relative to that of many East Asian states, a trend that is likely to continue as its economy and society modernize, globalization does not promise to make this power disparity substantially worse than it would otherwise be.[25] Small wonder that Chinese leaders and analysts are ambivalent about globalization, fearful of its consequences for political stability while needing the growth it facilitates to legitimize their government, and recognizing that the United States is in a better position to reap many of its benefits than they are.[26]

Thus, compared to China or Iran, let alone a state such as North Korea, the United States and like-minded powers should be able to cope relatively well with an environment in which international commerce, travel, and communication are becoming faster, denser, and more difficult for states to control without incurring excessive opportunity costs. The power of the United States should increase relative to that of its principal adversaries as a result of globalization, or else its adversaries should become less hostile as a result of reforming in order to reap greater benefits from globalization (a possibility of which contemporary Libya may provide an example). However, this emphatically does not mean that China will actually fall behind in its effort to catch up with American military capabilities, for even if globalization is impeding this pursuit, China's long-delayed economic modernization provides great impetus for it and makes China's eventual—albeit far from imminent—emergence as a superpower virtually certain (provided that it does not fragment into a set of smaller countries before this happens).[27] Moreover, China's ability to threaten U.S. security interests in East Asia does not necessarily depend on it being able to increase its overall military power relative to the United States.[28]

This prospect also does not mean that globalization will necessarily make the United States more secure in the future. As strategists and national leaders have understood at least since the 1930s, being more powerful relative to other states is not the same thing as being less vulnerable to attack, even though the two naturally do tend to vary together.[29] The relationship between power and security can diverge for a variety of reasons, some of which may be affected by globalization (such as the rise of nonstate enemies, as will be discussed below), although others will have little to do with it (for example, shifts in military technology such as the development of ballistic missiles making attacks intrinsically more difficult to defend against). At a minimum, the informational dimension of globalization is likely to facilitate both cyber attacks and propaganda-based information warfare threats,[30] while restricting opportunities for some other types of military action, such as attacks requiring the covert mobilization of forces that are more easily detected in a world of rapid, global communications by the press and other unofficial observers. States anticipating the possibility of conflict with the United States are especially likely to embrace opportunities for unconventional strategies and policy instruments because of the demonstrated effectiveness of U.S. military capabilities against conventional military opponents.

Making the World Safer for Liberalism

The third reason that globalization should be relatively benign for the United States is arguably the most important of all, though its subtlety makes it easy to overlook. Globalization as it currently exists is largely a manifestation of the success of liberal political and economic principles in the international system, particularly individual freedom of movement, expression, and communication.[31] Whether the United States deliberately laid the groundwork for globalization does not greatly matter—even to the extent that this is true, it is not necessarily the case that a state's actions will work to its advantage as intended over the long run. What is significant is that globalization is doing more to remake the world not in the image of the West, but in ways that are increasingly compatible with Western security interests than it is pushing it in the opposite direction.[32] These effects are very uneven, but even where globalization is not yet producing substantial liberalization, for example in most of the Arab Middle East, it generally does not appear to be making states substantially *less* liberal than they would otherwise have been, though it is certainly helping to make some of them less stable.[33]

Thus, although globalization gradually chips away at U.S. hegemony, as the importance of forces over which states do not easily have control increases, it also tends to make that hegemony progressively less essential to the achievement of many basic American foreign policy objectives. For example, if globalization creates incentives for states to eschew protectionism, it becomes less important for the United States to promote and defend openness in international trade. To say that globalization is simply the withering away of a system of hegemonic control whose purposes have been achieved would be a great exaggeration—after all, there are dimensions of state control over events that liberal statesmen certainly do not wish to see erode. However, much as Britain was relatively comfortable with the United States acceding to the role of global hegemon in an earlier era because the two states favored roughly the same future for the international system, so the United States should fear having its power displaced by globalization far less than an illiberal state would.

The Disruption of Change

That globalization is highly problematic for many other states poses problems for the United States, however. Economic and political instability as a result of changes in the distribution of wealth and the weakening of traditional cultural systems, for example, is a frequent consequence of globalization, both in states that resist it and in those that eagerly embrace it as the path to modernity and prosperity.[34] These in turn can lead to international security threats in at least three ways, though each is usually produced by a combination of forces of which only some are closely related to globalization. One is by generating internal conflicts, typically along lines of regional, class, ethnic, or religious divisions, that spill over into neighboring states. Some of these matter to United States foreign policy, if at all, only because of their humanitarian effects; others may impinge on deeper national interests. Second, regimes facing the threat of internal unrest may turn to aggressive international behavior either to distract their citizens or to gain wealth through conquest or coercion that can be used to shore up their domestic problems. Finally, instability can lead to partial or complete state failure, creating geographical or functional power vacuums that terrorist groups or other dangerous organizations can exploit, a threat to which the next section will return. Thus, for example, globalization may reasonably be said to have contributed significantly to the outbreak of the Yugoslav wars of secession, the Falklands War, and multiple conflicts in post-Soviet central Asia and the Caucasus, respectively. As instability in once peripheral parts of the world becomes more and more difficult for the United States to ignore safely (more on this below), in large part because of globalization, dealing with such events increasingly demands American attention and resources.

THE EMERGENCE OF TRANSNATIONAL THREATS

If the good news about globalization for U.S. national security is that it should tend overall, if inconsistently, to reduce the severity of traditional military threats from other countries, the bad news is that it facilitates the emergence of a new class of nonstate enemies. Specifically, globalization creates conditions under which transnational terrorist groups and other violent nonstate actors can better develop and perhaps thrive, among which the preeminent concern for American grand strategists is radical Islamist groups mounting terrorist attacks against the United States and its allies.[35] Although such enemies cannot imperil the national survival of a power such as the United States, they do have the capability to inflict serious harm and are more likely to attack than is any state.[36] The extent to which globalization will, on the whole, mobilize people to participate in such organizations is less certain, but it seems likely to continue to do so in the near term, even though over the long run the advance of modernity should diminish the threats posed by those who resist it.

Terrorists have, of course, existed for centuries, usually in the form either of insurgent or separatist groups internal to individual states that practice terrorism as a tactic of irregular warfare, sometimes creating serious local security problems but affecting the broader international security environment only slightly, or small groups of criminals or ideological or religious zealots that may present the states they attack with a significant law enforcement challenge but are of little consequence for national security.[37] However, there is another, more recent class of terrorist organization, currently but imperfectly exemplified by al Qaeda, that can actually pose a genuine security threat to the United States; for want of a better term, I use the label "hyperterrorist" for such groups.[38] The potential for them to exist and operate is intimately connected to globalization, and the motivations of their members may often be as well, though neither is a product of globalization alone.

Evolving Predators

A hyperterrorist group is essentially the terrorist ideal, the sort of terrorist organization that has been commonplace in movies for decades but is rarely approximated in real life, so it is best viewed as an ideal type rather than a description of existing groups.[39] It is defined by a combination of three characteristics, each of which makes such groups difficult to deal with by traditional means. The first is structural: hyperterrorist organizations are genuinely transnational political entities, neither dependent on nor beholden to any state or set of states for their survival and ability to function, although the policies of states will inevitably shape the spaces in which they can operate. Although a hyperterrorist group may exercise effective control over territory—potentially even over states themselves as al Qaeda did in Afghanistan prior to the destruction of the Taliban—and be the stronger for it, it is fundamentally nonterritorial in nature. Second, the destructive capabilities of hyperterrorist groups rival those of at least very small states and can be projected well beyond a single area of operations. This is partly a matter of scale, with the sheer size and wealth of a group like al Qaeda setting it apart from lesser terrorists. However, quality matters even more than quantity, and it is a terrorist entity's organizational sophistication, the specialized skills of its key personnel, and the sagacity of its leadership that make the greatest difference between being a manageable threat to its enemy's peace of mind and posing a significant threat to its national security. Finally, hyperterrorists are distinguished by the nature and intensity of their ideologies: their objectives are essentially unconditional and are unlimited, transcendental, or simply so extreme that any meaningful accommodation of them by their adversaries is difficult or even inconceivable, and their commitment to the pursuit of these objectives overrides any other goals they may seek.[40]

Dealing with terrorist groups that possess these characteristics is particularly problematic for national security strategists. Genuinely transnational terrorists possess little in the way of vulnerable targets against which to apply punitive coercive pressure and do not depend on sponsors who might themselves be susceptible to such threats.[41] Similarly, their resources and fanaticism, along with the inherent difficulty of defending against terrorist attacks, make deterrence by denial unlikely to succeed, while their ability to operate transnationally greatly complicates the problem of completely disabling them. Nor is accommodation feasible against an adversary that is committed to pursuing essentially unlimited goals, in contrast to its frequent utility when dealing with terrorists seeking more limited ends, such as regional autonomy for their homelands or better treatment of laboratory animals. In this sense, globalization limits state capacity to deal with such threats not by reducing defensive capabilities that previously existed, but by encouraging the emergence of enemies that are intrinsically difficult for traditional strategies to defeat.

Unfortunately, globalization does not only enable the emergence of occasional groups that approximate the full hyperterrorist model. It also facilitates threats from terrorists and other nonstate actors who possess only some of these characteristics, ranging from wealthy and powerful Colombian drug cartels and insurgents to locally focused but highly capable terrorist groups such as Hamas and the Tamil Tigers to fanatical antigovernment extremist groups in the American hinterland. So far, none of these has truly reached the point of appearing to pose a serious threat to U.S. national security, but they do imperil important U.S. allies and interests, threaten the safety of Americans at home or abroad, and as with al Qaeda, the worst may be yet to come.

Although it is common to discuss al Qaeda as if it were the greatest possible terrorist threat to the United States, and to place it at the far edge of the scariest corner of briefing chart graphics depicting terrorists' capabilities and objectives, this is highly optimistic. In fact, it is no more than an imperfect prototype of the hyperterrorist ideal, upon which any successor groups are likely to try to improve. With respect to ideology and motivation, al Qaeda would be fairly hard to surpass, for although the United States could face more ideologically extreme enemies, there are not likely to be many anti-American ideologies that would simultaneously exceed its jihadist Islam both in extremity and in their appeal to potential members and supporters. Organizationally, the ideal hyperterrorist group should exist entirely in what might be called virtual territory, even more fully exploiting the effects of globalization to organize and operate in myriad interstitial spaces within societies around the world. It should also be organized in a robust, nonhierarchical manner to minimize the effects of damage to the network without sacrificing operational effectiveness, something at which some Palestinian terrorist groups excel, and although al Qaeda may be evolving along such lines, it was far from having such a structure in its heyday. But it is with respect to its strategic and destructive capabilities that al Qaeda fortunately falls shortest of what a more advanced terrorist organization might look like on at least two levels. First, al Qaeda's attacks other than the September 11, 2001, operation have employed relatively modest means compared to the possibilities presented by the marketplace of modern unconventional violence. It is easy to picture (and unnecessary to list) ways in which future terrorist campaigns might potentially be far more destructive, with other possibilities paling beside that of nuclear terrorism.[42] Second, future hyperterrorist groups might also be much more capable than al Qaeda on the human dimension. Although al Qaeda is a large organization with thousands of members, relatively few of them possess specialized skills well-suited to conducting major terrorist operations against Western targets, and although many of its members are well-educated by Arab standards that adverbial qualifier is an important one.[43] An equally well-disciplined but smaller group consisting primarily of personnel capable of operating easily in the West could be far more dangerous.[44] All of these developments would be facilitated by globalization.

The Globalization of Insecurity

Globalization is a necessary prerequisite for powerful transnational terrorist groups to emerge and function, almost by definition, and it

is important to all three of the dimensions discussed above to varying degrees. Rapid, dense international travel and communication are
clearly central to the formation and the maintenance of dynamic transnational organizations, all the more so for decentralized ones and those
with powerful enemies. This may be especially crucial for the growth of
groups fighting to promote very extreme ideologies: although they can
be cultivated, true extremists tend to be in short supply,[45] but the "eBay
effect" of modern telecommunications, and particularly the Internet—
enabling small numbers of individuals who share an unusual interest or
goal to find each other and collaborate effectively—creates the opportunity to unite dispersed but like-minded enthusiasts for a cause into
a coherent organization, and IT greatly facilitates their operations.[46]
More subtly, globalization helps to create more potentially useful
recruits by expanding the range of education and information available
to them. The ability to move people, weapons, money, and information
across borders is also central to the operational effectiveness of international terrorists, and it increases their prospects for acquiring the
skills, knowledge, and tools required to cause destruction repeatedly
on a large scale.[47] Expanding international travel and migration also
makes terrorists better able to blend in to increasingly heterogeneous
societies far removed from their homelands, and globalization creates
new opportunities for innovative terrorists to cause harm by encouraging technological developments such as large airliners, container-
ized shipping, and widespread computer networks. Finally, although
transnational terrorists can by definition function without having use
of their own territory on a significant scale, almost all terrorist groups
benefit greatly from being able to control their own real estate. As overt
state sponsorship of international terrorists becomes less common, terrorist sanctuaries are increasingly likely to be the product of state failures, when a government either collapses altogether or loses the ability
to exercise effective control over part of its territory, and globalization
can contribute significantly to such failures.[48]

Yet hyperterrorist groups per se have appeared very infrequently—
indeed, al Qaeda is nearly the first to emerge[49]—even though they have
been feasible for many years. Although the potential for hyperterrorists
grows along with globalization, globalization is merely a new label for
a trend that has been actively underway at least since the eighteenth
century. And although the threat of nuclear, biological, and other
exotic forms of terrorist attack is relatively recent, major acts of terrorism merely require technology that was familiar a hundred years ago:
high explosives, repeating firearms, telegraphy, and a level of industrialization that concentrates large numbers of people in vulnerable

targets such as steamships, trains, and factories. For example, ninety years before the September 11 attacks, nineteen fanatical and well-trained anti-British terrorists could certainly have embarked aboard a pre–World War I transatlantic liner carrying with them the means to sink the vessel or to seize control and of the ship and scuttle it, killing thousands.[50] Nor have large, sophisticated, covert international organizations emerged only during the computer age.

Various factors contribute to this absence of hyperterrorists in the fossil record, beyond the fact that globalization used to be less advanced than it is today. For example, prior to the end of the Cold War, those desiring political change could do so by embracing states with different ideologies—and in some cases, such powers would work to prevent would-be revolutionaries from striking out on their own, or from turning to large-scale terrorism. Much of the explanation for hyperterrorists appearing on the scene only recently relates to the importance of entrepreneurial innovation: until Osama bin Laden came along, no one had combined the vision, leadership abilities, resources, motivation, and luck required to get such a hyperterrorist operation off the ground. However, globalization also plays a role by helping to create a target that appears worth forming an elaborate transnational network to attack: not only unipolarity but also modern communications and U.S. cultural hegemony help to make the United States into a worldwide lightning rod for discontent that usually begins at the local level.

Terrorism, like crime, requires more than mere opportunity; it also depends on motivation. The direct and indirect consequences of globalization—economic, political, and, perhaps most powerfully, cultural and social—can and do contribute powerfully to extremist motivations for terrorism in general and terrorism directed against the United States as the leading source and preeminent symbol of globalization in particular.[51] As Marc Lynch observes, "It is almost impossible to overstate the extent to which Arab intellectuals view globalization as a threat, in spite of its apparent empirical irrelevance to the region."[52] Globalization encourages its real and imagined victims to rally around those who offer an alternative future, and to the extent that globalization and Americanization appear—not without reason—to be synonymous, this should translate into opposition—and, to the extent that it appears potentially effective, active hostility—toward the United States. These effects on the political environment of the terrorists may also create incentives (and remove disincentives) for mounting spectacular, very high casualty attacks.[53]

Globalization increases the aggregate economic well-being of the international system, and the gradual spread of modernity, prosperity, and liberal political systems can be expected overall to diminish violent political conflict and unrest—eventually.[54] To the extent that hyper-terrorists are created by globalization, they should be a transitional phenomenon, but the period of transition will not be brief, and where states are particularly bad at adapting to the new reality, it could drag on almost indefinitely. On the other hand, as globalization proceeds, both the numbers and the resources of states with an interest in defending the system against adversaries such as al Qaeda should continue to grow, offering a more immediate silver lining to the relationship between terrorism and globalization.

THE GLOBALIZATION OF U.S. GEOPOLITICAL INTERESTS

In addition to increasing the power of the United States relative to its traditional rivals, while diminishing American control over the international system in absolute terms and contributing to new classes of threats, globalization will also tend to expand the scope of U.S. security interests by diminishing the traditional difference between core and periphery.[55] The increasing speed, density, and uncontrollability of the international movement of people, goods, and information reduce the physical and temporal barriers that separate states. One part of this pattern—the diminution of distance—is not a consequence of globalization, but rather one result of technological developments that also drive globalization to a considerable degree. Even those who have never heard of globalization are familiar with the idea that improvements in methods of transportation and communication are making the world a progressively smaller place, and it is hardly necessary to list the innovations that have accelerated travel, commerce, and communication between distant locations by many orders of magnitude over the centuries. The same sorts of forces have made it possible to project military power at ever-increasing speeds and ranges, compelling states to pay greater attention than they once did to distant neighbors or to potential enemies on the other sides of physical barriers such as oceans or mountain ranges. As the geography of warfare and trade becomes shaped less by shipping and railroads and more by air transport and telecommunications, MacKinder's global "heartland" is expanding, with the ranks of marginalized states on the periphery gradually decreasing.[56]

The other factors that contribute to this drift toward the formation of a geopolitical Pangaea are central to globalization per se, however.

International movement and contact are not only becoming easier and more rapid, but also far more frequent and more challenging for states to control, or even to monitor—although as Herrera notes, their ability to exploit IT for surveillance is greater than is often appreciated.[57] This increase in density is a natural result of technology making travel and communication easier and cheaper, but not an inevitable one, as a number of seclusionary states have demonstrated over the years. However, globalization punishes such states with serious opportunity costs: economic and informational isolation will interfere with creating the wealth that underpins national power (and is also likely to be politically unpopular among its domestic victims). The result is that most states are far less insulated from physical and intellectual contact with the outside world than they were even as recently as a generation ago.

International borders thus become increasingly porous to movements of people, goods, and information.[58] This increases the susceptibility of the United States to threats emanating from parts of the world that were once comfortably far away.[59] It also increases the potential for the transnational spread of local instability to states whose stability or friendship is important to U.S. security, not only across contiguous borders but also along lines of cultural and other communication. Most importantly, the United States has increasing reasons for concern about terrorist enemies establishing bases or sanctuaries in effectively ungoverned territory, even when these locations are in relative backwaters.

Other things being equal, this globalization of interests ought to point the United States (and the West) toward adopting an increasingly constabulary foreign policy, actively seeking to avert, contain, or quash potentially dangerous developments in states around the world on the grounds that threats to important national interests can now come from anywhere. Indeed, U.S. policy has already moved in this direction to a significant degree, albeit only by fits and starts. Truly embracing the constabulary option would be an interesting strategic course to pursue, but would also be difficult and expensive, for if the entire world matters, there is going to be a lot to do. Mobilizing and sustaining American domestic political support for spending substantial blood and treasure to deal with threats that are distant (both in geography and time), often highly ambiguous, and that must be addressed in many cases through patient, long-term engagement is challenging, and is likely to be all the more so as a result of the experience of occupying Iraq. It might nevertheless be cost-effective, however, if it could be conducted efficiently and if enough of the protothreats were expected to metastasize into true dangers sufficiently severe to make systematically interdicting them worthwhile.[60]

ADAPTING TO SECURITY CLIMATE CHANGE

Globalization is one of a number of forces that will shape the international security environment of the next several decades. Because it is not the only one and, for the United States at least, is probably not even the most important of these, understanding how to deal with the effects of globalization does not reveal what future U.S. foreign policy ought to look like. Nevertheless, there are a number of ways (in addition to the above) in which the design and conduct of American foreign policy ought to evolve to thrive in an increasingly globalized international system.

Before examining some of these prescriptions, however, it is appropriate to note that there is an alternative policy trajectory open to U.S. leaders, at least in theory. As Kirshner notes in his introduction to this volume, globalization is to a considerable extent the result of state policies, above all the policies of the United States, which has generally favored the march of globalization since 1945 and in some cases has acted energetically to promote it.[61] However, Washington could choose to pursue a different approach in the future, seeking systematically to retard and even to reverse globalization on the grounds that its security, economic, or other costs outweigh its benefits to the United States. Such a policy course would probably be supported by a number of domestic interests from both the protectionist left and the isolationist right, and even today, although it appears unlikely, it is not inconceivable. Given the right combination of catalysts, perhaps including a combination of domestic economic crisis and a major escalation of terrorist attacks against U.S. interests at home and abroad, it could become considerably more likely in spite of its potentially enormous costs.

But as other states have demonstrated in the past, most conspicuously the Soviet Union, rejecting globalization simply by opting out of it is a losing strategy. The U.S. economy would not collapse like North Korea's if Americans decided to fence themselves off from international exchange, information flows, and marketization, but it would be condemned to relative decline, as the rest of the international system adapted to the U.S. exit and carried on reaping the benefits of globalization.[62] Instead, the United States would need to fight globalization far more actively, working to promote barriers to trade and migration, inciting the fragmentation of the international community into regional and subregional blocs, and fomenting xenophobia—in short, persuading other states to join it in a comprehensive rejection of globalization. This would be difficult and expensive, even for the hegemon, and it would require the United States to embrace a set of preferences that fundamentally contradict the dominant American norms of the past sixty-five years.[63] Yet because globalization is not an unalloyed boon even for the United States, the possibility of such a policy will persist.

Distribution of Power: Keeping Your Friends Close

It is with respect to the balance of power that the security implications of globalization are the most positive for the United States. The differential effects of globalization generally favor the United States relative to the states most likely to pose security threats to it, reinforcing U.S. preeminence, particularly in the military arena. Yet it would be a mistake to interpret globalization as strengthening the case for unilateralism in American foreign policy.

There are at least four interconnected reasons why globalization actually increases the value of allies for the unrivaled liberal hegemon. The first follows from the tendency of globalization to contribute to the formation of transnational, stateless threats. Threats that are firmly rooted in individual states are the easiest to address through unilateral means, whether through brute force or coercive pressure against the local government. The closer the adversary moves toward the slippery, stateless end of the spectrum, the less able any single state, even the United States, will be to suppress it wherever it might decide to operate. Within this broad generalization, the need for allies and partners will vary by policy type: U.S. military force will often continue to be usable with essentially full effectiveness in a close-to-unilateral way, while effectively attacking adversaries' finances or conducting transnational policing against terrorists generally requires very extensive international cooperation if the target is not to slip through the net.[64]

Second, as U.S. security interests become even more global because enemies in the periphery are no longer safe to ignore, and the more the United States moves toward a constabulary security strategy as a result, the more important the participation of allies becomes. This is not so much because resource contributions from partners would be necessary to sustain an ambitious intervention strategy, true though this is, as it is due to the daunting challenge of having deep area expertise and skillful diplomacy available to use virtually everywhere in the world. Over the long run, globalization itself may help to provide capable and sympathetic allies by promoting economic growth and liberal modernity in regions of the world where this has been in short supply. In the nearer term, however, it may have greater impact as a catalyst of instability, complicating more than assisting with the challenge of stabilizing the decreasingly peripheral periphery.

Third, globalization increases the likely prominence of counterinsurgency and related types of warfare on the U.S. military task list, which creates resource problems for the U.S. armed forces of which recent personnel demands from the Iraq occupation are only the most recent and visible example. The problem for the United States is that improvements in military technology enable fewer people to achieve more on the battlefield, but this is far truer for high-intensity conflict against conventional armies than it is in low-intensity conflict, peace operations, and other military missions that depend on face-to-face contact with local populations. The United States is large and populous, but if it is going to conduct a lot of counterinsurgency warfare and other labor-intensive operations, assistance from allies will be indispensable.

Finally, as U.S. security interest proliferate, allies are necessary to provide bases and other support for American military forces. Although projecting power intercontinentally is more feasible than it used to be, it remains very inefficient, and is altogether impractical even for the United States in most types of sustained military operations. This does not necessarily mean that large U.S. forces must be permanently stationed around the world, but if they are to deploy forward from North America in times of crisis this will still work best if substantial infrastructure and equipment is already located in theater. Moreover, as potential adversaries develop improved capabilities to attack fixed bases, it will be desirable to have available more than a few easily predictable and irreplaceable basing options in each region of interest. Such facilities need not be American-owned, but they should not have to be hurriedly improvised if they are suddenly needed.

State Capacity: The Policy Integration Challenge

The more U.S. security policy comes to focus upon the sorts of diverse threats that should be favored and facilitated by globalization, the greater the extent to which effective policy measures will require means other than—or in addition to—military force, as the ongoing campaign against al Qaeda aptly illustrates. Addressing security threats has never been an exclusively military problem, especially when seeking to prevent the emergence of threats instead of waiting to fend them off after they appear. However, it is becoming more and more difficult to pretend that armed force is enough, and to get by pursuing policies built on the premise that the nonmilitary dimensions of security policy are mere appendices to the use of military force. This challenge is compounded by the ways in which globalization acts to erode state capacity, which further increases the need for the United States and its allies to employ the full spectrum of means that are available to them with efficiency and subtlety.

It would be rather peevish for a country that spent forty years obsessed with the Soviet menace to complain too strongly about finding that its principal security threats have now been reduced to ones usually best dealt with using police instead of armies, but this is in some respects bad news for American security policymakers. Of course, it is problematic for anything to limit the utility of military power when you possess so much of it. Perhaps more daunting in terms of practical policy, however, is that all of these considerations suggest that it is imperative for the United States to devote considerable effort to dramatically improving "interagency" coordination in its security policy—the integration of military, diplomatic, intelligence, law enforcement, and other efforts into a coherent whole that is more instead of less than the sum of its parts. This is a notoriously difficult problem for a host of reasons, as illustrated by the planning of the U.S.-led invasion, occupation, and reconstruction of Iraq, and by the checkered history of U.S. counterterrorism policy.

Axes of Conflict: War Is Politics

Finally, and closely related to the preceding issues, perhaps the most visible implication of globalization for the conduct of U.S. security policy is the growing importance of public diplomacy.[65] As global information networks expand and proliferate into the emergent hypermedia environment, and globalization makes public opinion increasingly important in many states, this dimension of foreign policy becomes evermore powerful as both a frequent threat to and a potential instrument of American policy.[66] Unfortunately, it is a realm in which the U.S. government and armed forces have not traditionally excelled, to put it kindly, as has been demonstrated during a number of recent military operations, though sometimes these deficiencies have been masked by similar or even worse performances by U.S. adversaries.

In general, the armed forces (and often the national leaders) of the United States tend to be vastly less adept at communicating persuasively with international audiences than with the American populace, who not only have been intrinsically receptive to official statements in recent years, but tend to be quite ill-informed about international events and to have little exposure to hostile sources of information.[67] To expect that globalization will make domestic U.S. audiences substantially more active and critical consumers of the news seems overoptimistic, so instead the purveyors of public information will need to take it upon themselves to improve the effectiveness of their product in the globalizing information marketplace.

One place where reform might begin in the military arena would be to reverse the developing subordination of public affairs to "information operations" (an extremely broad category also encompassing cyberwar, psychological operations, and other components), in which propaganda directed at the enemy looms particularly large. In the current hypermedia environment, the traditional doctrine separating public information from propaganda has become obsolete, forcing a choice to be made as to whether it is preferable not to lie when conducting public affairs and sacrifice some opportunities to mislead the enemy through propaganda, or to maximize the effectiveness of offensive information operations at the cost of deceiving U.S. and allied citizens about the military operations being conducted in their name. Similarly, it has become more and more difficult to conduct apparently contradictory or inconsistent policies in different parts of the world, because each audience will have the ability to see both local and distant actions. As General Chuck Horner, the coalition air commander in the 1991 Gulf War, argues,

> Sure we can try to manipulate the press, and the press can attempt to manipulate the truth; but in the end there is enough integrity in both the military and the media to make sure most of the truth gets out to the world…. The CNN Effect means that God's looking over your shoulder all the time, and I think it is a blessing. It is not pleasant, and you take hits, but in the end it brings out the best in mankind when he is out doing his worst, waging war.[68]

THE IMPORTANCE OF CHOICE

Globalization is only one of several factors contributing to the ongoing decline in state-based security threats to the United States and the rise of threats from nonstate adversaries. For all its disturbing features, this trend is to a considerable degree the product of American success in international politics, and while the new threats and axes of conflict, particularly the rise of rabid Islamist extremism, are less simple to deal with than the principal security threats the United States faced in the twentieth century, they are also less severe. Globalization does indeed threaten U.S. hegemony over the long run, but hegemony should be viewed not as the goal of liberal national security policy, but as a means to achieve more fundamental objectives, and these interests are served by globalization more than they are endangered by it.

This assessment of the impact of globalization upon the evolving constellation of security threats facing the United States is a relatively optimistic one, particularly over the long term. In spite of the dangers it poses, globalization is a trend with which the United States should be able to live more compatibly than the subjects of most of the other regional chapters in this volume—and this is fortunate for Americans, because globalization is for all practical purposes something with which we must live, whether we like it or not. However, this scenario is only potentially, not inevitably, rosy. The forces of globalization are powerful and failing to adapt appropriately to them could well make the difference between the United States gradually and comfortably slipping into hegemon emeritus status, enjoying similar benefits but with less work, or spending long years disconsolately reminiscing about how much nicer the world was before everything became so complicated.

NOTES

1. As Jonathan Kirshner explains in the introduction to this volume, globalization is not synonymous with unipolarity. Instead, the two are caused by some of the same factors and have tended at least since 1945 to be mutually reinforcing. Neither is globalization the same as Americanization, for although these two concepts usually overlap, either is possible without the other.
2. Scott D. Sagan, "Why Do States Build Nuclear Weapons? Three Models in Search of a Bomb," *International Security* 21(3) (Winter 1996/97): 54–86.
3. Cooley, chapter 7 of this volume. In addition, globalization makes the spread of information about nuclear weapon construction more difficult to limit, could facilitate the smuggling of nuclear materials, and in particular has played a very significant role in creating and shaping the "loose nukes" problem in Russia (ibid.), although this apparently has not yet been an important factor in the spread of nuclear weapons capabilities to nonnuclear states.
4. On imperial rise and decline, see for example Robert Gilpin, *War and Change in World Politics* (Cambridge: Cambridge University Press, 1981), and Jack Snyder, *Myths of Empire* (Ithaca, NY: Cornell University Press, 1991).
5. As the other First World giant, Western Europe enjoys similar economic benefits, although geography and its multinationality make the European Union less isolated than the United States in other respects.
6. Stephen G. Brooks and William C. Wohlforth, "Power, Globalization, and the End of the Cold War," *International Security* 25(3) (Winter 2000/01): 5–53.
7. Stephen D. Krasner, "State Power and the Structure of International Trade," *World Politics* 28(3) (April 1976): 317–347.
8. This would be an illusory distinction if states could not predict whence their next security threat would come, as John Mearsheimer maintains [*The Tragedy of Great Power Politics* (New York: Norton, 2001)]. However, even if states do not have permanent friends (a proposition that is frequently belied in international politics), they certainly do have considerable though imperfect abilities to anticipate whom their allies and enemies are reasonably likely to be in the foreseeable future.
9. Cooley, chapter 7 of this volume.

10. I do not count the European Union as a serious "peer competitor" threat to the United States, in spite of its power potential, because of the obstacles to its concerted wielding of superpower might in the near term [see, for example, Rachel Epstein's chapter (8) in this volume, and Stephen G. Brooks and William C. Wohlforth, "American Primacy in Perspective," *Foreign Affairs* 81(4) (July/August 2002): 25–26] as well as the unlikelihood of the European Union turning its military power against its principal overseas ally. However, it is still worth considering whether the United States might increasingly face security problems from fellow liberal states, such as an increasingly united and assertive European Union, that are equally or even more well-suited to thriving in a globalizing international environment. Although direct military threats from such powers appear improbable, indirect threats, for example working to obstruct U.S. security initiatives, may be more plausible. See Charles A. Kupchan, *The End of the American Era: U.S. Foreign Policy and the Geopolitics of the Twenty-First Century* (New York: Knopf, 2002).

11. Rogue status is almost always ambiguous and debatable—this is more a metaphor than a variable, especially a dichotomous one. Even some Western states—not excluding the United States—have a bit of a roguish streak; Israel has more than a bit.

12. Rogue states can directly threaten the United States by sponsoring terrorist attacks against it, of course, but this has become relatively uncommon as an act of deliberate national policy on a large scale (though state support for terrorists attacks against Israel and other states continues). The possibility of such a state, or of individuals within it, providing nuclear or sophisticated biological weapons to an anti-American terrorist group, either intentionally or inadvertently, is a serious concern for Washington, however.

13. Isobel Coleman, "The Payoff from Women's Rights," *Foreign Affairs* 83(3) (May/June 2004): 80–95.

14. Adamson, chapter 2 of this volume.

15. Although as Geoffrey Herrera argues (chapter 3 of this volume), modern IT is a less powerful threat to (and a more effective tool of) state control than is often supposed, globalization still has the potential to threaten the legitimacy and survival of regimes in states that fail to provide reasonable levels of prosperity and competent governance for their citizens.

16. Lynch, chapter 6 of this volume.

17. See Richard Rosecrance, *The Rise of the Trading State* (New York: Basic Books, 1986) for a parallel argument regarding interdependence.

18. This represents an interesting contrast with the earlier predictions of scholars such as A. F. K. Organski who saw China challenging for and ultimately assuming hegemony as the inevitable result of industrialization in a state of its size. That the prospect of a Chinese-dominated world appears remote today, though not out of the question, is due in considerable degree to the relative compatibility between globalization and the political and economic systems of the states supporting existing international regimes.

19. George J. Gilboy, "The Myth Behind China's Miracle," *Foreign Affairs* 83(4) (July/August 2004): 33–48; Charles Wolf, Jr., *Fault Lines in China's Economic Terrain*, (Santa Monica, CA: RAND, 2003); Gordon G. Chang, *The Coming Collapse of China* (New York: Random House, 2001).

20. Segal, chapter 10 of this volume.

21. On the nature and limits of U.S. military preeminence, see Barry R. Posen, "Command of the Commons: The Military Foundations of U.S. Hegemony," *International Security* 28(1) (Summer 2003): 5–46.

22. David Hale and Lyric Hughes Hale, "China Takes Off," *Foreign Affairs* 82(6) (November/December 2003): 36–53.

23. See, for example, David A. Shlapak, David T. Orletsky, and Barry A. Wilson, *Dire Strait? Military Aspects of the China-Taiwan Confrontation and Options for U.S. Policy*, (Santa Monica, CA: RAND, 2000), which also notes that China's military position vis-à-vis Taiwan would be considerably less favorable if the latter took a number of quite feasible defensive measures to which it has devoted far less attention than many other states exposed to the prospect of attack by much larger neighbors.

24. Stephen M. Walt, *The Origins of Alliances* (Ithaca, NY: Cornell University Press, 1987); Thomas Christensen and Jack Snyder, "Chain Gangs and Passed Bucks: Predicting Alliance Patterns in Multipolarity," *International Organization* 44(2) (Spring 1990): 137–168. There does remain a natural tendency for Japan to ally with the United States if for no other reason than because so many of its neighbors continue to distrust it as a military power (Midford, chapter 9 of this volume). See also "Back to the Future," *The Economist*, January 8, 1994, 21–23.

25. China's military modernization has relied heavily on importing weapons and military technology from abroad, especially from Russia, in state-to-state deals that have little obvious connection to globalization, other than the general pressures in favor of profitable arms exports that Rachel Epstein describes (chapter 8 of this volume).

26. Segal, chapter 10 of this volume.

27. George W. Bush, *The National Security Strategy of the United States of America* (Washington, DC: The White House, 2002) optimistically states that by maintaining apparently insurmountable military superiority over potential rivals, the United States can deter them from bothering to develop the capabilities required to challenge U.S. global military dominance (30), but does not suggest that the United States can prevent other major powers from developing the power potential to try to do so.

28. Thomas Christensen, "Posing Problems Without Catching Up: China's Rise and the Challenges for U.S. Security Policy," *International Security* 25(4) (Spring 2001).

29. See Uri Bialer, *In the Shadow of the Bomber* (London: Royal Historical Society, 1980) and many works addressing nuclear deterrence theory, notably Glenn H. Snyder, *Deterrence and Defense* (Princeton, NJ: Princeton University Press, 1961), and Thomas C. Schelling, *Arms and Influence* (New Haven, CT: Yale University Press, 1966).

30. See, for example, Charles J. Dunlap Jr., "Technology: Recomplicating Moral Life for the Nation's Defenders," *Parameters* 29(3) (Autumn 1999): 24–53.

31. Of course, when we discuss globalization we are really referring to a particular form of globalization. For example, it is possible to envision a very different globalization taking place if an antiliberal radical Islamist movement were to achieve true success on a nearly worldwide scale.

32. Fouad Ajami, "The Summoning," *Foreign Affairs* 72(4) (September/October 1993): 2–9.

33. Lynch (chapter 6 of this volume) observes that in pursuing economic reform, some Arab governments have scaled back their plans for political liberalization. Yet it seems unlikely that such liberalization would actually have been pursued aggressively in the first place in a world without globalization.

34. Robert Gilpin, *The Challenge of Global Capitalism* (Princeton, NJ: Princeton University Press, 2000), 293–306; Stanley Hoffman, "Clash of Globalizations," *Foreign Affairs* 81(4) (July/August 2002): 104–115; Robert O. Keohane, *Power and Governance in a Partially Globalized World* (New York: Routledge, 2002), 245; Lynch, chapter 6 of this volume.

35. Perhaps the most serious threat posed by Islamist extremists is that they will succeed in taking control of one or more important states such as Pakistan or Saudi Arabia, but even this prospect is disturbing primarily because of the magnification of terrorist threats that would potentially result from it.

36. Arguably the greatest threat posed to the United States by terrorists like al Qaeda is that their attacks will trigger a catastrophic overreaction in which the United States sacrifices some of the liberties and principles upon which it is based in order to increase the efficacy of its counterterrorist policies. This is the only way in which al Qaeda could plausibly destroy the "American way of life" that it is often said to imperil; fortunately, it is a path to victory that the United States can deny to the terrorists by refusing to play along.

37. On the evolution of terrorism, see Bruce Hoffman, "Terrorism Trends and Prospects," in *Countering the New Terrorism*, ed. Ian O. Lesser et al. (Santa Monica, CA: RAND, 1998).

38. Were the domain name available, "superterrorists" would be a better label, but this term is widely used to refer to terrorist employment of nuclear and other weapons of mass destruction. For further discussion, see Karl P. Mueller, "Hyperterrorists: Emergent Predators of the New World Order?" paper presented at the American Political Science Association Annual Meeting, Boston, MA, August 29, 2002.

39. Comparing al Qaeda with cinematic terrorist villains is neither facetious nor overly inaccurate. In many respects, al Qaeda has more in common with fictitious organizations such as "SPECTRE" (the megalomaniacal transnational villains in Ian Fleming's later James Bond novels and the movies of the 1960s and 1970s based on Fleming's books) than with the garden variety terrorists that the United States faced during the Cold War.

40. See Audrey Kurth Cronin, "Behind the Curve: Globalization and International Terrorism," *International Security* 27(2) (Winter 2002/03): 41–42.

41. Such groups do have valuable personnel and assets, but their attrition is expected in the normal course of events; moreover, their value is instrumental and would disappear if the organization abandoned its struggle, so threatening to destroy them unless they surrender is likely to be futile.

42. It is easy to exaggerate even the destructive potential of a terrorist group armed with an atomic weapon, or several, however. See John Mueller and Karl Mueller, "The Methodology of Mass Destruction: Assessing Threats in the New World Order," *Journal of Strategic Studies* 23(1) (March 2000): 165–168.

43. Of course, al Qaeda's ability to bring its resources to bear against U.S. targets was considerably enhanced by the arrival of large numbers of American and allied personnel in Iraq starting in 2003.

44. Comparing al Qaeda to Timothy McVeigh is worthwhile. McVeigh, certainly no intellectual giant, was able to wreak per capita destruction on an order of magnitude similar to that achieved by the September 11 hijackers and did so on a proportionally far smaller budget.

45. Terrorists being willing to employ extreme means is not unusual; doing so in pursuit of extreme ends is far more so, because the apparent attainability of a goal should play a major role in shaping whether it appears worth dying for. The recent popularity of suicide attacks among terrorists is instrumentally logical, but it is notable that most such attacks have been launched by groups—notably the Tamil Tigers in Sri Lanka and several Palestinian terrorist organizations—that are pursuing goals far less transcendental and more tangible than those of al Qaeda. See Robert A. Pape, "The Strategic Logic of Suicide Terrorism," *American Political Science Review* 97(3) (2003): 343–361.

46. Kevin Soo Hoo, Seymour Goodman, and Lawrence Greenberg, "Information Technology and the Terrorist Threat," *Survival* 39(3) (Autumn 1997): 138–140; Lynch, chapter 6 of this volume.

47. It can also be very important to intranational terrorists, which (especially in the absence of state sponsors) often depend on external sources of supply and frequently enjoy support from distant diaspora populations. See Cronin, "Behind the Curve."

48. See Cooley, chapter 7 of this volume, for example.

49. Japan's Aum Shinrikyo cult probably also qualifies for the label, although even in its heyday it was considerably less transnational in nature than al Qaeda.

50. Continuing with this scenario, the greatest obstacles to a terrorist attack on the *Titanic* might be less technological than sociological, especially if the terrorists hailed from Arabia. Acquiring the knowledge and skills necessary to seize or sabotage the ship, and even getting the terrorists aboard unrecognized, would probably have been more difficult for an al Qaeda precursor circa 1912 than preparing for and executing the multiple suicide hijackings of 2001 (although Virginia Woolf's famous success at gaining access to HMS *Dreadnought* while impersonating a robed and turbaned Abyssinian prince might cast some doubt on this assertion). However, it must be remembered that policing and identity checks have also became much more sophisticated during the course of the last century as well.

51. Lynch, chapter 6 of this volume.

52. Ibid, 188.

53. Cronin, "Behind the Curve," 51–52.

54. One important development along these lines, and one whose effects may be felt sooner than that of, say, the democratic pacification of the Arab world, is demographic: as birth rates fall in regions such as the Middle East—a trend to which several aspects of globalization contribute—the supply of young men, who are the preponderant ingredient of terrorist groups, will decline, as should the proportion of them who are encouraged to turn to extremist groups by a lack of other opportunities within their societies. See Phillip Longman, "The Global Baby Bust," *Foreign Affairs* 83(3) (May/June 2004): especially 68–71.

55. Keohane, *Power and Governance*, 275–276.

56. Halford MacKinder, "The Geographical Pivot of History," *Geographical Journal* 23(4) (April 1904): 421–437.

57. Herrera, chapter 3 of this volume.

58. Peter Andreas, "Redrawing the Line: Borders and Security in the Twenty-First Century," *International Security* 28(2) (Fall 2003): 78–111, notes however that contemporary states' ability to control movements across their borders is often underestimated.

59. There is an important offsetting consideration affecting the growth of security threats from the vanishing periphery, however. Although globalization and related developments are increasing the opportunity for enemies anywhere in the world to threaten U.S. interests, the end of the Cold War has reduced the sowing of seeds in this fertile ground. Through a combination of political revolution, cooptation, and exhaustion, the states that once did the most to promote hostility to the United States in the Third World have largely abandoned the effort, at least for the time being. Their place has more than effectively been taken by Islamist leaders, but only in the Muslim world.

60. If it were possible to distinguish, say, dangerous state failures from trivial ones, a more selective and affordable constabulary strategy would be possible. Of course, any such strategy in the real world would involve setting such priorities, but it is in the nature of globalization that this should only be possible to a limited degree—the more advanced globalization becomes, the more one failed state becomes as good a base for transnational subversion or international terrorism as the next.

61. Kirshner, chapter 1 of this volume. Of course, the United States has not always practiced what it has preached, for example engaging in protectionist trade policies to protect the interests of politically powerful industrial and agricultural sectors. Since September 2001, the United States has also implemented or advocated a number of counterglobalization measures to restrict the movement of people and money across its own and other international borders in order to impede the operations of terrorist groups.
62. Such an ill-advised turning away from economic openness at the national level is not difficult to imagine, however. See Ian Campbell, "Retreat from Globalization," *The National Interest* 75 (Spring 2004): 111–117.
63. An analogy might reasonably be drawn with the contemporary question of whether it is more sensible to invest in trying to stop global warming or in coping with its effects.
64. See Nora Bensahel, "A Coalition of Coalitions: International Cooperation Against Terrorism," *Studies in Conflict and Terrorism* 29(1) (January-February 2006): 35–49.
65. See, for example, Joseph S. Nye, "The Decline of America's Soft Power," *Foreign Affairs* 83(3) (May/June 2004): 16–20.
66. Jamie Frederic Metzl, "Popular Diplomacy," *Daedalus* 128(2) (Spring 1999): 177–192.
67. This is another arena in which allies can prove very useful, as in the preparations for the 2003 invasion of Iraq.
68. Tom Clancy and Chuck Horner, *Every Man a Tiger* (New York: Putnam, 1999), 219.

6

GLOBALIZATION AND ARAB SECURITY

Marc Lynch

IN CONVENTIONAL USAGE OF THE CONCEPT of globalization, the Arab Middle East is indisputably one of the least globalized regions in the world: state-dominated economies, relatively closed borders, controlled flows of information, low levels of domestic liberalization, and a highly ambivalent relationship with Western cultural products. Arab competitiveness has dramatically declined over the decades, as economies stagnate and population explodes. Outside of oil (and political violence), it produces few goods that are competitive on international markets. The region is almost completely excluded from the flows of private capital that have driven globalized finance—the Middle East attracts less private investment than even sub-Saharan Africa.[1] Attempts at regional integration have always failed. Perpetual risk of war and the fears generated by Islamist extremism allow states to justify extensive internal security apparatuses and tight border controls, as well as to postpone moves to democracy. Even the functional interdependencies of labor migration from the poorer and more populous Arab states to the Gulf have declined over the last decade, as the Gulf states turn to less politically suspect Asian and African workers in place of Palestinians and other Arabs.

This recitation of the region's economic failings misses the profound impact on security of the deeper underlying *processes* of globalization emphasized in this book.[2] For all its marginality in terms of global trade and financial flows, the Arab Middle East has been deeply affected by the transformation in the global flows of information and people. The impact of a market-seeking transnational Arab media arguably exceeds that to be found in any other part of the world. Labor migration and the impact of cheap travel and communications technology on the relationship between these diasporas and homeland politics have profoundly affected the region. The Arab Middle East stands at the center of the conflicts and fears associated with the backlash against the globalization and Americanization of culture. Both in terms of internal challenges to the domestic security and stability of Arab states, and in terms of the impact of regional actors on global security, tight and explicit causal relationships exist between particular processes of globalization and national security.[3]

Defining globalization as "relatively general phenomena that are stateless and uncoordinated, and that have little inherent regard for national borders" directs attention toward specific processes rather than to grand claims about systemic transformation. Although the Middle East has been largely excluded from economic globalization, it has been deeply reshaped by other processes of globalization. I emphasize three globalization processes that combine to produce a genuinely distinctive set of security challenges: marketization, information and communication technologies, labor migration. These processes together have reshaped the security environment for states, the region as a whole, and the wider international system. These changes have brought a more intense American involvement in the region while shifting local balances of power and restructuring perceptions of threat. More broadly, the intersection of blocked domestic political systems and struggling economies with a radically transformed information environment has presented great challenges to Arab states. Their responses—including the externalization of domestic challenges and defensive responses to a new public opinion—in turn create new security threats. Both states and their challengers have adapted creatively to the new conditions created by globalization. Indeed, the "war on terror" in the Middle East largely revolves around this competition between states and their challengers to seize the opportunities while minimizing the challenges presented by globalization processes.

It is important to be clear about what this chapter does not do. It does not examine all of the myriad security issues confronting the Middle East. Instead, I discuss only those security issues with a tight and explicit link to the processes of globalization that define this volume. In some areas, the linkages are clear and direct; in others, the linkages reflect more second-order security effects. I do not make a monocausal claim that globalization is uniquely responsible for these security problems. Nor do I argue that any one of the processes described is historically unprecedented. Instead, the argument is conjunctural: that globalization processes intervened and reshaped a range of challenges, problems, and incentives at a particular historical moment. The pressures of economic globalization, especially after the end of the Cold War, framed a set of undesirable political choices for most Arab states. Economic reform and demands for democratic opening alike threatened the power of entrenched elites. Limited political openings in many Arab countries in the early 1990s amounted to little, as regimes soon clamped down again. Tentative moves to privatization and economic liberalization similarly ran aground in most cases. As both political and economic conditions stagnated, the nature of political opposition began to change. Before the 1990s, Islamism primarily took the form of domestic challenges to the secular nationalist authoritarian regimes of the Arab world. With the Algerian and Egyptian descent into civil war, repression took the place of attempts at inclusion through much of the Arab world. This repression, although exacting a horrible human cost and devastating political and civil society, largely succeeded in either eliminating radical Islamists or driving them from their countries. The transnationalization of radical Islam follows directly from their domestic failures—they shifted their focus abroad because they had no other real alternative.

This shift of focus came at just the historical moment when globalization was creating new opportunities for transnational networks. Information (media and communications) globalization transformed political perspectives, both through transnational media and through vastly increased possibilities for communication and organization. The emergence of satellite television stations, especially Al Jazeera, focused political attention on broad regional issues—Palestine, Iraq, and later the war on terror—while blasting Arab states for their impotence in the face of these collective problems. Labor diasporas, more closely tied to homeland politics through new communications technology, further broke down geographical conceptions of state borders and security. The growing European and American Arab diaspora contributed to the globalization of Islamic dissent, as the Internet and easier international travel allowed groups like al Qaeda to organize in ways which would not have been previously possible. European cities such as London, Hamburg, and Paris became central nodes of the Islamist network, making it impossible to maintain a strictly geographical definition of the Middle East. American unipolar dominance and deep involvement in the politics of the region made it a strategic target for dissatisfied actors. Hence, 9/11 and the closing of the circle.

GLOBALIZATION PROCESSES

The demand for regional integration in the Arab world predates the current era of globalization, but has rarely been directly rooted in underlying material processes. Throughout the 1950s and 1960s, at a time of little inter-Arab economic interaction, Arab politicians and intellectuals pushed urgently, if unsuccessfully and hypocritically, for Arab states to unite into a single state.[4] The pan-Arabist momentum crashed to a halt after the 1967 war with Israel, which discredited Egyptian President Gamal Abd al Nasser and an entire generation of Arabist politics. Curiously, however, transnational migration and revenue flows—the stuff of economic integration from below—peaked during the 1970s and 1980s, precisely when pan-Arab ideologies were at their weakest, and before the explosion of globalization.[5] Arabist ideas have resurged powerfully in the second half of the 1990s, primarily driven by rapid and dramatic changes in the media and information environment rather than by any material economic forces.[6]

Many analysts explain the security problems of the region in terms of its failure to globalize economically, but fail to appreciate the ways in which the other globalization processes stressed in this volume have transformed the region's security environment. The conventional wisdom points out that the region has resisted the major economic and political processes of globalization, with strong states and stagnant economies defying global trends toward greater openness. Threatened by universalizing Western culture, unable to compete economically, saddled with top-heavy and nondemocratic states, the Arab Middle East exports political violence in no small part because of its failure to export anything else beyond oil. Failure to compete economically undermines regime legitimacy while dooming the people of the region to falling further and further behind. An exploding demographic pyramid exacerbates the problem, as ever-growing numbers of young people find few prospects. Desperate, corrupt regimes cling to power through repression, while carefully negotiating limited cooperation with the United States and with global economic institutions to stave off collapse. The combination of the absence of economic and political liberalism generates frustration, resentment, and alienation, driving more and more young people to Islamic extremism.[7]

The assumption that more globalized polities would ameliorate many of these security problems crosses political and theoretical divides. The Bush administration argues that bringing globalization to the Middle East will ease the security threat that the region poses to the United States.[8] Senator Joseph Lieberman agrees: the "problem of the Muslim world is not that there is too much globalization, but that there is too little."[9] The Broader Middle East Initiative adopted at the 2004 G8 Summit rests on the premise that economic and political reform in the Arab world would have direct and significant security payoffs. (The Group of Eight [G8] consists of Canada, France, Germany, Italy, Japan, the United Kingdom, the United States of America, and the Russian Federation.) Kofi Annan, secretary general of the United Nations, similarly calls on Muslim states to "embrace globalization" to escape their worsening predicament.[10] These arguments all assume that globalization would expand economic opportunities, which would stabilize regimes, advance political liberalization, and reduce the recruiting pool for terrorism. The proponents of globalizing the Middle East often seem curiously immune to the doubts that have been so widely expressed elsewhere about the political and economic implications of globalization. The region's record to date offers little reason for optimism. As in Cooley's discussion of the former Soviet areas in this volume, globalization can exacerbate rather than ease the institutional dysfunctions that plague Arab politics. The prioritization of economic reforms has led to a downgrading of political liberalization in "success stories" such as Jordan and Morocco. Globalization increases the impact of the West on all aspects of Arab life, which can exacerbate political and cultural resentments and drive anti-Americanism.[11] It remains an unproven counterfact that more globalization would reduce resentment of the West, reduce the pool of recruits to Islamism, or enhance the legitimacy of troubled Arab regimes.

The "failure to globalize" thesis exaggerates the relationship between economic globalization and political radicalism in the region and neglects the important ways in which other aspects of globalization have profoundly affected the region. Many of the problems in Arab societies most directly linked to security may in fact be caused by too much, rather than too little, globalization: forced reduction of the state sector leading to unemployment among previously favored constituencies; reduced state intervention in the economy increasing economic and social inequality and conspicuous consumption; increasingly intense exposure to global media triggering cultural defensiveness; greater levels of migration linked more tightly back to the homeland; increased opportunities for transnational mobilization; greater access to weapons of mass destruction and other weapons systems on a global arms market. Although economic globalization remains limited, the Arab world has a remarkably high level of transnational media, a disproportionate involvement in labor migration, and is at the center of the emergence of violent transnational networks such as al Qaeda.

Marketization

Defining marketization as "the intrusion of market mechanisms into new spheres of life" allows a conceptualization of its effect on the Middle East which its well-documented aversion to market globalization defined in purely economic terms.[12] As Paul Kingston concludes, "the region remains on the margins of—and indeed in many ways is detaching itself from—the accelerating processes of globalization."[13] The region has been virtually shut out of flows of private capital, attracting less than 2 percent of FDI in the developing world—and all told the entire region receives less foreign direct investment (FDI) than Sweden. Arab economies, rich and poor, remain largely at the mercy of oil markets.[14] Its share of world exports fell by more than half from 1980 to 2000, while its import tariffs average over 20 percent.[15] The Middle East region underperformed every other region in the world except for sub-Saharan Africa between 1975 and 1999. It currently shows few signs of improvement.

Some Arab governments have signaled a willingness to embrace economic globalization, but they are poorly equipped to handle its pressures and have been little rewarded for their efforts.[16] American officials have often held up Jordan as the model for how Arabs might embrace globalization not only as an escape from crushing poverty and debt but also as a bold move to protect national security. The Jordanian state enthusiastically pushed for globalization with King Hussein's peace treaty with Israel directly tied to his vision of a "New Middle East" linked both regionally and globally to the Western liberal international economy. King Abdullah's court has routinely tied Jordan's security to mastering globalization. As a result, policies such as joining the World Trade Organization (WTO), implementing International Monetary Fund (IMF) structural adjustment programs, encouraging foreign investment, and establishing free trade zones with the United States are presented not only as economic packages but also as vital to national security.

Despite Jordan's painful adjustments, however, its economy has continued to deteriorate. Privatization has fueled ethnic suspicions, as well as the predictable allegations of corruption. Poverty has skyrocketed, along with a frightening increase in inequality.[17] What is more, reduced public spending often directly harms those constituencies that have traditionally supported the regime, cutting into their patronage and entrenched benefits (in the case of Jordan, this means harming the trans-Jordanian population that dominates the public sector while helping the traditionally less favored Palestinian population that dominates the private sector). Despite its aggressive pursuit of neoliberal policy prescriptions, then, Jordan's per capita income has yet to return to 1985 levels, unemployment remains high (between 15 and 20 percent), and the qualified industrial zones (QIZs) and free trade agreements have done little for the vast majority of Jordanians.[18]

Jordan's experience mirrors that of other Arab states. Attempts to meet the demands of economic globalization have often proven dangerous to regimes, with few obvious payoffs. Many of the most dramatic riots and protests in the Arab world have responded to IMF-dictated economic reforms, and the short-term effects of liberalization have generally been to exacerbate inequalities and to undermine the well-being of the majority of the population. Implementing structural adjustment programs has often directly led to popular unrest, without doing much to strengthen economies. States such as Syria, which have taken a more defensive approach to globalization, see little in these experiences to change their minds. While economic reforms may have important long-term benefits, to this point their impact has been limited, ambivalent, and politically inflammatory.

Despite its near-complete exclusion from the core of contemporary economic globalization, the Middle East as a region has been deeply shaped over the last few decades by processes of marketization. Oil, which stands at the nexus of global finance and trade, is the most obvious driving force, affecting Middle Eastern oil producers and nonproducers alike. The security implications of the possession of oil are direct and obvious. The extensive network of American bases in the Persian Gulf—even before the invasion and occupation of Iraq—meant that the region might be seen as the forward deployment of American hegemonic power. The United States has always perceived a vital national interest in maintaining control over the flow of oil—keeping the Soviet Union out, preventing the Iraqi annexation of Kuwait, and maintaining a friendly Saudi regime. Relatively cheap oil has been a vital foundation of the liberal international economy, and challenges to that flow of oil represent a major challenge to American and to global conceptions of at least economic security.

Oil revenues have been an integral part of the global financial order, implicating Arab states directly in the globalization of finance. For oil producing states, the impact of changes in global finance is fairly direct, particularly as states such as the United Arab Emirates (UAE), Kuwait, and Saudi Arabia have diversified their portfolios beyond the oil sector. Indirectly, the other states of the Arab Middle East are all affected by the fortunes of the oil producers—through formal and private aid, labor migration and remittances, and some investment. The oil busts of the

1980s delivered a body blow to development plans, one from which few Arab states have recovered. The recycling of petrodollars beginning in the 1970s helped to stabilize the international financial system and arguably laid the foundations for the financial globalization of the 1990s.

At the same time, like the post-Soviet space described by Cooley (chapter 7 of this volume), the informal economy has been dramatically affected by globalization processes. The region is unusually tolerant of and dependent on "gray money," with financial institutions designed to minimize transparency and to facilitate the secretive movement of money.[19] The *hawala* structures of moving money that evolved in response to the demands of labor migration operate completely outside of formal economic institutions. Even within formal banking, "institutionalized corruption" has been the constitutive norm, to the interest not only of government ministers but also of drug traffickers, arms dealers, and terrorist groups. The free and unregulated movement of goods and money in the Middle East's gray economy offers a rather different picture than its stifled and obstructed formal economy. It also presented distinctive opportunities for nonstate actors to organize in ways that posed serious security challenges to states, both in the region and globally. Not all—or even a substantial portion—of these *hawala* financial transactions were terrorist-related, however. In the face of post-9/11 crackdowns on *hawala* networks, for instance, "millions of Somalis dependent on remittances from relatives abroad are now going without ... the closure of the hawala threatens to all but destroy Somalia's larger economy, which has been heavily dependent on the inflow of remittances for over three decades."[20]

The security implications of this informal economic globalization have not gone unnoticed. As the Council on Foreign Relations notes, "building al Qaeda's financial support network was Osama bin Laden's foremost accomplishment ... as long as al Qaeda retains access to a viable financial network, it remains a lethal threat to the United States."[21] Al Qaeda's financial network included earnings from legitimate businesses "then channeled to terrorist ends," but "the most important source of al Qaeda's money is its continuous fund raising efforts ... built from the foundation of charities, NGOs, mosques, Web sites, fund-raisers, intermediaries, facilitators, and banks ... that helped to finance the mujahideen in the 1980s."[22] Although Saudi Arabia was the largest source of these funds, significant funds have come from other Gulf states, Egypt, Jordan, South Asia, Europe, the United States, Asia, and virtually everywhere else. These transnational fund-raising efforts directly relied upon the mechanisms of globalization highlighted in this volume: media, financial flows, communications, and an effective framing of a common Islamic purpose in the face of the threat of an American-style globalization. Although Saudi Arabia originally dismissed accusations of terrorist funding, its attitudes changed after a series of terrorist attacks inside the kingdom beginning in May 2003. With an escalating perception of internal threat, the Saudi state began to crack down on terrorist financing, as well as other aspects of Islamist networks that had previously gone unchallenged.[23] Other Gulf states, such as the UAE, have responded unevenly to pressures to more closely regulate the banking sector.

Information

The media and information environment have been among the most profound areas in which globalization has transformed Arab politics.[24] The Arab media environment has changed almost unbelievably quickly.[25] The emergence of transnational satellite television broadcasting, the Internet, and so forth have dramatically altered the structure of political opportunity in the region. Although states have responded vigorously to the challenge of information globalization, their adaptations have themselves changed the security environment. Overall—and contrary to Herrera's expectation in chapter 3 of this volume—Arab states have been relatively more successful at controlling the Internet than they have been at combating the new media environment.

These media themselves represent an important marketization dynamic, as the most prominent new media are driven by an intensely competitive search for market share (even if advertising revenues remain elusive). This market-driven transnational broadcasting has facilitated a much stronger and more clearly articulated transnational public opinion by focusing upon regional issues such as Palestine and Iraq, which arouse interest across the entire region.[26] The new media have radically transformed the sense of distance among Arabs and Muslims, bringing them together in real time and in a common language alongside intense images and a shared political discourse. Although such media cannot directly produce political outcomes, they have at a minimum decisively broken the state's monopoly over information, even in more repressive states such as Saudi Arabia and Syria.[27] Arab audiences now have, and expect, a choice in news sources—something that they largely lacked even a decade ago. Ratiba Hadj-Moussa offers a telling description of the process in Algeria: "The national television network is so lacking in credibility that the only reliable sources of information about Algeria come from outside ... the advent of satellite television has created a circuit which begins in Algiers goes back to Paris or London and back again to Algiers."[28]

The widely cited radicalizing and mobilizing impact of this new media in the Arab context must, however, set aside conventional arguments that globalizing television has the reverse, depoliticizing effect, as a global, market-driven corporate media induces passivity and consumerist values in its audiences.[29] One key difference between the Arab transnational media and generically globalizing media is the preexisting collective identity and shared political interests across Arab state borders. Where a globalized media might "exclude much of local politics, citizen activism, public policy analysis, and deliberation," the new Arab satellite stations for the first time included exactly those things—with core Arab concerns such as Palestine and Iraq standing alongside demands for democratic reform as "local issues."[30] The preexisting political community, combined with the tedium of tightly controlled domestic state media, gave an arguably unique impact and salience to the new media in the Arab region.

As recently as the first Gulf War, there were no Arab satellite broadcasts. Arab satellites began broadcasting in growing numbers after the first Gulf War, but their entertainment content had little direct political impact. By 1994, at least 20 different regional satellites had been launched.[31] The impact of the incredibly rapid growth of transnational broadcasting permeates almost every realm of Arab politics, including security. Marketization processes can clearly be seen in the media realm, as some 200 Arab satellite stations compete fiercely for market share. Satellite dishes—legal or otherwise—have become ubiquitous. It was the creation of the Qatar-based satellite television station Al Jazeera in 1996, which revolutionized the Arab and Muslim media environment by adopting an overtly political focus. Speaking to an explicitly transnational audience addressed as fellow Muslims and fellow Arabs, Al Jazeera quickly moved to the center of an emerging Arab public sphere. Its coverage of the American strikes against Iraq in December 1998, and then of the second Palestinian Intifada beginning in 2000, captured the public imagination and focused attention squarely on politics rather than on music videos, game shows, and Egyptian soap operas. Al Jazeera coverage dramatically shaped public perceptions of the Afghan and Iraq wars by showing civilian casualties and by adopting a critical, Arabist political discourse that rejected the patriotic, nationalist discourse of American networks such as Fox and CNN.

Marketization of the media has meant the near-complete destruction of the voice monopoly formerly enjoyed by authoritarian regimes, as satellite television stations and other new media outlets compete furiously for market share. The particularly political focus and combative style of Al Jazeera and its competitors have quickly acclimated Arab audiences to the expectation of choice and disagreement. After rising to a position of near-hegemony by 2001–2002, Al Jazeera now faces numerous challengers for Arab market share. Market surveys demonstrate both the rapid rise of Al Jazeera as a challenge to the official media after 1997 and the fragmentation of the media market since 2003.[32] For instance, among those Jordanians who owned a satellite dish, 25 percent in 1998 saw Jordan TV as most credible for Arab news and 24 percent Al Jazeera while by 2000, the numbers were 25 percent and 49.4 percent, respectively. By 2003, about 35 percent of Jordanians viewed Al Jazeera as the most trusted source for Arab and international news—beating Jordan TV in both areas. Other countries showed a similar pattern. In September 1999, 51 percent of Palestinians named Al Jazeera as the most watched satellite television station, which grew to 58 percent in 2004.[33] In December 2004, 88 percent of Cairenes surveyed said that they watched Al Jazeera.[34]

The launch of the Dubai-based al-Arabiya in February 2003, with $300 million in start-up money from Saudi Arabia, technologically advanced facilities taken over from Saudi TV station MBC, and a veteran team of broadcasters, offers a clear marker of the evolution of a more competitive media environment. At around the same time, Abu Dhabi TV temporarily switched to an all-news format to compete with Al Jazeera. Others combined news programming with popular entertainment, such as the Lebanese stations LBC and Future TV's mix of reality TV shows and political content. Some competitors have chosen to cultivate niche audiences—such as CNBC Arabiya or Dubai TV's focus on businessmen—or on particular countries or regions. In June 2004, a survey by Shibley Telhami found that Al Jazeera ranked as the primary station for 62 percent of Jordanians, 54 percent of Moroccans, 44 percent of Lebanese, 44 percent of Saudis, and 46 percent in the UAE, with a variety of other stations scoring well in particular markets.[35] In November 2005, Telhami found that Al Jazeera was the first or second choice of 65 percent of respondents in six Arab countries, while al-Arabiya was first or second for 34 percent, Abu Dhabi TV for 19 percent, MBC for 19 percent, LBC for 16 percent, and al-Manar for 9 percent.[36] Again, that masked significant regional variation. Surveys by Ipsos-Stat on behalf of al-Arabiya found the Saudi-owned station overtaking Al Jazeera in the Saudi market in late 2005, while numerous surveys showed Al Jazeera scoring poorly in Iraq.

In short, intense market competition increasingly drives the Arab media realm. There are limits, however. Few of these stations rely on advertising revenues, and advertising choices in the region are still driven more by politics than by market rationality. Al Jazeera, most dramatically, is shut out of the large Saudi market for political reasons despite its huge audience. Al-Arabiya's experience also shows both the realities and the limits of marketization. Despite al-Arabiya's mandate to be "moderate," during the war in Iraq it found itself adopting a more Arabist and radical voice in response to competitive market pressures. In 2004, however, its Saudi owners changed the management of that station in order to produce more pro-American coverage even at the risk of losing market share.

Broadcasting and the Internet have also revitalized the Arab press. Despite continuing high levels of illiteracy, the rapid expansion of mass education, combined with the traditionally high value placed on texts in Islamic culture, ensure that these globalizing processes encompass the print media as well.[37] As Abdullah Schliefer points out, "the first major impact of new satellite technologies upon Arab media was in the eighties, not the nineties, and it was the satellited daily newspaper, not television."[38] Newspapers such as *Al Hayat*, *Al Sharq al Awsat*, and *Al Quds al Arabi*, published in London and aimed at a pan-Arab audience, offered an early challenge to state control over information. Globalization has helped newspapers to overcome their traditional difficulty in reaching an audience in the Middle East, whether because of their price and because governments could stop them at the border or censor their contents. But these papers now widely circulate among elites, and most now post their content free online. What is more, satellite television news broadcasts routinely read from these newspapers, which allows them to reach a far wider audience. These papers therefore have a disproportionate impact among influential Arab elites, and "are a fundamental link between expatriate Arab communities … and the Arab world itself."[39] In an earlier study, for example, I found that 68 percent of the letters to the editor published in one newspaper in 2001 and 2002 came from Europe or the United States.[40]

Governments take the destabilizing power of the new Arab media quite seriously and have worked to influence their coverage even against prevailing market forces.[41] The United States increasingly saw the new Arab media as a principle enemy in the region, pressuring Qatar to rein in Al Jazeera and harassing its correspondents in the field.[42] Arab governments have issued literally thousands of complaints against Al Jazeera and have regularly closed down the offices of satellite stations for airing offensive programs. When pro-Iraqi advocates managed to organize a rally outside the Iraqi embassy in Jordan, for example, the Al Jazeera camera operator was the first target of Jordanian security forces—the Jordanian government did not want to project an image of instability, or a pro-Iraqi image, or to attract undue attention to its repression of the rally.[43] As in China (see Segal, chapter 10 this volume), the new media may not have created democracies, but they have created a situation where even authoritarian rulers cannot afford to ignore public opinion.[44]

The Internet has been less pervasive and more easily countered than the satellite television revolution, even if over the long term it has great potential for reshaping the security environment of the Arab world.[45] In the spring of 2005, bloggers and Internet activists played a significant role in organizing democracy protests in Arab countries such as Egypt, Lebanon, and Bahrain. Jihadist groups rely heavily on Internet chat rooms and other online sites to organize the jihad and recruit new members. Still, as a recent RAND report puts it, "most of the countries of the Middle East and North Africa show no signs of impending information revolutions."[46] The Middle East remains one of the regions of the world least connected to the Internet—one commonly cited statistic showed only 2 million total Internet users in the Middle East out of a total population of more than 220 million—but the distribution patterns range widely. Egypt, Jordan, and Lebanon, for example, have many easy and inexpensive Internet cafes. For the elite, Internet access is increasingly widespread and the trend is clearly upward, but this could in turn create new problems:

> the irregular pattern of ICT diffusion and use ... favoring the wealthy and privileged ... will increase the standard of living and opportunity gaps between the richest and poorest sectors of MENA [Middle East and North Africa] societies, resulting in continuing unrest—including armed rebellion and the export of terrorism—and justification for a government's strict controls, which contributed to the problem in the first place.[47]

Outside the geographic Middle East, information technology has had a more direct and clear impact on security. The Internet has played a hugely important role in coordinating and maintaining the transnational Islamist networks in the diaspora, especially in Europe and North America. Chat rooms, Web sites, and e-mail lists allow Arabs and Muslims in the diaspora to maintain contact with their communities.[48] Islamist groups have been particularly active on the Internet, creating sophisticated and well-designed Web sites for news, fatwas, Quranic and sharia texts and interpretation, and community building. But as with other aspects of globalization, these changes have also been used by radical groups for organization and mobilization.[49]

At the micro level, mobile phones and text messaging have played an important role in changing communication patterns and the dissemination of information. For example, Jordanian activists arranging a demonstration against the sanctions on Iraq managed to circumvent close scrutiny by state security agencies by "blasting" the location of the protest over instant messaging only at the last minute. By the time the police reacted, the protestors had already been filmed by Al Jazeera and their message broadcast to a wide audience.[50] Even before the explosion of satellite television dish ownership, videotapes of the most exciting and controversial Al Jazeera programs circulated freely to be played on already ubiquitous VCRs. These mid-tech communications technologies pose real difficulties for regime control, given their centrality to business and their widespread integration into daily life.[51] Early challenges to the legitimacy of the Saudi regime by Islamist dissidents such as Mohammad al-Masa'ri, for example, deployed information collected from local sources or from Western media, and then used fax machines, and later the Internet and e-mail, to distribute information damning to the Saudi regime into the kingdom. The Ayatollah Khomeini famously used cassette sermons taped abroad to rally and mobilize Islamic protests against the shah of Iran.[52]

States have battled back against the challenges of new information and media technologies. They have been far more successful in the former than the latter. Contrary to widespread expectations about the revolutionary impact of the Internet, Arab states have proven quite adept at developing new mechanisms of surveillance and control. Indeed, these Arab states have harnessed these information technologies in many cases to increase their surveillance and control capabilities—particularly since 9/11.[53] Arab governments have used techniques ranging from sophisticated censorship regimes to state-controlled Internet service providers and proxy servers to highly publicized crackdowns on Internet users to intimidate or prevent political uses of the Internet.[54] A study by the Berkman Center found that Saudi Arabia blocked over 2,000 Web sites for various reasons.[55] RAND claims that "as poorly as the governments might be doing, they are still light years ahead of the opposition ... [which have] not taken to the Information Age, and none is more technically savvy or well-wired than the government."[56] This conclusion, I suspect, rests on a narrowly conceived notion of "the opposition," however. It is clearly the case that Islamists in general have proven remarkably adept at using the Internet; al Qaeda specifically has used the Internet creatively and effectively; and the measuring of "success" focuses too much on outcomes and not enough on the underlying processes by which opposition groups come together, mobilize, organize, and reach out to a wider public.[57]

The Arab states have proven less adept at responding to the dramatically changed media environment, however. Almost every state has harassed or shut down the bureaus of independent satellite stations, banned circulation of independent newspapers, or arrested independent journalists. Most have attempted to compete by launching their own satellites to "get their message out." Even relatively liberal Lebanon introduced, in January 1997, laws featuring prior censorship of news programs and authorizing the blocking of "the transmission of any news or political item affecting state security," and Jordan issued a series of evermore restrictive media laws in the late 1990s.[58] But these heavy-handed efforts have largely backfired. Satellite dishes have spread even in rigidly authoritarian regimes such as Syria and Saudi Arabia. Arab audiences have become rapidly acclimated to having a genuine choice of engaging, independent media and have little to no interest in stodgy, politically controlled state broadcasting.

Migration

As Adamson argues in this volume, the impact of migration on security is mediated by the transformations in information and communications technology described above. The movement of people has long been an integral part of the political economy of the Middle East, escalating to a central position with the oil boom beginning in 1973 and persisting even after the oil busts of the mid-1980s. Indeed, in terms of labor, migration in the Middle East seems to be on the vanguard of globalization rather than a laggard. A large number of Arabs from poorer states went to the Gulf to work, sending home remittances that helped to finance extended family networks. Migrants to the Gulf proved a key link in spreading more conservative conceptions of Islam through the region. Arabs, particularly North Africans, also went to Europe, where they found growing and vibrant communities; as Adamson notes in chapter 2, some 10 percent of the Moroccan population lives in Europe.[59] Over the course of the 1990s, replacement migration has dominated the Gulf, as wary Gulf states have turned to supposedly apolitical South Asians and other non-Arabs instead of Palestinians or other Arabs, which has cut back on the intraregional migration to some extent. Kuwait, for example, expelled some 350,000 Palestinians and 110,000 Syrians after the Gulf War; Saudi Arabia expelled some 800,000 Yemenis.[60]

Labor migration to the Gulf helped to regionalize the political economy of the Arab world in the 1970s and 1980s in ways that the political ideologues of Arab nationalism could have only dreamed in the 1950s.[61]

Egypt, for example, received remittances from its workers in the Gulf averaging $3 billion to $4 billion a year through the 1980s and 1990s. Jordan went from around $21 million in remittances in 1972 to over $1 billion in 1982, and some $6 billion in 1996.[62] Even Syria, with its closed economy, had remittance income averaging over $1 billion a year over these decades—interestingly, with a far wider geographic distribution than the Gulf. Returnees from the Gulf impacted domestic societies in a number of ways, not only economic; for example, the conservative culture and religious ideas to which the migrant workers were exposed—and their relative wealth upon their return—had noticeable effects on public life.

The role of immigrant labor poses important security challenges in Arab states. Prior to the decision to replace Palestinian and other Arab labor, states carefully monitored these Arab communities for signs of politicization. The current situation poses a new kind of challenge, however. Saudi Arabia—to say nothing of the new Iraq—relies heavily upon foreign contractors to provide vital services in areas ranging from regime security to oil production. As terrorist attacks targeting foreigners raise the costs of such contractors or even drive them from the region, such countries could face serious threats to their abilities to maintain viable levels of security and economic productivity.

Migration to Europe, particularly from North Africa, has developed to such a degree that it has become difficult to even speak of "the Middle East" as a geographic region. Life in Europe exposes Arabs to ideas and experiences that deeply affected their attitudes to local cultures and politics. The European Union, recognizing this reality, has pushed its Euro-Med initiative to develop North African economies and societies, in large part to reduce the push factors driving this Arab migration north.[63] Large Arab and Muslim immigrant communities are now well-established in almost every European country, and—due to the transformation of information and communications technology—are far more attuned to the political life of their homelands than in the past. Concern over the "threat" posed by this large-scale Muslim immigration has pushed migration to the top of European security agendas—both for the threat to cultural integrity and for more direct concerns about terrorism and the externalization of Middle Eastern conflicts.[64] As I discuss below, the role of networks linking Moroccan communities in Spain back to North Africa in the March 2004 Madrid terrorist attacks, of London-based radical Islamist mosques in wider political movements, or of the Arab students in Germany in the 9/11 attacks all attest to the importance of these migration patterns for wider questions of international security.[65]

IMPACTS

How have these processes affected national security as defined in this volume? There are three broad areas in which direct and clear impacts can be seen: the balance of power and the threat of war, cultural conflicts, and violence associated with Islamist terrorist networks. The final section of this chapter then looks briefly at how the American-led war on terror intersects with globalization processes in these issue areas.

The Balance of Power and the Threat of War

As Mueller discusses in chapter 5, the transformation of American conceptions of its vital national interests driven by globalization has radically increased American involvement in the Middle East. Because such involvement often takes conflictual forms—from the imposition of sanctions to war—growing American intervention clearly represents a major security issue. American forces invaded and occupied Iraq in 2003, and there have been serious discussions of possible military interventions—as well as the actual leveling of economic sanctions—against many other Arab states (Lebanon, Syria, Sudan, Libya, Saudi Arabia), as well as Iran. In short, as American presence in the region has increased, so has the level of threat perceived by many regional actors. The growing identification of globalization with Americanization intersects with the spiraling levels of anti-American sentiment in the region to reinforce hostility to both.[66] This radicalized anti-American opinion in turn increases both the pool of recruits for terrorist movements and the political incentives for public attacks on American targets.

The interminable Arab-Israeli conflict has little to do with globalization, but the processes of globalization may have contributed significantly to shifting the military balance of power in Israel's favor in the 1990s as that country's high-tech modern economy thrived even as Arab states struggled to adapt. But Israel's military supremacy has not prevented a horrific spiral of violence since the fall of 2000, with suicide bombings and terrorism inflicting great physical and psychological harm upon Israeli society. The marketization processes making weapons of mass destruction more available (as described next) raises the risk of catastrophic terrorism—precisely the fear that led the late Yitzhak Rabin to pursue the peace process in the early 1990s. The unifying and mobilizing impact of coverage of the second intifada in the new Arab media arguably has had a magnifying and even distorting effect on Palestinian resistance. What is more, as authoritarian Arab governments pay more attention to a public opinion empowered by the forces described above, they are likely to adopt more confrontational rather than more conciliatory policies toward Israel.

As Epstein points out in chapter 8, the role of globalized production networks in making accessible weapons of mass destruction (WMD) components, along with the market incentives driving arms companies to seek out Middle Eastern markets, has important implications for national, regional, and international security. It is not only European companies, of course. Chinese sales of sophisticated antiaircraft systems to Iraq were motivated more by profit than by politics. Perhaps the most troubling instance of this concerns the Pakistani "nuclear Wal-Mart," which demonstrates the very real possibility that any state with the financial resources—from Saudi Arabia to Libya—could purchase nuclear weapons off the shelf. Although there have been initiatives to reassert political and state control over the nuclear market, globalization processes would seem to cut against the ability of states to successfully do so.[67]

Cultural Conflicts

For many Arabs and Muslims, like the Chinese leaders described by Segal in chapter 10, globalization itself represents a major threat to security. Memories of the era of colonialism, and anger at what is widely seen as the neoimperial aspirations of the West, deeply permeate Arab and Islamist political culture. The bookstores of Cairo and Amman, the columns of the major Arabic newspapers, the preaching in Islamist mosques are all full of explicit condemnations of globalization. In these conceptions, globalization is part of the American (and Western) hegemonic project, which seeks to finally eradicate the Arab-Islamic identity.[68] Cast in cultural terms as much as economic and political terms, the Arab-Islamist discourse places globalization and "the Western cultural invasion" firmly in the realm of security threat.[69] As one Egyptian commentator put it, "globalization is another term for capitalism and imperialism and all Arabs and Muslims need to consider it an imminent danger that is endangering our political, social, cultural, and economic stability."[70] This view of a cultural threat tends to conflate globalization with Americanization in important ways: "in light of unipolar [American] hegemony in international politics ... we must return to the concept of globalization which brings together politics and the economy and culture and thought."[71]

It is almost impossible to overstate the extent to which Arab intellectuals view globalization as a threat, in spite of its apparent economic irrelevance.[72] For the Egyptian Islamist Hassan Hanafi, just as for the

Marxist Galal Amin, globalization's essence is "the north's desire to control the south." For Yusuf al Qaradawi, probably the most important politically moderate Islamist public intellectual today, globalization is simply "the old imperialism presented under a new name." Qaradawi warns that globalization

> from the beginning has been linked to the expansion of the American model and widening it to encompass the whole world ... it is not only about a mechanism of the expansion of modern capitalism, but also the call to build a specific model ... as an economic model it is also an ideology expressing this system and serving it and consolidating it ... that is why some authors call it "Americanization."[73]

Many worry about whether a place will remain for Islam in a globalizing world in the face of Americanization and a global culture of modernity. One response to American support for Israel and the war on terror has been a largely symbolic but impressively self-sustaining popular boycott of American products and chains such as McDonald's. Although this has had little economic impact, it has given its participants some sense of empowerment against these distant and impersonal forces shaping their lives.

Fear of this cultural onslaught has driven the efforts of Islamist conservatives, who have focused their energies on policing the public sphere for signs of blasphemy.[74] Their efforts were not purely defensive, even if they seemed somewhat quixotic in the face of the rapidly globalizing media environment. These Islamists saw the realm of culture as the primary battleground for the defense of Islamic authenticity and identity. They also tended to pick fights they could win. Egypt again offers the best example. To diffuse Islamist opposition to the regime, Egypt delegated increasing power over public affairs and the media to the conservatives at Al-Azhar. Furthermore, Islamists had an increasingly central place within the Egyptian legal system, with judges and lawyers sympathetic to the Islamist trend willing to push for the recognition and implementation of sharia.[75] In this instance, then, the fears generated by globalization played into the hands of cultural conservatives, which arguably in turn enhanced the domestic position of Islamists who could in principle threaten the regime's security.

The explosion of satellite television and access to information has been one of the most transformative dimensions of globalization for the region. As Michael Hudson points out, "the lower classes in the Middle East ... may be falling behind, but they can also see that they are falling behind."[76] It is quite simply no longer possible for even highly authoritarian states to confidently control the dissemination of information and political opinion. It has also triggered some of the more extreme instances of backlash and cultural defensiveness. Beyond the usual conservative complaints about *Baywatch*, concerns are widely expressed about the spread of consumer culture and of encoded Western ideas.

The rise of Islamism in its current form is directly linked to the processes of globalization. Islamism rose to the forefront of the politics of the Middle East in the early 1970s, in response to the failure of secular development models and foreign policy, not during the 1990s (the period in which globalization is generally considered to have peaked). It was not the downtrodden and uneducated, for the most part, who drove Islamism's rise. On the contrary, it was educated, politicized university graduates who took the lead of what was overwhelmingly an urban movement of the educated middle class. What has changed in recent years has been the emergence of a new kind of Islamist, territorially detached and politically radical. Al Qaeda represents a globalized form of Islamism that challenges the older forms of Islamist political and social activism as profoundly as it does Arab regimes or the West.

The conventional view of Islamism as a defensive reaction to globalization profoundly misunderstands the creative and aggressive ways in which Islamist movements engaged with globalization. Indeed, some go so far as to argue that Islamism is "self-consciously advancing the cause of an alternative form of globalization from the currently dominant, and made to seem inevitable, Western capitalist one."[77] Islamism's emphasis on transnational activism—including both political action and the construction of a dense array of Islamic NGOs and voluntary associations—anticipated the kind of global civil society made possible under conditions of globalization. Islam is not tied to territory and has never accepted the division of the *umma* into nation-states. It is embodied in people—mobile, deterritorialized people carrying ideas and practices. But Islamism has been powerfully reshaped by globalization processes, particularly information and migration. Islamism has taken on a more universalist focus, moving away from a state-level focus that had come to dominate Islamist practice in the 1980s, and has also taken on a more confrontational hue with regards to the United States and its allied regimes.

The transnational nature of Islamism is not new, but the intensity and global focus—both organizationally and in the new kinds of media described above—suggests something qualitatively new. Political Islam is inherently a transnational movement, and there have been linkages among Islamist groups for years. Muslim Brothers, Deobandis, Tablighis, Wahhabis, and other groups have long traveled through the region proselytizing (*dawa*), setting up mosques and schools, and collaborating on social and cultural ventures. Islamism has been organized in network structures since long before Western sociologists of globalization became enamored with the concept. The initial rise of Islamism in the 1970s was aided, but not caused, by the investment by the suddenly massively wealthy Saudi state in a far-flung network of mosques and charities aimed at spreading both a religion and a conservative political ideology. At the time, this seemed desirable to the United States and to Western-oriented Arab rulers who saw Islamism as a useful balance to the more dangerous leftist groups. Because they generally shared modernization theory's view that economic progress and social mobilization would weaken religious forces over time, they were not greatly worried about the future of this Islamist trend.

Nevertheless, for the first decades of the Islamist revival, most Islamist activism focused at the level of nation-states, with political parties contesting elections and local movements challenging governments. The Gulf war transformed the profile of Islamism, setting it on a more globalized trajectory. As the first global media war, it enabled Islamist movements for the first time to witness one another engaged in common protests over the same issue in real time. The main transnational components came from the Saudi role in financing networks of mosques and social welfare organizations. Oil wealth and labor migration both played a major role in this process. Saudi support for the vast expansion of religious institutions and services throughout the Middle East and the world helped to create the infrastructure for Islamist opposition. Although Saudi Arabia sometimes withdrew or shifted its official financial support, sympathetic Saudi citizens continued to finance them. Saudi dissidents, such as bin Laden, furious at the Saudi alliance with the United States, at this time began organizing their global jihad from bases in sympathetic but weak states such as the Sudan and Afghanistan. In the 1990s, this radical jihad became increasingly global in outlook, fitting conflicts everywhere from Bosnia to Chechnya, Kashmir to Indonesia, into a single common narrative.[78] This does *not* mean that there exists a single, unified Islamist movement, under the command of an Islamist International. It does mean that globalization—media, travel, and the common experience of international politics in the post–Cold War era—heightened mutual awareness of "Islamic" issues, sharing of strategies and theories, and a general transcending of the nation-state. This network of charities, mosques, and NGOs fits well within the tight definition of globalization in terms of uncoordinated individual decisions having a direct impact on traditionally defined security. This Islamist transnational civil society is empowered by the same forces as the presumably more benign global civil society, operates in much the same way, and helps to engender similarly cosmopolitan—though not Western—worldviews.[79]

The crisis over the publication of cartoons deemed offensive to Islam in a Danish newspaper in the fall of 2005 illustrates powerfully how these globalization processes can interact to produce security threats. Originally published as a local political provocation, the cartoons initially generated little response—even after being republished in at least one Egyptian newspaper. Over a period of several months, however, Islamist activists cultivated outrage over the Internet and through the dissemination of inflammatory dossiers through mosque networks. In January, several major Islamist figures publicized Islamic anger over the cartoons on satellite TV, with Yusuf al-Qaradawi on Al Jazeera calling for Muslim rage in response. Protests erupted across the Arab and Muslim world, with the issue rising to the top of the political agenda and a boycott of Danish products biting into that country's exports. When consulates were burned in Damascus and Beirut, Qaradawi and others called for calm, "rational rage": defending the boycott and the expression of anger but condemning violence. In a fascinating example of the marketization of Islamist politics itself, other Islamist would-be leaders offered competing plans (the televangelist Amr Khaled organized a dialogue in Copenhagen heavily publicized by al-Arabiya, for instance), while al Qaeda reaped the fruits of Muslim outrage with the West. Rather than an example of a timeless clash of civilizations, the Danish cartoons crisis exemplified how the processes of globalization—from restive immigrant populations in Europe to the mobilizing impact of the Internet and satellite television—can drive cultural conflict.

Organized Violence

Europe became central to Arab and Islamist politics in the 1980s. London hosted the most influential new Arab media, especially newspapers, and a vibrant Arab and Islamist cultural and political scene. Within these European capitals, Arabs and Islamists of all nationalities found the opportunity to network, form alliances, and to carry on localized but intensely transnational dialogues. The new media also allowed this diaspora to actively participate in the politics of the region. At times this took a direct form, as when the vicious war between the Armed Islamic Group and the military in Algeria externalized itself to France and to local Algerian communities in France, in alarming ways. At other times, the relationship is more indirect.

Egypt offers an outstanding example of the connections between domestic and globalized violence. From roughly 1992 to 1997, Egypt waged a brutal campaign of repression against an equally brutal Islamist insurgency. Its success in this campaign had several unintended consequences. First, although the fierce campaign did largely defeat the Islamist insurgency, the broadly based offensive against Islamist movements in general, and the state's refusal to distinguish between moderate and radical Islamists, drove ever deeper the wedge between the state and society. Second, the state's success in crushing the insurgency led many of its leaders and cadres to flee the country. In exile from Egypt, these radical Islamists found themselves placed into close proximity with other Islamists living in exile, including the "Afghan Arabs." The first attack on the World Trade Center in 1993 was planned and executed by Egyptian radicals associated with the blind Islamist Shaykh Omar Abd al Rahman. Ayman al Zawahiri, leader of Al Gihad al Islami, took advantage of his exile from Egypt to join forces with Osama bin Laden, exiled from Saudi Arabia, to form al Qaeda. Even though bin Laden has been the most prominent public face of the al Qaeda network, the Egyptian presence has been crucial to its development. Mohammed Atta, of course, was an Egyptian who had studied in Europe and had come to al Qaeda through Zawahiri's network.[80]

The shift to globalized networks and direct action against the United States is a function of both the technological and political possibilities created by globalization and the successful repressive campaigns of Arab states such as Egypt and Saudi Arabia that forced dissidents such as Osama bin Laden and Ayman al Zawahiri to work outside their homelands. The jihad against the Soviet Union in Afghanistan produced a hard core of "Afghan Arabs" who were highly motivated and well-trained in guerrilla warfare and terrorist methods. When these Afghan Arabs returned to their homes, in Egypt and Algeria especially, they often pushed Islamist opposition in a more radical and more effectively violent direction. Successful repression of these challengers tended to externalize rather than eliminate these security problems, as Egypt, Algeria, and other troubled Arab states exported their problems. Saudi Arabia most explicitly attempted to actively orient opposition activity outside of its borders by continuing to fund otherwise hostile groups as a way of keeping their attention elsewhere.

The high levels of violence and uncertainty in the region help perpetuate a self-fulfilling prophecy with regard to globalization. As Noland and Pack point out, "close integration with producers beyond the region requires cross-border investment and frequent personal contact, which immediately raises issues relating to political risk." The targeting of international workers by al Qaeda in Saudi Arabia and by the insurgency in Iraq, like earlier campaigns against tourism and foreign workers in Egypt and Algeria, adds to the perception and the reality of such risk.

A regional political economy heavily shaped by oil and by geopolitics, including the ongoing conflict between Israel and its Arab neighbors, has contributed to unusually heavy militarization.[81] Militarization—often directed inwardly more than externally—and an overdeveloped state, has plagued the Arab world; the "oil curse," concentrating economic resources in the state, exacerbated the trend.[82] War and oil together have justified—and made possible—an unnaturally large state sector. Pervasive autocracy, repression, corruption and patronage politics, and tight control over information followed. The militarization of the region and the exaggerated role of the state stand firmly against transparency or the easy movement of goods, people, and information upon which globalization depends.

THE WAR ON TERROR: GLOBALIZATION STRIKES, STATES STRIKE BACK

The terrorist attacks of September 11 emerged from this interaction of globalization and security. The al Qaeda network associated with Osama bin Laden used globalized communications technologies to link together frustrated diasporas and externalized oppositions to wage their campaign before a globalized media. The war on terror has in turn concentrated precisely on those areas where globalization processes have most impacted the Middle East: global Islamic networks and their connection to an Arab (Muslim) diaspora, immigration, communications and media, and the movement of money (*hawala* system and terrorist financing). The war on terror can in large part be read as the state striking back, adapting to the security challenges posed by globalization.

The concrete impact of the war on terror has been decidedly negative in terms of globalization processes. Tighter control over Arab immigration to the West, greater surveillance over diaspora communities, and an uneven but real attempt to assert control over financial networks and banking all target core globalization processes. Arab and Islamist civil society is under siege, especially global NGOs and charities coming under scrutiny as potential sources of terrorist financing.[83] The greater attention to tracking the movements of "potential terrorists" raises the costs of and obstacles to labor migration, and has made it vastly more difficult for Arabs to enter the United States (and to a lesser extent Europe) for work, study, or tourism. But these statist responses cut against powerful underlying globalization forces. Migration responds to the very real incentives of the market and may be beyond the power of states to seriously control or regulate. It is difficult to imagine the large Muslim communities resident in Europe easily repatriating; indeed, the trend is toward a more consolidated Muslim presence. But if the war on terror does significantly reduce labor migration, the loss of remittances will have a devastating economic effect on many states in the region. The inability to export unemployed young men, combined with growing economic problems, will place greater stress on these governments. And this may increase the potential recruits to violent opposition movements. This may alleviate international security problems by reducing the ability of states to externalize their problems, at the cost of the security of the increasingly besieged states in the region.

For all the talk of democratization and reform by the Bush administration, greater priority has been given to granting Arab governments leeway to control highly mobilized populations intensely opposed to the invasion of Iraq. The war on terror, by giving Arab and Muslim governments a free hand to repress domestic Islamist opposition, has tended to encourage repression while undermining pressures for political and economic reform. This increased repression may well increase the likelihood of externalized violence.

The war on terror has, if anything, increased the importance of the Arab and Islamic transnational media—in spite of intense but ineffectual American efforts to contest that influence.[84] Al Jazeera and its competitors have prospered covering the wars in Afghanistan and Iraq and have locked in enormous audiences. The battle for Arab and Muslim public opinion has been one of the greatest failures of the American "war on terror." The United States created its own Arabic language satellite television station, Al Hurra, to have a voice in the new Arab public sphere, but this statist response to a market problem has to this point been a failure.

The last several years have seen the arrest or killing of significant portions of the al Qaeda leadership (although not the top leadership). But in response, al Qaeda and like-minded groups have become more globalized and less centralized.[85] The terrorist attacks in Morocco and Saudi Arabia in recent months—not to mention the escalating violence in Iraq—certainly suggest that regional targets will be hit when the opportunity and incentive arise.

To the extent that American policy makers consider economic reform in the Middle East to be a vital security interest, American initiatives could provide a spur to increased marketization processes in the region. However, as this chapter argues, increased marketization would not necessarily enhance security. It might well increase, rather than mitigate, much of the impact of globalization described above. It might paradoxically increase the perception of threat by those concerned that globalization really means subordination to American interests. The war on terror, therefore, can be read in large part as a response to the impact of the globalization processes emphasized in this book on the Arab and Muslim worlds. Attempts to reestablish state control over areas increasingly driven by marketization cut against the idea that globalization holds the key to normalizing the Middle East.

NOTES

1. Paul Kingston, "Avoiding Globalization?" *International Journal* 53 (Winter 2002–2003): 201–212, 203 (quote). Also see Clement Henry and Robert Springborg, *Globalization and the Politics of Development in the Middle East* (Cambridge: Cambridge University Press, 2001). One exception is the recycling of petro-dollars through the Western financial system; see David Spiro, *The Hidden Hand of Hegemony* (Ithaca, NY: Cornell University Press, 1996).

2. Toby Dodge and Richard Higgott, eds., *Globalization and the Middle East* (London: Royal Institute of International Affairs, 2002).

3. Audrey Kurth Cronin, "Behind the Curve: Globalization and International Terrorism," *International Security* 27(3) (2002/03): 30–58.

4. Michael Hudson, ed., *Middle East Dilemma* (New York: Columbia University Press, 1999) reviews the various dimensions of attempts at Arab unification.

5. Hudson, *Middle East Dilemma*, 2.

6. Anabelle Sreberny, "Mediated Culture in the Middle East," *Gazette* 63 (2–3) (2001): 101–119.

7. For a sophisticated presentation of this argument, see Herbert Kitschelt, "Origins of International Terrorism in the Middle East." *Internationale Politik und Gesellschaft* 1 (2004), available at http://www.fes.de/ipg/online1_2004/artkitschelt.htm.

8. See Mueller, chapter 5 of this volume. This strategic justification was clearly articulated in Bush's speech promising a U.S.-Middle East Free Trade Area within a decade (May 9, 2003); speech available at http://www.whitehouse.gov/news/releases/2003/05/20030509-11.html. Also see Charlene Barshefsky, former U.S. trade representative, "The Middle East Belongs in the World Economy," *New York Times*, February 22, 2003.

9. Joseph Lieberman, "The Theological Iron Curtain," *The National Interest* (Fall 2003): 5–9.

10. Kofi Annan, quoted in *Arab News*, October 20, 2002, available at http://www.globalpolicy.org/globaliz/cultural/2002/1029annan.htm. A report issued by the U.N. agency Economic and Social Commission for Western Asia (ESCWA) in July 2003 made similar recommendations.

11. Marc Lynch, "Anti-Americanisms in the Arab World," in *Anti-Americanisms in World Politics*, edited by Peter J. Katzenstein and Robert O. Keohane (Ithaca, NY: Cornell University Press, forthcoming 2006).

12. Marcus Noland and Howard Pack, "Islam, Globalization, and Economic Performance in the Middle East," Institute for International Economics, International Economics Policy Briefs PB04-4 (June 2004).

13. Kingston, "Avoiding Globalization,"201.
14. Paul Sullivan, "Globalization: Trade and Investment in Egypt, Jordan and Syria since 1980," *Arab Studies Quarterly* 21(3) (1999): 35–50; Karen Pfeifer and Marsha Pripstein Posusney, "Arab Economies and Globalization: An Overview," in *Women and Globalization in the Arab Middle East*, eds. Eleanor Doumato and Marsha Posusney (Boulder, CO: Lynne Rienner, 2003), 25–54.
15. George T Abed, "Unfulfilled Promise," *Finance and Development* 40(1) (2003): 10–15; Noland and Pack, "Islam, Globalization, and Economic Performance," 2.
16. Pfeifer and Posusney, "Arab Economies and Globalization."
17. Peter W. Moore, "The Newest Jordan: Free Trade, Peace, and an Ace in the Hole," *Middle East Report Online*, June 26, 2003, available at http://www.merip.org/mero/mer0062603.html; also see Moore and Andrew Schrank, "Commerce and Conflict," *Middle East Policy* 10(3) (2003): 112–120.
18. Moore and Schrank, "Commerce and Conflict,"116.
19. John Sfakianakis, "Gray Money, Corruption and the Post-September 11 Middle East," *Middle East Report* 222 (Spring 2002): 32–39.
20. Khalid Medani, "Financing Terrorism or Survival?" *Middle East Report* 223 (2002): 2–9.
21. Council on Foreign Relations, "Terrorist Financing," report of an independent task force sponsored by the Council on Foreign Relations, October 2002; and Council on Foreign Relations, "Update on the Global Campaign against Terrorist Financing," second report of the task force, Council on Foreign Relations, June 15, 2004.
22. Council on Foreign Relations, "Terrorist Financing," 6–7.
23. Council on Foreign Relations, "Update on the Global Campaign."
24. Marc Lynch, "Beyond the Arab Street," *Politics and Society* 31(1) (2003): 55–91, and *Voices of the New Arab Public: Iraq, al-Jazeera, and Middle East Politics Today* (New York: Columbia University Press, 2006). For discussion of the wider context of media globalization, see W. Lance Bennett, "Global Media and Politics," *Annual Reviews of Political Science* 7 (2004): 125–148.
25. Naomi Sakr, *Satellite Realms: Transnational Television, Globalization, and the Middle East* (New York: I. B. Tauris, 2001). Jon Alterman, *New Media, New Politics?* (Washington, DC: WINEP, 1998); Hassan Mneimah, "The New Intra-Arab Cultural Space," *Social Research* 70(3) (2003): 907–930. Marwan Kraidy, "Arab Satellite Television between Regionalization and Globalization," *Global Media Journal* 1 (2002).
26. Charles Kurzman, "The Globalization of Rights in Islamic Discourse," in *Islam Encountering Globalization*, ed. Ali Mohammadi (New York: Routledge Curzon, 2002), 131–153.
27. On Syria's struggles to adapt, see Najib Ghadbian, "Contesting the State Media Monopoly: Syria on Al Jazira Television," *MERIA* 5(2) (2001).
28. Ratiba Hadj-Moussa, "New Media, Community and Politics in Algeria," *Media, Culture and Society* 24 (2003): 451–468. On the new media environment in Lebanon, see Yves Gonzalez-Quijano, "The Birth of a Media Ecosystem: Lebanon in the Internet Age," in *New Media in the Middle East*, eds. Eickelman and Anderson, rev. ed. (n.p.: n.p., 2003).
29. Bennett, "Global Media and Politics."
30. Bennett, "Global Media and Politics," 126.
31. Sakr, *Satellite Realms.*
32. Center for Strategic Studies at the University of Jordan, "Democracy in Jordan," annual surveys conducted by the Center for Strategic Studies at the University of Jordan. Available at http://www.css-jordan.org/polls/democracy/2003/index.html.
33. Center for Palestinian Studies and Research, Public Opinion Poll No. 43, September 2–4, 1999, and Public Opinion Poll No. 47, February 24–26, 2000. http://www.pcpsr.org/survey/polls/2004/p12b.html

34. http://tbsjournal.com/ArabAdvisors.html.

35. Zogby International poll for Shibley Telhami, University of Maryland, June 2004, available at http://www.bsos.umd.edu/sadat/.

36. My calculations from the original data, which can be found at: http://www.bsos.umd.edu/SADAT/PUB/Arab-attitudes-2005.htm and http://www.bsos.umd.edu/sadat/pub/unweighted.htm.

37. Dale Eickelman, "Islam and the Languages of Modernity," *Daedalus* 129 (2000): 119–136.

38. Abdullah Schleifer, "Media Explosion in the Arab World," *Transnational Broadcasting Studies Journal* 1 (Fall 1998).

39. Jon Alterman, "The Information Revolution and the Middle East," in *The Future Security Environment in the Middle East,* eds. Dan Byman and Nora Bensahel (Santa Monica, CA: RAND, 2004), 230–231.

40. Lynch, "Beyond the Arab Street," 65.

41. Asef Bayat, "The 'Street' and the Politics of Dissent in the Arab World," *Middle East Report* 226 (2003): 10–17.

42. Marc Lynch, "Not the Enemy," *Arab Reform Bulletin* (April 2004).

43. Jillian Schwedler, "More than a Mob: the Dynamics of Political Demonstrations in Jordan," *Middle East Report* 2256 (2003): 18–23.

44. Marc Lynch, *Voices of the New Arab Public: Iraq, Al Jazeera, and Middle East Politics Today* (New York: Columbia University Press, 2006); Shibley Telhami, *The Stakes* (Boulder, CO: Westview, 2003).

45. The Internet appears to play a larger role in stimulating dissent in Iran; see Babak Rahimi, "Cyberdissent: the Internet in Revolutionary Iran," *MERIA* 7(3) (2003).

46. Grey Burkhart and Susan Older, *The Information Revolution in the Middle East and North Africa* (Santa Monica, CA: RAND, 2003).

47. Burkhart and Older, *The Information Revolution,* x.

48. Gary R. Bunt, *Islam in the Digital Age* (London: Pluto Press, 2003).

49. Lawrence Wright, "The Terror Web," *The New Yorker,* August 2, 2004.

50. Personal interview, Aida Dabbas, Amman, May 2002; see Jillian Schwedler, "More than a Mob," *Middle East Report* 226 (2003): 18–23.

51. Dale Eickelman, "Kings and people," in *Iran, Iraq and the Gulf States,* ed. J. Kechichian (New York: Palgrave Macmillan, 2003).

52. Ali Mohammadi and Annabelle Sreberny Mohammadi, *Small Media, Big Revolutions* (Minneapolis: University of Minnesota, 1994).

53. Shanthi Kalathil and Taylor Boas, *Open Networks Closed Regimes* (Washington DC: Carnegie, 2003), 103. Thanks to Ron Deibert for suggestions on this point.

54. Kalathil and Boas, *Open Networks Closed Regimes,* 2003; Burkhart and Older, *The Information Revolution,* 2003.

55. Jonathan Zittrain and Benjamin Edelman, "Documentation of Internet Filtering in Saudi Arabia," Berkman Center for Internet & Society, Harvard Law School, Cambridge, MA (2003).

56. Burkhart and Older, *The Information Revolution,* 38.

57. For an interesting discussion, see W. Sean McLaughlin, "The Use of the Internet for Political Action by Dissident Actors in the Middle East," *First Monday* 8(11) (2003).

58. Sreberny, "Mediated Culture," 111.

59. Gregory White, "Risking the Strait: Moroccan Labor Migration to Spain," *Middle East Report* 218 (2001): 26–29.

60. David McMurray, "Recent Trends in Middle East Migration," *Middle East Report* 211 (1999): 16–19.

61. Malcolm Kerr and El Sayed Yassin, eds., *Rich and Poor States in the Middle East* (Boulder, CO: Westview, 1982); Laurie A. Brand, *States and Their Emigrants* (New York: Cambridge University Press, 2006).

62. Sullivan, "Globalization: Trade and Investment."

63. Sheila Carapico, "Euro-Med," *Middle East Report* 220 (2001): 24–28.

64. For example, see chapter 6 "Societal Security" in Barry Buzan and Ole Waever, *Security: A New Framework for Analysis* (Boulder, CO: Lynne Rienner, 1999), and Bill McSweeney, *A Sociology of Security* (Cambridge: Cambridge University Press, 2001).

65. Christopher Rudolph, "Security and the Political Economy of International Migration," *American Political Science Review* 97(4) (2003): 603–620.

66. Pew Global Attitudes Survey 2003; a Zogby International survey in June 2004 found that a stunning 98 percent of Egyptians had negative views of the United States.

67. Graham Allison, "How to Stop Nuclear Terror," *Foreign Affairs* 83(1) (2004): 64–74.

68. "The Future of the Arab identity in Light of American Pressure," *No Limits*, Al Jazeera, October 8, 2003. All translations from the Arabic by the author.

69. "The Western Cultural Invasion," *The Opposite Direction*, Al Jazeera, February 26, 2002.

70. *Gulf News*, March 22, 2002.

71. Tawfiq Taha, interviewing Egyptian culture minister Farouq Husni, "Arab Culture in an Age of Globalization," *Today's Interview*, Al Jazeera, November 19, 2003. A sample of recent Al Jazeera programs on this topic includes "The Western Cultural Invasion," *The Opposite Direction*, February 26, 2002; "The Future of the Arab Identity in the Face of American Pressure," *No Limits*, November 8, 2003; "Effects of Western Culture and Thought on the Arab Nation," *The Jazeera Platform*, September 22, 2003: "The Dangers of Western Programming in the Arab Media," *No Limits*, March 2004.

72. A cross-section of views on globalization: Galal Amin, *The Globalization of Conquest* (Cairo: Dar al-Sharouq, 2002); Burhan Ghalyoun and Samir Amin, *The Culture of Globalization and the Globalization of Culture* (Beirut: Dar al-Fikr, 1999); Hassan Hanafi and Sadiq Jalal al-Azm, *What is Globalization?* (Beirut: Dar al-Fikr, 1999); Yusuf al-Qaradawi, *Muslims and Globalization* (Cairo: Dar al Tawzi wa al Nashr al Islamiyya, 2000).

73. Qaradawi, *Muslims and Globalization*, 4.

74. Salwa Ismail, "Confronting the Other," *International Journal of Middle Eastern Studies* 30 (1998): 81–94.

75. Carrie Rosefsky-Wickham, *Mobilizing Islam* (New York: Columbia University Press, 2001).

76. Michael Hudson, "Managing Unruly Regions in an Age of Globalization," *Middle East Policy* 9(4) (2002): 65.

77. Stephen Vertigans and Philip Sutton, "Globalisation Theory and Islamic Praxis," *Global Society* 16(1) (2002): 31–53, quote on 32. Also see Said Amir Arjomand, "Islam, Political Change, and Globalization," *Thesis Eleven* 76 (2004), 9–28.

78. Jason Burke, *Al Qaeda: Casting a Shadow of Terror* (New York: St. Martins, 2003).

79. Ann Florini, *The Coming Democracy* (Washington, DC: Island Press, 2003).

80. Dan Benjamin and Steve Simon, *The Age of Sacred Terror* (New York: Random House, 2002), gives a good (if somewhat apologetic) account of the Clinton administration's approach to al Qaeda in the 1990s.

81. Etel Solingen, *Regional Orders* (Princeton, NJ: Princeton University Press, 1999).

82. Steven Heydemann, ed., *War, Institutions, and Social Change in the Middle East* (Berkeley: University of California Press, 2000); Nazih Ayubi, *Over-Stating the Arab State* (New York: I. B. Tauris, 1995).

83. Council on Foreign Relations, "Terrorist Financing."

84. Marc Lynch, "Taking Arabs Seriously," *Foreign Affairs* 82(5) (September/October 2003): 81–94.
85. Daniel Byman, "Al Qaeda as an Adversary," *World Politics* 56 (2003): 139–163; Jason Burke, "Al Qaeda after Madrid," *Prospect* (June 2004), available at http://www.prospect-magazine.co.uk/ArticleView.asp?P_article=12678.

7

GLOBALIZATION AND NATIONAL SECURITY AFTER EMPIRE

The Former Soviet Space

Alexander Cooley

BY MOST ACCOUNTS, GLOBALIZATION PLAYED a critical role in the collapse of the Soviet Union. The Soviet Union was unable to bear the opportunity costs of maintaining a completely self-sufficient system of economic organization and, by the late 1980s, no longer could compete with a Western economic community that reaped the efficiency advantages of global production chains, international financial markets, and a liberal international trading system.[1] Transnational movements and a global civil society of policy makers, peace activists, and scientists provided ideas and information that further undermined entrenched hard-line Soviet defense policies.[2] By the time that Mikhail Gorbachev ushered in the "new thinking" that favored constructive engagement with the West,[3] global forces had undermined the Soviet monolith to the point that it rapidly unraveled under the weight of economic stagnation, nationalist mobilization, and a new environment of political openness. With the end of the Cold War, Russia and its former imperial satellites were thrust into a period of internal transition and geopolitical uncertainty, as many debated the merits of reorienting themselves away from Eurasia and toward the West.[4]

Although international relations scholars have pointed to how globalization contributed to the Soviet collapse, few have systematically theorized about the effects of globalizing processes on the state formation and national security of the post-Soviet states.[5] Unlike the other regions under consideration in this volume, the very formation and development of the *post*-Soviet space has coincided with the era of globalization, making an examination of how global exchange, marketization, and the rise of nonstate actors affect post-Soviet security all the more analytically instructive.

Lately, media depictions of Eurasian politics have produced images of terrorist insurgencies in the Caucasus, al Qaeda–type suicide operations in Moscow, and the smuggling of radioactive materials, weapons, and narcotics across Central Asia, suggesting that the nefarious elements of globalization have infiltrated even the previously insulated Eurasian region. Indeed, even Russian President Vladimir Putin observed in December 2003, that "drugs, terrorism and money laundering are links of one chain."[6] This image also fits the broader emerging narrative in security studies that globalization has created a category of nonstate actors such as criminal organizations and terrorist movements that now threaten the fundamental security of nation-states.[7]

As I will argue later in this essay, there is much that is actually correct about this alarmist view, although the involvement of the state and its security institutions in these globalizing processes is much more instrumental than the Russian president and many globalization theorists acknowledge. But, as Jonathan Kirshner underscores in chapter 1, the claim that globalization inevitably undermines state security is neither analytically helpful nor empirically new.[8] Missing from most analyses of globalization and national security is not so much an identification of the global actors that might challenge state security and authority, but a theoretical explanation of why states' capacities for coping with these global threats vary so greatly. The post-Soviet cases suggest that globalization not only weakens the capacity of states in security matters, as other contributors to this volume also point out, but that the global processes of exchange and marketization can alter, condition, and even "criminalize" the very functions and organizational purpose of a state's security apparatus.

This essay advances an organizational theory of the relationship between globalizing processes and the evolution of national security within a particular institutional domain: the postimperial state. My central argument is that the fragmented organizational structures of postimperial states, especially in the security sphere, differ significantly from those of traditional states. Whereas Western states maintain a clear differentiation among security functions, organs, and agencies, postimperial states lack these distinctions and an overall rationalization of their state security structures. As in Robert Jackson's "quasi-states" formulation, postimperial states lack positive sovereignty and the ability to effectively monopolize, organize, and control the use of violence within their boundaries.[9] Given this starting point, the global processes under consideration in this volume—particularly the legal and illegal international economic exchange described by Kirshner; the market for private security as described by Deborah Avant; the flows and the networking of people as described by Fiona Adamson—tend to criminalize the operations of security institutions, diminish the capacity of states to cope with external security threats, and blur distinctions between the various functions associated with internal and external security.

Much like Marc Lynch suggests in chapter 6 on the Middle East, globalization has significantly affected the security of the post-Soviet space, but not in the sanguine "liberalizing" or interdependence-promoting manner in which the term is popularly understood. In fact, rather than promote the normalization of security institutions, globalization has exacerbated these institutional dysfunctions across the post-Soviet states. It will continue to do so unless a set of international organizations or other external actors, such as the North Atlantic Treaty Organization (NATO) or the European Union (EU), impose a comprehensive institutional conditionality that can standardize and reorganize the security apparatus of these states.

I begin by contrasting the organization forms of two types of states, the traditional state and the postimperial state, and show how the security institutions of the latter are characterized by declining functional differentiation, organizational corruption and chronic rent-seeking, and severe control or agency problems. After specifying certain hypotheses concerning globalization and postimperial state security, I examine the organizational legacies of the Soviet collapse and the security structures of the region's states. Next, I illustrate these theoretical claims about the effects of globalization on the region's security apparatus with evidence from the post-Soviet space, focusing on elements of the arms trade and weapons smuggling, the rise of mercenaries and private security actors, and the expansion of illicit markets. I find that the global processes of exchange and marketization, in particular, have exerted a profound impact on the capacity and very nature of the post-Soviet state. In the final section, I explore how these state dysfunctions have prevented post-Soviet authorities from adequately coping with the security threats posed by emerging nonstate actors such as criminal and terrorist movements, before offering some tentative conclusions.

THE ARGUMENT: GLOBALIZATION AND POSTIMPERIAL SECURITY INSTITUTIONS

The Organizational Structure of Traditional and Postimperial States

Traditionally, states follow a centralized organizational form in which various functional divisions of governance correspond to certain ministries or departments. Ministries, in turn, are responsible for implementing general policies within their particular functional or issue areas. Usually, the center determines the state's general priorities, overall goals, and jurisdictional responsibilities and provides the revenues necessary to finance each ministry's operations. Although the scope of state functions may vary somewhat (i.e., a totalitarian state may perform a wider array of functions than a more limited liberal state), this type of organizational structure holds for most modern states with some degree of bureaucratic capacity.

The organization of political violence and security-related functions also follows such an organizational structure. Different security-related functions such as the armed forces, internal security, law enforcement and policing, border patrol, and intelligence services all usually operate as distinct entities or agencies within the state, and each functional division plays a specified and well-defined role. Of course, the exact functional divisions and security-related jurisdictions will vary across states, as will the centralized state institutions responsible for coordinating them (national security agencies, joint chiefs of staff, etc.), but traditional state security policies are predicated on some variation of this functionally differentiated state structure.

Now consider the organizational structure of a postimperial state or other fragment of a collapsed larger hierarchical entity. In all likelihood, the new state will not inherit intact the broad array of functional bureaucracies from the larger polity. Instead, the state structure is likely to be composed of a mix of agencies and branches that were locally based during imperial times, as well as a number of collapsed functional divisions that were centrally controlled. Rather than a unitary organizational structure, such states will be characterized by a patchwork-type organizational structure, with various agencies, bureaucratic fragments, and informal networks all co-existing with various levels of capacity, resources, and ties to the new state center. The more centrally organized a particular branch was at the time of hierarchical collapse, the more likely that the postimperial fragment will lack the well-developed organizational characteristics of a coherent agency or mature bureaucratic division. In both the Yugoslav and Soviet federal structures, for example, the armed forces and other external security-related functions were typically tightly controlled by the center and were, therefore, the most likely to disintegrate or unravel within peripheral republics upon hierarchical collapse. As Charles Fairbanks Jr. notes:

> In the Soviet Union and in Yugoslavia, state institutions were much more weaker in the federal units than in the national capitals because the economy, foreign policy, the security police, ideology, and the official appointments were controlled from the center. Thus from the moment of the federal republics' secession their state structures were decisively weaker than the earlier state structure.[10]

The Organizational Imperatives of the Postimperial State

As a result of this patchwork organizational structure, three features will distinguish the political dynamics of postimperial states that would be absent or tempered in traditional states and their security agencies. First, postimperial state agencies are more likely to develop independent mechanisms for revenue extraction. Xiaobo Lu has referred to the process of autonomous rent-seeking by state agencies as "organizational corruption" and has noted that many underfunded state organs in China and other parts of the developing world must raise revenues in this illicit manner to sustain their operations.[11] Obviously, the types of revenue activities will depend on that agency's particular function, asset base, or expertise but may include trading in goods and services, as well as the granting of unofficial regulatory licenses. For security agencies, this will mean commercializing in some manner their security-related activities.

Second, agencies within a postimperial state are more likely to aggressively compete over new areas of functional jurisdiction. Although it is a fundamental characteristic of bureaucracies to fight turf wars against other bureaucracies,[12] both the scale and scope of this dynamic are greatly heightened in the setting of a postimperial state. Wholesale functions once executed by the center may now exist in the most rudimentary or fragmented form, thus becoming prime targets for an organizational "takeover" by other agencies. This is particularly relevant in the security sphere, where the distinctions among security activities can become blurred. Armed forces are liable to step into internal policing and security roles and vice versa, depending on which one had the greater organizational capacity upon the start of independence and which one has maintained stronger institutionalized links to the new central government.[13] Furthermore, new jurisdictional areas related to the control of political violence, such as border patrols or customs posts, can provide enticing revenue-enhancing targets for such agencies. As state agencies undertake multiple tasks, distinctions between various security-related functions such as policing, defense, and the border patrol will become increasingly obscured.

Finally, the patchwork structure of the postimperial state greatly increases the control loss or agency problems faced by the center vis-à-vis its various state organs. As in any set of hierarchical relations, traditional states also face agency problems as a result of the regular process of political delegation.[14] Again, the issue in postimperial states is one of degree. Postimperial agencies that independently pursue rent-seeking activities and expand their jurisdictional scope will be much more difficult for the center to monitor than agencies with a clearly designated functional purpose. The center may even purposefully allow a great deal of "organizational slack" to security agencies, especially if they happen to also serve as the guardians and protectors of the regime in question. At the extreme, warlords and militias that command state resources for substate political purposes may even be tolerated by a weak center that views its political standing as precarious or lacks the resources to combat such defections.[15]

In sum, the organizational differences between postimperial states and traditional states also create distinct organizational imperatives for postimperial security agencies. The proliferation of organizational corruption and revenue-seeking, the expansion of jurisdictional scope, and the exacerbation of control loss problems all come together to reduce the functional differentiation of state agencies and their activities. In the security sphere, this undermines the ability of the state to effectively control, monitor, and organize political violence on its territory.

Globalization and Security in a Postimperial Setting

As defined by the essays in this volume, globalization refers to the "rise and influence of unorganized and stateless forces." Of these forces, the most important for the development of the postimperial state are the processes of exchange—the increasing volume of legal and illegal cross-border transactions—and marketization—the encroachment of market forces into noneconomic areas of social organization. Overall, global exchange and marketization will tend to magnify each of these previous state imperatives and diminish the postimperial state's overall capacity to effectively and exclusively perform security-related functions. The following three hypotheses further specify these processes and interactions.

Hypothesis 1: Globalization offers alternative markets and exchange opportunities for security-related agencies to rent-seek and fund their organizational activities Globalization allows weak or unfunded state institutions to continue their activities by other means rather than restructure their activities or fold their organization. In terms of this volume's analytical framework, global exchange and marketization (processes) undermine and transform state capacity. First, exchange and marketization allow state security agencies to independently raise revenue. Security agencies with access to weaponry, military technology, or other marketable items can engage in asset-stripping and export these items to private clients. State agencies can also offer their services to the global marketplace, either independently or with tacit official acquiescence. In the realm of security, the proliferation of a global market for private security services allows agencies facing budget cuts or other financial constraints to find alternative revenue opportunities and clients.[16] States, therefore, can be suppliers as well as consumers of the global market for security-related goods and services. In addition, the existence of smuggling networks allows state agencies involved with internal security matters to rent-seek and network with the criminal groups that organize these illicit exchange activities. As Peter Andreas suggests, organized smuggling networks always involve some degree of state complicity, usually an agency that must be co-opted or bribed, and the illicit international political economy often intersects with the activities of security-related actors.[17] Again, positions that bring state officials in contact with smuggling or trafficking networks are particularly lucrative for the presiding security agency and the individuals who staff them. As illicit global markets develop, state security agencies are uniquely well-positioned to act as their *de facto* regulators. Diego Gambetta has argued that the mafia and other organized crime groups perform the economic function of regulating unofficial markets.[18] By offering protection services, guaranteeing contracts, and managing dispute settlements, organized crime becomes a de facto regulator of illegal markets in which the state is not present. As analysts of globalization suggest, the worldwide retrenchment of the state, the opening of borders and liberalization of exchange, and the advent of new communications technologies have contributed to the proliferation of global underground markets for illegal goods and finance.[19] The very fact that a security agency might itself be responsible for border patrolling or policing smuggling routes makes these clandestine activities more likely to become encompassed within its informal organizational jurisdiction.

Finally, the involvement of the state within the illicit political economy of smuggling and trafficking has led security analysts to increasingly incorporate these criminal actors and their activities into their analyses of contemporary internal warfare as well as to formulate distinctions between recent and previous wars based on these factors.[20] Indeed, as the Bosnia and Kosovo conflicts suggest, the state's very ability to effectively conduct warfare or perform security functions may be contingent on the success of its various security agencies in regulating and profiting from these illicit markets.[21]

Hypothesis 2: Globalization increases the security threat posed by nonstate actors by weakening the capacity of postimperial states to cope with such transnational actors Second, globalization, perhaps paradoxically, diminishes the capacity of states to respond to transnational security threats such as insurgents, terrorists, and organized crime networks. Effectively combating the threat of nonstate actors requires that states and their security agencies maintain adequate border controls, share information, coordinate tasks with other state agencies, and effectively infiltrate such networks without being co-opted.[22] Such interagency capacity, coordination, and purpose do not typically characterize postimperial states.

Hypothesis 3: Globalization prevents the postimperial state from normalizing its malformed security institutions Finally, as a result of these unofficial organizational activities, globalization actually inhibits the internal processes necessary for the "normalization" of these dysfunctional and criminalized security institutions within a postimperial state. Rather than develop the internal institutions necessary for state building and consolidation, the presence of the global processes of exchange and marketization will hinder effective state formation. The acute agency problems that already characterize relations between central governments and security agencies in postimperial states will only be exacerbated by global processes. Corruption in border patrols and policing, trafficking in arms and military hardware, and the use of state assets to pursue private profits all diminish domestic and international confidence in state-related security institutions. However, the very ability to pursue alternative revenue-seeking activities within the global market might itself be a *quid pro quo* for a certain security agency to maintain its loyalty to a particular regime. Contrary to the expectations that interaction with the international system will homogenize or inevitably rationalize these organizational characteristics, interactions with global markets and economic flows are only likely to institutionalize these types of organizational activities as a normal state of affairs. Similarly, the counterfactual should also hold: effective state formation and internal consolidation would be more likely to transpire in the *absence* of globalization. For example, studies of European state formation and the development of the modern state system have highlighted the importance of the state's ability to develop an effective apparatus for taxation, monopolize the institutions of violence by promoting national militaries, and expand centralized, bureaucratic control.[23] Tellingly, these state formations occurred during eras when the global processes of exchange and marketization were relatively muted.

SOVIET AND POST-SOVIET ORGANIZATION OF SECURITY AND STATE VIOLENCE

Under the Soviet system, security and economic activity were vertically integrated under unionwide ministries and centralized state control. Of the main security functions, the five distinct functional divisions of the armed forces (Ground Forces, Strategic Rocket Forces, Air Forces, National Air Defense Troops, and the Navy) represented the highest priority function of the Soviet state and were assigned to various military districts (noncontiguous with individual republics) under the auspices of the Ministry of Defense.[24] The Committee for State Security (KGB) controlled internal security, intelligence services, and the border patrol, while the Ministry of Internal Affairs (MVD) retained jurisdiction over routine policing and militia matters. Branches of each of these bureaucracies were placed within each Soviet republic, each with varying degrees of accountability to regional organs. Usually, the more sensitive the security function, the more likely that the branch organ would be exclusively accountable to its functional division located in Moscow.

When the Soviet Union collapsed, so too did the various unionwide organizational entities and administrative hierarchies responsible for various security-related functions.[25] The Soviet army was left in organizational disarray, with various ex-republics inheriting varying numbers of Soviet-era troops and nontitular national officers, military hardware, institutional legacies, and nonmovable installations on their respective territories.[26] Moreover, the growth of clandestine security actors, criminal organizations, and ethnically motivated paramilitary organizations during the Gorbachev era further contributed to the unclear division of security-related institutions and functions in the immediate post-Soviet era.

As a result, upon their independence, the post-Soviet states failed to develop well-institutionalized national armed forces, especially as several post-Soviet states (Azerbaijan, Armenia, Georgia, Moldova, and Tajikistan) descended into violent conflicts in 1992 and 1993.[27] Instead, national defense units were pragmatically cobbled together as an assembly of national guardsmen, paramilitary organizations with ties to certain individuals or state agencies, mercenaries, and external forces (usually Russian) charged with specific duties such as peacekeeping or border patrols.[28] Underfunded, ridden with corruption and desertions, and lacking in any organizational capacity, the national militaries of the post-Soviet states are far weaker organizations than they were during Soviet times. Indeed, in most post-Soviet countries, police agencies—the organizational benefactors of the locally organized MVD associations of the Soviet era—have assumed many of the broader security functions that were previously performed by the Moscow-based KGB or even defense forces (see Table 7.1).

For example, a recent International Crisis Group report on Central Asian policing and internal security found that:

> the military in Central Asian states plays a more limited role in everyday political life than the interior ministries. Police forces in the region are much more powerful than the militaries and include their own armed units designed for internal control. They have a considerable role in political life that may grow further in the future. Although the role of militaries in Central Asian societies should not be ignored, the internal security forces pose the greater threat to stability and the greater opposition to deeper economic and political reform.[29]

In sum, the unitary and clearly functionally defined security institutions of the Soviet military gave way in the post-Soviet era to a patchwork of official and nonofficial security organizations with unclear functional roles, organizational mandates, and weak capacities.

GLOBALIZATION AND SECURITY IN THE POST-SOVIET SPACE

Two particular processes of globalization—global exchange and marketization—have exacerbated these organizational legacies and dysfunctions of the post-Soviet states. First, post-Soviet state security agencies have actively used global exchange to further enhance their organizational interests. They have sold their assets and services on both the official and unofficial global markets and, by so doing, managed to maintain their operations after the Soviet collapse. Security agencies have also regulated the structure and operation of illicit markets, as the

Table 7.1 Comparative Number of Internal and External Security Troops, 2003

Country or Region	National Armed Forces	Police and Internal Security	Ratio External: Internal Forces	Armed Forces per Population	Police Forces per Population
		CIS			
Russia	860,000	700,000	1.23	1:168	1:206
		Western NIS			
Belarus	82,900	98,000	0.85	1:125	1:105
Moldova	8,500	16,000	0.53	1:522	1:277
Ukraine	303,800	386,000[a]	0.79		
		Caucasus			
Armenia	44,667[b]	50,000[c]	0.89	1:74	1:67
Azerbaijan	64,820[e]	50,000[d]	1.30	1:121	1:157
Georgia	18,200	80,000[i]	0.23	1:271	1:62
		Central Asia			
Kazakhstan	60,150	69,000[ii]	0.87	1:279	1:243
Kyrgyzstan	11,000	19,000	0.58	1:445	1:258
Tajikistan	6,000	28,800[iii]	0.21	1:1144	1:238
Turkmenistan	17,500	25,500	0.69	1:273	1:187
Uzbekistan	70,000	200,000	0.35	1:371	1:130
		Other			
Hungary	39,000	37,000	1.05	1:258	1:271
Belgium	39,655	40,000	0.99	1:259	1:257
New Zealand	8,750	7,100	1.23	1:452	1:557
Guatemala	32,200	9,800	3.29	1:432	1:1419
Peru	120,000	89,000	1.35	1:237	1:319
Cameroon	13,650	9,000	1.52	1:1154	1:1750
Botswana	7,800	4,695	1.66	1:202	1:335
Jordan	100,500[d]	25,000	4.02	1:54	1:218
Sri Lanka	110,000	80,000	1.38	1:179	1:247
Thailand	240,000	120,000	2.00	1:268	1:536

(continued)

smuggling and trafficking of illegal goods such as narcotics have become vital components of their operations. The origins of such illicit activities can be traced to the Perestroika era when official decentralization

Table 7.1 (continued) Comparative Number of Internal and External Security Troops, 2003

created an environment for the systematic stripping and selling of state-owned assets;[30] however, the general lawless environment encouraged by Russia's radical shock-therapy-style economic reforms in the early 1990s created unprecedented opportunities to expand this unofficial international exchange, especially in security sectors.[31] Thus, although the tendencies for illicit exchange were evident in the late Soviet era, the post-Soviet states' interaction with global processes afforded them immediate opportunities to profit from their security-related assets and activities.

Post-Soviet Security Agency Revenue-Seeking and Exchange in Official Markets

Much of the security-related exchange activities involve the direct descendants of the old Soviet military-industrial complex. Officially, the military-industrial complex remains an important domestic influence in Russian politics and the Russian government seems determined to support and promote strategic sectors.[32] Given a very limited and cash-strapped domestic market for these specialized military goods, globalization has afforded various defense-related industries the opportunity to reorient their production for the new global market for military hardware. As Rachel Epstein notes in chapter 8, ailing post-Soviet defense industries face stiff competition from European companies that also desperately seek new global clients and markets. The emergence of a truly global market for weapons and military hardware has allowed former Soviet state defense companies to continue their production, but, unlike the European Union suppliers that Epstein describes, post-Soviet producers and their governments do not seem overly concerned with dealing with unsavory international clients. The Russian state-owned company Rosvooruzhnie (Russian Armaments) increased its export sales in the year 2000 to $2.8 billion in sales (out of a total of $3.4 billion) to 49 different countries, helping to make Russia the fourth largest exporter of arms in the world.[33] The Russian nuclear energy ministry (Minatom) has also stepped up its export activities to about $2.6 billion in 2003, including continuing a major project (worth $800 million and 20,000 Russian skilled jobs) to construct a nuclear complex in Bushehr, Iran, over the public objections of US officials.[34] This has raised concerns over Iran's weapons of mass destruction (WMD) production potential and Russia's role in global nuclear proliferation.

Even though buyers such as Iran and China may be out of favor with the West, the global market for security-related industries offers an important source of hard currency for Russia's producers, and Moscow has demonstrated a commitment to reinvigorating these sectors.[35] As Robert Legvold observes of the link between Soviet-era military-industrial organization and post-Soviet economic developments in Ukraine and Belarus,

> not only do the remnants of the Soviet architecture create dependencies whose organizational and economic imperatives compel leaderships to live with a fragmented, non-viable military-industrial base, they also push them to hawk their arms abroad, even when selling in some markets adds to international instability and angers potential supporters.[36]

Similarly, Kimberly Marten Zisk has observed that across a broad array of former Soviet defense-related industries, enterprise managers opportunistically initiated a number of new spin-offs and start-ups from the larger enterprise, thus ensuring their survival in a time of economic crisis.[37] As Zisk suggests, the activities of these "daughter enterprises" are by their very nature secretive and make it difficult for the Russian state to accurately assess, monitor, and tax these enterprises, let alone regulate their production and exports within the global marketplace.[38]

Asset Stripping and the Unofficial Markets for State-Produced Military Goods

Unofficially, the exchange opportunities afforded by international markets have allowed state security agencies to both appropriate and illegally sell state assets and resources on the global market as well as to engage in explicitly illegal activities such as drug and human trafficking. In both cases, international exchange has been facilitated by the cooperation of organized criminal networks with well-developed international business contacts and networks. The illicit exchange opportunities afforded by globalization have been every bit as significant, if not more so, as official exchange.

The collapse of the Soviet army generated seemingly unlimited numbers of minimally guarded supply depots, ammunitions dumps, military garrisons, and arms-producing plants. For instance, in 1992, the Ukrainian-Siberian Commodity Exchange switched from brokering commodity trades to selling Soviet-era fighter planes, tanks, and antiaircraft systems, as global buyers rushed to find military hardware at bargain prices.[39] Russia's military procurator's office estimates that from 1995 to 2001, over 8,000 firearms were stolen from army storage, with 184 servicemen convicted of illicit arms trafficking in 2001 alone.[40] In 2003, the military procurator estimated that 1,700 crimes were committed against federal property, with criminal proceedings initiated against 1,100 military service members.[41] Clients for these assets have ranged from global arms traffickers, to international criminal organizations, to local private actors undertaking security-related and protection activities.

As Graham Turbville observes of the scope of these unofficial activities, the Russian armed forces since independence have been involved in

> smuggling crimes of all types (particularly drugs and armed trafficking), the massive diversion of equipment and materials, illegal business ventures, and coercion and criminal violence … financial crimes and schemes involving a spectrum of banks and financial organizations, real and dummy corporations, joint ventures with foreign partners, and overseas money laundering schemes.[42]

The proliferation of such criminal activities has even led some to speculate that Russian criminal organizations and their state security collaborators actively constitute a global security threat.[43] For example, in April 2001, Italian authorities arrested Russian and Ukrainian members of a crime network that had smuggled over 13,400 tons of weaponry to various fighting factions in the Balkans (including the Croatian army) and, just a few months later, dismantled a similar network that was trafficking weapons to Charles Taylor's forces in Sierra Leone.[44]

Stripped and smuggled military assets have also been used within post-Soviet conflict settings. For example, the weapons pipeline to rebel factions in Chechnya has regularly been supplied by Russian personnel and even soldiers stationed in the region. In addition, the Russian military in Chechnya is widely rumored to be siphoning off oil and facilitating smuggling, thereby further entrenching themselves in the region as a result of these lucrative spin-off activities.[45] In the spring of 2002, a discovery of Russian-manufactured Igla man-portable air defense system (MANPADS) missile launchers in Vedeno prompted Russian security officials to accuse Georgia of selling these weapons systems to Arab mercenaries operating in Chechnya.[46] Georgian officials countered that, in fact, troops at the sovereign Russian military base of Akhalkalaki (in southern Georgia) had illegally sold the systems to the Chechen rebels.[47] In fact, many observers have reported that unmonitored Russian military personnel on these bases regularly smuggle weapons and hardware. Russian troops are also accused of having smuggled arms to factions in Abkhazia, Ossetia, Nagorno Karabakh, and Moldova during the early 1990s (although some would argue with tacit government approval).

Illegal Exchange: Rent-Seeking and the Market for Illicit Goods

The exchange, regulation, and financing of illicit goods has been another source of revenue extraction for many state security agencies. The tacit regulation of illegal economic sectors is a function that post-Soviet agencies are undertaking, also usually in cooperation with various international criminal networks and other transnational actors with global links.

Of all the smuggling networks within the post-Soviet space, the most lucrative remains the drug trade, especially in the former Central Asian republics. The United Nations estimates that about 75 percent of the world's opium (and all of European and Russian supply) is produced in Afghanistan and about half that Afghan production passes through the post-Soviet Central Asian states.[48] Drug trafficking is a major revenue source for various involved parties in transit countries. Kyrgyz Deputy Prime Minister of National Security Miroslav Niyazov estimated that narcotics trafficked through Kyrgyzstan alone is worth about $1 billion annually to international crime syndicates.[49] The United Nations Office on Drugs and Crime (UNODC) estimates that income from drug trafficking accounts for about 35 percent of Tajikistan's gross domestic product (GDP).[50] Although the amount of opium seized by Central Asian border guards has increased every year, these interdictions have been minor compared to the rise in production over the same time. The border guard, police units, and government officials receive kickbacks for allowing the majority of shipments to pass through.[51] The International Crisis Group estimates that the internal security forces of Kyrgyzstan and Tajikistan have become so dependent on these illicit markets that the central government provides only 25 percent of their operating budgets.[52] In addition to the Central Asian countries, all three countries of the Caucasus are regularly cited as transshipment points for narcotics. The freelancing military units of the breakaway Transdniestria region in Moldova also allegedly structure and manage the trafficking of drugs and weapons—about $2 billion worth a year—in order to finance their activities.[53]

The global smuggling of people, in addition to drugs and contraband, is also a lucrative business in the Eurasian region and another illicit market that is regulated by state security agencies in collusion with organized crime. The trafficking in women from various former Soviet republics is now a multibillion dollar business with well-established supply chains throughout the Eurasian space.[54] In 1998, the Ukrainian Ministry of Interior estimated that over 400,000 Ukrainian women had been illegally trafficked since independence, a number that domestic and international NGOs dispute as too low.[55] In 1999 alone, four thousand Kyrgyz women and girls were illegally sold abroad as sex workers to the Gulf states, China, Turkey, and Eastern Europe.[56] In certain conflict-ridden areas, kidnapping and ransoms can also provide important sources of revenue. In Chechnya, various militant and rebel groups have used ransoms from the kidnapping of foreign aid and humanitarian workers as their primary source of hard currency.

Those political entities or quasi states that lack access to official international sources of revenue seeking—IMF, World Bank, international capital markets, and bond issues—have little alternative but to rely on the underground world economy to raise revenues and establish payments systems. This seems to be especially applicable to the *de facto* states that have been established in the Eurasian territories of Nagorno-Karabakh (in Azerbaijan), Abkhazia (in Georgia), Ossetia (Georgia), Transdniestria (Moldova), as well as portions of Chechnya (Russian Federation). Charles King has observed that the police and militia forces of these regions are the main facilitators of commerce, regulating the transit of everything from petrol to cigarettes and narcotics.[57] Indeed, the involvement of international humanitarian agencies and international organizations in these conflict areas provides the only internationally "legal" injection of foreign exchange into these territorial economies.

Of course, the greatest US security concern in the area of illicit exchange remains that nuclear-related materials will be illegally sold on the black market and may be acquired by organizations with links to international terrorist networks. Several interdictions of Russian uranium and fissile materials in the mid-1990s further added to the Western perception of a "loose nukes" problem. According to Rensselaer Lee III, the nuclear black market involves two types of criminal syndicates—career criminals and "bureaucratic criminals"—composed of active or retired state employees, including military officers, naval personnel, and KGB operatives.[58] However, these criminal groups also act pragmatically and do not maintain any permanent organizational structure to traffic these materials in the way they do other contraband sectors. Major seizures of Soviet-era fissile materials in Munich and Prague in 1994 revealed that even though the traffickers were immersed in a dense international trading network, they were still actively looking for buyers for the materials.[59] Moreover, although certain terrorist organizations such as al Qaeda would undoubtedly like to procure nuclear materials, the exact market demand outside of international sting operations is almost impossible to assess with any certainty.[60]

Post-Soviet Security Agencies and the Marketization of Security Services

As described by Deborah Avant in chapter 4, the rise of a global private security industry over the last decade has been remarkable,[61] but its growth within Russia and the other ex-Soviet republics is especially noteworthy. With the downsizing of the Soviet "power ministries" (the KGB/Federal Security Service [FSB], MVD, and Defense Ministry) in the 1990s, a flood of security personnel was unleashed into a rapidly privatizing economy and relatively lawless environment.[62] With minimal initial regulatory oversight and the liberalization of financial transactions, the demand and financing for private security quickly created a glut of private security firms that became both the guardians and beneficiaries of the Russian economic transition. The sheer number of private security businesses in Russia is staggering, having more than doubled from 4,540 in 1993 to 11,652 in 1999, absorbing about 50,000 former officers of Soviet state security agencies (see Table 7.2).[63]

Table 7.2 Growth of Private Security Sector in Russia by Year

	1992	1993	1994	1995	1996	1997	1998	1999
Total number of private agencies	0	4,540	6,605	7,987	9,863	10,487	10,804	11,652
Private protection companies	0	1,237	1,586	3,247	4,434	5,280	5,995	6,775
Private security agencies	0	2,356	2,931	4,591	5,247	5,005	4,580	4,612
Agencies closed by authorities	0		73	690	622	978	1,364	1,277

Source: Vadim Volkov, *Violent Entrepreneurs* (Ithaca: Cornell University Press, 2002), p. 138, Table 3.

Private security businesses include private protection companies and private security services and, by a 1992 law detailing licensing procedures, all Russian enterprises are entitled to establish security-related subdivisions.[64] Analytically, distinguishing between PSCs and other forms of extrastate violence-wielding groups such as the mafia is often difficult given that both groups employ former Soviet security personnel, both provide protection services for various commercial enterprises, and both maintain institutionalized links to various state agencies and bureaucracies.[65] In November 2000, the head of Russia's Interior Ministry's Main Administration for Public Order observed that half of the country's 12 largest private security firms (employing over 200,000) served as fronts for organized crime and explained that his agency had revoked the licenses of over 2,000 such firms.[66] Although the Russian state is now trying to more carefully monitor and clamp down on the activities of PSCs, as Avant observes, the marketization of security functions in the post-Soviet era undoubtedly has redistributed power away from the central state toward certain powerful groups and organizations within Russian society.

Military-related or mercenary activities have also proliferated within the post-Soviet space. With their national militaries in economic and organizational disarray, former skilled fighters such as pilots or special operatives initially found lucrative opportunities for employment in regional conflicts precipitated by the Soviet collapse. For instance, Ukrainian and Russian pilots (mostly stationed from a recently disbanded unit in Latvia) were hired by the Azerbaijani Defense Ministry to fly MIG-25 sorties into Nagorno-Karabakh.[67] Azerbaijan was also accused of hiring Afghan troops in an attempt to bolster its failing ground campaign in the same area during the summer of 1992.[68] At some point in the early 1990s, Russia, Armenia, Azerbaijan, Transdniestria, Uzbekistan, Chechnya, Taliban, and Northern Alliance Afghanistan, as well as international networks of Islamic militants, had all reportedly financed some private military activity outside of their borders in the post-Soviet space.[69] The most publicized deployment remains the Russian government's increasing use of hired soldiers or *kontraktniki* in Chechnya, a group that have acquired a formidable reputation for their harsh attitudes and brutal actions against civilians.[70]

Post-Soviet private security forces have also supplied personnel and services to external clients outside of Eurasia. In addition to buying a wing of Russian Su-27 fighters, the Ethiopian government hired a number of Russian military experts in a private capacity to run critical military functions such as air defense, radar warfare, and artillery as well as to advise the Ethiopian government on basic military strategy.[71]

According to Peter Singer, every meeting of the Ethiopian General Staff during its Eritrean campaign included the guiding participation of hired Russian advisors, and other accounts have speculated that Russian pilots were flying aircraft for both sides during the Ethiopian-Eritrean border conflict.[72] Ukrainian soldiers have been reportedly hired for combat services in the former Yugoslavia, North Africa, Southern Africa, and the Middle East,[73] and a reported band of 300 mercenaries fought on behalf of rebels in Sierra Leone in 1997 and 1998, an allegation that the Ukrainian government continues to deny.[74] It is now widely acknowledged that a number of different Russian mercenaries fought for Serbian forces in Kosovo, thereby making the injection of Russian peacekeepers after the conflict more difficult for the Kosovar population to accept. Finally, other ex-Soviet PSCs have formally folded themselves into larger international or Western-based security-related corporations. For example, the Moscow-based Alpha firm, a descendant of the Soviet-era elite special forces organization, was acquired by ArmorGroup to enhance its capacity for operations in the former Soviet states.[75] As Avant observes about the ambiguous relationship between the US government and the activities of US-based MPRI in Croatia, the expanding international market for force affords opportunities to post-Soviet military personnel to offer a broad range of services to global clients, while simultaneously allowing the post-Soviet governments to deny any official responsibility, complicity, or accountability for these groups' activities.

Empirical Reprise: The Effects of Global Exchange and Marketization on the Postimperial State

The involvement of state security agencies in the global underground economy testifies to the weakness of central authorities to both adequately fund and control political violence within and outside of their territories. Through their asset-stripping, provision of services to other clients, and regulation of illicit markets, the security agencies of the post-Soviet state have used the exchange opportunities afforded to them by globalization to pursue self-interested organizational imperatives. Charles Fairbanks goes even further to suggest that a network of patron-client relations has become institutionalized within the post-Soviet state, with central governments ceding significant leeway to security agencies to the pursuit of unofficial revenue-raising activities in exchange for supporting the governing regime.[76]

Taken altogether, the processes of exchange and marketization have eroded the ability of the post-Soviet states to maintain adequate control of their various security agencies. Such principal-agent problems have been aggravated by the patchwork nature of the post-Soviet security state, but the empirical trends suggest that globalization is making the security apparatus in various post-Soviet states less, not more, coherent over time. Without a doubt, the organizational corruption, rent-seeking, and entrepreneurial activities of the post-Soviet security agencies can be starkly contrasted to the centralized and relatively well-maintained military apparatus of the pre-Gorbachev era.

THE RISE OF NONSTATE SECURITY THREATS
AND POST-SOVIET SECURITY INCAPACITIES

Finally, the criminalization of the post-Soviet state, nurtured by globalization, also hampers these governments' ability to successfully eradicate new transnational security threats such as mafia organizations and terrorist groups. Although ethnic and regional conflicts proliferated throughout Eurasia after the Soviet collapse, most are now relatively calm as nonstate actors have now emerged as the primary sources of instability throughout the post-Soviet space.[77] The rise of both militant Islamic insurgent movements as well as the activities of organized transnational criminal networks constitute important challenges to state authority and, in some cases, even regime stability. Although we should be wary of the fact that certain governments might overstate the threat posed by these Islamic groups in order to justify broader crackdowns on political dissidents, the post-Soviet state security agencies seem to lack the capacity to adequately deal with these nonstate groups.

Islamic movements with international ties emerged as a primary security threat in the Central Asian states in the late 1990s.[78] For example, the Islamic Movement of Uzbekistan (IMU) had developed extensive ties with al Qaeda in Afghanistan and Osama bin Laden reportedly made its leader—Juma Namangani—an al Qaeda deputy before the Uzbek was killed in fighting in Afghanistan in the fall of 2001.[79] Prior to the US campaign in Central Asia, the IMU had launched multiple guerrilla-like assaults throughout Uzbekistan and its neighbors. IMU forces were remarkably effective in their guerrilla campaign and managed to finance their operations through extensive drug smuggling made possible through collusion with local law enforcement officials and a notoriously corrupt Central Asian border guard. The IMU insurgents also mounted raids into Kyrgyzstan and kidnapped foreign workers, including a group of Japanese geologists in the south of the country, prompting the Kyrgyz government to appeal to the international community for help. Most recently, the rapidly growing militant Islamic movement Hizb ut-Tahrir, a movement born out of a Palestinian group and currently based in London, has been identified as a growing threat to regional governments. The movement, which officially advocates nonviolent means to establish an Islamic government, is active in all the Central Asian republics and is rumored to be networking and unifying a number of previously distinct regional groups such as the IMU, Uighur separatists, and isolated al Qaeda cells.[80] The April 2004 coordinated suicide attacks and market bombings in Uzbekistan, which killed about 50 people and were blamed on Hizb ut-Tahir, signal that radical Islamic elements continue to reorganize, network, and mount periodic attacks on the Central Asian governments.

In the Caucasus, a striking rise in Islamic militant activity has been accompanied by a dwindling state capacity to intercept and eradicate these movements. A flood of Islamic militants in the republic of Dagestan helped to provoke the second Russian military campaign in Chechnya. Elements of the Chechen resistance cemented their status as a terrorist organization when in October 26, 2002, a Russian special forces operation in a Moscow theater hostage crisis resulted in 170 deaths. Among the dozens of Chechen factions that are fighting Russian troops in the small breakaway republic, some are financed by external patrons such as Saudi Arabia, Jordan, and Pakistan, with some possibly having received training and funds from al Qaeda.[81] Russian Presidential Aide Sergei Yastrzhembsky declared in 2001 that Russian intelligence estimated that about 200 foreign mercenaries were hired by rebel militias and actively involved in the region.[82] Perhaps no other incident symbolizes the global links of these transnational actors better than the accusation that Chechen rebel forces were actively recruiting for their cause in English universities, including the London School of Economics.[83] The Russian government, like its Central Asian governments, has an interest in exaggerating the links of Islamic and terrorist insurgents to foreign Islamic networks in an effort to conflate their domestic anti-insurgent campaigns with the ongoing "war on terror."

Similarly, neighboring Georgia's Pankisi Gorge has become an infamous safe haven for criminal organizations and Islamists involved in drug trafficking and kidnapping, as well as a hiding place for Chechen rebels. With endemic corruption, two breakaway provinces within its borders, and the dominance of regional warlords at the expense of the center, Georgia is very much a failing state with little capacity to police internally, let alone patrol its borders and mount effective counterinsurgency campaigns. In the summer of 2002, Russia engaged in covert operations against Chechen rebels in the gorge and even threatened to send troops into Georgian territory.[84] Concerns over Pankisi were so great that in 2002, then Georgian President Edward Sheverdnadze invited 200 US troops to train the Georgian army in counterinsurgency operations. Currently, Russia and Georgia partly defused tensions by agreeing to joint border patrols of the region.[85] Although Georgian-Russian relations have improved under the leadership of President Mikhail Saakashvili following the "Rose Revolution" in late 2003, the country's institutions remain mired in organizational disarray and institutionalized corruption. Until Georgia and the other institutionally weak post-Soviet states find a way to normalize their security services and state structures, authorities will lack the capacity to adequately address the growing security challenge posed by transnational actors.

But perhaps no other events illustrate how security agency dysfunctions have reduced the ability to effectively combat terrorism than reports indicating that in three of the biggest terrorist incidents in Russia in recent years—the 2002 Moscow theater hostage crisis, the September 2004 suicide bombings, and the Beslan attack—terrorists bribed Russian security forces prior to committing their acts.[86] The investigation of the Moscow theater hostage crisis indicated that the Chechen gunmen had bribed over 100 police and security officials at checkpoints between Chechnya and Moscow, including a group of police officers at railway stations who were about to inspect the gunmen's bags.[87] In September 2004, it was revealed that one of two Chechen suicide bombers, who simultaneously blew up two Sibir Air flights from Moscow, had bribed her way on to the plane.[88] Underscoring the point, Aleksandr Torshin, chairman of the parliamentary commission inquiry into the Beslan attack, commented about the area's security forces that, "Corruption, total corruption [is what we see] in the North Caucasus."[89] In a post-Beslan story on police corruption and Russia's ineffective response to terrorism, one Russian newspaper noted, "some police chase terrorists while others cover the latter for bribes. And now we are surprised that caches with weapons and TNT are found right near Moscow everyday."[90]

CONCLUSIONS: GLOBALIZATION AND SECURITY IN THE POSTIMPERIAL STATE

I have argued that the patchwork of post-Soviet security agencies, their lack of clear functional distinctions, and their organized corruption are nourished and even exacerbated by the processes of globalization under consideration by this volume. Although much of the globalization literature points to the rationalizing and homogenizing impacts that international flows have on state economies, my findings suggest that in conditions where institutions are initially underdeveloped, globalization serves to exacerbate, not correct, such institutional dysfunctions.

The basic problem currently confronting the post-Soviet states is that because these globalized networks symbiotically developed during the state formation and consolidation following their independence, these legal and illicit multiple functions have become institutionalized as part of their security agencies' organizational missions. State security agencies and markets exist not in tension, as formulations of international political economy often frame the relationship, but in a transformative and mutually reinforcing symbiosis that should be a cause for concern. Cash-strapped and underfunded, central governments have seemingly little choice but to tacitly allow this criminal freelancing on behalf of security forces. The provision of security, in both the private and public spheres, has become an increasingly lucrative and entrepreneurial activity. Accordingly, the very ability of the state to conduct other activities that require a functioning and credible security apparatus will be increasingly constrained. For example, international investors are now skeptical of the ability of post-Soviet security agencies to enforce the security for high-priority direct investments in fixed assets, such as the oil wells, transit pipelines, and mines. As a result, international companies have turned to the international security services market to guarantee their property rights.

Although this essay has focused empirically on the post-Soviet space, the basic argument can be applied to a number of settings, most notably to other postcolonial states after they gained their independence. Postcolonial states lack internal state capacity, must simultaneously manage internal and external threat, and are primarily supported by international legal recognition as opposed to domestic control. Their increasing penetration by various global processes and actors should only further fragment and erode their overall institutional capacity.[91] Perhaps the most analogous organizational structure to the Soviet case is that of the former Yugoslav states, where a mix of former federal institutions and local institutions created a similar patchwork-type state security structure when the Yugoslav state disintegrated. The arguments developed in this paper should be readily testable in both of these settings.

Alternatively, examining the cases in Eastern European states and the Baltic states where security institutions have been normalized since the Communist collapse suggests that international organizations and their accessions requirements could play a constructive role in reversing this dysfunctional development. The extensive reform-oriented conditionality imposed by both the European Union and NATO played a critical role in their institutional development.[92] For example, in Romania and Bulgaria, NATO's conditionality expedited the process of defense industry conversion and forced authorities to more effectively deal with smuggling and trafficking on their non-EU borders.[93] From this perspective, the expansion of NATO even further eastward may be beneficial purely from the standpoint of encouraging comprehensive institutional reforms that would otherwise not be attempted by the post-Soviet governments. Similarly, if Russia were to join the WTO, its ability to provide subsidized energy exports, which it currently uses to exercise political leverage within the post-Soviet space, would be curtailed as a discriminatory practice.[94] Thus, membership in international organizations, not the unchecked processes of global exchange and marketization, may offer the best hope of standardizing the institutional behavior, practices, and policies of the post-Soviet states.

In this era of globalization, the lines distinguishing the operations of state security agencies, security contractors, criminal groups, terrorists, and other militant insurgents are increasingly becoming blurred, but they also demand analytically rigorous explanations. Criminal and terrorist networks may threaten global security, but, conversely, criminalized states are in no position to adequately deal with these global security challenges. Understanding the organizational imperatives facing state security institutions is a necessary step to theorizing the relationships between national security and the political impact of globalization.

NOTES

1. On the material sources of Soviet collapse, see Stephen Brooks and William Wohlforth, "Power, Globalization, and the End of the Cold War: Reevaluating a Landmark Case for Ideas," *International Security* 24(3) (Winter 2000): 5–53.
2. Matthew Evangelista, *Unarmed Forces: The Transnational Movement to End the Cold War* (Ithaca, NY: Cornell University Press, 1999).
3. This literature is vast. For representative examples, see Jeffrey T. Checkel, *Ideas and International Political Change* (New Haven, CT: Yale University Press, 1997); and Robert G. Herman, "Identity, Norms, and National Security: The Soviet Foreign Policy Revolution and the End of the Cold War," in *The Culture of National Security,* ed. Peter Katzenstein (New York: Columbia University Press, 1996).
4. See Dmitri Trenin, *The End of Eurasia: Russia on the Border between Geopolitics and Globalization* (Washington, DC: Carnegie Endowment for International Peace, 2002).
5. There are some notable exceptions. See Georgi M. Derluguian, *Bourdieu's Secret Admirer in the Caucasus: A World-System Biography* (Chicago, IL: University of Chicago Press, 2005); Robert Legvold and Celeste Wallander, eds., *Swords and Sustenance: The Economics of Security in Belarus and Ukraine* (Cambridge, MA: MIT Press, 2004); Rawi Abdelal, *National Purpose in the World Economy: Post-Soviet States in Comparative Perspective* (Ithaca, NY: Cornell University Press, 2001); Rajan Menon, ed., *Russia, the Caucasus and Central Asia: The 21st Century Security Environment* (Armonk, NY: M. E. Sharpe, 1999); and Barnett R. Rubin and Jack Snyder, eds., *Post-Soviet Political Order: Conflict and State-Building* (Boulder, CO: Routledge, 1998).

6. "Drugs, Terrorism, Money Laundering Links of One Chain—Putin," *ITAR-TASS News Agency*, December 5, 2003.

7. For example, see Audrey Kurth Cronin, "Behind the Curve: Globalization and International Terrorism," *International Security* 27(3) (Winter 2002–2003): 30–58.

8. Also see Stephen Krasner, *Sovereignty: Organized Hypocrisy* (Princeton, NJ: Princeton University Press, 2000).

9. Robert Jackson, *Quasi-States: Sovereignty, International Relations and the Third World* (New York: Cambridge University Press, 1990).

10. Charles H. Fairbanks, Jr. "Weak States and Private Armies," in *Beyond State Crisis: Postcolonial Africa and Post-Eurasia in Comparative Perspective*, eds. Mark Beissinger and Crawford Young (Baltimore, MD: Johns Hopkins University Press), 146.

11. Xiabo Lu, "Booty Socialism, Bureau-preneurs, and the State in Transition: Organizational Corruption in China," *Comparative Politics* 32(3) (2000): 273–295.

12. See James Q. Wilson, *Bureaucracy: What Government Agencies Do and Why They Do It* (New York: Basic Books, 2000); and Graham Allison, *Essence of Decision*, 2nd ed. (New York: Pearson Longman, 1999).

13. Indeed, the mode of imperial extrication may determine which type of security actor monopolizes the use of force in the independence era. For instance, in many British colonies, a well-maintained police service became increasingly militarized during decolonization and thus formed the nucleus of the security forces of the postimperial state. See D. M. Anderson and David Killingray, eds., *Policing and Decolonisation: Politics, Nationalism and the Police, 1917–1965* (Manchester: Manchester University Press, 1992).

14. See David Epstein and Sharyn O'Halloran, *Delegating Powers* (New York: Cambridge University Press, 1999).

15. See William Reno, *Warlord Politics and African States* (Boulder, CO: Lynne Rienner, 1998).

16. Peter Singer, *Corporate Warriors* (Ithaca, NY: Cornell University Press, 2003).

17. Peter Andreas, *Border Games: Policing the U.S.-Mexico Divide* (Ithaca, NY: Cornell University Press, 2000), 21–25. Also see Andreas, "Illicit International Political Economy: The Clandestine Side of Globalization," *Review of International Political Economy* 11 (3): 641–652.

18. Diego Gambetta, *The Sicilian Mafia: The Business of Private Protection* (Cambridge, MA: Harvard University Press, 1990).

19. See Andreas, *Border Games*; James Mittelman, *The Globalization Syndrome* (Princeton, NJ: Princeton University Press, 2000), chap. 11; and R. T. Naylor, *Wages of Crime: Black Markets, Illegal Finance, and the Underworld Economy* (Ithaca, NY: Cornell University Press, 2002).

20. See Mary Kaldor, *Old and New Civil Wars: Organized Violence in a Global Era* (Palo Alto, CA: Stanford University Press, 1999), and Stathis Kalyvas, "'New' and 'Old' Civil Wars': A Valid Distinction?" *World Politics* 54(1) (1999): 99–118. See also the World Bank's ongoing research program on "The Economics of Civil Wars, Crime and Violence."

21. On criminality and warfare in Bosnia, see Peter Andreas, "The Clandestine Political Economy of War and Peace," *International Studies Quarterly* 48(1) (Spring 2004): 29–51. On Kosovo, see Adamson, chapter 2 of this volume.

22. On the state requirements to combat such internal security threats, see Peter Andreas and Richard Price, "From War-fighting to Crime-fighting: Transforming the American National Security State," *International Studies Review* 3(3) (Fall 2001): 31–52.

23. On institutional development and state formation in the modern international system, see Hendrik Spruyt, *The Sovereign State and Its Competitors* (Princeton, NJ: Princeton University Press, 1994). On the consolidation of military capacity, see Charles Tilly, *Capital, Coercion and the Formation of European States: AD 990–1990* (Cambridge, MA: Blackwell, 1990). On bureaucratic expansion and administrative centralization, see Thomas Erstman, *Birth of the Leviathan* (New York: Cambridge University Press, 1997); and Reinhard Bendix, *Kings or People: Power and the Mandate to Rule* (Berkeley: University of California Press, 1978).

24. For an organizational overview, see Robert V. Barylski, "The Soviet Military before and after the August Coup: Departization and Decentralization," *Armed Forces & Society* 19(1) (Fall 1992): 27–45.

25. On the collapse of Soviet administrative hierarchies, see Alexander Cooley, *Logics of Hierarchy: The Organization of Empires, States and Military Occupations* (Ithaca, NY: Cornell University Press, 2005).

26. Alexander Cooley, "Imperial Wreckage: Property Rights, Sovereignty and Security in the Post-Soviet Space," *International Security* 24(3) (Winter 2000): 100–125; and Daniel W. Drezner, *The Sanctions Paradox: Economic Statecraft and International Relations* (Cambridge: Cambridge University Press, 1999), 130–230.

27. For an overview of these conflicts, see Barnett Rubin and Jack Snyder, eds., *Post-Soviet Political Order: Conflict and State Building* (New York: Routledge, 1998).

28. Charles H. Fairbanks, "The Post-Communist Wars," *Journal of Democracy* 6(4) (1995): 18–34.

29. International Crisis Group, "Central Asia: The Politics of Police Reform," 1. Accessed at http://www.crisisweb.org/projects/showreport.cfm?reportid=843.

30. Steven Solnick, *Stealing the State* (Cambridge, MA: Harvard University Press, 1998).

31. See William E. Odom, *The Collapse of the Soviet Military* (New Haven, CT: Yale University Press, 1998).

32. For a discussion, see Celeste Wallander, "Economics and Security in Russia's Foreign Policy and the Implications for Ukraine and Belarus," in Legvold and Wallander, *Swords and Sustenance*, 63–100.

33. Michael R. Gordon, "Russia is Pushing to Increase Share in Weapons Trade," *New York Times*, July 14, 2000; and Guy Chazan, "Russia's Defense Industry Launches Bid to Boost Sales," *Wall Street Journal*, July 14, 2000.

34. Eve Conant and Adam Piore, "Open for Business," *Newsweek* (International ed.), September 8, 2003, 31.

35. Wallander, "Economics and Security in Russia's Foreign Policy," 75. Wallander also notes that Russian aircraft manufacturers sell more to China than to the Russian military.

36. Robert Legvold, "The United States, the European Union, NATO and the Economics of Ukrainian and Belarusian Security," in Legvold and Wallander, *Swords and Sustenance*, 195.

37. Kimberly Marten Zisk, *Weapons, Culture, and Self-Interest: Soviet Defense Managers in the New Russia* (New York: Columbia University Press, 1997), chap. 4.

38. Ibid., 125–130.

39. Naylor, *Wages of Crime*, 100.

40. "Supreme Court to Advise on Illegal Arms Trafficking Cases," *ITAR-TASS News Agency*, January 31, 2002.

41. "Russian Military Prosecutor Discusses High Profile Crime in Armed Forces," *Rossiskaya Gazeta*, December 24, 2003.

42. Graham H. Turbville, Jr., "Organized Crime and the Russian Armed Forces," *Transnational Organized Crime* 1(4) (Winter 1995): 63–64.

43. See Jeffrey Robinson, *The Merger: The International Conglomerate of Organized Crime* (New York: Overlook Press, 2000).

44. Louise Shelley, John Picarelli, and Chris Corpora, "Global Crime, Inc." in *Beyond Sovereignty: Issues for a Global Agenda*, ed. Maryann Cusimano Love (Belmont, CA: Wadsworth Publishing, 2002), 149.

45. Remarks by Glenn Howard, president of the American Committee on Chechnya, presented to the Carnegie Council Roundtable on Ethics and Foreign Affairs, New York, April 21, 2004. Also see Yuri Zarakhovic, "Profits of Doom: A Russian Special Ops Commander Says the Chechen War Is Really Being Fought for Oil, Arms and Money," *Time* (Europe), September 28, 2003.

46. Adam Geibel, "Potential MANPAD Threat in Central Asia," *Journal of Electronic Defense* 25(1) (June 2002): 29. On the hybrid governance arrangements that underpin these post-Soviet basing arrangements, see Cooley, "Imperial Wreckage."

47. Geibel, "Potential MANPAD Threat," 29–30.

48. Nancy Lubin, *Narcotics Interdiction in Afghanistan and Central Asia: Challenges for International Assistance* (New York: Open Society Institute, 2002), 5.

49. Lubin, *Narcotics Interdiction in Afghanistan and Central Asia*, 5.

50. See UNODC, *Illegal Drug Trade in Russia* (Freiburg: Max Planck Institute for Foreign and International Criminal Law, 2000), 5.

51. For a sobering account of drug trafficking and corruption on the Tajik-Afghan border, see Aram Roston, "Central Asia's Heroin Problem," *The Nation*, March 25, 2002, 23–25.

52. ICG, "Central Asia: The Politics of Police Reform," i.

53. Eugen Tomiuc, "Presidents from Moscow, Kyiv and Chisnau Discuss Transdniester Trafficking," *RFE/RL Report* (March 2002). Accessed at http://www.rferl.org/nca/features/2002/03/18032002105939.asp. Also see ICG, *Moldova: Regional Tensions Over Transdniestria*, Europe Report No. 157, June 14, 2004 (Brussels/Chisnau: ICG, 2004).

54. See Louise Shelley, "The Trade in People in and from the Former Soviet Union," *Crime, Law & Social Change* 40 (2003): 231–249. Also see Shelley, "Trafficking in Women: A Business Model Approach," *The Brown Journal of World Affairs* 10(1) (Summer/Fall 2003): 119–131.

55. International Migration Organization, *Trafficking in Migrants* 23 (April 2001): 5.

56. Quoted in Ahmed Rashid, *Jihad: The Rise of Militant Islam in Central Asia* (New Haven, CT: Yale University Press, 2002), 129.

57. Charles King, "The Benefits of Ethnic War: Understanding Eurasia's Unrecognized States," *World Politics* 53(4) (2001): 524–552.

58. Rensselaer W. Lee, *Smuggling Armageddon: The Nuclear Black Market in the Former Soviet Union and Europe* (London: St. Martin's Press, 2000), 47–72.

59. Of the six Central European seizures of weapons-usable materials in 1994 and 1995, in five of the cases authorities traced the materials to a supplier in Obninsk, Russia. Lee, *Smuggling Armageddon*, 89.

60. Lee, *Smuggling Armageddon*, 140–141.

61. See also P. W. Singer, *Corporate Warriors* (Ithaca, NY: Cornell University Press, 2003).

62. See Vadim Volkov, *Violent Entrepreneurs: The Use of Force in the Making of Russian Capitalism* (Ithaca, NY: Cornell University Press, 2002), 126–154. On the lack of state capacity during Russian privatization, see Michael McFaul, "State Power, Institutional Change, and the Politics of Privatization in Russia," *World Politics* 47(2) (January 1995): 210–243.

63. Volkov, *Violent Entrepreneurs*, 138. According to Volkov, as of July 1, 1998, "out of total of 156,169 licensed private security employees in Russia, 35,351 (22.6%) came from the MVD, 12,414 (7.9%) from the KGB-FSB, and 1,223 (0.8%) from other security and law enforcement organizations," 133.

64. Vadim Volkov, "Who is Strong when the State is Weak? Violent Entrepreneurship in Russia's Emerging Markets," in *Beyond State Crisis? Postcolonial Africa and Post-Soviet Eurasia in Comparative Perspective,* eds. Mark Beissinger and Crawford Young (Baltimore, MD: Johns Hopkins University Press, 2002), 94.

65. On the origins and rise of the Russian mafia, see Volkov, *Violent Entrepreneurs;* and Stephen Handelman, *Comrade Criminal: Russia's New Mafiya* (New Haven, CT: Yale University Press, 1997).

66. *RFE/RL Security Watch* 1(16) (November 6, 2000). Accessed at: http://www.rferl.org/reports/securitywatch/2000/11/16-061100.asp. Accessed April 18, 2006.

67. Sergei L. Loiko, "Ex-Soviet 'Top Guns' Shot Down, Face Possible Death as Mercenaries," *Los Angeles Times,* July 19, 1993.

68. Jon Auerbach, "Azerbaijan Hires Afghan Mujahideen to Fight Armenia," *Boston Globe,* November 8, 1993.

69. Charles H. Fairbanks, Jr., "Weak States and Private Armies."

70. On Chechnya, see Mathew Evangelista, *The Chechen Wars* (Washington, DC: Brookings, 2003). Also see the background information provided by Human Rights Watch at http://www.hrw.org/campaigns/russia/chechnya/docs.htm.

71. P. W. Singer, *Corporate Warriors,* 173.

72. Ibid.; and Kevin Whitelaw and Richard J. Newman, "The Russians are Coming," *US News & World Report,* March 15, 1999, 40.

73. "Ukrainian Mercenaries Serve in Many Conflict Areas," *Special Warfare* 11(2) (Spring 1998): 41.

74. "Sierra Leone Seeks UN Action on Liberia, Burkina Faso Intervention," *Agence France Presse,* January 29, 1999.

75. Singer, *Corporate Warriors,* 84.

76. Charles H. Fairbanks, Jr., "Weak State and Private Armies."

77. For a theoretically informed overview, see Rubin and Snyder, *Post-Soviet Political Order.*

78. For overviews, see Rashid, *Jihad;* and Gregory Gleason, "The Politics of Counterinsurgency in Central Asia," *Problems of Post-Communism* 49(2) (March/April 2002): 1–11.

79. Rashid, *Jihad,* chap. 8.

80. For an overview, see International Crisis Group, *Radical Islam in Central Asia: Responding to Hizb ut-Tahrir,* Asia Report No. 58, June 30, 2003 (Brussels: ICG, 2003).

81. Charles H. Fairbanks, Jr., "Weak State and Private Armies," 138–139.

82. Pyotr Akopov, "Sergei Yastrzhembsky: There Are No More Than 200 Mercenaries in Chechnya," *The Current Digest of the Post-Soviet Press* 53(41) (November 7, 2001): 14.

83. Amelia Gentleman and Jamie Wilson, "LSE 'Has Links' with Chechen Terrorists," *The Guardian,* February 25, 2001.

84. Fiona Hill, "Central Asia and the Caucasus: The Impact of the War on Terrorism," in *Nations in Transit, 2003* (New York: Freedom House, 2003), 43.

85. Hill, "Central Asia and the Caucasus," 47.

86. For an overview, see Victor Yasmann, "Russia—Between Terror and Corruption," RFE/RL Report, September 26, 2004. Accessed at: http://rferl.org/featuresarticle/2004/09/3cab44ec-da1d-4a9a-9366-d66c2381c27c.html. Accessed April 18, 2006.

87. *Komsomolskaya Pravda,* October 27, 2004, 8-9.

88. "Russian Plane Bombers Exploited Corrupt System," *Washington Post,* September 18, 2004, A1.

89. Interview on NTV Mir, Moscow, November 5, 2004.

90. *Komsomolskaya Pravda,* October 27, 2004, 9.

91. For similar arguments, about Africa see Reno, *Warlord Politics and African States*; Jeffrey Herbst, *States and Power in Africa* (Princeton, NJ: Princeton University Press, 2001); and Nicholas van de Walle, *African Economies and the Politics of Permanent Crisis, 1979–1999* (Cambridge: Cambridge University Press, 2001).
92. On the logic of NATO criteria and admissions bargaining, see Andrew Kydd, "Trust-Building, Trust Breaking: The Dilemma of NATO Enlargement," *International Organization* 55(4) (2001): 801–828.
93. On NATO conditionality and institutional change, see Alexander Cooley, "Western Conditions and Domestic Choices: The Influence of External Actors on the Post-Communist Transition," in *Nations in Transit: Democratization in East Central Europe and Eurasia*, eds. Amanda Schnetzer et al. (New York: Rowman and Littlefield and Freedom House, 2003).
94. I am thankful to Rawi Abdelal for suggesting this point. For further analysis of the potential political consequences of WTO membership, see Igor Burakovsky, "Economic Integration and Security in the Post-Soviet Space," in Legvold and Wallander, *Swords and Sustenance*, 159–188.

8

DIVIDED CONTINENT

Globalization and Europe's Fragmented Security Response

Rachel Epstein

GLOBALIZATION HAS OSTENSIBLY CHANGED THE COMPETENCE of states—increasing their capacity to govern in some areas, diminishing it in others.[1] Extending this argument to European security, globalization may well undermine the state's ability to provide certain public goods, including defense, at a level of expenditure acceptable to European publics.[2] Arguably, national defense competence is largely an economies of scale problem for all but the wealthiest states with the biggest markets. Thus Europe's mid-range powers have since the close of World War II been increasingly susceptible to defense denationalization for economic and political reasons. The question I pose here is whether globalization, defined in this volume as the rise of purposeless and stateless forces, affects national security in the European context. In particular, I explore whether the encroachment of markets impinges on the ability of European states, both individually and collectively, to defend the increasingly integrated political and economic order painstakingly constructed over decades.

In key areas of European integration, politics has followed an economic logic (as in creating a single market) or politics has shaped economic arrangements (as in the case of monetary union). With respect to national security, however, my thesis is that politics and economics have so far moved in opposite directions. Forces of globalization, namely markets, are pushing European states toward greater defense industry integration, both within Europe and beyond Europe's borders.[3] At the same time, Europeans remain deeply divided on the politics of European foreign and security policy—a fact that was first reflected in the early exclusion of the defense industry from the common market.

Likely results of a continuing divergence between politics and economics in security include a long-term marginalization of Europe as a foreign policy player and security provider, continuing dependence on U.S. defense dominance, and vulnerability to security threats stemming from proliferation and terrorism. In the post–Cold War era, it is no longer clear that the United States is willing to indefinitely provide a security guarantee.[4] Thus, the failure of European defense could have real world consequences that were threatened, but never realized, in the early debates when the European Defence Community (EDC) failed.[5]

It should be noted that Europe is among the toughest cases in which to observe the effects of globalization. Layers of formal and informal political institutions regulate and scrutinize disorganized and purposeless forces of markets and technology both carefully and constantly. Where veto players abound and where consensus building is a powerful ideology, Europe may seem an unlikely venue for globalization to manifest a strong influence.[6] This is in stark contrast to other areas under consideration in this volume, particularly the former Soviet space and the Middle East (see Cooley [chapter 7] and Lynch [chapter 6] in this volume, respectively), where the absence of encompassing political structures would appear to allow stateless and purposeless forces to penetrate more easily. Although I do not argue that globalization in the European context goes unmediated by political authority, the increasing salience of markets and technology, even for Europe, highlights how powerful the forces of economic integration have become.

THE ARGUMENT

I argue in this chapter that for Europe, globalization poses both opportunities and threats. Whether globalization in due course bolsters or undermines European security, and specifically the capacity of European states to exercise ultimate authority over organized violence in defense of their interests, depends on Europe's political response to globalizing trends. The most salient form of globalization in the context of European security is the rise of markets and by extension the unprecedented marketization of relations between defense firms and governments.[7] Practical manifestations of globalization in the European context include the fact that national governments are no longer necessarily the biggest purchasers of systems and components originating in a given country. Cross-national defense industry integration is increasingly the norm. States prefer to foster quality and price competition at the expense of supply self-sufficiency. Firms are ever more keen to pursue global market share rather than political favoritism as a means of survival.

All of these trends present an opportunity for European security in so far as defense industry integration could reduce overcapacity, increase competitive efficiency, and diminish costs.[8] Most important, it could provide an integrated industrial base that transcends long-standing political conflicts over *juste retour*, security of supply and information, and even definitions of national interest. Defense industry integration could therefore provide the material base for a uniform and enforceable export code and a centralized procurement policy based on a pan-European conception of security. Such subordination of economic trends to political priorities would provide the EU with increased bargaining power vis-à-vis the United States and enhance Europe's capacity to defend its territory at home and interests abroad. In this regard, the Europeans could count themselves among the lucky, for as Paul Midford points out in chapter 9 on Japan, not even the second largest economy in the world has as promising an array of defense production and procurement options as do the Europeans. Indeed, massive experience in pushing regional integration forward and supranational institutions that could be refashioned for foreign and security policy coordination leave Europe uniquely poised to exploit globalization and the relative power to be gained from new economies of scale.[9]

But whether defense industry integration has a fortifying effect on European security is inextricably linked to whether European institutions develop channels of political authority that adequately harness globalizing trends—and herein lies the threat. Against the backdrop of continuing marketization of the armaments sector, Europe's failure to exercise political control at a commensurate, supranational level promises to make all European states worse off. This is because globalization increases the relative costs of maintaining nationally based production, which in turn diminishes the willingness of politicians and publics to sustain arms industries on a domestic level. Giving up domestic production, however, also necessarily means yielding political authority over issues of historically vital concern to states—export codes, weapons sales as a tool of foreign policy, and procurement according to national needs.[10] Moreover, jettisoning weapons development may dampen technological competitiveness and cut into long-term job growth. If states forego their domestic capabilities and political authority but simultaneously fail to replace it with anything else, Europeans will lose relative power in the international system and experience a diminishing capacity to defend their territory at home or to follow through on foreign policy goals abroad.

That globalization poses a threat to European security by diminishing Europe's ability to take part in military actions abroad assumes that Europeans generally agree on the utility and desirability of military power—an admittedly contested claim. Arguably, the reluctance of European states to spend massively on defense, their very pragmatic approach to governing that prioritizes social welfare over preparing for warfare, and their narrow threat perceptions that have nothing to do with one another are all cause for celebration. Certainly to the extent that integration has demilitarized European political culture, we are witnessing a radical and welcome departure from times past.

Nevertheless, there is still a strong case to be made for Europe enhancing its military capability. Looking back over more than a decade, military and foreign policy disunity prevented the Europeans from initiating decisive action in the Balkans. Failures of interoperability there and in the first Gulf War dissuaded the Americans from embarking on meaningful military coordination with their European partners in Afghanistan, limiting the latter's role in determining both how the war would be fought and how Afghanistan would be governed in the aftermath. Iraq provides another example in which European fragmentation contributed to American unilateralism, and the Madrid bombings demonstrated that Europe is far from immune to a range of threats that lead not only to loss of life at home but also to instability abroad. Thus, the range of security challenges highlights the potential benefits of a European military capability and underlines also the advantages of European unity, both in terms of carrying out missions autonomously and in terms of possibly shaping U.S. actions in ways that reflect European interests as much as American ones.

Importantly, the kinds of foreign policy fragmentation that have plagued Europe in the past and that threaten to undermine the continent's influence in the future are not a consequence of globalization. Globalization does not cause political fragmentation. The rise of markets and the changing nature of military technologies do render Europe's security situation more precarious in light of this fragmentation, however, because without the capacity to take advantage of new economies of scale, individual European states' power will erode. The erosion will be relative to the United States and relative to other states and nonstate actors who will benefit both from proliferation of weapons of mass destruction and dual-use technologies. Even as the Soviet Union's demise has improved Europe's strategic situation in monumental ways, new uncertainties are materializing—namely the uncertain durability and character of the American security guarantee and by extension the credibility of the North Atlantic Treaty Organization (NATO), the ongoing threat of terrorism, regional instability in the Caucuses and Africa, and war in the Middle East.

In the remainder of this chapter, I begin by defining what globalization refers to in the European context. I then assess three propositions that concern the degree to which the rise of purposeless forces on a global scale have affected the ability of European states to provide for their security. I conclude with some observations about the likely consequences of two different scenarios in Europe—one in which the globalization of the arms industry is subject to only sporadic controls at the national level, and one in which European states institutionalize new channels of authority at the supranational level in an effort to subordinate globalizing economic trends to coordinated political objectives.[11]

DEFINING GLOBALIZATION IN THE EUROPEAN CONTEXT

Although globalization refers to the rise of stateless and purposeless forces, the liberalization of transnational flows is a phenomenon with political origins. Globalization in the arms industry is no exception. The political event that mattered most in this connection was the end of the Cold War and the shrinking of markets for arms. In response to diminished demand, states and firms looked for ways of cutting costs and increasing economies of scale, respectively. The globalization option, already advanced in finance and some industries, thus provided firms with the opportunity to effectively expand the size of their markets by pursuing transnational mergers and joint ventures, assuming they could win state support for such strategies.[12]

Pressed by increasingly costly welfare systems and convergence criteria for the European Monetary Union, states' interests overlapped with those of firms in so far as states were increasingly concerned with fostering competition and suspending previous commitments to sustain national defense firms by guaranteeing contracts.[13] Certainly not all states and firms have followed this globalizing logic—there are still plenty of ways in which the European arms industry remains fragmented and bound by national orientations.[14] But where market integration has started to occur, globalization has taken on a logic and force of its own. Such observations about the political origins of globalization do nothing to change this volume's central claim about its essentially stateless and purposeless character, however. For once competitive pressures are unleashed, the costs of not submitting to their logic rise relative to embracing marketization.

Acknowledging that there are political origins in both the movement of goods, capital, services, and people and in the decision to advance particular technologies, I also argue that changes in these areas have indeed created trends that are no longer contained by, or easily reversed by, any single European power. Manifestations of globalization in European security include the penetration of a market logic in organizing European defense industries including the marketization of relations between states and firms. A second feature of globalization is the changing nature of technologies, especially their soaring costs and dual-use character. Globalization also refers to the internationalization of the defense industry and the incidence of transnational mergers and joint ventures as a means of gaining access to larger and more markets. Proliferation of weapons is a fourth feature of globalization that, although certainly not new, potentially amplifies threats posed by both rogue regimes and transnational terrorist organizations. All of these trends affect the capacity of European states to defend their interests through military means principally by undermining the national logic on which security has traditionally been based.

For the purposes of this volume, globalization also refers to a range of other phenomena, including the movement of people and the empowerment (through communications technology) of transnational political groups (see Adamson [chapter 2] and Herrera [chapter 3] in this volume, respectively). Although these developments are crucial for European security, the EU has mobilized some political resources to cope with their increasingly integrated economic space.[15] With the creation of a single market and the legal system needed to facilitate the movement of goods, capital, and individuals, the Europeans have started to develop parallel police structures. Europe-wide policing regulates admission to the European space (through the Schengen Agreement) and is increasingly engaged in monitoring illicit activities under centralized authority. Because France in particular has been reluctant to allow NATO to take on either internal counterterror (policing) responsibilities or tasks associated with "consequence management" (civilian efforts to deal with the aftermath of terrorist attacks), European institutions have been the logical repository for developing such capabilities.[16] Thus the EU, in large measure through EUROPOL, the Europe-wide police agency, has since 1999 enhanced transnational police cooperation, harmonized legal instruments and definitions of financial crimes, increased the transparency of financial transactions, and strengthened air security.[17]

The primary focus here on markets and the defense industry rather than on migration and terrorist threats serves three purposes. First, because the focus of the volume is to establish how globalization affects the capacity of states to provide for their security, I argue that the transformation of the armaments industry and its connection (or lack thereof) to policy has greater implications for the dependent variable than does migration and terror. In other words, although emerging threats around migration and terror provide new challenges to security, they do not necessarily impinge on the ability of states to mount defenses. Rather, threats stemming from terror and migration, even if new, expanded, or changed, require continuity of states in their capacity to build and deploy systems that meet such challenges. The second purpose is to shed light on an area in which the Europeans have generally failed to forge political institutions despite repeated rhetorical commitments to do so. Harmonizing foreign, security, and defense policy may prove to be increasingly intractable as, with EU enlargements, an ever-larger number of voices compete to have their own threat perceptions institutionalized at the supranational level. The final purpose of focusing on defense industries is to reflect on Europe's potential as a unified global actor, which, considering trends toward industry integration, would be a logical policy objective.

The evidence that follows largely speaks to three propositions about the extent to which the European arms industry is undergoing globalization and whether globalization, defined as "stateless forces—especially but not exclusively markets," has undermined the capacity of European states to pursue national defense strategies, including the preservation of "national champions." The evidence also concerns the degree to which globalization undermines traditional sources of political authority and correspondingly enlarges the discrepancy between some Europeans' federalist ambitions and operational reality. This is especially important in light of emerging threats, including global terror networks and proliferation. Globalization, I will argue, produces production specialization that increases states' vulnerabilities by imposing interdependence. Although the post–World War II embedded liberal compromise between economic integration and national autonomy shielded states from having to choose between competing priorities, globalization, and particularly the mobility of capital, has resulted in the encroachment of markets on the defense industry.[18] It is unclear whether events will substantiate the third proposition regarding the reconstitution of authority at the supranational level given faltering governance at the national level. Although several shocks have repeatedly renewed efforts at creating European defense independence, it is still not clear whether the EU will emerge as an empowered military and foreign policy player.

PROPOSITION 1: GLOBALIZATION AND EUROPEAN DEFENSE INDUSTRY CONSOLIDATION

Defense industry consolidation has taken place on two fronts: both within states and transnationally. The structure of defense industries matters to national security because traditionally, states have preferred an "internal arming" capacity to avoid dependence on foreign suppliers—as was the tendency among European powers following World War II.[19] Although one might have anticipated that the end of the Cold War would provoke a return to greater defense self-sufficiency as the U.S. commitment to Europe diminished from its peak,[20] the reverse trend has instead been the case. European levels of defense spending have declined and defense industry consolidation is on the rise.[21] The political explanation is self-evident: Europe no longer faces the same level of threat given the Soviet Union's demise and the epochal changes in Western Europe's own immediate environment. Yet there is a globalization explanation as well—one that suggests the changing nature of technology (most notably its growing expense and complexity) and increasingly competitive markets have made it more difficult for states to arm themselves.

The globalization argument I present here is not meant to replace a political explanation for intra- and interstate defense consolidation. If Europeans were willing to commit 6 percent of their GDP on military expenditures as the United States routinely did during the Cold War, maintaining a range of national defense industries might still be possible. Clearly, it is a political choice not to do so.

At the same time, the very significant resistance among European powers to forego a modicum of indigenous capacity[22] suggests economic infeasibility is as important as the relatively benign security environment in limiting national defense capabilities. Moreover, even in the wake of the Cold War, it is not the case that European states do not face threats—instability in the Balkans, Africa, the Middle East, and the Former Soviet Union all impinge directly on European security. Europeans certainly share with their American counterparts an interest in meeting the challenges posed by proliferation and terrorism. The European Union may in one way be well-served by the United

States fighting the Afghanistans of this world by simply enjoying the role of a free rider. It is also clear, however, that without making its own military contributions, the EU has much less voice in how and whether such wars should be fought, or in how such regions are governed in their aftermath. Thus defense industry consolidation, if it occurs in the absence of political coordination, threatens to marginalize Europe as a foreign policy power.

Although significant defense industry restructuring has been underway in Europe since 1985, the intense period of consolidation began in the mid-1990s such that by 2002, there were only three major contractors left in the European market. The multinational enterprises European Aeronautic, Defence and Space Company (EADS), BAE Systems (formerly British Aerospace), and Thales dominated European military electronics and aviation by 2002, with land systems and ship building undergoing restructuring on the national level that was expected to lead to further transnational consolidation, as well.[23] Although the leading European states had tried to exercise political authority over consolidation trends, they were in the end relatively unsuccessful in their bid.

From the outset of European integration, arms manufacturing has been among the most protected of industries. Beginning with the Treaty of Rome in 1957, defense contractors were excluded from trade liberalization in Europe. Because political leaders deemed national security a strategic concern, they refused to subject arms production to the common market.[24] The national approach to weapons production was affirmed as recently as 1997 when the Treaty of Amsterdam preserved Article 223 (renamed Article 296) as a guiding principle in defense industry organization, excluding weapons manufacturing from common market regulation.

In the intervening decades, Britain, Germany, and France all developed successful arms industries such that each country was largely able to provide for its own defense needs, albeit at considerable expense to European taxpayers. To the extent that weapons systems were jointly produced among European partners, *juste retour* was strictly enforced. This means that a state's economic gains from cooperative projects (in terms of production, for example) were commensurate with a state's financial contribution. Led at various times by the United States and France, a number of European defense initiatives were proposed—but then ultimately buckled under political pressure.[25] Even with respect to joint weapons projects, national procurement agencies and oligopolies consistently interfered with efforts for greater cooperation and integration that governments and even militaries had supported.[26] Although there was considerable defense industry consolidation between the 1950s and the

1990s, it was mostly within European nations rather than among them, leading to overcapacity and duplication in the European market.[27]

The end of the Cold War, American defense industry consolidation, the changing nature of defense technology, and new European priorities concerning monetary union reversed earlier trends favoring nationally organized defense industrial and technological bases (DITB) in Europe. The end of the bipolar standoff meant shrinking markets for arms the world over. In response, the U.S. government subsidized consolidation among American companies. At a meeting between U.S. Secretary of Defense William Perry and defense company CEOs in 1993 that has since been dubbed the "last supper," the U.S. government made it clear that not everyone would survive the downturn. This ushered in a period of U.S. neglect in enforcing antitrust law, aggressive marketing of international arms sales, and government assistance in financing consolidation of up to $1.5 billion.[28]

New economies of scale in the United States left European weapons producers in a more vulnerable position than ever before, especially in light of the changing nature of military technology. No longer would they be able to sustain indigenous production capacity and therewith defense self-sufficiency. The blurring of lines between civilian and military components, coupled with diminished demand for weapons, shifted manufacturers' attentions to commercial markets and undermined the traditionally privileged positions of defense contractors vis-à-vis governments. Further exacerbating European defense manufacturers' vulnerability was the drive from the early 1990s onward to meet the Maastricht criteria for economic policy convergence in preparation for the single currency, itself a response to the pressures of globalization. Strict limits on public spending sent national treasurers looking for places to cut. The end of the Cold War and the sanctity of social welfare made defense budgets the logical target.[29]

In response to sagging demand and material constraints, partly the result of market trends and partly the result of political developments, governments gradually began giving way to cross-national consolidation for the first time in European history. The creation of EADS and the growth of BAE Systems into a transatlantic conglomerate with a U.S. workforce and access to U.S. markets were industry responses to political failures.

Prior to market-led rationalization, however, Europeans attempted political integration. France, Britain, Germany, Spain, Sweden, and Italy committed in December 1997 to consolidating their national champions through greater integration and restructuring in an enterprise that would have been called European Aerospace Defence Company

(EADC). The deal fell apart, however, because of competition for jurisdiction over certain spheres of production and over the ownership structure. This last point concerned the role of shareholders in an enterprise that might still in part be state owned by several of the participating countries, including France, Italy, and Spain.[30]

Massive consolidation did take place shortly after the failure of EADC, but with politics trailing rather than leading. British-dominated BAE Systems came close to merging with Germany's Dasa but opportunistically changed course and merged with Marconi in the United States instead, permanently damaging relations between BAE Systems and its would-be German partner. In keeping with European defense firms' fears that merging on unequal footing would essentially mean being overtaken, BAE Systems was then excluded from further European consolidation because it had grown too powerful. As Dasa contemplated merging with the recently privatized CASA (the Spanish aircraft manufacturer), the German firm simultaneously pursued plans with France's Aerospatiale. The end result was EADS, the first "European champion," in this instance from Germany, France, and on a smaller scale, Spain. Specializing in civil and military aviation and space technology (including Airbus), EADS is poised to compete with its American counterparts.

Although market-led, the making of EADS was not free from political authority. The French and Spanish governments both took significant steps in divesting themselves of these traditionally state-owned defense industries, but their withdrawal was not complete. With France and Spain being shareholders in the new enterprise, both came under pressure to renounce excessive political interference but at the same time are not legally bound to abide that commitment. Moreover, political sensibilities may circumscribe the economies of scale that participants hope to realize. The political imperative to geographically balance production among Germany, France, and Spain will limit market-based rationalization. And because common market law does not cover defense industries, EADS will not be subject to European norms governing labor law reconciliation.[31] This could further complicate the enterprise's efforts to operate as a coherent entity, restricting basic business decisions such as shifts in production.

Defense industry consolidation and the creation of three major players, Franco-German-Spanish EADS, British-American BAE Systems, and Franco-British Thales, should in theory provide the organizational basis for political harmonization in defense planning and procurement in Europe. Forces of globalization, including the changing nature of military technologies, the disproportionate rise in the costs of research and development relative to other expenditures in defense, and the increasing competitiveness of markets have contributed to unprecedented levels of transnational defense restructuring. Market-led integration could in turn facilitate greater cooperation. Thus far, however, very little in the way of political cooperation has materialized.

Another consequence of the inability of European states to arm themselves has been the internationalization of supply. Only the United Kingdom, France, Germany, Sweden, Spain, and Italy have substantial armaments sectors and account for 90 percent of defense production in Europe; the rest of Europe buys nearly all its weapons from abroad and prefers to keep European markets open to gain access to the best products at the lowest cost. Moreover, Europe is already heavily and disproportionately dependent on the United States. Whereas half of all European contracts go to American companies, the number of U.S. contracts that go to European suppliers is only 3 percent.[32] Another way to demonstrate the same trend is to assess the proportion of a country's imports and exports. Over the 10 year period spanning from 1993 to 2003, the United Kingdom exported 215 systems and imported 66, and France exported 316 systems and imported 21. In sharp contrast over the same period, the United States exported 1,087 systems and imported 63.[33] What these figures show is that as individual nation-states, European powers are already dependent on both regional and global markets in a way the United States is not. Thus, the size of markets clearly matters to defense self-sufficiency.

The key point with regard to globalization and European security, whether we perceive economic integration to be politically driven or unintended, is that political control has atrophied. As examination of the following two propositions suggests, excessive marketization of Europe's defense industry without encompassing political authority will likely limit the continent's political power, compromise its defense and especially its power-projection capabilities, and leave Europeans vulnerable to ongoing weapons proliferation.

PROPOSITION 2: GLOBALIZATION WITHOUT POLITICAL AUTHORITY: EMERGING THREATS

The second proposition under consideration here is that globalization has generated security challenges that Europe would not otherwise face. Globalization potentially poses three threats. The first is that Europe will fail to realize its stated ambition of becoming a credible global player, and will, through its continuing defense dependence on the United States, remain a marginal and fragmented presence in international affairs. This risk includes the possibility that transatlantic mergers could seriously undermine European defense independence. Second, in light of globalizing trends, both within Europe and beyond, Europe, along with everyone else, risks becoming more vulnerable vis-à-vis developing countries that have increasingly sophisticated weapons programs of their own. This threat is not limited to direct attack but rather includes general instability that accompanies the spread of arms and other dual-use but deadly technologies. Third, without political institutions capable of rationalizing and enforcing export controls, Europe is in danger of contributing to the proliferation that could very likely compromise its own security.

Europe's Marginalization

A survey of post–Cold War conflicts, including the first Gulf War, Bosnia, Kosovo, Afghanistan, and the Iraq war, corroborate the claim that individual European nation-states are marginal, and as a single entity, the European Union has been a nonplayer. Depending on the crisis, Europeans' roles have ranged from passive to supporting to obstructionist. The fragmentation of European foreign and security policy since the end of the Cold War cannot be traced to uncoordinated and purposeless forces of globalization. Rather, it is largely historical experience, national tradition, and commercial interests that define challenges and their responses. Nevertheless, market trends described in the previous section do threaten to exacerbate preexisting divisions by dissolving national authority and making all European states militarily more vulnerable in the process.

Although it is true in the most recent period that declining demand and increasingly competitive markets have undermined European states' ability to sustain their national champions, this alone cannot explain Europe's defense dependence. Rather, U.S. dominance stems from post–World War II transatlantic security arrangements that were largely path-dependent. Although the United States encouraged European defense cooperation, the Europeans themselves were eager to limit such integration.[34] In addition, West Europeans were, within NATO, charged with the task of defending their territories. Assuming that the most likely war scenario was one in which Soviet forces would come to them, West Europeans invested heavily in large forces and personnel rather than in research and development. By contrast, U.S. military planning revolved primarily around deploying the most sophisticated systems in the world and power-projection capabilities that would carry the American military across oceans.[35] Whereas the Cold War division of labor created mutual dependence between the United States and Europe, following Communism's collapse, many more U.S. military assets have been adaptable to an uncertain security environment than those of the Europeans.

The capabilities gap between Europe and the United States by the turn of the twenty-first century spanned just about every area of military technology. Specifically, U.S. assets outstripped those of its European counterparts in strategic mobility, precision-guided munitions, electronic warfare, long-range air and missile strike capability, and command, control, communications, and reconnaissance. The problem is not limited to technology. With nearly 2 million troops on the continent, mobilizing even 40,000 to 50,000 for deployment elsewhere presented a challenge in the late 1990s.[36] Moreover, the very low value of what the Europeans receive for the money invested, coupled with initially low levels of investment, suggests it is unlikely that the capabilities gap will narrow any time soon.[37]

Proliferation and Global Instability

Globalization potentially poses a second threat. The changing nature of military technology (particularly its dual-use character) and arms production (integrative licensing arrangements) may close the gap in capabilities between European powers and developing nations.[38] The marketization of relations between governments and defense contractors drives technological leveling between industrial and developing nations. During the Cold War, governments supported the cordoning off of military research from civilian society in order to prevent the proliferation of sensitive technologies.[39] Dissemination of civilian spin-offs from military innovation was controlled. As firms have come under increasing economic pressure, however, they have moved toward developing dual-use technologies that promise larger markets. Greater market coverage is one way of compensating for the growing relative costs of research and development.[40] Because of dual-use, governments are increasingly dependent on technology suppliers that are not necessarily susceptible to the same political oversights that have routinely been applied to defense manufacturing.[41] The competitiveness of markets and the increasing costs of technology have also heightened the appeal of offset agreements even though they contribute to the dissemination of military technology that could in turn compromise European security. Ironically, despite the opposition of European defense ministries, finance ministries, procurement agencies, and militaries, offset arrangements and a national approach to weapons deals persist. The buyer's market in arms explains this conundrum. Offsets are expensive for the supplier, both in terms of short-term costs and longer-term security challenges. But as long as buyers demand such arrangements, the abundance of suppliers and the lack of any coordinated, enforceable prohibition of offsets ensures that buyers will be able to extract them. Defense industry preferences aside, governments purchasing weapons would rather move toward "long-term international development contracts" to improve their own technological capability when they acquire systems from abroad. For this reason, offset arrangements will not go away and may increase in light of market competition.[42]

More than any other country, the United States has contributed to escalating market pressures and to lowering the bar on export controls. This makes it evermore difficult for the European powers to enforce mutual and self-restraint. Between 1992 and 1997, U.S. spending on arms decreased as a percentage of gross national income (GNI) from 4.8 to 3.3 percent,[43] but then resurged in the wake of terror attacks in 2001. Although U.S. spending has shifted up and down through the 1990s and beyond, the post–Cold War business orientation of the defense industry has not. By 1994, the Coordinating Committee for Multilateral Export Controls (CoCom) had been dismantled. The Clinton administration, in addition to financing the defense industry's consolidation, took new steps to allow the export of dual-use technologies.[44]

Examples of how arms exports and technology transfers compromise the security of suppliers abound in the Middle East. During the 1970s, the United States sold $11 billion in military equipment to Iran and trained eleven thousand Iranian officers prior to the revolution there. In the 1980s, the Iran-Iraq war was fought with $80 billion worth of arms imports.[45] Over the course of decades, the United States supplied nuclear power programs around the world (including in Iraq) although the Nuclear Non-Proliferation Treaty (NPT) has proven insufficient to limit their use to exclusively peaceful purposes. More recently, the United States faced Taliban fighters armed with weapons and training provided by the United States during the Cold War.[46] Further, in the war against terrorism, the United States rescinded arms sanctions that had been in place against Pakistan, India, Azerbaijan, and Tajikistan. The U.S. government has also promoted additional arms sales and military assistance around the world in a coalition-building effort—an effort that benefits U.S. arms manufacturers, perhaps at the expense of both regional and global security.[47]

Globalization has contributed to proliferation generally as the integration of markets, the diminishing costs of transport, and increased sophistication of communication have facilitated the circumvention of the export laws that currently exist. The dual-use character of many deadly technologies exacerbates the problem of control. Chemical weapons components, for example, are almost exclusively dual-use.[48] Although much trade in arms occurs without government knowledge, governments are also complicit. They use "commercial confidentiality" to avoid timely reporting to parliamentary overseers and the media.[49] Moreover, export of final products is no longer the issue in many instances of proliferation. As more integrative modes of arms manufacturing develop, technological leaders export the means of production rather than the products themselves. If the transfer is taking place between a European or North American state and a developing country, we can assume the recipient country has even more permissive export practices.

Proliferation and Threats to European Security

The European powers have a series of technology and arms exports to their credit, as well. The long history of European contributions to the diffusion of potentially lethal technology cannot be traced exclusively to America's relatively recent aggressive marketing. However, the intensity of market pressures that have prevailed since the 1990s, driven by a combination of competition and evolving technologies, no doubt complicates Europe's efforts to formulate a coherent political response. A brief review of Europe's most regrettable exports lends some credence to the notion that globalization will strengthen the export imperative still further, creating both general instability around the globe as well as specific threats to European security. France, the United Kingdom, and Germany are among the world's five biggest arms traders.[50] France in particular has taken an increasingly active role in promoting arms exports as a means of reforming the country's military-security apparatus. French reforms included moving from conscription to a volunteer force, large-scale privatization of the defense industry, and a renewed commitment to foreign weapons sales to support national companies in the wake of the Cold War.[51] France was one of only a few countries in the world whose arms exports as a percentage of total exports increased between 1992 and 1997 from 0.9 percent to 2 percent.[52] Reported French arms exports have increased since then, although according to one source, "the French government is generally not transparent about its arms exports."[53]

France has long used trade in weapons and technology as a strategy for supporting domestic industry, even before the U.S. defense company consolidation of the early to mid-1990s that in turn provoked European consolidation. On several occasions, French exports have in retrospect proven disastrous. It was French Exocet missiles that destroyed the British HMS *Sheffield* in the Falklands War and badly damaged the USS *Stark* in 1987, the latter event killing 37 sailors.[54] French arms sales not only contributed to Israel's and Iraq's nuclear weapons program, but also ultimately compromised France's military contribution to the Persian Gulf War. The American-led force against Iraq confronted French Exocet missiles and Franco-German surface-to-air misssiles (SAMs), for example. In addition, France was prohibited from using its own Mirage jets in the campaign because the country would not be able to distinguish its own fighters from those of the Iraqi force—to whom France had sold the Mirage F-1 (along with its air-to-air missiles) in the previous decade.[55]

A 2003 report by Amnesty International also chronicles French sales in small arms and light weapons, larger arms, and instruments of torture (including "security equipment"). France also engages in licensing agreements, global arms brokering, and military training. At least one of the recipients has been engaged in civil war (Angola) while many other regimes are engaged in various levels of political repression (Indonesia, Kenya, Egypt, Cameroon, Zimbabwe, Ivory Coast, and Turkey).[56] Whether arms transfers to such states will compromise European security is contested, depending on how states construe threat perceptions. If industrialized states continue to claim that defending democratic order and human rights around the world is critical for long-term stability, however, then there is little doubt that weapons proliferation, even in small arms, undermines those basic principles.

Much like France, Germany's contribution to Iraq's weapons programs is well documented. Before the Persian Gulf War, Germany was among Iraq's biggest trading partners in weapons, especially in components and technology for biological and chemical weapons in addition to missile technology.[57] Additionally, in the 1980s, the German company Imhausen-Chemie designed a chemical weapons plant for Libya.[58] Germany has taken legal measures to reverse some of these trends, but as late as 2002, a German small arms manufacturer [Heckler-Koch (HK)] had a contract pending with Nepal.[59] Although Germany came under intense pressure to deny HK an exporting license, there is evidence that the assault rifles were conveyed to Nepal via the United Kingdom as they were in use as of 2003. Other conventional weapons produced in Germany span the globe, often reaching their final destination through indirect exports.[60]

Jack Straw, the British foreign minister, claimed in early 2003 that the United Kingdom's annual report provided the most complete information about its arms export of any country in the world. Critics on the other hand have argued that the U.K. system of reporting excludes such vital information as the recipients within a country, the reasons for denying export licenses, the quantity of arms exported, and the banks involved in arms transactions—aspects of arms transfers that other European states do reveal. At the same time, Amnesty International has criticized the United Kingdom for exporting myriad arms ranging from crowd control devices to electronics to everything in between. The war on terrorism has extended the geographical reach of U.K. exports to many states neighboring Afghanistan despite these countries' illiberal ideologies and practices.[61]

From this evidence, two effects of globalization stand out. Because of the end of the Cold War and declining demand for weapons in its wake, arms manufacturers are compensating for losses with dual-use technologies and increasingly aggressive efforts to market their products overseas. Firms do this with the assistance of governments. Second, globalization structures opportunities in ways that impinge upon states' perceptions of gain and security. As globalization limits the authority of states domestically (by, for example, making the preservation of national champions untenable), globalization also creates new channels for realizing profit. The post-9/11 tendency, particularly by the United Kingdom and United States, to trade long-term prudence for short-term security cooperation and economic advantage suggests that globalization has indeed altered the strategies and interests of states since the end of the Cold War.

PROPOSITION 3: GLOBALIZATION AND THE RECONSTITUTION OF POLITICAL AUTHORITY

The third proposition under consideration here, derived from the literature on globalization (e.g., Cerny 1995), is that the erosion of authority on the national level will drive states to reconstitute authority at the supranational level. Market-led consolidation of European defense industries and threats of proliferation sparked by the changing nature of technology and new forms of weapons collaboration would suggest an urgent imperative for European defense cooperation. To the extent that globalization proceeds without an adequate political response, defense dependence and foreign policy marginalization endanger European security. Moreover, the leveling of technological capacity between European powers and developing countries threatens to create new challenges, or at a minimum, sharpen the challenges that Europeans already face vis-à-vis defending their interests at home and pursuing their objectives abroad. As of 2004, there was evidence both for the argument that Europe is responding to globalization through policy coordination and for the argument that long-standing barriers to foreign and security policy rationalization will persist.

Analysts have pointed out that European defense industry consolidation has paved the way for unprecedented coordination among European powers in the areas of foreign policy and defense.[62] In repeated attempts, however, the Europeans have failed to produce an effective Common Foreign and Security Policy (CFSP). The divisions within Europe over policy in Iraq suggest one explanation for the divergence of political possibility from material reality. Despite the effects of globalization that necessitate a high degree of procurement and export control coordination, European powers remain divided on fundamental issues of national interest. Divisive subjects include threat perceptions, the utility of force in fomenting change, and the role of the United States in European and global security. National suspicions and the nature of transatlantic ties pose barriers to European unity that were salient in the 1940s and 1950s, as well. The divide over Iraq in Western Europe was brought into even sharper relief by the widespread support of U.S. policies through much of central and eastern Europe—a division that derives from diverging national experiences of the Cold War.[63]

The post–Cold War period has generated mixed evidence as to the direction of Europe's foreign and security policy. The EU's 2004 enlargement to central and eastern Europe was certainly a foreign policy success, but the security dimensions of that endeavor were slim. It is true that exclusively European post–World War II foreign and security policy achievements pale in comparison to the range of European initiatives in the post–Cold War period. It is also the case, however, that none of the existing institutions transcends a decidedly intergovernmental logic. Europe's Common Defence Policy/Defence Policy (CDP/DP) depends on the role of the CFSP. The latter is dependent in most cases on both NATO and U.S. assets. In this connection, even the Combined Joint Task Force (CJTF) cannot boast true European independence. Even the putatively most Europeanist powers are ambivalent about moving forward with CFSP because such integration "poses special challenges to *national* values and even identity since much of a state's history, for better or worse, is wrapped up in armed forces."[64]

Despite national sensitivities around yielding sovereignty in foreign policy and defense, different constellations of European powers have made initial efforts to reconstitute authority at the supranational level. Institutional innovation in procurement and export controls, if successful, could signal a regional response to globalization's challenges. With respect to procurement, Germany, France, Italy, and the United

Kingdom created the Organisation for Joint Armaments Cooperation (OCCAR) in 1996. In 1998, these countries plus Sweden and Spain signed the Letter of Intent (LoI) aimed at harmonizing procurement regulations. OCCAR manages a number of joint European projects including the A-400M transport aircraft, the Tiger combat helicopter, an air defense system, and two antitank missile programs. The LoI, on the other hand, is meant to ensure the security of supply and information as well as the harmonization of export procedures and of military requirements. Finally, all 15 then-EU member states agreed to the terms of an EU Code of Conduct on arms sales in 1998.[65]

These initiatives, in concert with the European Foreign and Security Policy (EFSP) and the EDC, do not yet, however, represent the coherent political response necessary to thwart the effects of globalization that threaten European security. With respect to the LoI, there has been more progress in technical areas than in political ones. States still cling to the premise of national autonomy such that on issues such as "security of supply" they are allowed to reconstitute national capabilities if necessary.[66] The LoI also calls for a "common military concept" but in reality this is intended for future, rather than current, attention. Moreover, the LoI does not assess the political foundations that must precede a common military concept.

The EU Code of Conduct on arms exports is similarly impressive on paper, but so far lacking in political effect. The central barrier to fundamentally new practices in arms proliferation among European states is that nothing in the code is legally binding and everything is subject to individual states' interpretation. In the wake of 9/11 and the United States' renewed commitment to arms exports, it is likely that the Europeans will opt for a looser application of the code. One such example is a discontinuation in 2001 of the arms embargo against the Northern Alliance in Afghanistan that had been in place due to concerns about human rights abuses. France has likewise resurrected military ties with Pakistan as Germany has with Uzbekistan. As of 2000, it was also not clear whether a key feature of the code, bilateral consultations on export licenses that had been denied, was having any effect on the practice of "undercutting."[67] Undercutting refers to an instance of one European country stepping in to fill a contract that another had rejected because the client presented a proliferation, human rights, or terrorist risk.

Given the range of institutions in place, market-led transnational defense industry consolidation, and well-established procedures for reaching agreement, Europe could be on the verge of giving substance to supranational arrangements. Such arrangements would prevent Europe's marginalization and allow the continent to protect itself against proliferation. Spillover resulting from conflicts over defense industry integration, the harmonization of export controls and procurement policy might encourage states to cede their national autonomy to supranational institutions, much as has been the case in markets and money. There have already been a number of exogenous "shocks" in European security, however, that might have elicited deeper cooperation—including the then end of the Cold War; the wars in the Balkans; weapons programs in Libya, Iraq, and elsewhere; 9/11; and the bombings in Madrid. Because European defense arrangements still do not allow for a unified European security policy and are moving only haltingly in that direction, doubts remain about whether Europe is positioned to translate its growing economic power into commensurate global influence.

CONCLUSION

Shrinking markets for arms have made globalization a survival strategy for defense firms. The perceived imperatives to capture new markets and economies of scale have driven contractors toward cross-national mergers, joint ventures, and licensing arrangements. Competitive markets, oversupply, and increasing attention to financial returns in light of declining state support also provide incentives to export, enter into offset arrangements, and otherwise pursue short-term gains at the expense of suffering long-term security costs of destabilizing proliferation. As noted elsewhere in this chapter, undesirable proliferation is evermore likely to take place as (1) national control over exports erodes and is not replaced by supranational control given cross-national production and as (2) dual-use technology in WMD and communications makes it more difficult for any political authority—national or supranational—to prevent dangerous actors from arming themselves. States have been slow to respond to the threats that the globalization of the arms industry poses because they have been more concerned with near-term resource constraints than with more distant strategic considerations—but at their peril.

Analysts are quite right to point out that within the globalizing trends listed above are the seeds of tremendous opportunity—especially for Europe.[68] These include all the economic gains that medium-sized European states would enjoy if they integrated their arms market according to the same logic they have integrated other sectors—specialization, reduction of oversupply, economies of scale, and, if American firms are allowed to continue to compete for European contracts, robust competition. At the same time, politics has a vital role to play because of all of the economic and national security implications that naturally accompany the organization of a defense-industrial base. As I have argued throughout this chapter, although globalization does provide Europe with some potential advantages, Europe will never realize them without the simultaneous exercise of political authority.

This is not to say, of course, that all supranational political authority is equal. Within the context of European security and globalization, there have been both constructive as well as counterproductive episodes of political intervention in the procurement and production of multinational projects. Although there have been some successful projects delivered on time and at or near anticipated cost, such as the Eurofighter, the M-400A transport aircraft, and the Horizon with plans for a commonly built air defense frigate, all encountered either serious problems or fell apart completely because of national differences—in some cases over specifications or work sharing arrangements. Indeed, one survey, conducted in 1999, found that cost overruns were 30 percent higher for European multinational projects than for commensurate national ones.[69]

For greater defense industry integration to yield benefits in terms of increased security for Europe at lower costs, the political problem is not just achieving greater multinationality. It is, rather, achieving greater multinationality that fully embraces the logic of globalization and with it defense denationalization. Most important, this means forgoing *juste retour,* developing procurement strategies for a common conception of European security, and enforcing an export code consistent with long-term European security concerns.

The stakes are high because without defense industry rationalization in which the Europeans improve on the returns to security they achieve for the money they spend, they will not be able to make contributions to global operations on a scale equal to their economic power. Continued European military impotence puts NATO at risk by undermining its credibility as a truly transatlantic security organization, limits Europe's voice with respect to American-led military operations, and seriously circumscribes the extent to which Europe can defend both its territory at home and interests abroad. Even with a more powerful and uniform export code it is virtually inevitable that each European state's military capabilities will erode relative to the rest of the world and especially to states and nonstate actors that seek to acquire deadly military technologies. Whether globalization, and the technical erosion of power among individual European states that accompanies it, then translates into a downward spiral of compromised security for the continent as a whole depends on Europe's organizational capacity.

The encroachment of markets and the changing nature of technology (particularly its increasingly dual-use character) promise to limit government control, both over development and over distribution. It is clear that European national defense firms are too small to stay competitive. More important, current trends, if unaddressed, threaten not only to increase the capabilities gap between Europe and the United States still further but also to diminish the capabilities gap between Europe and the rest of the world.

NOTES

1. See Philip G. Cerny, "Globalization and the Changing Logic of Collective Action," *International Organization* 49(4) (Autumn 1995): 595–625.
2. Richard Bitzinger, "The Globalization of the Arms Industry: The Next Proliferation Challenge," *International Security* 19(2) (Autumn 1994): 170–198; and Barry Buzan, "The Interdependence of Security and Economic Issues in the 'New World Order,'" in *Political Economy and the Changing Global Order*, eds. Richard Stubbs and Geoffrey R.D. Underhill (Houndsmills, UK: Macmillan Press Ltd., 1994).
3. Keith Hayward, "The Globalisation of Defence Industries," *Survival* 42(3) (Summer 2000): 115.
4. John Mearsheimer, "Back to the Future: Instability in Europe after the Cold War," *International Security* 15(1) (Summer 1990): 5–56.
5. The threat was that the lack of cooperation on the continent would leave Europe vulnerable. In light of lingering European mistrust and the rising antagonism of the Soviet Union, the United States provided a security umbrella that ultimately obviated the need for an independent European defense capability. Simon Duke, *The Elusive Quest for European Security: From EDC to CFSP* (New York: St. Martin's Press, 2000), 295.
6. Duane Swank, *Global Capital, Political Institutions, and Policy Change in Developed Welfare States* (New York: Cambridge University Press, 2002).
7. Deborah Avant in chapter 4 of this volume also highlights the political effects of a similar kind of marketization in defense—specifically the use of private defense companies in lieu of national defense forces.
8. The potential for such gains now is even greater than it was during the Cold War within NATO. There was of course significant defense coordination among NATO members, but most of Europe's two million troops were nevertheless organized around the principle of territorial defense. NATO realized few efficiency gains as a consequence of their cooperation, especially vis-à-vis the United States. Overall, the Europeans spent proportionately more on personnel than on research and investment than the United States, although the latter was continually engaged in perfecting force projection capabilities. Thus the defense capabilities gap between Europe and the United States was long in the making. See David S. Yost, "The NATO Capabilities Gap and the European Union," *Survival* 42(4) (Winter 2000–2001): 97–128.
9. Midford points out that whereas European powers already engage in cross-national production networks with one another in defense (and to a lesser extent with the United States) such arrangements in the Asian context remain "unthinkable."
10. The question of whether the privatization of security undermines state control of violence is a central motivating question in Deborah Avant, *The Market for Force: The Consequences of Privatizing Security* (Stanford, CA: Stanford University Press, 2005).

11. Michael Mastanduno notes that through history, "economic policies are subordinated to and supportive of security concerns" in "Economics and Security in Statecraft and Scholarship," *International Organization* 52(4) (Autumn 1998): 827. To the extent that such subordination no longer obtains in the European context, globalization has indeed changed the fundamental relationship between states and defense contractors.

12. On how defense firms have engineered globalization, see John Lovering, "The Defense Industry as a Paradigmatic Case of 'Actually Existing Globalization,'" in *The Place of the Defense Industry in National Systems of Innovation*, ed. Judith Reppy, Cornell University, Peace Studies Program, Occasional Paper No. 25 (Ithaca, NY: Cornell University Press, 2000), 13–23.

13. The British defense industry has in some respects been among the most internationalized since World War II (see Andrew D. James, "The Place of the UK Defense Industry in its National Innovation System: Co-evolution of National, Sectoral and Technological Systems," in Judith Reppy, *The Place of the Defense Industry*, 96–124), but more recently has made unprecedented moves to privatize and internationalize even further. See Mark Odell and Jean Eaglesham, "Lowering Defences: Britain Throws the Doors Open to Foreign Contractors, but are the Rules of the Game Clear Enough?" *Financial Times*, May 28, 2004.

14. On how France has maintained a more national approach to defense innovation and procurement, see Claude Serfati, "The Place of the French Arms Industry in its National System of Innovation and in the Governmental Technology Policy," in Judith Reppy, *The Place of the Defense Industry*, 71–95.

15. But on all the initiatives that had been agreed to after September 11, 2001, but that had still not been implemented by the time of the Madrid Bombings in March 2004, see Judy Dempsey and James Blitz, "EU Urged to Work Together in Fight against Terrorism," *Financial Times*, March 15, 2004, 3.

16. Nora Bensahel, *The Counterterror Coalitions: Cooperation with Europe, NATO, and the European Union* (Santa Monica, CA: RAND, 2003), 31–32.

17. See Bensahel, *The Counterterror Coalitions*, 34, 37, 42. She also points out that there are limits to each of these advances including the European Union's limited intelligence gathering capacity and the tendency for EU rules on internal policing to be within national jurisdictions of enforcement. Nevertheless, since 1999 and especially after September 11, 2001, European powers have made substantial advances in coordinating surveillance and legal action with the European territories.

18. Krasner, Lake, and Keohane and Nye all discuss international vulnerability in terms of degree of domestic economic diversity and the ability of states to adjust. See Stephen D. Krasner, *Structural Conflict: The Third World Against Global Liberalism* (Berkeley: University of California Press, 1985); David Lake, "Power and the Third World: Toward a Realist Political Economy of North-South Relations," *International Studies Quarterly* 31(2) (1987): 217–234; and Robert O. Keohane and Joseph Nye, *Power and Interdependence: World Politics in Transition* (Boston and Toronto: Little, Brown and Company, 1977). Consistent with these insights, Ruggie argues that industrialized states were able to maintain domestic diversity and thereby limit their vulnerability to external shocks via the embedded liberal compromise in John Ruggie, "International Regimes, Transactions, and Change: Embedded Liberalism in the Postwar Economic Order," *International Organization* 36(2) (Spring 1982): 379–415. More recently, however, the "varieties of capitalism" literature has shown that economic integration, rather than leading to convergence, actually produces greater specialization. Peter Hall and David Soskice, eds., *Varieties of Capitalism: The Institutional Foundations of Comparative Advantage* (Oxford and New York: Oxford University Press, 2001). As weapons markets become increasingly competitive and independent from states, production specialization threatens to raise

the relative costs of indigenous defense procurement for some countries, making them more dependent on foreign producers. On the specific role of global capital in defense industries, see Ann Markusen, "Should We Welcome a Transnational Defense Industry?" In Judith Reppy, *The Place of the Defense Industry*, 24–46. Also see Lovering and Serfati in the same volume.

19. Ethan B. Kapstein, "Allies and Armaments," *Survival* 44(2) (Summer): 142. This began much earlier, of course, when in the mid-1800s "defense industries became one element of national sovereignty." See Hayward, "The Globalisation of Defence Industries," 116.
20. Mearsheimer, "Back to the Future."
21. Kapstein, "Allies and Armaments," 143–144, 147.
22. Hayward, "The Globalisation of Defence Industries," 118.
23. A German merger of Howaldtswerke-Deutsche Werft (HDW) and ThyssenKrupp shipyards was reported to set the stage for creating a larger European enterprise for naval shipbuilding. See "ThyssenKrupp and HDW Take First Step down the Aisle: Firms Sign Non-binding Declaration of Intent," *Lloyd's List*, May 18, 2004.
24. Frederic Merand, "Soldiers and Diplomats: The Institutionalization of European Defense Policy in France, Germany and the United Kingdom" (Ph.D. dissertation, University of California–Berkeley, 2003).
25. Pierre de Vestel, *Defence Markets and Industries in Europe: Time for Political Decisions?* Chaillot Paper No. 21 (Paris: Institute for Security Studies, 1995); and Steve Weber, "Shaping the Postwar Balance of Power: Multilateralism in NATO," *International Organization* 46(3) (Summer 1992): 633–680.
26. Andrew Moravscik, "Armaments Among Allies: European Weapons Collaboration, 1975–1985," in *Double-Edged Diplomacy: International Bargaining and Domestic Politics*, eds. Evans, Jacobson and Putnam (Berkeley: University of California Press, 1993).
27. See de Vestel, *Defence Markets*, 14. NATO, the West European Union (WEU), and the Independent European Programme Group (IEPG) tried on more than 20 occasions to limit the proliferation of national armaments projects beginning in the mid-1950s but mostly failed to undermine the perceived imperative to develop nationally based defense industrial and technological capacities. De Vestel, *Defence Markets*, 5.
28. Burkard Schmitt, *From Cooperation to Integration: Defense and Aerospace Industries in Europe*, Chaillot Paper No. 40 (Paris: Institute for Security Studies, 2000), 23–25.
29. Merand, "Soldiers and Diplomats." The United Kingdom cut budgets first. Between 1985 and 1997, defense expenditures declined by 10 percent in France, 22 percent in the United Kingdom, and 33 percent in Germany.
30. Schmitt, *From Cooperation to Integration*, 31–32.
31. Schmitt, *From Cooperation to Integration*, 47–49.
32. See Daniel Keohane, "The EU and Armaments Co-Operation," Centre for European Reform Working Paper, London, December 2002, 10, 13.
33. These and additional figures are from the SIPRI database "FIRST" available at http://first.sipri.org/.
34. See de Vestel, *Defence Markets;* and Weber, "Shaping the Postwar Balance."
35. Yost, "The NATO Capabilities Gap."
36. Yost, "The NATO Capabilities Gap," 98–99.
37. In 1999, the then U.S. Secretary of Defense William Cohen estimated that although the Europeans collectively spent 60 percent of what the United States spends on defense, they accrue only about 10 percent of the capability. See Elizabeth Becker, "European Allies to Spend More on Weapons," *New York Times*, September 22, 1999. On this point, also see Keohane, "The EU and Armaments Co-Operation."
38. Bitzinger, "The Globalization of the Arms Industry."

39. William Keller, *Arm in Arm: The Political Economy of the Global Arms Trade* (New York: Basic Books, 1995), 41–42.
40. Keller, *Arm in Arm*, 9–10.
41. Hayward, "The Globalisation of Defence Industries," 118.
42. Kjell A. Eliassen and Markus Skriver, *European Defence Procurement and Industrial Policy: A Comparative 6 Country Analysis* (Oslo: Centre for European and Asian Studies at Norwegian School of Management, 2002), 6.
43. United Nations, World Development Indicators, 2001, 296.
44. Keller, *Arm in Arm*, 30; and Markusen, "Should We Welcome a Transnational Defense Industry?"
45. These figures are from Keller, *Arm in Arm*, 2–5.
46. This included $2 billion in light weapons between 1979 and 1989. "This US aid continued openly until 1991, despite the fact that thousands of Afghan civilians were deliberately and arbitrarily killed by Mujahideen fighters," suggesting that these factions might one day constitute a security threat to the West generally. Amnesty International, *A Catalogue of Failures: G8 Arms Exports and Human Rights Violations* (New York: Amnesty International, 2003), 13–14. Available at http://web.amnesty.org/library/Index/ENGIOR300032003.
47. On these points, see Sybille Bauer, "Arms Exports Post 9/11—and the Flood Gates Open?" *European Security Review* 11 (March 2002): 6–7.
48. Jonathan B. Tucker, The Proliferation of Chemical and Biological Weapons Materials and Technologies to State and Sub-State Actors. Testimony before the Subcommittee on International Security, Proliferation, and Federal Services of the U.S. Senate Committee on Government Affairs (2001), 5.
49. Amnesty International, *A Catalogue of Failures*, 2.
50. France has 10 percent of the global trade, the United Kingdom 7 percent and Germany 5 percent. They follow the United States (28 percent) and Russia (17 percent). Stockholm International Peace Research Institute, *SIPRI Yearbook 2002: Armaments, Disarmament, and International Security* (Oxford: Oxford University Press, 2002), 374–378.
51. *Jane's Defence Weekly*, May 20, 1998.
52. United Nations, World Development Indicators, 294.
53. Amnesty International, *A Catalogue of Failures*, 32.
54. Kenneth M. Pollack, *The Threatening Storm: The United States and Iraq: The Crisis, the Strategy, and the Prospects after Saddam* (New York: Random House, 2001), 19.
55. Keller, *Arm in Arm*, 5.
56. Amnesty International, *A Catalogue of Failures*, 32–43.
57. Pollack, *The Threatening Storm*, 19; Keller, *Arm in Arm*, 4, 21.
58. Tucker, testimony, 3.
59. Bauer, "Arms Exports Post 9/11," 7.
60. Amnesty International, *A Catalogue of Failures*, 62–64.
61. On these points, see Sybille Bauer, Select Committee on Defence. The United Kingdom Parliament. Memorandum from Sybille Bauer, Institute for European Studies: Comments on the evidence of 27 February 2003; and Amnesty International, *A Catalogue of Failures*, 47.
62. De Vestel, *Defence Markets*; and Schmitt, *From Cooperation to Integration*.
63. Timothy Garton Ash, *In Europe's Name: Germany and the Divided Continent* (London: Jonathan Cape, 1993).
64. Duke, *The Elusive Quest for European Security*, 303.
65. This information comes from Schmitt, *From Cooperation to Integration*, 60; Kapstein, "Allies and Armaments;" and Keohane, "The EU and Armaments Co-Operation."

66. Schmitt, *From Cooperation to Integration*, 67. "Security of supply" traditionally requires firms to abide by government directives to prioritize national arms supply needs in times of crisis, possibly temporarily diverting production from other contracts. European states are currently negotiating how "security of supply" could be guaranteed transnationally.
67. See Sybille Bauer, "The Council's Report on the EU Code of Conduct on Arms Exports: Still no Transparency Breakthrough," *European Security Review* 3 (December 2000): 5–6; and Bauer, "Arms Exports post 9/11."
68. For the free market logic behind why states should want open competition in the defense industry, see Joanne Gowa and Edward Mansfield, "Power Politics and International Trade," *American Political Science Review* 87(2) (June 1993): 408–420.
69. This information is from Keohane, "The EU and Armaments Co-Operation," 21–23.

9

GLOBALIZATION AND NATIONAL SECURITY
Is Japan Still an Island?

Paul Midford

JAPAN HAS OFTEN BEEN HELD UP as a model of how to resist the forces of globalization, defined here as unorganized and purposeless forces, above all markets, with little regard for national borders. Taming market forces to the purposes of the state is said to be a Japanese specialty.[1] Recent evidence and closer inspection reveals, however, that globalization (or *gurobaruka* in Japanese) is increasingly influencing Japan economically in ways that challenge state manipulation.[2]

The effects of globalization are beginning to influence Japan's national security. In one sense, this is not surprising, because Japan has always defined its security "comprehensively," ranging beyond military security to encompass economic, technological, and political aspects (discussed further below). The common denominator in all these areas is a quest for autonomy, thereby ensuring greater degrees of freedom in foreign (and even domestic) policy. Even in traditional military security, however, globalization is beginning to have an impact on Japan.

This chapter focuses on the challenge globalization poses to Japan's goals of preserving and enhancing autonomy. It begins by identifying Japan's conception of security as comprehensive autonomy and how this conception was crafted in response to the state's security environment. The focus then shifts to how globalization is challenging Japan's capacity for autonomy in three areas: financial autonomy (exchange, and tangentially information and marketization), technological autonomy in civilian and military production (exchange and marketization), and

259

autonomous command and control of its military (transborder information flows). Specifically, globally mobile capital threatened Japan's regional production networks, trading partners and followers, the fragmentation of production has undermined Japan's long-term quest for the indigenization of production and technology (what the Japanese call *kokusanka*) in military aerospace. In addition, the fragmentation of production combined with cross-border flows of information promoted by information and communications technology (ICT), and embodied in the so-called Revolution in Military Affairs (RMA), is undermining Japan's long-cherished autonomous command and control of its military.

As stressed throughout this volume, however, states are hardly helpless in the face of the forces of globalization. They have choices: to pursue accommodating strategies, sheltering strategies, or harnessing strategies. An accommodating strategy entails adjusting to a loss of autonomy in exchange for some gain in capacity. A sheltering strategy entails accepting some loss of capacity for preserving or enhancing autonomy. A harnessing strategy involves exploiting globalization forces to enhance both autonomy and capacity. The have-your-cake-and-eat-it-too harnessing strategy is only available to those with significant structural power: the hegemon and to a much smaller extent regionally dominant powers such as Japan.

Japan has chosen different strategies in different areas, exacerbating, at least in the short-run, the Cold War bifurcation of its economic and military strategies. In finance, Japan has chosen a sheltering strategy, reaching for regional solutions to buffer itself and East Asia from globally footloose capital, in the process gaining greater autonomy also from the United States while sacrificing only a modicum of autonomy to other Asian nations. As discussed below, this sheltering strategy appears to have achieved some success, although it will take another financial crisis to know for sure. Critics suggest that Japan is sacrificing efficiency, and ultimately capacity, by trying to shelter itself and the region from globalized capital flows. However, as Kirshner points out in chapter 1, there is little evidence that liberalized capital flows are economically efficient. Thus, Tokyo's sheltering strategy does not necessarily entail sacrificing much capacity.

Japan has adopted a harnessing strategy expanding its domestic production networks into the region and reaching for neo-techno-nationalist cooperation with other states in Northeast Asia. However, Tokyo has chosen to accommodate itself to globalization by sacrificing autonomy in military security (*kokusanka* in military aerospace and full command and control of its military), mostly to the American unipole, in exchange for greater capacity. Overall, Japan's response to globalization is deepening its dependence upon the United States for military security while driving it to seek greater regional cooperation in order to maintain autonomy economically and financially in the face of global capital flows and American efforts to harness these flows for national gain.[3] As discussed in the conclusions, this bifurcated response to globalization may prove difficult to maintain, because policies such as financial regionalism and collaboration on missile defense may alienate the United States or China (and other Asian states), or both simultaneously.

A key challenge for this chapter is disentangling Japan's attempts to shelter itself from the forces of globalization with its attempts to maintain and enhance its autonomy vis-à-vis the American unipole. This is made all the more difficult, because as discussed by Mueller in chapter 5, the United States has often seen its national interests as promoted by the advancement of globalization. As described in the finance section of this chapter, the United States has attempted to harness the wave of globally mobile capital flows in order to promote its national interests in East Asia. Moreover, to the extent that American power has actually been advanced by globalization (as opposed to the mere perception), the degree of US preponderance that faces Japan is, itself, at least a second-order effect of globalization. Nonetheless, this chapter will distinguish between the influence that the globalization processes identified in this volume have had on Japanese national security versus those linked more directly to American choices and power.

JAPAN'S CONCEPTION OF SECURITY: COMPREHENSIVE AUTONOMY

Although this volume defines national security as political violence that affects the vital interests of the state, as noted above, Japan defines its national security much more broadly. Although maintaining the state's monopoly over the use of force internally and its relative military position externally are important to Tokyo's conception of security, Japan defines security "comprehensively," extending beyond force to include economic, political, and technological aspects.[4] The common denominator is autonomy. Although security can be defined as an absence of threats, autonomy connotes an absence of the threat of dependence. It is the search for autonomy and the management of dependence, when inevitable, that have been the central concerns in Japan's conception of security.[5] Japan seeks to limit its dependence upon other states or outside actors in order to increase its degrees of freedom in overall policy making.

By defining its security more broadly as comprehensive autonomy, Japan has given greater emphasis to nonmilitary aspects than is often the case elsewhere. To a large extent, this emphasis reflects real limits on the postwar Japanese state's ability to respond directly to military threats. The formal source of these limits is Japan's war pacifist postwar constitution. The deeper political cause stems from profound distrust internally,[6] and especially externally,[7] of the Japanese state's ability to wield the sword.[8] Japanese and Asian wartime experiences and collective memories of Japan's behavior as a military power up to 1945 continue to anchor expectations about Japan's future behavior should it reemerge as an independent military power.[9] To avoid an adverse domestic reaction, and especially to avoid counterbalancing by neighboring Asian states, Japan has chosen to limit its military autonomy. Yoshida Shigeru, the Japanese prime minister who defined Japan's postwar security strategy (the so-called Yoshida Doctrine), identified Asian mistrust of Japan's character as a military power as an important reason for avoiding rearmament and military autonomy: "many of the countries with which we had been at war still held Japan in distrust, a distrust which could easily be fanned into active hatred."[10] This concern was a central motivation for relying upon the United States for military security.

Japan's self-imposed limits upon its politico-military autonomy have gradually lessened over time. Beginning with purely economic roles in Asia, Japan gradually assumed political roles as well. Nonetheless, as enunciated by the 1977 Fukuda Doctrine, Japan's growing economic and political roles in Asia have been predicated upon a promise to never again become a "military power," defined as a power with the offensive capabilities to attack others.[11] To ensure the credibility of this doctrine, continued dependence upon the United States for security has been crucial. In a widely read 1990 essay, career diplomat and Vice Foreign Minister Kuriyama Takakazu explicitly identified defense dependence upon the United States as a key prerequisite for Japan's expanding economic and political role in Asia. "Regionally, the [US-Japan] security system builds international trust in Japan's fundamental position that it will never become a military great power. The security system makes it easy for neighboring countries to accept a large political and economic role from Japan."[12]

Since the end of the Cold War, Japan has sought not only to discourage counterbalancing but also to slowly improve its reputation as a military power. It has done so through the demonstration effect of a gradual and benign assumption of greater and greater security roles. Examples include Japan's emergence as an architect and active participant in regional security dialogues and the dispatch of the Self-Defense

Forces (SDF) overseas for peacekeeping, humanitarian missions, and more recently, for noncombat rear area support of American and allied military forces.[13]

The net result of these efforts is that although Japan remains heavily dependent upon the United States for its military security, it enjoys an increasing range of foreign policy tools. Beginning with reparations payments and then economic assistance in the early postwar period, by the 1990s, Japan had developed sufficient regional trust and institutional capacity to provide leadership in the construction of regional multilateral frameworks covering economics, politics, and to some extent, even security.[14] Japan has concentrated on using these tools to compensate for its lack of military autonomy. The very fact of Japan's heavy dependence upon the United States for military security has made reducing dependence upon the American unipole in other areas a priority.

The expansion of Japan's foreign policy options, a result of successfully reassuring other Asian states, has occurred as its traditional domestic tools for enhancing economic and technological autonomy have been eroding due to the pressures of globalization. Traditionally these tools have centered on market conforming planning and intervention, including industrial policy. The goal has been the promotion of autonomous and closed domestic production networks. However, as has been the case with European nations (see Epstein, chapter 8 of this volume), the effectiveness of these domestic policy tools has been declining as a result of globalization. Consequently, Japan has begun to slowly and inconsistently abandon these tools, gradually opening its markets to greater foreign direct investment and international market forces. Yet, as discussed below, at the same time Japan has tried to preserve its domestic production networks by regionalizing them. Japan has utilized its growing political role to organize regional multilateral cooperation to shield these production networks, and increasingly the region as a whole from some of the forces of globalization, most notably globally footloose capital flows. Although Japan's decision to reach for regional solutions has the potential to limit its autonomy vis-à-vis other Asian states, these limits appear to be minimal given Tokyo's advantages in terms of economic size and technological and financial sophistication compared with most of its Asian neighbors. Conversely, these regional solutions have offered the promise of greater insulation against globalizing forces, especially globally mobile capital, and equally important, the promise of expanded economic autonomy vis-à-vis the American unipole, and its attempts to exploit global capital flows to its own advantage.

EXCHANGE: INTERNATIONAL FINANCE

This section discusses the impact of globalized finance on Japan and its major East Asian trading partners. It focuses on how Japan has understood these impacts and responded. Japan's reaction has been different domestically and regionally: Tokyo has gradually opened up its own markets to greater capital liberalization and foreign investment while simultaneously seeking to shelter the wider region from globalized capital flows. American attempts to exploit these global flows to promote its political and economic power have enhanced Japan's incentive to pursue a sheltering strategy while simultaneously making this strategy more difficult to realize.

Domestic Finance

Because of globalized financial markets, Japanese policy makers face increased exposure to adverse market reactions when policy decisions appear to threaten investor interests. Growing capital mobility, especially the emergence of 24-7 virtualized capital, undergirded by the digital information, is driving momentum toward greater integration of national market standards and regulations.[15] This increasingly poses a challenge for Tokyo's distinctive form of capitalism and its autonomous regulatory regimes.

One notable example from the banking sector is the imposition of the Basle Accord or Bank for International Settlements (BIS) standards. The Basle standards imposed uniform risk-based capital requirements on commercial banks operating in Organisation for Economic Cooperation and Development (OECD) economies. These standards were in no small part aimed at Japanese banks, which were perceived elsewhere to benefit (or alteratively to pose a risk) from comparatively low and loosely defined Japanese capital ratios.[16] The imposition of international standards such as the BIS is undermining the very autonomy that Japanese decision makers so jealously guard. Although it initially fought the BIS, more recently, the Japanese state has attempted a more proactive harnessing strategy toward globalization. With the so-called Financial Big Bang of 1998–2001, the state has attempted to enhance the international competitiveness of Tokyo financial markets.[17]

To be sure, Tokyo's loss of autonomy remains minimal compared with most other states. Although Japan's position as the world's premier source of capital implies a high degree of exposure to financial globalization, in practice this position has shielded the country from many pressures associated with financial globalization while presenting opportunities for exerting influence globally and especially regionally.

This position has also allowed Japan to mitigate the effects of international standards upon its own economy and those of its neighbors. For example, Japan has parlayed its dominant regional financial position into primary management responsibility for the regional East Asian BIS office in Hong Kong, partially softening the impact of BIS on Japanese banks.[18]

Japan has traditionally received relatively little in the way of inward FDI. According to one account, this is because "Japan has protected itself ... by effectively limiting the ability of multinationals to gain control of Japanese companies." Although Japan is said to jealously guard the nationality of its firms,[19] the late 1990s witnessed marked increases in inward investment as overall foreign direct invement (FDI) flows increased and foreign companies bought controlling stakes in leading Japanese corporate entities such as Nissan, Mazda, Mitsubishi Motors' truck division, and the Long-Term Credit Bank. Although inward FDI continued to average less than 0.1 percent of GDP in the 1980s and early 1990s, it began to climb significantly in 1998, and by 2000, it had reached 0.6 percent of GDP (although inward flows fell to 0.4 percent in 2001). If the Japanese state once tried to discourage inward FDI, its position has recently changed, with Ministry of Economy, Trade, and Industry (METI) now actively encouraging greater inward FDI flows. This may be one cause for increased inflow since the late 1990s,[20] and this new policy suggests reduced sensitivity to corporate nationality.[21]

If the 2000 peak becomes the average for the next ten years, foreign ownership of the Japanese economy will reach almost 6 percent, approximately ten times the level in 2001. However, even this level would still be far below the current norm for OECD countries; the FDI inflow peak of 0.6 percent of gross national product (GNP) constitutes less than a quarter of the rate for a typical OECD country. Although barriers to capital inflow have been reduced, the role of foreign capital in the Japanese economy remains modest. Consequently, Japan is not as subject to international capital markets as are other OECD countries, or as exposed as France was in 1982.

Regional Finance

Although relatively insulated from globally mobile capital flows, Japan has nevertheless worried about the degree of exposure faced by its Asian economic partners and followers. To defend the legitimacy of its economic system, Asian social and political stability, and its region encompassing production networks, Japan has reached for regional solutions, under its own leadership, to shield East Asia from ever freer and larger capital flows and the market-opening agenda of unipolar America. Regionally, Japan has never been willing to pursue an accomodationalist strategy regarding globalized capital flows. The most notable examples of Japan's sheltering strategy emerged from the Asian Financial Crisis (AFC).

In response to the spreading Asian currency crisis of mid-1997, Japan used the annual IMF and World Bank meeting, held in Hong Kong in September, to propose establishing an Asian Monetary Fund (AMF), to be capitalized at $100 billion. The AMF would provide a regional financial surveillance mechanism and an emergency loan facility to detect and preemptively suppress financial crises. Most significantly, the United States was not included in the AMF and the use of the fund was not tied to IMF conditionality. Japanese diplomats resorted to their favorite tactics of extensive low-key consensus-building consultations (what is known in Japanese as *nemawashi*) using various regional channels, including the Executives' Meeting of East Asia-Pacific Central Banks (EMEAP) and informal meetings of Association of Southeast Asian Nations (ASEAN) and East Asian finance ministers, to try out the AMF proposal. Notably, these channels did not include the United States. Japan succeeded in building considerable regional support, especially among ASEAN, for the AMF proposal.[22]

The proposal met with immediate and intense American opposition.[23] The United States argued that the AMF proposal threatened IMF conditionality, undermining pressure for reform of "crony capitalist" economic systems that were supposedly the root cause of the AFC.[24] Second, and perhaps more importantly, US officials at the Hong Kong IMF–World Bank meeting argued that the AMF would undermine US leadership and influence, creating a divide across the Pacific. This charge came despite the presence of regional financial institutions in Europe, which exclude the United States and which have the same (and much greater) capabilities than those envisaged by Japan's AMF proposal.[25] To defeat this perceived challenge to American leadership, then Deputy Treasury Secretary Lawrence Summers even alluded to the unpleasant specter of regional domination by a Japan not unlike the militarist Japan of the past. US leadership "is crucial to avoid a descent into the kind of regionalism and protectionism that we saw in the periods between the first and second world wars."[26] This rhetoric persuaded China, and to a lesser extent, South Korea, to join the United States in opposing the AMF initiative.[27] Despite support from the rest of East Asia, especially ASEAN, the combined weight of US and Chinese opposition forced Japan to withdraw the initiative in November.

As Kirshner discusses in chapter 1, a world of completely unregulated capital is least risky for those with the largest and deepest economies and capital markets. The United States bears a disproportionately small share of the costs from financial crises, and the United States may even attract capital as investors "flee to quality." Most significantly, the United States can determine whom to help and whom not to and the conditions under which assistance will be extended. Thus, the United States has the most to gain and the least to lose from a world of unregulated capital flows. During the AFC, the United States used its influence over the IMF and its relatively sheltered position to harness the rising wave of global capital flows as a means to promote its own national interests. These interests included opening up East Asian economies for US goods, acquisitions of local firms, and, more broadly, spreading pro-American democracies, human rights, and free-market economics. US officials were at times candid about using IMF conditionality to promote narrow US interests: US Trade Representative Mickey Kantor called the IMF a "battering ram" for opening up Asian markets.[28] Summers boasted, "the IMF has done more to promote America's trade and investment agenda in East Asia than 30 years of bilateral trade negotiations."[29]

To a lesser degree, Japan's position parallels the American position that Kirshner identifies. As the world's leading source of capital, the world's second largest economy, and one of the leading global financial centers, Japan is also relatively sheltered from globalized capital flows. Nonetheless, Japan's voice in international financial institutions such as the IMF, although not negligible, is simply insufficient to ensure desired policies, even in Asia. Beyond the relative lack of influence at the IMF, Japan's economic and political exposure regionally in East Asia gave Tokyo an incentive to extend its own financial shelter to protect the entire region from the effects of globalized capital flows.

Globally footloose capital flows and US attempts to harness these flows to open markets and promote American interests were believed to threaten Japanese interests in at least four ways. First, IMF-imposed conditions and reforms threatened regional political stability, as the fall of Suharto and subsequent instability in Indonesia suggested. According to one Japanese economist, Japan has an important role to play in preventing American intervention from "leading to a collapse of political stability" in Southeast Asia.[30] Second, by giving US firms greater access to Asian markets and acquisitions, American rivals could improve their ability to challenge Japanese firms in markets long dominated by Japanese firms or at least Japanese licensed technology.[31] Third, by attacking the Capitalist Development Model[32] in other Asian states so directly, IMF bailout packages were attacking the long-run legitimacy of Japan's

own domestic system. This danger was driven home to Japanese officials at an Asia-Pacific Economic Cooperation (APEC) trade ministers'
meeting in June 1998, where the US and East Asian states united to
pressure Japan to liberalize marine and forestry product trade under
the Early Voluntary Sector Liberalization (EVSL) rubric. MITI officials
apparently came away convinced that the United States had used IMF
restructuring plans to force upon East Asian states an American neoliberal trade agenda.[33] Finally, expanded IMF conditionality threatened
regional Japanese production networks, especially to the extent that
these networks enjoy access to preferential governmental policies and
capital in host Asian nations (these networks are discussed at length in
the next section).

The common denominator to all these threats was globalized footloose capital flows exploited by a unipolar America. This US strategy
added to Japan's incentive to attempt to control these flows. If massive
and highly mobile capital undermined autonomous economic policy
making, concurrent intervention by the American hegemon seemed to
threaten the obliteration of such autonomy, at least for Japan's Asian
partners. In addition, Japan's strategy challenged Washington's agenda.
As a counterfactual exercise, one can speculate that had Japan's proposed AMF been in place (or at least a serious prospect) by November
1997, Washington's ability to leverage a $58 billion IMF bailout into a
massive opening of the Korean economy, or a $42 billion IMF bailout
into a similar opening of the Indonesian economy, would have been
greatly diminished.[34]

In the wake of the AMF proposal's defeat, Tokyo, rather than accommodating itself to globalized capital flows harnessed by the US hegemon,
persisted in its sheltering strategy. Japan switched tactics, shunning
high profile formal proposals by openly challenging the United States
in favor of more traditional low-key diplomatic methods. First, Japan
invoked bilateral currency intervention agreements with EMEAP partners as a partial substitution for AMF-type funding, jointly intervening
in November 1997 with Indonesia and Singapore to support the Thai
baht. Japan began to revive its regional multilateral financial diplomacy
by supporting the establishment of the Manila Framework in November
1997. This framework performed essentially the same regional capital
market surveillance functions contained in the original AMF proposal,
but with the subtraction of the non-IMF tied loan facility and with the
addition of the United States as a member.

The following year Japan revived the non-IMF tied loan facility
through a low-key step-by-step process. In October 1998, Finance Minister Miyazawa Ki'ichi announced a US$30 billion initiative to fund

short- and long-term needs. Known as the New Miyazawa Initiative, this fund was used to recapitalize ailing banks and corporations, presumably strengthening them against hostile takeovers. Although some claim that New Miyazawa Initiative funding is tied to IMF conditionality,[35] in fact, this loan facility offered softer conditionality than IMF funds and entirely avoided corporate governance and market-opening conditionality.[36] Indeed, Japanese leaders openly claimed that Miyazawa funds would be disbursed before IMF funds, arguing that "harsh conditionality" produces protracted negotiations, thereby ensuring that IMF funding is too late to head off a crisis.[37] In 1998 and 1999, a number of Asian states received funding from the New Miyazawa Initiative (Indonesia, $2.4 billion; Korea, $5 billion; Malaysia, $2.2 billion; the Philippines, $1.6 billion; Thailand, $1.9 billion). Japan also issued up to $22.5 billion in export credits to promote intraregional exports, thereby helping to sustain its regional production networks.[38] New Miyazawa Initiative and other crisis-related assistance from Japan eventually totaled $80 billion.[39] Japanese funding for recapitalizing troubled Asian companies helped Asian nations resist US and IMF pressure. For example, this funding probably contributed to what US Treasury Secretary Lawrence Summers claimed was Indonesian "foot-dragging" over liquidating failed companies.[40]

Malaysia was a primary, and indeed the first, beneficiary of Japanese funding. Tokyo generously assisted Kuala Lumpur despite the later's open challenge to the United States and the IMF by imposing capital controls. Japan started pumping assistance funding into Malaysia almost immediately after Kuala Lumpur imposed capital controls, despite Washington's opposition.[41] The use of New Miyazawa funding to help Malaysia is also the clearest example of delinkage from IMF conditionality. The eventual success of Malaysia's capital controls advertised the promise of Japan's sheltering strategy in helping Asian nations reestablish policy autonomy.

In May 2000, Japan took a further step toward creating the functions of the AMF with the adoption the Chiang Mai Initiative (CMI). Ostensibly an ASEAN initiative, but in reality an example of Japanese "proxy diplomacy," the CMI, adopted at a meeting of ASEAN-Plus-Three [(APT): the ASEAN states plus China, Japan, and Korea] finance ministers, brought a substantial expansion of the existing bilateral currency swap and currency repurchase facility agreements. Essentially a system of multiple bilateralisms, the CMI provides de facto regional multilateral funding to help members fight off speculative attacks on national currencies.[42] China's support[43] was clinched by greater Japanese efforts at informal consultations with Chinese counterparts and by a shift in Chinese thinking away from worrying about the threat of Japanese hegemony and toward worrying more about the threat of American hegemony after the Kosovo War and the bombing of its Belgrade embassy.[44]

Chinese participation and the extensive foreign reserves held by China and other members (over $800 billion in total) suggest that the CMI may be effective.[45] Although 90 percent of the funds committed to these currency swaps are in theory tied to IMF conditionality,[46] there is continued ambiguity about whether Japan's commitments are (or would be in a crisis) actually tied (tightly or otherwise) to IMF conditionality.[47] These doubts are fueled by the continued existence of the untied $15 billion loan facility created by the New Miyazawa Initiative for short-term financial stabilization.[48] Moreover, as one study notes, more important than the current declaratory policy on IMF conditionality or the current level of committed funds, "the simple process of negotiating and concluding these agreements has had a major impact on the ability of countries in the region to fend off future speculative attacks by giving rise to dense networks of communication."[49] These networks increase the ability of Japan and its APT partners to transcend formal agreements and cooperate on the fly during a crisis and are contributing to more ambitious projects, most notably the creation of Asian regional bond markets[50] and longer term efforts toward creating an Asian Monetary Union (AMU).[51] As a first step toward an AMU, the APT finance ministers agreed in May 2004 to consider various proposals for strengthening the CMI framework by the end of the year, including lifting the pre-IMF 10 percent cap or a tenfold increase in CMI funding.[52] The creation of the CMI mechanism within the APT, itself a reaction to the AFC and an organization that excludes the United States, reinforces the impression that Japanese policy makers were "able to nudge the APT framework towards regional financial cooperation and thereby create in all but name another AMF."[53]

Although Susan Strange argued as early as 1990 that global financial integration has enhanced US structural power,[54] some are now concluding that Japan's

> position at the centre of the East Asian political economy is not easily lost and provides it with a good deal of structural power … the actual outcome of the East Asian currency crisis may not be to undermine Japanese leadership and the model of the developmental state in the region, but against all expectations, actually to consolidate them.[55]

If Japan really has clawed its way back from defeat, its determination reflects a desire to shelter East Asia from globalized flows of "hot money." Tokyo believes that these flows, especially when harnessed by the American unipole to advance its own interests, undermine the stability of Japan's Asian partners, challenge the legitimacy of it's own economic system, and threaten Japan's growing regional production networks.

As is evident elsewhere in this chapter, the influence of the US hegemon is intertwined with the stateless and purposeless forces of globalization. Financial globalization, and especially capital liberalization, is at least in some part the result of policies pursued by the United States. Even if the United States had not actively sought to exploit the AFC for its own interests, Japan would nonetheless have had sufficient incentive to pursue a sheltering strategy to protect its partners from the vagaries of unregulated global flows of capital. The AFC demonstrated how disruptive these flows could be for Japan's regional production networks, its major trading partners, and followers. Indeed, the AMF proposal was initially promoted at a time when Washington appeared to be ignoring the emerging financial contagion. As a counterfactual exercise, we can speculate that had Washington continued the initial disinterest it showed during the Thai baht crisis in July 1997, the proposed AMF probably would have been realized. However, over the longer run, Washington's decision to cede regional financial leadership to Japan might have encouraged greater Chinese opposition to this leadership. In sum, the pressures of globalized capital flows, combined with the American efforts to exploit these flows, increased not only Japan's incentives for pursuing a regional sheltering strategy but also regional receptivity to this strategy.[56]

TRADE AND PRODUCTION I: REGIONAL PRODUCTION NETWORKS AND COOPERATION

This section examines Japan's strategy of harnessing the stateless and purposeless forces of globalization to enhance economic capacity and autonomy through the creation of private regional production networks and formal regional cooperation. Beyond the extension of Japan's private-sector industrial networks, Japan has recently promoted a more formal model of regional corporate-state cooperation in Northeast Asia. The initial objective of this model is challenging the dominance of the Windows operating system (OS) and preventing its spread beyond personal computers. This new cooperative model reflects deepening dependence upon regional partners to avoid much greater technological dependence upon a single multinational corporation or superpower and appears to reflect what has been identified as a neo-techno-nationalist strategy. Like finance, the promotion of regional production networks and cooperation reflect efforts to enhance autonomy, especially vis-à-vis the United States, albeit at the cost of slightly increased dependence upon East Asian partners.

Regional Production Networks

Harnessing the forces of globalization, Japan has extended its distinctive form of capitalism—the Capitalist Development State—to Asia through the force of example and regional hierarchically integrated production networks.[57] Arguably, Japan has been building its own system of systems in Asia, sometimes identified as the "complex production" links model.[58] A derivation of Japan's "flying geese model"[59] of sequential (hierarchical) economic development, with Japan as the lead goose, this model, unlike the flying geese model, argues that the follower geese (other Asian nations) remain dependent upon Japanese technology and expertise and therefore cannot close production cycles to create their own export industries.[60]

These networks have allowed Japan to realize economies of scale while exploiting regional abundancies in productive factors (e.g., inexpensive abundant labor). These Asian production networks also allow Japanese companies to move their production and exports beyond the framework of the Japanese polity, thereby redefining trade imbalances and frictions with the United States and Europe as imbalances between these two and the East Asian region, on the one hand, and between Japan and East Asia, on the other. Japan is extending national industries into regional production networks, achieving significant economies of scale, tapping into diverse production factor abundances (e.g., abundant labor), and preferential access to Asian markets in the process.[61] In fact, this has been a stated goal of MITI/METI, namely "the creation of open [sic] industrial networks" in East Asia.[62] Japan's Asian production networks are significant for another reason: they represent a form of globalization clearly divorced from the policies and interests of the American hegemony, an "alternative" non-American form of globalization.

Trade data suggest the growing importance of Japan's regional production networks. Before the outbreak of the AFC in 1997, Asia experienced the world's fastest growth of intraregional trade, a large part of which consisted of the export of technologically sophisticated parts and capital goods from Japan to subsidiaries in Asian nations for use in manufacturing finished goods, a substantial proportion of which were then exported beyond the region.[63] The growth and composition of this trade reflects the regionalization of Japan's production networks. Another reflection of the growth of these networks has been the tendency of many Asian nations (especially the ASEAN states and South Korea) to run persistent trade deficits with Japan. Technological dependence is a major reason—since the mid-1990s, half of all technological imports in East Asia came from Japan, and more than half of technical experts dispatched by the Japanese government are sent to Asia.[64]

Beyond purely Japanese production networks, East Asian states sometimes utilize Japanese capital and technology for promoting targeted industries. A prominent example is Malaysia's national car, the Proton, which has been dependent upon technology and other inputs from Mitsubishi.[65]

During the AFC, IMF structural reforms that led to market opening and the demise of industrial policy obviously threatened Japanese stakes in national industrial projects such as the Proton. These reforms also threatened long-term hierarchical ties (based on technology and capital transfers) with Asian firms, and even Japanese subsidiaries hit by currency crisis induced illiquidity and the contraction of local markets. It is not surprising then that the Japanese government made $22.5 billion in trade insurance and trade-related loans available to kick-start intraregional Asian trade again[66] and that a significant portion of New Miyazawa funds were used to bail out Japanese small and medium enterprises in Asia.[67]

Japan's Asian production networks demonstrate the structural power that can be derived from being a systems integrator. This is illustrated by MITI/METI's self-appointed role as the technological manager of Asian nations, especially ASEAN. METI saw the AFC as partly resulting from the "Chinese goose overtaking the ASEAN geese," thereby creating destabilizing market competition. METI's solution was to raise the technological level of ASEAN (keep the geese flying in order) to stay clear of Chinese competition.[68]

Regional Cooperation

The emergence of such "systems of systems" across a range of areas is arguably one of the key characteristics of globalization. The increasing mobility of trade, capital, labor, and information is creating pressure for the harmonization of national standards and systems into transborder and global standards and systems.[69] One purposeless and stateless driver behind the rise of transborder and globalized systems of systems is the digital revolution. The revolution in digital information flows increases pressure for national systems to integrate into larger systems. The rise of virtualized 24-7 global finance is one obvious example. The RMA, discussed below, represents the emergence of a digital system of systems in traditional security. The rise of the Internet is another obvious example; the emergence of a dominant OS for personal computers is perhaps the most compelling case. A system of systems creates clear externalities: the systems integrator (creator of the overall system) gains structural power (in the form of privileged knowledge and control) over the behavior of subsystem creators, and overall control over the system's operations.

The power conferred by being a digital systems integrator can be best seen in the Windows OS—what I will call the "Windows Effect." OS software integrates application software into the overall functioning of a computer. As is well known, this role has given Microsoft the opportunity to mold, if not limit, the access that application software makers have to personal computer (PC) users. What is less appreciated is that Window's closed code has also transferred power from even large and sophisticated users, such as multinational corporations and national governments, to Microsoft. As one observer remarked, "if you are the Japanese Government and you're installing Microsoft software on all of your systems, if anything goes wrong with it, it's up to Microsoft to fix it, and you have to rely on them and their programmers."[70] Behind this power lays a massive externality: the convenience of using an OS allowing smooth communication with other computers using the same system. This is the essence of the Windows Effect. It is what allows a mediocre OS to gain commanding global dominance. This externality is evident in other digital systems of systems, including missile defense.

Strikingly, Japan is tackling the original Windows Effect head on. Tokyo is reaching for a regional alliance to challenge the dominance of Windows. This alliance is characterized by public-private cooperation among three Northeast Asian nations. By September 2003, Japan had committed $85.5 million and built a regional coalition with China and South Korea (and implicitly backed by Malaysia) to promote joint research and development of open-source OS alternatives to Windows. In November, with governmental encouragement, sixteen computer (including IBM Japan) and consumer electronics makers agreed to form a Japan Open Source Software Promotion Forum, which was followed by the creation of a bilateral Japan-Korea forum. At an April 2004 meeting in Beijing involving bureau heads from the economic ministries and representatives from private industry, including local multinational affiliates such as IBM China and IBM Japan, the three nations agreed to form a Japan-China-Korea "Northeast Asia Open Source Software Promotion Forum." National, bilateral, and trilateral efforts focus on using Linux OS as the basis for developing new open OSs for computers, fourth-generation cell phones, digital broadcasting, and so forth.[71]

The first goal appears to boast the competitiveness of Linux and encourage its wider adoption in East Asia if not beyond. A second goal is to address the danger that the continued dominance of Windows for computers will quickly spread to OSs for servers, personal digital assistants (PDAs), digital cameras, car navigation systems, and so forth. Japan fears that the spread of Windows to these other products will subordinate, if not stymie, most of Japan's high-tech digital industries, subjecting them to the whims of Microsoft. This explains government and industry focus on building a consumer electronics (CE) Linux for use in PDAs, cell phones, and so forth.[72] A broader goal is to reassert national control over OSs, including governmental computers. "If you've installed Linux, your programmers can actually get in there, find the problems and fix them themselves."[73] Japan might even share China's fear that Windows has "back doors" allowing Microsoft or the U.S. government to spy on users.[74] (For a broader discussion of backdoor threats, see Herrera, chapter 3 of this volume.)

A recent report's conclusions about China's prospects for successfully challenging Microsoft Windows arguably ring even more true for the regional alliance of China, Korea, and Japan: "market power ... and the dynamics of competition among multinational corporations for access ... highlights opportunities for China [Korea and Japan] to alter the balance of structural power in the international political economy by challenging the architectural leader."[75] More broadly, Japan's promotion of a regional Northeast Asian software alliance illustrates what has been termed "neo-techno-nationalism." Whereas technonationalism is state-led and closed to foreigners, and technoglobalism is open but insensitive to national interests, neo-techno-nationalism attempts to promote national interests through public-private partnerships and is open to foreign participation under some circumstances.[76]

At this point, a skeptic might ask whether the structural power conferred by being a systems integrator is not more an artifact of American hegemonic power rather than a consequence of the digital revolution. In short, would Microsoft enjoy the power it does were it not an American corporation? Although there is undeniably a relation between the distribution of power among states, the nationality of firms, and firms' ability to exploit the structural power inherent in digital systems of systems, this relationship does not limit such structural power only to the corporations of the hegemon. Although Microsoft has dominated the OS market for personal computers, Japanese firms have achieved similar dominance and structural power in the market for embedded OSs. Japan's The Real-time Operating System Nucleus (TRON) OS controls 60 percent of the global market for build-in OSs (automobile engines, home appliances, digital cameras, cell phones, and so forth). Rather than challenge TRON, Microsoft capitulated and agreed to cooperate in making Windows and TRON compatible.[77] TRON shows the power that even a non-American digital system of systems can realize once it achieves global dominance.

TRADE AND PRODUCTION II: MILITARY AEROSPACE AND AUTONOMY

This section examines how globalization has affected Japan's long-standing efforts to promote autonomous production (*kokusanka*) of weapons, especially in military aerospace, and to maintain autonomous command and control of its military. It finds that Japan is responding to the forces of globalization in military aerospace by adopting an accommodating strategy—Japan is accommodating itself to a loss of autonomy in exchange for greater capacity. This highlights the second half of the bifurcation dynamic identified in this chapter: Japan is accommodating itself to greater dependence upon the American hegemon for security even while pressing ahead with efforts to achieve greater autonomy financially and economically. The reasons behind Japan's surrender of further autonomy in military production have much to do with the very different and more hostile environment that Japan faces for regional security cooperation versus economic cooperation. This section focuses upon the production of combat aircraft and missile defense.

Indigenous Combat Aircraft

Stateless and purposeless global forces are creating incentives for Japan to move away from its long-term goal of *kokusanka,* or indigenization, in defense production.[78] *Kokusanka* reflects a long-term goal to ensure Japan's military and economic security by promoting an independent techno-industrial base, especially in defense industries, a goal that Richard Samuels has labeled "technonationalism."[79] In many areas, Japan's drive for *kokusanka* has been very successful: most weapons systems used by the SDF are domestically produced and many are domestically designed. However, the peak of Japan's ambition for indigenous weapons production has been indigenously produced high-performance combat aircraft (fighters and ground attack jets). Globalization has caused Japan to abandon this goal and accommodate itself to technological dependence.

As Epstein notes (chapter 8 of this volume) regarding Europe, globalization is producing purposeless technological and economic forces that are having a transformative effect on weapons production in three respects. First, the changing nature of technology in terms of growing complexity and expense makes national production increasingly difficult. Second, as increasing economies of scale in military aerospace have come to exceed that capturable by the nation-state, these economies of scale have become a salient force for globalization.[80] Third, increasingly competitive markets have increased the opportunity costs to states that choose national production as a goal instead of relying upon global markets to guide procurement. As Epstein notes, however, a nonsystemic force, namely US government-promoted consolidation in military aerospace, contributed to the increased competitiveness of markets, increasing pressure on non-US aerospace producers to also consolidate beyond national level firms.

Japan's strategy of gradually increasing *kokusanka* in defense production was relatively successful up to the late 1980s; Japan was gradually climbing the technological ladder toward indigenous design, development, and manufacture of high-performance combat aircraft.[81] The turning point came in the late 1980s when Japan began planning to indigenously develop and produce a state-of-the-art fighter support and ship-attack plane, known as the FSX (later designated the F-2). This was to be a replacement for an indigenously developed but technologically second-rate ground attack plane known as the F-1. Eventually, Japan abandoned indigenous development in favor of codevelopment based on the US F-16.[82] The true significance of the FSX decision transcended a single combat aircraft development program, because along with giving up indigenous development of the FSX (a technological long shot according to critics) came the recognition that indigenous production of high-performance combat aircraft was an unrealistic goal. Although important indigenization efforts continue in Japanese military aerospace (e.g., development of an indigenous follow-on to the P-3C anti-submarine patrol plane—the P-X),[83] the cancellation of indigenous FSX development also marked the end of a decades long drive to eventually produce high-performance indigenous combat aircraft.[84]

To be sure, US pressure played a significant role in the decision to abandon indigenous development of the FSX itself and also discouraged Japan from considering Europe as an alternative codevelopment partner.[85] Nonetheless, American pressure had little appreciable role in the larger decision to abandon the long-cherished goal of developing an indigenous high-performance combat aircraft. Rather, the increasing difficulty of producing such aircraft entirely within the national boundaries of a single economy, even the world's second largest, was the main reason for this broader decision.[86] As Epstein finds in chapter 8 of this volume, European nations have found it increasingly necessary to transcend national-scale production to remain viable in military aerospace. The same reality faces Japan (and increasingly even the United States), prompting Tokyo to tap into a global production network in order to remain viable in military aerospace.[87] Through the FSX dispute, Japan came to focus increasing attention on dominating codevelopment, especially by assuming the systems integration role, rather than on preparing for a future of fully autonomous design and development.[88]

Of course, Japan can, and has at times opted to, purchase less than state-of-the-art products for the sake of promoting greater autonomy, as is evident in the original decision to produce the indigenous but inferior F-1 and its more recent decision in 1998 to procure indigenous spy satellites with relatively mediocre resolution.[89] These satellites also lack infrared sensors for detecting missile launches (an increasingly important function), involve the purchase of key components from the United States, and rely upon the United States for processing the data from these satellites.[90] Conversely, building the satellites themselves provides Japan with the all-important role (and learning curve) of systems integrator.[91] Similarly, Japan has pursued an extremely expensive, and not especially successful, independent rocket development program for the sake of *kokusanka* and maintaining autonomy. Although Japan will likely continue to choose autonomy over capacity for a wide variety of military aerospace systems, the decision to abandon indigenous high-performance combat aircraft production represents a retreat from aerospace *kokusanka* that is best explained by the purposeless and stateless forces of globalization. Moreover, as discussed below, globalization will likely prompt Japan to abandon an increasing range of other indigenization projects in military aerospace.

Missile Defense

The problem of increasing economies of scale pushing aerospace production to a scale beyond the grasp of the world's second largest economy to capture, indeed, even for the world's largest economy to fully capture, is exacerbated by the increasing scale of the weapon systems themselves. Some weapons are expanding in scale beyond that capturable within a single nation's borders. This reflects the dawning of the

RMA. The RMA entails the emergence of digital military information networks that exceed national boundaries, systems of systems, that are used to dominate the information dimension of war.[92] These systems typically revolve around widely deployed sensors, linked by high-speed digital data streams to data analysis and command and control systems, and to weapons systems designed to respond to gathered, analyzed information and the decisions made upon the basis of this information. Missile defense is the most concrete embodiment of this concept of a military system of systems to date, but it will gradually spread to include other areas, such as intelligence and antisubmarine warfare.[93]

Despite the tremendous dominance of Microsoft, tackling the original Windows Effect is easier than tackling this effect in military systems of systems. Whereas Linux offers an open-source alternative to Windows, there are not obvious open-source alternatives for military systems of systems such as missile defense. And just as the efficiency gains for computer networks are imperiled by the presence of multiple OSs, or procurement by the lack of an overall information system linking suppliers and users, so too the efficiencies realized by a military system of systems, such as a missile defense system, are imperiled by national components imperfectly integrated. Independent national military commands beget further losses in efficiency. By challenging its conception of security defined as autonomy, the emergence of globalized military systems of systems has imposed a painful dilemma for Japan.

Since regaining independence in 1952, Japan has jealously guarded command and control of its military. Japan is the only major US ally with which there is no mechanism for joint (United States) command of its military.[94] Formally, this reflects the government's interpretation of Japan's war-renouncing constitution as forbidding participation in "collective defense." In other words, Japan has the right to cooperate with its ally, the United States, only for the sake of defending Japanese territory. Cooperation to help defend the United States or its interests, not to mention other nations, is deemed to be an example of the unconstitutional exercise of collective defense.[95]

Behind this legal argument lay at least three deeper political issues. One is the fear of weakening civilian control over the Japanese SDF. Given Japan's experience of the 1930s, when the military spun out of control and hijacked the state, postwar elites have been perhaps understandably paranoid about again losing control.[96] Another reason is the fear that the creation of a joint control mechanism might facilitate American efforts to commandeer the Japanese military for involvement in regional conflicts. Thus, the lack of a joint command mechanism has allowed Japan to minimize the risk of "entrapment" by its American ally.[97] As discussed above, the Japanese state has been deeply committed to guarding and increasing autonomy as central to its definition of security.

Although Japan is the only major US ally lacking a mechanism for integrated command and control with US forces, missile defense threatens to change this. As a digital system of systems, it involves integrating reconnaissance, space-based and ground-based sensors with data analysis, command and control functions (C3ISR), and interceptor missiles over a wide area far beyond Japanese territory.[98] Because of the short warning times involved, and the need for tight integration, there is little opportunity for Japanese leaders to opt out in a crisis. In effect, Japanese forces would be placed in an integrated system under US command. As one study notes, "given the physical realities of very short warning times, it will be absolutely necessary to achieve effective, seamless, and unimpeded command and control of disparate sensors and weapons.... Japan and the United States will have to learn to integrate command and control functions, either implicitly or explicitly."[99] In short, the design of a missile defense system would greatly exacerbate the alliance dilemma of entrapment or abandonment for Japan. As Christopher Hughes notes, "Japan might be unable to take an independent decision to deploy BMD in a crisis situation unless it has secured the consent of the US and has demonstrated that this action was compatible with its ally's interest."[100]

Again, the Windows Effect means that the United States, as the digital systems integrator, will be in the driver's seat technologically. As the study cited above notes, "systems and components will be overwhelmingly American in origin, and the United States will have to step up to political and technical leadership for design and integration. Japan will have to come to grips with this fundamental reality."[101] Thus, the development and deployment of a missile defense system threatens to further subordinate Japan's military aerospace industry[102] in the same way that the Windows OS can subordinate software applications and hardware producers, or a dominant financial power can force others to adopt its financial standards and regulations. Although purposeful state behavior, in this case that of unipolar America, plays an undeniable role, beneath this lays the same stateless, purposeless force discussed elsewhere in this chapter: Windows Effect compatibility externalities for digital systems that transcend national boundaries.

The key difference between indigenous development of combat aircraft and missile defense, on the one hand, and regional cooperation in finance, tackling Windows, and the extension of Japan's production networks, on the other, is the absence of a viable regional option for Japan. As Epstein notes in chapter 8, globalization and American defense industry consolidation has promoted European defense industry consolidation, albeit without a corresponding consolidation of political authority. Although Asia is enjoying increasing levels of regional cooperation across a wider range of issue areas, regional defense industry consolidation and cooperation in Asia remains virtually unthinkable. One reason is the presence of a nascent strategic competition between Japan and China.[103] A more serious problem for Japan is continued distrust across the region of Japan as a military power, a mistrust that renders defense industry cooperation even with other American allies (Japan's de facto allies)[104] out of the question. Although Epstein finds that regional defense consolidation has improved the competitive position of European defense firms, regional defense consolidation is not an option for Japanese firms. Neither is another important option for European weapons manufacturers: third party export markets. Another consequence of regional distrust of Japan as a military power has been a long-standing ban on weapons exports (with exceptions made for the United States).[105] Thus, while Europe is matching greater economic integration and autonomy from the United States with greater defense industry integration, Japan is pursuing an increasingly bifurcated strategy: greater regional economic and financial cooperation to limit dependence upon the United States while simultaneously deepening its dependence upon the United States for military technology and hardware.

CONCLUSIONS

Japan is responding to globalization differently in different areas. Economically, Tokyo is pursuing a regional sheltering strategy with respect to finance and a harnessing strategy by promoting regional production networks and technological cooperation. Indeed, Japan's regional production networks represent an alternative non-American form of globalization divorced from the interests and policies of the United States. Also, Tokyo is accommodating itself to a loss of autonomy in military aerospace and a significant degradation of autonomous command and control of its military. Thus, Japan's response sharply bifurcates between economic and military security. Although this bifurcation was also characteristic of Japan's grand strategy during the Cold War, globalization is exacerbating it.

Some argue this bifurcation is Tokyo's desired outcome: Japan pursues a strategy of "mercantile realism" that distinguishes balancing against techno-economic threats versus military ones. Thus, Japan is willing to offer at least limited military cooperation to the United States while simultaneously utilizing potential military threats, most notably China, in its efforts to balance American techno-economic competitiveness.[106] However, this chapter has presented a different interpretation. Rather than being Tokyo's desired outcome, economic-military bifurcation is in no small part a legacy of Japan's difficult postwar position in East Asia. Deep Asian and domestic mistrust of the Japanese state's ability to wield the sword forced Japan to accept deep dependence upon the United States for military security.[107] Japan compensated for this dependence by focusing upon enhancing economic autonomy.

During the Cold War, Japan was able to gradually reassure Asian states, and this reduced mistrust allowed Japan to expand its regional role, first economically and then politically. Since the 1990s, reduced mistrust of Japan has allowed the country to assume a leadership role in promoting regional multilateral cooperation. This has opened up greater opportunities for promoting regionalism as a means to respond to globalization. Although promoting regionalism has entailed some loss of autonomy for Japan, given the nation's regionally dominant position, this loss has been minimal. Indeed, despite China's rise, Japan's regional dominance, especially in finance and regional production networks, to some extent parallels America's global dominance.

In the area of military production, however, nascent Sino-Japanese rivalry, and above all regional and domestic mistrust of Japan as a military power, has rendered a regional option for weapons production unthinkable. Although Mitsubishi can use regional networks to produce automobiles, the political barriers to producing combat aircraft this way remain formidable. Although Japan has continued to demonstrate its desire for techno-industrial autonomy in weapons procurement by purchasing its own spy satellites, even at the cost of effectiveness and a higher price tag, increasing economies of scale in defense production are prompting Japan to give up the goal of autonomous production for high-combat aircraft and for an increasing range of other military aerospace projects. Moreover, participating in a missile defense system where the United States acts as the systems integrator greatly increases Japan's alliance dilemma of entrapment or abandonment and perhaps irrevocably impairing autonomous command and control of its military. Participation will further limit, and ultimately subordinate, Japan's military aerospace industry for decades to come.

Globalization not only exacerbates bifurcation in Japan's security strategy, it also appears to be deepening the consequences of this bifurcation. Embracing missile defense with its principle military partner, the United States, undermines Japan's ability to pursue financial and economic regionalism with its principle regional partner, China, and vice versa. Indeed, military dependence upon the United States was an important motivation for Japan to scrap its original AMF proposal.[108] Given China's strong opposition to missile defense,[109] Japan might have to eventually choose between further developing regional financial cooperation (such as the CMI) and collaborating with the United States on missile defense. In short, Japan risks alienating the United States, or China (and perhaps ASEAN and other Asian states), or both simultaneously.

In the medium to long run, however, Japan has a chance to decrease its dependence upon the United States for security by building Asian and domestic trust in its ability to wield the sword. Japan has been attempting to reassure these audiences through a combination of bilateral and regional security dialogues, and by the demonstration effect of the Japanese military serving benignly and professionally overseas. Indeed, Japan's decision to dispatch SDF troops to Iraq appears to have more to do with efforts to relegitimate a "normal" security role for the Japanese state than with satisfying Washington's "demands."[110] Moreover, growing cooperation with China and other East Asian nations on financial and technological issues may have a positive spillover effect, building Asian trust in Japan as a partner in other areas, including security.[111]

At the same time, Washington's strategy of riding the tide of globalization to promote its national interests, and more generally its behavior as a unipole, may be creating new US-focused mistrust in Asia that is beginning to negate mistrust of Japan. These trends may make it easier for Japan to eventually scrap its ban on weapons exports and take a more active leadership role in promoting regional military cooperation in East Asia paralleling expanding economic cooperation. Nonetheless, there is little reason to expect much progress on this front before the end of this decade.

NOTES

1. For a study that identifies and favorably evaluates a distinctive Japanese market intervention strategy within the context of grand strategy, see Eric Heginbotham and Richard J. Samuels, "Mercantile Realism and Japanese Foreign Policy," *International Security* 22(4) (Spring 1998): 171–203. For a less favorable evaluation of Japan's market intervention strategy see Richard Katz, *Japan: The System that Soured* (Boulder, CO: Lynne Reinner, 1998).
2. See William W. Grimes, "Japan and Globalization: From Opportunity to Restraint," in *East Asia and Globalization*, ed. Samuel S. Kim (New York: Rowman and Littlefield Publishers, Inc., 2000), 55–79; Katz, *Japan: The System that Soured*.

3. Eric Heginbotham and Richard J. Samuels make a somewhat similar argument, identifying a Japanese tactic of double or dual hedging: "One the one hand, Japan relies on its alliance with the United States as a hedge against military threats. On the other hand, it relies on different partners, including some that the United States identifies as present or potential adversaries, as a hedge against economic uncertainties and dangers." See Eric Heginbotham and Richard J. Samuels, "Japan," in *Strategic Asia 2002–03: Asian Aftershocks*, eds. Richard J. Ellings and Aaron L. Friedberg (Seattle: The National Bureau of Asian Research, 2002), 122.

4. "Comprehensive security" as a concept was developed by an advisory council to Prime Minister Ohira Masayoshi. See Sogo Anzenhosho Kenkyu Gurupu, *Sogo Anzen hosho Senryaku* [Comprehensive Security Strategy] (Tokyo: Okurasho Insatsu kyoku, 1980).

5. For a discussion of the philosophical and historical underpinnings of this desire, see Paul Kowert and Katja Weber, "Cultures of Order in Postwar Japan," paper prepared for presentation at the 99th Annual Meeting of the American Political Science Association, Philadelphia, Pennsylvania, August 28–31, 2003. Regarding the ideology of "technonationalism" in Japan, see Richard J. Samuels, *"Rich Nation Strong Army" National Security and the Technological Transformation of Japan* (Ithaca, NY: Cornell University Press, 1994), especially 33–78.

6. Thomas U. Berger, *Cultures of Antimilitarism: National Security in Germany and Japan* (Baltimore, MD: Johns Hopkins University Press, 1998).

7. Paul Midford, "The Logic of Reassurance and Japan's Grand Strategy," *Security Studies* 11(3) (Spring 2002): 1–43; Midford, "Making the Best of a Bad Reputation: Japanese and Russian Grand Strategies in East Asia" (Ph.D. dissertation, Columbia University, 2001); Barry Buzan, "Japan's Future: Old History versus New Roles," *International Affairs* 64(4) (1988): 557–573; and Buzan, "Japan's Defence Problematique," *The Pacific Review* 8(1) (1995): 25–43.

8. Paul Midford, "Cartelization Versus Democratization: The Prospects for a Revival of Japanese Overexpansion," paper prepared for delivery at the Annual Meeting of the American Political Science Association, Washington DC, August 31–September 3, 2000.

9. Midford, "Making the Best of a Bad Reputation," chap. 4. For a more recent and Constructivist approach to this issue, see Thomas U. Berger, "The Construction of Antagonism: The History Problem in Japan's Foreign Relations," in G. John Ikenberry and Takashi Inoguchi, eds., *Reinventing the Alliance: U.S.-Japan Security Partnership in an Era of Change* (New York: Palgrave Macmillan, 2003), 63-84.

10. Shigeru Yoshida, *The Yoshida Memoirs* (London: Heinemann, 1961), 274. On Yoshida's position, also see Chihiro Hosoya, "Japan's Response to U.S. Policy on the Japanese Peace Treaty," *Hitotsubashi Journal of Law and Politics* 10 (1981): 18.

11. Sueo Sudo, *The Fukuda Doctrine and ASEAN: New Dimensions in Japanese Foreign Policy* (Singapore: Institute of Southeast Asian Studies, 1992).

12. Takakazu Kuriyama, "Gekido no 90 nendai to Nihon gaiko no shintenkai: Atarashii kokusai chitsujyo kenchiku e no sekkyokuteki kouken no tame ni," *Gaikou Forum*, May 1990, 20. The author thanks Noguchi Kazuhiko for valuable comments on this point and elsewhere.

13. Paul Midford, "Japan's Response to Terror: Dispatching the SDF to the Arabian Sea," *Asian Survey* 42(2) (March/April 2003): 329–351; and Midford, "Japan's Leadership Role in East Asian Security Multilateralism: The Nakayama Proposal and the Logic of Reassurance," *Pacific Review* 13(3) (2000), 367–397.

14. Midford, "Japan's Response to Terror"; Midford, "Japan's Leadership Role in East Asian Security Multilateralism"; Kuniko P. Ashizawa, "Japan and the United States, and Multilateral Institution Building in the Asia-Pacific: APEC and the ARF," in *Beyond Bilateralism: U.S.-Japan Relations in the New Asia-Pacific*, eds. Ellis S. Krauss and T. J. Pempel, (Palo Alto, CA: Stanford University Press, 2004), 248–271; and Paul Midford, "Explaining Japan's Leadership in East Asian Security Multilateralism," paper prepared for the Annual Meeting of the International Studies Association, Portland, Oregon, February 25–March 1, 2003.

15. For a Japanese perspective on the impact of virtualized and digitized finance, see Eisuke Sakakibara, *Kokusai kin'yuu no genba: Shihonshugi no kiki wo koete* (Tokyo: PHP Shinsho, 1998).

16. Grimes, "Japan and Globalization," 63; and Thomas Oatley and Robert Nabors, "Market Failure, Wealth Transfers, and the Basle Accord," *International Organization* 52(1) (Winter 1998): 35–54.

17. Grimes, "Japan and Globalization," 63–66; Richard Katz, *Japanese Phoenix: The Long Road to Economic Revival* (Armonk, NY: M. E. Sharpe, 2003), 212–216; and more generally, Steven Vogel, *Freer Markets, More Rules: Regulatory Reform in Advanced Industrial Countries* (Ithaca, NY: Cornell University Press, 1996).

18. Jennifer Holt Dwyer, "US-Japan Financial-Market Relations in an Era of Global Finance," in *New Perspectives on US-Japan Relations*, ed. Gerald L. Curtis (Tokyo: Japan Center for International Exchange, 2000), 98.

19. Heginbotham and Samuels, "Mercantile Realism and Japanese Foreign Policy," 188.

20. Ibid., 189; Katz, *Japanese Phoenix*, 166–169.

21. Regarding the Japanese state's partial opening of its research and development system to foreign participation, see Atsushi Yamada, "Neo-Techno-Nationalism: How and Why It Grows," paper presented at the International Studies Association's annual meeting, March 14–18, 2000, available at www.ciaonet.org/isa/yaa01, 3.

22. Midford, "Explaining Japan's Leadership in East Asian Security Multilateralism"; Glenn D. Hook et al., "Japan and the East Asian Financial Crisis: Patterns, Motivations, and Instrumentalisation of Japanese Regional Economic Diplomacy," *European Journal of East Asian Studies* 1(2) (2002): 177–197, especially 184–186; Christopher W. Hughes, "Japanese Policy and the East Asian Currency Crisis: Abject Defeat or Quiet Victory?" *Review of International Political Economy* 7(2) (2000): 219–253; and Dwyer, "US-Japan Financial-Market Relations in an Era of Global Finance," 97–102. For more on the EMEAP, see http://www.emeap.org.

23. Michael J. Green, *Japan's Reluctant Realism: Foreign Policy Challenges in an Era of Uncertain Power* (New York: Palgrave Macmillan, 2003), 230, 244–249.

24. On this narrative, see Rodney Bruce Hall, "The Discursive Demolition of the Asian Development Model," *International Studies Quarterly* 47(1) (2003): 75–81. Also see Robert Gilpin, *Global Political Economy: Understanding the International Economic Order* (Princeton, NJ: Princeton University Press, 2001), 321–333; and Tetsuo Kubota, "Ajia tsuuka kiki to IMF kaikaku—Atarashii shuppatsu ni mukete [The Asian Currency Crisis and IMF Reform: Toward a New Start]" and Sachio Konishi, "Ajia no kinyu kiki to seiji fuhai [The Asian Financial Crisis and Political Decay]," in *Ajia no tsuuka kiki to kin'yuu shijyou* [The Asian Currency Crisis and Financial Markets], ed. Yutzuru Imai, Kwansei Gakuin University Industrial Research Institute Report No. 27 (Tokyo: Ochanomizu Shobou, 2003), 24–29, 38–41, 97–118.

25. C. Fred Bergsten makes this point by comparing the Asian Financial crisis with the European monetary crisis of 1992 and 1993. See "The New Asian Challenge," Working Paper 00-04, Institute for International Economics, March 2000, 3–4, available at http://www.iie.com/publications/wp/2000/00-4.pdf.

26. David Wessel and Bob Davis, "Global Crisis Is a Match for Crack US Economists," *Wall Street Journal,* September 25–26, 1998. Hall observes that "apocalyptic past and future" narratives were used by US Treasury officials throughout the Asian financial crisis to warn against any departure from neoliberal orthodoxy or US leadership. The two world wars and the Great Depression were favorite specters invoked by officials. See Hall, "The Discursive Demolition of the Asian Development Model," 83.

27. Wessel and Davis, "Global Crisis Is a Match for Crack US Economists," 8.

28. *International Herald Tribune,* January 14, 1998. Former World Bank Chief Economist Joseph Stiglitz described these structural reform conditions as a "crude power play." Joseph E. Stiglitz, "Failure of the Fund: Rethinking the IMF Response," *Harvard International Review* 23(2) (Summer 2001): 17.

29. Quoted in David Hale, "Dodging the Bullet—This Time," *Brookings Review* 16(3) (Summer 1998), 24. Also see Lawrence H. Summers, "Address to the Economic Strategy Institute," May 5, 1998. Available at http://www.ustreas.gov/press/releases/pr2983.html.

30. Kubota, "Ajia tsuuka kiki to IMF kaikaku," 49. Kubota points to American intervention in Indonesia's domestic politics during the Asian financial crisis as a major reason not only for that country's subsequent political instability, but also for the rise Islamic fundamentalist terrorism there. See Kubota, "Ajia tsuuka kiki to Indoneshia," 119–120, 141, 154–161.

31. On the significance of Korean imports of Japanese technology, see Reinhard Drifte, "The Japanese-Korean High Technology Relationship: Implications for Weapons Proliferation and Arms Control Regimes," Center for Pacific Asia Studies at Stockholm University, Occasional Paper 31, August 1997.

32. Regarding this model, see Chalmers Johnson, *MITI and the Japanese Miracle: The Growth of Japanese Industrial Policy, 1925–1975* (Palo Alto, CA: Stanford University Press, 1982); and Meredith Woo-Cumings, ed., *The Developmental State* (Ithaca, NY: Cornell University Press, 1999). For a perspective on the Japanese model by a leading financial bureaucrat, see Eisuke Sakakibara, *Shihonshugi wo koeta Nippon* [Japan Beyond Capitalism] (Tokyo: Toyo Keizai Shinposha, 1990).

33. *Asahi Shimbun,* June 26, 1998; and Hughes, "Japan and the East Asian Crisis," 232–233.

34. On US policy toward Indonesia, see Lawrence Summers, "Indonesia and the Challenge of Lasting Recovery," Jakarta, Indonesia, January 24, 2000, accessed at http://www.ustreas.gove/press/releases/pr248.html. On IMF policy, see Robert Dalrymple, "Indonesia and the IMF: The Evolving Consequences of a Reforming Mission," *Australian Journal of International Affairs* 52 (1998): 233–239; Hall, "The Discursive Demolition of the Asian Development Model," 82. For a Japanese view on Indonesia and the Asian Financial Crisis, see Tetsuo Kubota, "Ajia Tsuuka kiki to Indoneshia [The Asian Currency Crisis and Indonesia]," in Imai, *Ajia no tsuuka kiki to kinyuu shijyou,* 119–166.

35. Green, *Japan's Reluctant Realism,* 230, 254–257.

36. Dwyer, "US-Japan Financial-Market Relations in an Era of Global Finance," 98, 120, n. 31; Hook et al., "Japan and the East Asian Financial Crisis," 185–186; Hughes, "Japan and the East Asian Crisis," 222, 245–248. In a personal communication with the author on April 4, 2004, Christopher Hughes confirmed his view that New Miyazawa funding was given on softer (or no) conditionality, noting that there were no formal memoranda or publicly announced conditions for the dispersal of these funds. The most notable characteristic of New Miyazawa funding was (and continues to be) its virtually impenetrable intransparency.

37. "Shin Miyazawa kousou wo kakudai, Okurasho, betonamu ni tekiyou-IMF nado ni senkoushi shien mo," *Nihon Keizai Shimbun,* May 3, 1999.

38. Hook et al., "Japan and the East Asian Financial Crisis," 185.

39. The Ministry of Foreign Affairs of Japan, "Asian Economic Crisis and Japan's Contribution," at http://www.mofa.go.jp/policy/economy/asia/crisis0010.html. As of October 2000, $70 billion had been distributed with another $10 billion still in the implementation stage.
40. On these complaints, see Summers, "Indonesia and the Challenge of Lasting Recovery." To the extent that Miyazawa funding did mitigate "firesale FDI," this accorded not only with the national interests of Japan and its Asian partners, but even with neoliberal economic theory, reemphasizing Kirshner's point that US and IMF policies during the financial crisis were anything but politically neutral. See the observations of prominent neoliberal economist Jagdish Bhagwati, "The Capital Myth," *Foreign Affairs* 77(3) (May/June 1998): 9; and Paul Bowles, "Asia's Post-Crisis Regionalism: Bringing the State Back in, Keeping the (United) States out," *Review of International Political Economy* 9(2) (Summer 2002): 230–256, quote at 237–238.
41. "Seifu, Ajia yuushi ni boueki hoken, minkan shikin wo katsuyou—Mare-shia ni mazu 700 oku en," and "Tai Mare-shia kinyuu shien keikaku, seifu, keizai gaikou no shisei tenkan (kaisetsu)," *Nihon Keizai Shimbun*, September 23, 1998; "Bei-zaimuchoukan, shihon idou kisei ni hantai," *Nihon Keizai Shimbun*, October 31, 1998.
42. "Tsuka suwappu kyouka goui Chugoku fukumi kyoutei kakujyutsu," *Asahi Shimbun*, May 7, 2000; "ASEAN nichukan kurashyou, Gaika yushutsu de goui-tsuka kiki saihatsu wo boushi," "Gaika yushutu goui, shin miyazawa kousou no jisseki haikei ni," *Nihon Keizai Shinbun*, May 7, 2000. Hook et al., "Japan and the East Asian Financial Crisis," 185–187.
43. By November 1999, Chinese Premier Zhu Rongji claimed to be "very supportive" of the AMF concept. See Bergsten, "The New Asian Challenge," 2. Also see "Gaika yuutsu goui."
44. Regarding the connection with the Kosovo War, the author heard this view from a Japanese researcher at the Chinese Academy of Social Sciences during an academic workshop in Stockholm, August 2000. Bowles, "Asia's Post-Crisis Regionalism," 242–244, also identifies the Kosovo War along with several perceived "hostile" US acts as reasons for China's more receptive attitude toward Japanese regional financial leadership. Regarding the post-Kosovo reassessment in Chinese perceptions of the United States and greater receptiveness to Japanese regional leadership, see Michael Pillsbury, *China Debates the Future Security Environment* (Washington, DC: National Defense University Press, 2000), 95, 134; Paul Midford, "China Views the Revised US-Japan Defense Guidelines: Popping the Cork?" *International Relations of the Asia-Pacific* 4 (2004): 140–143; and Gilbert Rozman, "China's Changing Images of Japan, 1989–2001: the Struggle to Balance Partnership and Rivalry," *International Relations of the Asia Pacific* 2(1) (2002): 112–113. By the end of 1998, South Korea had also become more favorable toward the AMF concept. See Hook et al., "Japan and the East Asian Financial Crisis," 187.
45. For a skeptical view of the CMI, see Markus Hund, "ASEAN Plus Three: Towards a New Age of Pan-East Asian Regionalism? A Skeptic's Appraisal," *The Pacific Review* 16(3) (2003): 407–408. For less skeptical views, see Graham Bird and Ramkishen S. Rajan, "Regional Arrangements for Providing Liquidity in a Financial Crisis: Developments in East Asia," *The Pacific Review* 15(3) (2002): 370–372; and Masayuki Tadokoro, "Ajia ni okeru chiiki tsuka kyouryoku no tenkai," in *Nihon no Higashi Ajia Kousou*, eds. Yoshihide Soeya and Masayuki Tadokoro (Tokyo: Keio daigaku shyuppankai, 2004), 117–122.

46. The inclusion of conditionality appears to reflect Chinese and Korean desires to decrease their exposure to bailout Southeast Asia during a future currency crisis rather than Japan's policy. See Jennifer A. Amyx, "Japan and the Evolution of Regional Financial Arrangements in East Asia," in *Beyond Bilateralism: U.S.-Japan Relations in the New Asia-Pacific*, eds. Ellis S. Krauss and T. J. Pempel (Palo Alto, CA: Stanford University Press, 2004), 213–216.

47. Aside from the Sino-Japanese swap, which is unambiguously untied, questions about possible IMF conditionality for Japan's contributions to these swaps is perhaps another example of strategic ambiguity on Japan's part—Japan's traditional low profile diplomacy of challenging US leadership quietly rather than openly. The history of the New Miyazawa initiative suggests this is the case. Regarding these doubts, see C. Randall Henning, *East Asian Financial Cooperation* (Washington, DC: Institute for International Economics, 2002), 41–42. For recent evidence of Japanese efforts to tailor Chiang Mai declaratory policy to mollify US concerns, see "Safety Net: Asia Slow to Build Multilateral Currency Framework," *Nikkei Telecom*, April 21, 2004.

48. Other untied facilities created by Japan include a $3 billion Asian Currency Crisis Support Facility within the Asian Development Bank, and various forms of trade insurance valued at over $2 billion. See The Ministry of Foreign Affairs of Japan, "Asian Economic Crisis and Japan's Contribution," at www.mofa.go.jp/policy/economy/asia/crisis0010.html.

49. Amyx, "Japan and the Evolution of Regional Financial Arrangements in East Asia," 26.

50. "Ajia saiken kikin setsuritsu happyou," *Nihon Keizai Shimbun*, June 3, 2003; "Thailand's Asia Bond Faces Uphill Battle," *The Nikkei Weekly*, May 24, 2004; and Jae-Ha Park, "Prospects for Regional Financial Cooperation in East Asia," paper prepared for the Government of Japan/ABAC Japan Symposium on "Regional Cooperation in East Asia," May 16, 2003, 13–15, available at http://www.mofa.go.jp/policy/economy/apec/symposium/symp00305/session2-2.pdf.

51. Saori N. Katada, "Japan's Counterweight Strategy: U.S-Japan Cooperation and Competition in International Finance," in Krauss and Pempel, *Beyond Bilateralism*, 195.

52. Masahiro Kawai and Haruhiko Kuroda, "Asia's New Financial Architecture Needs Support," *Financial Times*, June 17, 2004. Kuroda is a former Japanese vice finance minister for international affairs. If the CMI funding were to be increased tenfold, it would surpass the IMF in capitalization.

53. Dwyer, "US-Japan Financial-Market Relations in an Era of Global Finance," 98, Hook et al., "Japan and the East Asian Financial Crisis," 193.

54. Susan Strange, "Finance, Information and Power," in *Authority and Markets: Susan Strange's Writings on International Economy*, eds. Roger Tooze and Christopher May (New York: Palgrave Macmillan, 2002), 71, 79, originally printed in *Review of International Studies* 16(3) (July 1990).

55. Hughes, "Japanese Policy and the East Asian Currency Crisis," 250–251.

56. On regional resentment of the United States and the IMF and growing receptivity to Japanese leadership, see Bowles, "Asia's Post-Crisis Regionalism," 238–244.

57. Walter Hatch, "Japanese Production Networks in Asia: Extending the Status Quo," in *Crisis and Innovation in Asian Technology*, eds. William W. Keller and Richard J. Samuels (Cambridge: Cambridge University Press, 2003), 23–56; and Richard F. Doner, "Japan in East Asia: Institutions and Regional Leadership," in *Network Power: Japan and Asia*, eds. Peter J. Katzenstein and Takashi Shiraishi (Ithaca, NY: Cornell University Press, 1997), 197–233, especially 212–215.

58. Bernard Mitchell and John Ravenhill, "Beyond Product Cycles and Flying Geese: Regionalization, Hierarchy and the Industrialization of East Asia," *World Politics* 47(2) (1995): 171–209.

59. Kaname Akamatsu, "A Historical Pattern of Economic Growth in Developing Countries," *Developing Economies* 1 (1962): 3–25.

60. Mitchell and Ravenhill, "Beyond Product Cycles and Flying Geese." For a discussion of this literature, see Hughes, "Japanese Policy and the East Asian Currency Crisis," 224–229.

61. See Walter Hatch and Kozo Yamamura, *Asia in Japan's Embrace: Building a Regional Production Alliance* (Cambridge: Cambridge University Press, 1996).

62. MITI, *Tsuushou Sangyou Seisaku no Jyuuten: Heisei 8 Nendo* [Commercial and Industrial Policy Priorities for 1996] (Tokyo: MITI, 1995), 25, as cited in Hatch, "Japanese Production Networks in Asia," 32–33. For other functions of these networks, see Hatch, "Japanese Production Networks in Asia," 31, 40, 43–44.

63. It should be noted that these regional production networks have been more successful in some industries (automobiles) than others (computer peripherals). See Hatch, "When Strong Ties Fail: U.S.-Japanese Manufacturing Rivalry in Asia," in Krauss and Pempel, *Beyond Bilateralism*, 154–175.

64. Hatch, "Japanese Production Networks in Asia," 28–29. The same has held true even for relatively advanced Korea. See Drifte, "The Japanese-Korean High Technology Relationship." However, as Drifte notes, the 1990s witnessed increasing equality in the technology relationship between Japan and Korea, with the emergence of joint ventures for technological development, Japanese imports of Korean technology, and Korean acquisitions of Japanese technology through the purchase of small and medium Japanese corporations.

65. Hatch and Yamamura, *Asia in Japan's Embrace*, 33–34, 168. On the ability of Japanese companies to convert minority stakes but technological dominance into effective control of Asian joint ventures, see Hatch, "Japanese Production Networks in Asia," 49.

66. Hughes, "Japanese Policy and the East Asian Currency Crisis," 245.

67. Hatch, "Japanese Production Networks in Asia," 43–46; Hughes, "Japanese Policy and the East Asian Currency Crisis," 244–246.

68. Hughes, "Japanese Policy and the East Asian Currency Crisis," 235–240, 245.

69. For an overview of "strategic standards setting," see Peter Grindley, *Standards, Strategy, and Policy: Cases and Stories* (New York: Oxford University Press, 1995).

70. "East Asia plans Windows Rival," BBC News, September 8, 2003, accessed at http://news.bbc.co.uk/1/hi/technology/3090918.stm on September 12, 2003.

71. "Rinakkusu hyoujyunka goui, Nichukan, Ninshou kenkyuu nado suishin," *Nihon Keizai Shimbun*, April 4, 2004; "Datsu Uindouzu Nichukan ga renkei [Dumping Windows-A Japan-China-Korea coalition]," *Asahi Shimbun*, August 31, 2003; "Kyodou OS kaihatsu, Chuu-kan to Kyoryokushi jyunbi chyaku jyaku [Joint OS Development, China-Korea Cooperation Progressing]," *Asahi Shinbun*, November 14; "Japan, China, ROK eye Linux-based OS," *Daily Yomiuri*, March 31, 2004; "Asian Trio Embark on Quest to Lead in Cutting Edge Tech," *The Japan Times*, April 6, 2004.

72. For sources, see note 71. Japanese market-leader NTT Docomo chose Linux as the operating system for its third-generation cell phones launched in the fall of 2004. *Asahi Shinbun*, December 2, 2003.

73. "East Asia Plans Windows Rival."

74. On China's fears, see Richard P. Suttmeir and Yao Xiangkui, *China's Post-WTO Technology Policy: Standards, Software, and the Changing Nature of Techno-Nationalism*, NBR Special Report (Seattle: National Bureau of Asian Research, 2004), 36–42, especially 38; and Barry Naughton and Adam Segal, "China in Search of a Workable Model: Technology Development in the New Millennium," in William W. Keller and Richard J. Samuels, *Crisis and Innovation in Asian Technology*, 183–184.

75. Suttmeir and Xiangkui, *China's Post-WTO Technology Policy*, 42.

76. Yamada, "Neo-Techno-Nationalism."

77. "Tron Aims at Global Standard," *Daily Yomiuri*, October 4, 2003. Also see *Aera Weekly*, October 13, 2003.

78. Michael J. Green, *Arming Japan: Defense Production, Alliance Politics, and the Postwar Search for Autonomy* (New York: Columbia University Press, 1995).

79. Samuels, *"Rich Nation Strong Army."*

80. Increasing economies of scale, a purposeless, stateless force with little respect for national boundaries, becomes a salient force for globalization when the scale of production begins to exceed the scale of the national state. On this point, see Philip Cerny, "Globalization and the Changing Nature of Collective Action," *International Organization* 49(4) (Autumn 1995): 597.

81. Samuels, *"Rich Nation Strong Army,"* 231–244.

82. Ibid., 227–228; and Arthur Alexander, *Of Tanks and Toyotas: An Assessment of Japan's Defense Industry* (Santa Monica, CA: The Rand Corporation), Rand Note N-3542-AF, 30–35. A Japanese aerospace executive later captured the bravado of indigenous production advocates when he boasted "the next generation fighter support plane (FSX) could have been easily developed by adapting technologies currently used for non-military products." "In Self Defense," *Business Tokyo*, February 1988, 53, as cited in Alexander, *Of Tanks and Toyotas*, p. 2.

83. However, even the P-X follow-on to the P-3C is not a fully indigenous project, because the onboard avionics are being jointly developed with the United States. See Japanese Defense Agency, *Defense of Japan 2002* (Tokyo: Urban Connections, 2002), 197; and more generally, see Paul Jackson, ed., *Jane's All the World's Aircraft 2003–2004* (Coulsdon, UK: Jane's Information Group, 2003), 308.

84. A half-hearted attempt was made in the mid-1990s to develop a fully indigenous fighter, including the plane's jet engine. After repeated delays and false starts, the program was deleted from the defense budget in 2002. See *Jane's All the World's Aircraft 2003*–2004, 307.

85. Japan did turn to European aerospace for assistance when developing the F-1 ground-attack jet in the mid 1970s. See Alexander, *Of Tanks and Toyotas*, p. 39.

86. Green, *Arming Japan*, 108–124.

87. Although Japan has so far mostly (although not always) tapped into US-based production networks, European aerospace companies, especially Airbus, have emerged as candidate codevelopment partners for Japanese plans to develop new transport (C-X) and maritime patrol (P-X) planes. See Jackson, ed., *Jane's All the World's Aircraft 2003–2004*, 308.

88. Green, *Arming Japan*, 124, 129, 132–133, 154–155.

89. Michael J. Green, "The Challenges of Managing U.S.-Japan Security Relations after the Cold War," in *New Perspectives on U.S.-Japan Relations*, ed. Gerald L. Curtis (Tokyo: Japan Center for International Exchange, 2000), 247.

90. Ibid.; Christopher W. Hughes, "Ballistic Missile Defense and Sino-Japanese Relations: Japan's Inescapable Security Dilemma?" paper presented for the Workshop on the Chinese-Japanese Relationship, Swedish Institute for International Affairs, Stockholm, August 17–19, 2000, 27; Jiyuu Minshutou Seimu Chousakai, "Joho Eisei ni kansuru Purojekuto Chimu," *Joho Shuhshu Eisei Duunyuu ni tsuite Teigen*, October 29, 1998; and Barbara Wanner, "Japan's Push to Develop Spy Satellites Presents New Challenges to Bilateral Armaments Cooperation," *JEI Report* 21A (Washington, DC: Japan Economic Institute).

91. On Japan's emphasis on systems integration, see Mark Lorell, *Troubled Partnership: A History of US-Japan Collaboration on the FS-X Fighter* (Santa Monica, CA: RAND, 1996), 81–84.

92. Green, "The Challenges of Managing U.S.-Japan Security Relations after the Cold War," 248; Joseph Nye and William Owens, "The Information Edge," *Foreign Affairs* 75(2) (1996): 20–26; and Office of the Secretary of Defense, *United States Security Strategy for the East Asia-Pacific Region 1998* (Washington, DC: Department of Defense, 1998), 16–17.

93. Green, "The Challenges of Managing U.S.-Japan Security Relations after the Cold War," 248.

94. Green, "The Challenges of Managing U.S.-Japan Security Relations after the Cold War," 246; and Hughes, "Ballistic Missile Defense and Sino-Japanese Relations," 15–16.

95. Masamori Sase, *Shudanteki Jieiken—Ronsoh no tame ni* (Kyoto: PHP, 2001); and Hughes, "Ballistic Missile Defense and Sino-Japanese Relations," 15.

96. See Berger, *Cultures of Antimilitarism*; and Midford, "Making the Best of a Bad Reputation," chap. 3.

97. Hughes, "Ballistic Missile Defense and Sino-Japanese Relations," 15–16. For a theoretical discussion of the alliance dilemma dangers of abandonment or entrapment, see Glenn H. Snyder, *Alliance Politics* (Ithaca, NY: Cornell University Press, 1997), 180–186. For how fear of entrapment influenced Japan's early postwar defense posture, see John W. Dower, *Empire and Aftermath: Yoshida Shigeru and the Japanese Experience, 1978–1954* (Cambridge, MA: Harvard University Press, 1979), 388–389.

98. Michael D. Swaine et al., *Japan and Ballistic Missile Defense* (Santa Monica, CA: RAND, 2001), 65.

99. Patrick M. Cronin, Paul S. Giarra, and Michael J. Green, "The Alliance Implications of Theater Missile Defense," in *The US-Japan Alliance: Past, Present, and Future*, eds. Michael J. Green and Patrick M. Cronin (New York: Council on Foreign Relations, 1999), 181.

100. Hughes, "Ballistic Missile Defense and Sino-Japanese Relations," 27. Also see Swaine et al., *Japan and Ballistic Missile Defense*, 64.

101. Cronin, Giarra, and Green, "The Alliance Implications of Theater Missile Defense," 181–182.

102. Swaine et al., *Japan and Ballistic Missile Defense*, 65; and "Theater Missiles Defenses in the Asia-Pacific Region," A. Henry L. Stimson Center Working Group Report No. 34, June 2000, 70–71.

103. Regarding China's position, see Kori J. Urayama, "Chinese Perspectives on Theater Missile Defense: Policy Implications for Japan," *Asian Survey* 60(4) (July/August 2000): 599–621.

104. On Japan and Korea as "de facto" allies, see Victor D. Cha, *Alignment Despite Antagonism: The US-Korea-Japan Security Triangle* (Palo Alto, CA: Stanford, University Press: 1999).

105. Marie Soderberg, *Japan's Military Export Policy* (Stockholm: University of Stockholm, 1986).

106. Heginbotham and Samuels, "Mercantile Realism and Japanese Foreign Policy." This strategy might not be unique to Japan, Michael Mastanduno observes that the first Bush administration and the Clinton administration generally pursued defensive realist policies in military security but offensive realist policies in economic security. See Michael Mastanduno, "Preserving the Unipolar Moment: Realist Theories and U.S. Grand Strategy after the Cold War," *International Security* 21(4) (Spring 1997): 49–88.

107. Even Heginbotham and Samuels appear, at least in passing, to acknowledge Japan's need to reassure Asian nations: Japan "had to reassure the United States that it is becoming a military partner, while reassuring others that it is not." "Japan," in Ellings and Friedberg, *Strategic Asia 2002–03*, 122.

108. A senior Bank of Japan official cited this reason in an interview with Jennifer Holt Dwyer, "US-Japan Financial-Market Relations," 120–121, n. 38, and 97, 101.

109. Urayama, "Chinese Perspectives on Theater Missile Defense."

110. For a Japanese view on the importance of overseas military cooperation with the United States for the sake of promoting Japan's reputation as a military power, see Hisahiko Okazaki, "Dispatch of MSDF Vessels Historic, but Only First Step," *Daily Yomiuri,* November 26, 2001. Also see Midford, "Japan's Response to Terror."

111. Japan's ability to parlay a leadership role in regional economic multilateralism into a role in promoting regional security multilateralism suggests this positive spillover effect is already occurring. See Midford, "Japan's Leadership Role in East Asian Security Multilateralism."

10

GLOBALIZATION IS A DOUBLE-EDGED SWORD
Globalization and Chinese National Security

Adam Segal

THIS CHAPTER ADDRESSES THE NATIONAL SECURITY implications of globalization for China.[1] It does so by arguing that Chinese decision makers define national security as encompassing both internal and external threats, and that in both realms globalization presents challenges and opportunities. As Chinese security analysts and writers in the more popular press are fond of noting, globalization is a "double-edged sword."

Domestically, globalization highlights the Chinese Communist Party's (CCP) central paradox of trying to further engage the world economy, manage domestic reforms, and still maintain one-party rule. Globalization brings the capital, technology, and ideas needed to promote economic development, a cornerstone of regime legitimacy. But decision makers also fear that uncontrolled capital and trade flows could undermine "economic security" and sustainable economic development, creating social and political unrest that could lead to the toppling of the regime. In the end, the Chinese leaders must welcome forces that they fear will weaken their control over the economy, but at the same time are essential for continued economic growth.

The global diffusion of telecommunication and information technologies has a similar double-edged effect. The current regime clearly believes that future economic growth in China will depend in large measure on the extent to which the country is integrated with the global information infrastructure. Like their predecessors Jiang Zemin and Zhu Rongji, China's new leaders Hu Jintao and Wen Jiabo see the Internet as a key engine of growth in the new economy, and China continues to devote massive material and political resources to what it calls "informatization"—the application of modern information technology (IT) tools to other economic sectors. At the same time, there is widespread fear that the spread of new technologies may degrade the state's control of information and empower opponents of the regime such as the Chinese Democratic Party and Falun Gong.

In regards to the external environment, globalization, especially of IT production and research and development (R&D), could strengthen Beijing's position in its relations with Taiwan and in its military competition with the United States. The fragmentation of IT production over the last ten years has increased China's access to global technology, and China is an increasingly important importer and exporter of technology products. Total technology trade was $229.3 billion in 2003. China has become the world's third largest manufacturer of electronic and information technology, and China is increasingly the site of not only lower-end manufacturing but also research and design.[2] Within the larger trend of the geographical dispersion of IT manufacturing, the relocation by Taiwanese IT manufacturers to the mainland has yielded perhaps the most important political outcome: the increasing interdependence of the Taiwanese and Chinese economies.

The end result of the globalization of IT production may be a reduction of the likelihood of conflict across the Taiwan Strait. Trade with and dependence on the mainland has created political interests within Taiwan who are supportive of Beijing's stance on closer economic ties. Prominent business people and industrial associations have called for the lifting of restrictions on trade with and investment in China. Moreover, globalization may improve Beijing's economic leverage over Taipei and thus diminish the need for military force. Before the two economies were tightly linked, China's response to a unilateral change of the status quo across the strait was limited to doing nothing or using force. China can now signal the seriousness of its threat and leverage a range of coercive economic measures before it has to resort to a military attack.

Here it is important to echo a distinction made by Kirshner in chapter 1. Globalization across the Taiwan Strait is not an extreme form of interdependence.[3] Rather, China and Taiwan are more interdependent because of the globalization of IT sectors. Globalization is the force behind interdependence. Although attracting Taiwanese investment to places such as Shanghai, Guangzhou, and Fujian was certainly the goal of Chinese economic policy, the driving force behind the increasing integration of the two economies is the changing nature of global

IT production, not state action. The uncoordinated firm behavior and technological changes that have reshaped the development, production, and distribution of ITs have reinforced and intensified interdependence across the strait.

The globalization of IT and R&D may also help narrow the gap between Chinese and American military capabilities. This may happen through three channels. First, China may purchase commercial, off-the-shelf technologies to improve significantly its current military capabilities. Widely available sensors, imaging and space technologies, and computer and networking technologies could all be used to improve the effectiveness of the People's Liberation Army (PLA). As a 1999 Defense Science Board Task Force on Globalization and Security argued: "Over time, all states—not just the U.S. and its allies—will share access to much of the technology underpinning the modern military."[4]

Second, the globalization of IT may improve the productivity of Chinese defense industries. Although the Chinese defense sector has had success in producing fighters, missiles, and nuclear devices, it has been notably less able to provide the modern weapons the PLA currently requires, as evidenced by the purchase of advanced systems from Russia and other foreign suppliers. Technologically backward, geographically isolated, and poorly managed, the defense science and technology system lags behind and remains separated from more innovative commercial producers. The commercialization of defense technologies and the globalization of R&D might provide access to both technological "hardware" and "software" more advanced than what China could produce on its own.

Third, as the introduction to the volume notes, China is clearly interested in developing information warfare or "cyberwar" capabilities. Information warfare capabilities might allow China to degrade the strength of U.S. military forces in Asia and, combined with other asymmetric strategies, may play a leading role in an attack on Taiwan. Information warfare is attractive to China not only because cyberwar extends the power projection capabilities of the PLA beyond the range of its current arsenal of conventional weapons, it may also allow the PLA to attack the U.S. forces anonymously.

Like the other chapters in this volume, this chapter uses globalization to refer to the rise of stateless, unorganized forces, in particular trade and capital flows as well as technological change, especially the spread of IT. These forces have affected China through all three of the conduits of globalization discussed in chapter 1: exchange, information, and marketization. The state has had to respond, react, and try to control increases in the volume and intensity of economic transactions, in the ease, speed, and forms of communication, and in the range of activities governed by economic forces.

China's interaction with and acceptance of these forces across a range of issues has been halting, especially in areas of national security and territorial sovereignty.[5] The response of Chinese leaders to the outbreak of severe acute respiratory syndrome (SARS) exemplifies how China is being pulled in two different directions. Chinese leaders were widely criticized, both inside and outside of China, for failing to accept the responsibilities of a more global world. Beijing initially hid the extent of the epidemic, controlled media reports, and restricted World Health Organization (WHO) access to China. Yet after the epidemic, Pang Zhongying argues, "China's government has recognized that, in the age of globalization, a nation needs to take a global attitude in treating domestic events that emerge, including making information publicly available and engaging in regional cooperation."[6]

Beijing's ambivalence toward globalization stems from at least two overlapping concerns. First, in the back of most Chinese leaders' and policy analysts' minds is likely to be an argument made in chapter 1: globalization is not politically neutral and it is the action of states—especially the United States—that is critical in defining the structures and processes that shape financial, technology, and information flows. Globalization may affect all states, but it is the United States that is uniquely positioned to exploit these changes. As Wang Yizhou, the head of Chinese Academy of Social Sciences, argues, "in the present period of globalization, the United States of America's dominant role is undeniable."[7] In many ways, China's attitude toward globalization is reflected in its conflicted relationship with the United States. Beijing requires good, stable relations with Washington in order to achieve most of its major goals—economic development, reunification with Taiwan, regional stability—but the United States is also the country most likely to be able to block the outcomes Beijing desires most. China's enthusiasm for globalization stems from its belief that, although it threatens regime stability, it is essential for continued economic growth. When the United States, through the CIA or Voice of America, funds efforts to undermine China's control of information, these two concerns merge.

Second, despite China's size and economic power, many of the fears and concerns Chinese leaders have about the processes of globalization are very similar to those of policy makers in smaller, more vulnerable states. Beijing continues to struggle with the balance between globalization and the political goal of unifying a multinational state.[8] Beijing wants to preserve autonomy from the international economy so as to be able to attend to critical domestic reforms. In this context, instead of being a benign or value neutral force, globalization undermines state capacity and may even act as a new form of imperialism, imposing Western values. Like the Middle Eastern leaders described by Lynch in chapter 6, Chinese policy makers fear that globalization is a threat to a unique identity and culture.

This chapter consists of four main parts. The first introduces Chinese definitions of national security and globalization. The second looks at the effects of globalization on domestic security and regime stability. The third section considers the possible impact of the globalization of IT on China's external security concerns, especially Taiwan and defense modernization. The fourth and concluding section summarizes the findings of this chapter.

CHINESE DEFINITIONS OF SECURITY AND GLOBALIZATION

As noted by other analysts of Beijing's security policy, Chinese definitions of security have tended to be comprehensive (*zhonghe*), consisting of both external and internal threats. These conceptions map over the more expansive definitions of national security as used in this volume, entailing organized political violence between states as well as the state's ability to defend its own interests, especially its own survival. Thomas Christensen's discussion of Beijing's grand strategy contains a clear overlap between external and internal security concerns. As Christensen notes, Chinese policy makers must balance among defending regime security and domestic stability, maintaining territorial integrity (primarily the question of Taiwan, but also policies regarding Tibet and Xinjiang), and enhancing material power (comprehensive strength) and economic development.[9] In fact, the more comprehensive definitions of security may prioritize domestic concerns. David Shambaugh, for example, argues that in these more encompassing views, "domestic 'stability' is always paramount, and external threats are usually perceived in the context of aggravating domestic instability."[10]

Chinese scholars and analysts began to address the question of globalization (*quan qiu hua*) during the last years of the 1990s, particularly after the 1997 Asian Financial Crisis. These writings defined globalization as the flow of capital, goods, technology, and ideas but tended to focus on "economic" as the most developed of the types of globalization.[11] Globalization, in the words of one commentator, is the "globalization of the market economy controlled by market forces and market laws."[12] Another analyst notes that the three areas most involved in globalization are "international trade, international finance, and international production."[13]

The most obvious benefit of globalization is that integration into the world economy results in an increased pace of domestic development and thus greater national strength. Foreign funds will flow into China, making up shortages in domestic capital and strengthening the construction of infrastructure and basic industries.[14] Opening to global forces is also expected to push domestic structural reform forward, furthering the transformation of state-owned enterprises, financial markets, and the legal system.

Chinese analysts argue that increased trade interdependence also raises the cost of possible conflicts, linking the world "more tightly together through common markets, mutual trade, and shared interests."[15] Some scholars have adopted more liberal interpretations of globalization, implicitly questioning the relevance of the sovereign nation-state as the unit of analysis or traditional realist measures of relative power. In addition, globalization may thwart efforts to contain China.

These potential positive outcomes are always balanced with negatives. Globalization is a double-edged sword—strengthening and threatening China at the same time. Chinese analysts often refer to globalization as "an objective condition in the world economy" independent of American power, yet many see the stronger powers—and the United States in particular—as being better positioned to exploit the changes of globalization. Globalization allows developed nations to "redraw the political, economic, and cultural map of the world using 'warfare without the smoke of gunfire.'"[16]

Globalization is often used synonymously with the increased international competition among countries over the means to create wealth within national economies.[17] Wang Yizhou notes that although "in theory all states are equally placed to compete," with greater access to capital, more rational industrial structures, quicker access to information, and better managers, "the developed countries are in a more favorable position."[18] Globalization has been especially harmful to the interests of Third World countries, widening the gap between rich and poor, degrading state capacity, and exacerbating ecological destruction.[19]

Moreover, although "cultural blending is beyond reproach," some "American's view the 'big stick of culture' as an important tool to carry out the American concept of values and ideology."[20] As in the Middle East, there is a tendency in China to equate globalization with the diminishing of a culturally distinct identity and the spread of American or Western values. Marketization is seen to corrupt domestic political culture, bringing consumerism and ideological pollution.

The degree of perceived threat in Beijing, however, is much less, in no small part because of the increasing sense of confidence Chinese analysts have about the strength of the domestic economy and of the state as well as China's growing importance as a global power. As Marc Lynch notes in chapter 6 of this volume, Middle Eastern intellectuals often portray globalization as a hegemonic project that ultimately seeks to eradicate the Arab-Islamic identity. Globalization allows Western countries to "promote their own values."[21] Yet Chinese views are not nearly as apocalyptic as those in the Middle East. Rather, Chinese leaders are more likely to describe the negatives as an inevitable and controllable aspect of globalization. For example, in response to conservative criticism that opening to the world led to "spiritual pollution," Deng Xiaoping responded that "when you open the window, a few flies fly in" and continued to push for greater integration with the international economy.

GLOBALIZATION AND DOMESTIC SECURITY: ECONOMIC SECURITY AND REGIME LEGITIMACY

Domestically, globalization is most clearly conceived as a threat to "economic security" and to the regime's monopoly over information. For the CCP, the source of regime legitimacy has gradually shifted from Communist revolution to revolutionary ideology to economic performance.[22] Rising living standards and national wealth, not Communism and egalitarianism, are what the party uses to justify continued rule. In addition, the CCP has consistently pushed economic reform over political changes that might increase the efficacy and legitimacy of the party. In this context, slow economic growth can call the CCP's legitimacy into question and so political, economic, or social forces that could derail continued growth, either internal or external, must be managed. Former President Jiang Zemin explicitly linked political power with continued economic development in his July 2001 speech commemorating the eightieth anniversary of the founding of the Communist Party: "If we deviate from development, it will be impossible for us to talk about upholding the Party's advanced nature and its steadfastness."[23]

Globalization reinforces and in some cases strengthens the destabilizing forces unleashed by the economic reform program begun in 1978. Chinese leaders fear that globalization will overwhelm moribund state-owned enterprises, aggravate rising unemployment, and destabilize political order, and Chinese writers have focused on how global capital, trade, and technology flows undermine the ability of national economies to create wealth within their own territories—or "China's ability to manage internal problems without outside intervention."[24] The 2000 Defense White Paper notes, "financial and economic risks are increasing, and economic security has become a concern for all countries."[25] As one analyst argues, the central goal of the grand strategy in the twenty-first century is "to provide the space and time for sustainable development and economic construction." Simply put, "without economic security, there can be no genuine national security."[26]

In China, the Asian financial crisis was seen to have obvious security implications, diminishing state autonomy and threatening domestic stability. Chinese analysts noted that in developing Asia, the international crisis led to the collapse of domestic economies and rising unemployment. In the case of Indonesia, the domestic political outcome was clear to see and more threatening; popular frustration was directed against the ruling regime, and the Suharto government eventually tumbled from power.[27] Even in "economic stars" such as Thailand and Korea, the crisis had a corrosive effect on state-society relations and the government's ability to manage growth and social stability. As Kirshner notes in chapter 1, in the Korean case, the terms of IMF bailout included many provisions unrelated to the financial crisis but which American negotiators had tried and failed to get Seoul to adopt in bilateral trade talks. Chinese analysts noted that United States and Japan appeared to use the crisis to seek opportunity for strategic gains.[28] Increasingly dependent on global finance to sustain economic growth, Chinese policy makers fear that someday they too could be forced to adopt reforms that not only reduce state autonomy but also serve U.S. export interests.

Much of Beijing's resistance to revalue the yuan can be understood as the desire to maintain insulation against the world economy because capital account liberalization is associated with an increased likelihood of financial crisis and the loss of an independent monetary policy. Even with stringent controls on convertibility, China is not immune to the pressures of globalized finance. According to the Chinese press, rumors of imminent revaluation have caused some $25 billion in "hot money" to flow into China between January and July 2003. This money, in search of "arbitrage profits," causes "considerable difficulties for our country in implementing monetary policy."[29] More generally, China's leaders fear that yuan revaluation will be deflationary, reduce the attraction of China as an investment location for FDI, damage exports, reduce enterprise profits and increase unemployment, increase the fiscal deficit, and undermine the stability of monetary policy.[30]

GLOBALIZATION AND DOMESTIC
SECURITY: INFORMATION CONTROL

The dual nature of globalization is especially apparent in China's embrace of the Internet and IT. Beijing is strongly committed to making IT central to its national ambitions—from transforming Chinese society at home to pursuing its ambitions as a world economic and political power. At the same time, the diffusion of information technologies and the free flow of ideas that these technologies support could, in the long run, undermine the CCP's ability to control access to and dissemination of restricted information. Despite having only 15.9 computers for every 1,000 people,[31] China is still set to surpass Japan as the world's second largest Internet nation (after the United States).[32] In June of 2002, China's 16.13 million host computers were used by China's 45.8 million Internet users.[33] China now ranks first in the size of its mobile telephone market (206 million users, an estimated 300 million by the end of 2005).[34]

Chinese security analysts speak of "information security problems" and the "flow of information that carries political influence."[35] Western states can exploit the globalization of information using new and expanding mediums to promote political change within China and thus directly challenge Chinese state security.[36] Globalization and the spread of Western ideas may even threaten the CCP's control of the military. Although officers will benefit from managerial ideas entering China, there is also the risk that they may adopt more "Western bourgeoisie" values such as such as "money worship, pleasure-seeking, and extreme individualism." Perhaps even more threatening, ideas about "cutting the army from the party" and "depoliticizing" and "nationalizing" the army could undermine the party's absolute leadership over the military.[37]

Groups both inside and outside of China have been able to use the Internet, satellite broadcasts, and mobile phones to disseminate restricted information. The recent SARS epidemic gives a sense of how the diffusion of IT could undermine central control. At the beginning of the outbreak, China aggressively tried to limit domestic reporting about the spread of SARS, but Chinese citizens accessed other news sources. In Guangzhou, the cell phone text message, "There is a fatal flu in Guangzhou" was resent 40 million times on February 8, 41 million times the next day, and 45 million times on February 10, according to the *Southern Weekend* newspaper.[38] Shortly after Chinese leaders acknowledged hiding information on the epidemic, traffic on DynaWeb—a technology that allows access to any Web sites without being filtered or monitored—increased by 50 percent within one day.[39]

New technologies can also be used to coordinate new forms of organization and publicize opposition to the regime. Falun Gong's ability to mobilize between ten and fifteen thousand members to surround the leadership compound at Zhongnanhai in April 1999 was only the most visible example of what underground movements and new technologies might be able to accomplish. In June 2002, Falun Gong interrupted nine channels run by China Central Television (CCTV) and 10 provincial channels, replacing official broadcasts with Falun Gong programs. In October 2003, Falun Gong jammed signals carried by the Sinosat-1 of China's first manned spaceflight. Other groups have also exploited new technologies; dissidents used e-mail to develop, organize, and expand the Chinese Democracy Party from 12 activists in one region to more than 200 spread through China in only four months.[40] Tibetan activists have been particularly successful in using new forms of communication, the global media, and globalized nongovernmental organizations (NGOs) to promote their causes.[41]

Finally, the state's control of information has been diminished by what the introduction calls the "least appreciated conduit of globalization"—the expansion of market forces into ever-broader ranges of human activity. In the Chinese case, the marketization of media, although still limited, has encroached on the center's ability to determine what citizens can read in the newspapers and watch on television. Twenty-five years ago, China had fewer than 200 newspapers; today it has more than 2,000 newspapers, 9,000 magazines, and 2,000 TV stations.[42] Beijing announced in June 2003 that it would cut off state funding for all but three newspapers and one journal. Moreover, the CCP is considering allowing foreign and domestic private investment in publications not specifically designated as an official mouthpiece of the Communist Party, with a maximum 49 percent equity stake to private investors.[43]

For all media, advertising and subscription income have become the major sources of revenue, and all must increasingly vie for audience share. As a result, newspapers and TV shows now compete for viewers often by developing hard-hitting investigative reporting. Regional newspapers such as the *Southern Weekend* (*Nanfang Zhoumou*) have been instrumental in breaking stories of corruption and malfeasance, although they are likely to pursue stories that occur in other provinces in the hope of creating some political protection. *Southern Weekend,* based in Guangdong, was banned in Henan Province for its reporting on the AIDS epidemic in that province. Despite the move to commercialize the media, the state still tightly controls content, purging editors and reporters and, in some cases, closing papers when they publish articles deemed too critical or controversial.

In the short term, the state has had unexpected success in controlling the political impact of openness.[44] The Ministry of Public Security, the Ministry of State Security, and the Public Security Bureau have developed a multilayered strategy to control Internet content and monitor online activities at every level of Internet service and content networks. Control is built on a mixture of legal regulations and blocking, filtering and surveillance technology, and physical intimidation.[45] A 1997 Public Security Bureau regulation titled "Computer Information Network and Internet Security, Protection and Management Regulations" places most of the onus for monitoring, reporting, and preventing antiregime use of the Internet on domestic providers. In 2002, the Chinese Web companies signed a pledge to promote self-discipline in Web usage and encourage "the elimination of deleterious information [on] the Internet."

All Internet traffic must go through government-controlled servers, and between May and November 2002, Zittrain and Edelman identified at least four distinct types of Internet filtering.[46] Foreign Web sites are routinely blocked and news forums are monitored and censored. In February 2004, China launched a crackdown on Internet news discussion groups, banning discussions on economic instability and party corruption; in June 2004, the Ministry of Information Industry issued a new series of measures to regulate content, crackdown on unregistered Internet cafes, and increase controls over online bulletin boards.[47] Journalists and civil rights campaigners have been detained for "using the internet to subvert state power," and several have been given jail sentences of up to ten years. China has also benefited from the willingness of some foreign companies to sell censorship technology and, in return for access to the Chinese market, to compromise on content.[48] In serious crises, the Chinese government has shut down networks temporarily in order to gain control.

Longer term, it is possible that power will shift from the state to individual citizens due to technological progress.[49] Newer forms of technology may prove more difficult to monitor. State control may also come apart on the paradox of trying to maintain tight controls over the Internet at the same time as aggressively promoting the development of information and communication technologies. Restrictive policies could increasingly limit the competitiveness of Chinese firms.[50]

But recent evidence does little to support the argument that opening new flows of information will threaten the stability of authoritarian regimes. In many ways, China exemplifies Herrera's argument in this volume that the severity of threat posed by IT to states will be determined by the evolution of the Internet and related technologies. Open networks with rapidly dropping access costs make it less likely that the state will be able to control content and opposition over the long term. By contrast, in cases of centralized development of the Internet and state ownership of the media, as in China, authoritarian regimes will be better able to respond. Even when faced with new technologies—text messaging, for example—China has been able to use state control of the telecom market to develop controls. New regulations have been issued to allow mobile phone service providers to filter messages for political, pornographic, or "fraudulent" content.[51]

In the near term, it makes more sense to focus our thinking less on the zero-sum battle between the state and its opponents and more on the ways that new technologies have reshaped the environment in which Chinese leaders make decisions. As Herrera notes, modern technologies have added to the capacity of the Chinese state to extend its political authority. But although the mechanism of delivery has improved, it is no longer true that the message carries the same weight. Authority is no longer unquestioned. Internet technologies and a more open media have significantly changed the political calculus of central leaders in Beijing. Whether in the domestic or foreign policy sphere, decision makers can no longer afford to ignore public opinion. For example, almost 50,000 people posted commentary on an Internet news discussion after a Heilongjiang province court handed down a suspended sentence to a woman who ran her BMW into a crowd, killing one and injuring 12, after a farmer and his wife scratched her car with their cart. The court eventually revisited the case, and although the sentence was upheld, the fact that public anger convinced the government to review the case is noteworthy.[52] Here the political outcomes echo those in the Middle East that were described by Lynch. New media has not (yet) directly produced political outcomes, but it has at a minimum decisively weakened the state's monopoly over information.

Foreign policy, traditionally even more insulated from public opinion than domestic politics, also no longer operates in a vacuum. New technologies, especially the Internet, have strengthened a popular, more aggressive nationalism, sometimes in the face of officially sanctioned nationalism. This contrast is especially apparent in cases involving Japan. Activists in Beijing started the Patriots' Alliance Web to argue that the Railway Ministry should reconsider German and French bids for a $15 billion bullet train between Beijing and Shanghai. Referring to Japanese atrocities during World War II and relying on anti-Japanese nationalist sentiment, the Web site collected 87,320 signatures to a petition within 10 days, and eventually the ministry dropped the Japanese bid. As the administrator of the Ministry of Foreign Affairs Web site put it, "Policy-makers can't make decisions based on public opinion, but they can't ignore it either."[53]

In the short term, regime security and survival is more likely to depend on how well Beijing manages all of the economic and social challenges of globalization, rather than simply on the narrower question of how it manages and controls information. A well-managed opening could enhance the CCP's claim that social stability, economic prosperity, and authoritarian rule are all interlinked and mutually supportive.[54] By contrast, globalization that creates greater social dislocation will greatly weaken regime stability.

A number of chapters in this volume argue that globalization makes most developing countries weaker while it strengthens more economically developed, institutionally sophisticated states. China is a hybrid case, sharing many of the weaknesses of a developing state trying to retain control and at the same time benefiting enormously from globalization. Greater exposure to the international economy and freer flows of information threaten regime legitimacy and domestic stability, but China, unlike many other weak states, has benefited economically from its greater engagement with globalization. China has, so far, managed to stay on the right side of globalization's double-edged sword.

EXTERNAL SECURITY

In their discussions of globalization and international security, Chinese analysts have concentrated on the need to respond to diverse, new threats from nonstate and subnational actors and the growing importance of nontraditional security areas such as the environment. Globalization, according to one commentator, has caused a multiplication of security threats. Although warfare traditionally stemmed from conflicting economic interests, globalization forces different cultures to rub up against each other, fomenting religious and political conflict. Sovereign states and standing militaries are being displaced by subnational actors such as terrorists, drug smuggling networks, and secret religious organizations. Moreover, these nonstate actors do not rely simply on conventional weapons. Instead, they may use civilian aircraft or chemical and biological weapons.[55]

Despite these new dangers, the globalization of IT manufacturing and R&D could provide benefits to China, especially in regard to Beijing's desire to prevent Taiwan from moving closer to independence and to narrow the technological gap between the PLA and American military.

During the 1990s, manufacturing and R&D have gradually been more disbursed across national boundaries. Production is increasingly divided into discrete functions along the value chain and contracted out to producers in different national and regional economies. Internet technologies and improvements in transportation have made it easier to locate part of the production process in one part of the world and research and design in another. As a result, trade among multinational corporations makes up an increasing share of global trade. In 2002, intrafirm trade accounted for around one-third of goods exports from Japan and the United States, about one-third of all US goods imports, and one-quarter of all Japanese goods imports.[56]

Similarly, R&D is spreading through licensing agreements, R&D alliances, or the establishment of subsidiaries abroad.[57] China may be increasingly part of this globalization as over 200 foreign R&D centers and labs were established on the mainland from 1990 to 2002,[58] but for now its relative importance is small. In 1998, almost two-thirds of US R&D conducted abroad was located in Canada, France, Germany, Japan, and the United Kingdom; Japan is the largest foreign R&D investor in the United States.[59]

To be sure, even if China plays a larger role in a globalized process of R&D, its ability to leverage political and military goals from this process is uncertain. In the case of Taiwan, the increasing sense of dependence on the mainland created by globalization plus Beijing's reliance on the threat of force and failure to offer attractive policy incentives appear to have reinforced a separate sense of Taiwanese identity. The prospects of the PLA "leap-frogging" past the United States appear remote. The United States is at least twenty years ahead in terms of military capability and technology, and, with continued US defense spending, that gap is likely to remain beyond the next twenty years.[60] As Robert Ross argues, "should there be a revolution in military affairs (RMA), it will be a largely American revolution."[61]

Taiwan

China has clearly defined interests regarding Taiwan, and the defense of these interests is of utmost importance at present and for the foreseeable future. China's long-term core objective vis-à-vis Taiwan is to achieve reunification. Beijing's near-term objective is to stabilize the relationship and to make tangible progress toward some sort of reunification with Taiwan. Beijing's current Taiwan strategy consists of four parts: military leverage; squeezing Taiwan on the international stage; economic integration; and "united front" tactics of reaching out to

Taiwanese business people and factions of the Kuomintang while isolating President Chen Shui-bian.[62]

The surge of capital, technology, and skilled personnel across the Taiwan Strait during the late 1990s is a major source of leverage for China and one of the few sources of confidence for Chinese leaders as they consider the long-term prospects of Taiwan. The existence of these flows is the result of a policy decision to promote Taiwan's economic dependence on the mainland. Yet the pace and scope of the movement of high-technology products to the mainland has been influenced more by the changing international electronics industry than by Chinese policy. With Chinese incentives alone, there probably would have been a steady stream of electronic and IT manufacturers moving to the mainland. With Chinese incentives and the globalization of IT production, the stream has become a flood.

Since 1978, China has actively tried to encourage the integration of the two economies. The results of this policy have been dramatic. Accounting for 25 percent of Taiwan's export, China displaced the United States as Taiwan's largest export market in 2001. Japan, the United States, and the European Union have all declined in importance as export markets as China's has risen. China plays a similarly large role in shares of Taiwan's outward foreign direct investment. In 2002, cumulative Taiwanese investment in China totaled more than $21.43 billion [the official People's Republic of China (PRC) number is $31 billion as of 2003, and the real number probably higher still], and in 2002 China exceeded 50 percent of outward investment.[63]

Taiwanese IT producers have also become gradually more dependent on the mainland. Taiwan firms began moving the most labor-intensive stages of electronics production to China, beginning with assembly of keyboards, mice, and monitors. Now the movement has gradually expanded to include nearly all assembly operations as well as some research and design. According to the Institute for Information Industry's Market Intelligence Center, by the first quarter of 2002, the share of Taiwan's IT hardware actually produced in Taiwan was only 38 percent (down from 47 percent in 2001), and the share produced on the mainland was 49 percent (up from 37 percent for 2001).[64] Industry analysts predict that within five years, 80 percent of Taiwan's technology output will be made on the mainland.[65]

In Taiwan, politicians are increasingly worried about economic dependence on the mainland. President Chen Shui-bian has placed a ceiling on Taiwanese investments on the mainland, proposed a "national technology protection law" to regulate the flow of high-tech products, and attempted to lure Taiwanese- and foreign-invested firms back to

Taiwan by offering preferential tax exemptions and other incentives.[66] These policies are unworkable, and the result has been a rush to establish new ventures in China with only mild efforts to disguise getting around current regulations.

Despite the flow of IT manufacturing across the Taiwan Strait, the political outcome has not been what Beijing expected. From the beginning of economic contact between the two sides, Chinese policy makers have had a clear view of the political objectives of cross-strait trade. In the terms of Albert Hirschman's classic discussion of foreign trade as an instrument of national power, asymmetric trade would increase China's coercive power over Taiwan.[67] Because cross-strait trade is a much smaller share of China's economy than Taiwan's, implicit or explicit threats to break commercial relations give China greater coercive power.

For the most part, coercive threats have remained in the background of cross-strait relations. In the run-up to and in the immediate aftermath of the 2000 and 2004 Taiwanese presidential elections, Beijing did use economic coercion, but in an extremely limited manner. The message was sent to specific businesses with strong political ties to Chen Shui-bian, the Democratic Progressive Party (DPP), or others seen to "favor independence." After the 2000 election, state-owned enterprises were ordered not to do business with the Chi Mei Group, and the company faced constant scrutiny from zealous tax inspectors.[68] After the 2004 election, Beijing again criticized Hsu Wen-lung, chairman of Chi Mei and a leading supporter of Chen. Still, after both elections, China moved quickly to reassure Taiwanese businessmen about the safety of their investments. Vice Premier Qian Qichen traveled around Guangdong, in 2000, holding meetings with Taiwan businesspeople and telling them "under any circumstances, the mainland's policy of welcoming Taiwan compatriots to carry out economic activities on the mainland will not change, and so Taiwan compatriots can completely feel assured."[69]

Despite the insecurity it creates for Taiwan, China's ability to use economic coercion may reduce the chance for military conflict across the strait. Currently China's options to use military power are fairly limited. The PLA is likely to fail in an invasion of the island, and a limited naval interdiction, blockade, or missile strikes are not without tactical and strategic challenges, with or without a U.S. military response. But there are clearly circumstances under which Beijing feels the need to respond to what it sees as provocations, such as the revision of the constitution, and Beijing now has a wider range of coercive choices before resorting to force. China can apply pressure to individual firms or sectors and shift trade and investment patterns. As Morrow argues, expanding trade "increases the menu of options for signaling resolve in a dispute by opening up a range of possible trade sanctions."[70]

In addition to coercive power, as Abdelal and Kirshner note, the expansion of asymmetric trade across the strait also creates an influence effect.[71] As an internal 1990 Chinese document explained, expanding trade with Taiwan would contain separatist trends and help "interest groups involved closely with the mainland emerge in Taiwan's politics in the future and facilitate peaceful unification."[72] Chinese President Yang Shangkun noted at a December 1990 National Conference on Taiwan Work that the "emphasis should be placed on economic and other exchanges in order to use business to press politics (*yi shang wei zheng*) and use the public to pressure the official (*yi mi bu guan*)."[73]

Beijing's hope that economic trade would create interest groups that would push for greater economic opening appears to have borne fruit. From the first business people who funneled money illegally through Hong Kong to invest on the mainland to the industrial leaders claiming to be too restricted by the "Go Slow, Be Patient" policy, Taiwanese businesses have pressured the Lee and Chen administrations to hasten the pace of economic integration. For example, in a 1998 survey, 70 percent of Taiwanese businesses had investments in China and 50 percent hoped for greater relaxation of restrictions on investments.[74] Industries with direct interest in trade such as shipping lines and computer manufacturers have been up front in the campaign for greater cross-strait ties.

Yet it is not clear that economic interdependence will necessarily lead to political leverage and influence for Beijing. There has been no evidence of business leaders moving from lobbying on behalf of economic rights to political concessions, nor of Taiwanese businesses calling for unification or negotiation on China's terms. In fact, especially after the March 2004 presidential elections in which Chen received a fraction over 50 percent of the popular vote (compared to when he won in 2000 with 39 percent), it appears that China lacks a mechanism for converting economic power into political influence. In the absence of any consensus about what Taiwan's identity is and in the face of a growing military threat, the view of economic relations as a "Trojan horse" has significant support in Taiwan.[75]

Moreover, the globalization of IT and economic integration promote at least two political trends that work against China's ultimate objective of reunification. First, economic integration polarizes Taiwan domestic politics, with one pole around Chen Shui-bian and supporters of independence, and another around the business community and closer ties to China. Politicizing the relationship may undermine the role commerce plays as a bridge between the two sides. Second, the more integrated the economy has become, the greater the pressure on Chen to expand and tighten military ties with the United States and to continue promoting the development of a separate Taiwanese national identity.

Military Capability

Globalization is broadly defined as the expansion of economic flows that may play a significant role in a state's ability to mobilize resources for military modernization. As Rowe argues, expanding trade alters the relative prices of domestic economic resources and thus of the cost of using these resources to pursue security goals. Building on Stolper-Samuelson, he notes that increasing exposure to international trade benefits the holders of the resource in which the domestic economy is relatively well-endowed compared to the rest of the world; if labor is more abundant, it benefits more from expanding trade. The more a resource earns in the economy, the harder it is for the state to mobilize that resource for security concerns.[76] So in the case of China, the state should have less difficulty in mobilizing capital as exposure to the international economy rises. This clearly appears to be the case as Chinese defense spending has grown at a double-digit rate for thirteen of the last fourteen years (and the year it was below double digits, the increase was 9.6 percent).

The globalization of IT could also significantly improve the PLA capabilities to fight technology intensive wars. Chinese doctrine currently calls for the development of a military able to fight "limited wars under high-technology conditions"—conflicts employing high-technology weapons and joint operations, and highly reliant on information and command, control, computers and communication and intelligence, surveillance, and reconnaissance (C4ISR).[77] Despite the recent purchase of high-tech weapons from Russia and other foreign suppliers, the PLA has continued difficulties in waging these types of wars. Currently the efficacy of advanced weapons systems acquired from Russia such as the Su 30 and the Sovremenny—and thus China's power-projection capabilities—is limited by weaknesses in systems integration, and the PLA suffers from a telecommunications infrastructure characterized by outmoded technology and lack of secure communications.

The commercialization and globalization of IT means that the PLA—or any other military with a sizable enough budget—can address weaknesses in integration and command and control capacities by going shopping. All states have access to advanced technologies because they can be purchased on the open global market. Space, surveillance, sensors and signal processing, high-fidelity simulation, and telecommunication technologies are now widely available. As a result, according to the Defense Science Board, "the so-called revolution in military affairs is, at least from a technology availability standpoint, truly a global affair."[78]

In the face of an American military dominance partly based on information superiority, China's interest in developing information warfare (IW) capabilities can be traced to at least three rationales. First and at the most general level, the ability to wage high-technology cyberwarfare is seen as a critical symbol of China's development into a modern and technologically advanced power. Second, given the relatively backward nature of the PLA and the military gap between China and the United States, IW is an arena in which China hopes it will be able to compete. The IW arena remains relatively open—no one power is predominant—and Beijing hopes that it can exploit the global revolution in IT to leapfrog to a position of equality in IW.[79] Finally, and perhaps most important, China could employ IW as a strategy of asymmetric warfare.

In their studies of the American military during the Gulf Wars I and II, Kosovo, and Afghanistan, Chinese strategists have noted the close link between information superiority and military victory. Despite the success of U.S. forces in these conflicts, Chinese analysts appear to believe that the United States is too dependent on civilian networks as well as on the NIPRNET, the Department of Defense's unclassified network.[80] American military systems, especially those related to command and control, could be attacked. In addition to their use in a Taiwanese scenario, cyber attacks also have a role in political competition with Washington and Taipei and have occurred during periods of major tension in Sino-U.S. and China-Taiwan relations. Incidents of "nationalist hacking," which include defacing Web sites, denial of service attacks, and virus writing, broke out during the May 1999 NATO bombing of the Chinese embassy in Belgrade, President Lee Teng-hui's August 1999 declaration of a "two-state theory," the inauguration of Taiwanese President Chen Shui-Bian in May 2000, and the April 2001 collision involving a U.S. reconnaissance plane and a Chinese fighter aircraft.[81]

IW capabilities are tightly linked to a potential Taiwan scenario in which cyberwarfare tactics might be used to attack both the will of the Taiwanese people to resist and the ability of U.S. military to respond to a Chinese attack on the island. In one potential scenario, PLA operators would crash American-coordinated logistics networks, delaying the arrival of a U.S. carrier battle group, while simultaneously launching short-range ballistic missile, "fifth column," and IW attacks against Taiwan's communication, financial, and power infrastructure. With the American forces delayed and the public panicked, the Taiwanese leadership could collapse and quickly surrender to Beijing. As Mulvenon notes, this strategy

> is available to the PLA in the near term; (2) it does not require the PLA to be able to attack/invade Taiwan with air/sea assets, which most analysts doubt the PLA is capable of achieving for the next ten years or more; and (3) it has a reasonable level of plausible deniability, provided that the attack is sophisticated enough to prevent tracing.[82]

There are real reasons to doubt that the globalization of IT will enable China to narrow the gap with the United States significantly. Perhaps most importantly, the United States is not standing still. The United States continues to dedicate significant resources to transforming its military forces to be able to take advantage of the revolution in military affairs. As Herrera notes in chapter 3, in the "short-to medium-term future the United States will retain a sizeable, if not massive lead in 'information-enabled' weaponry."[83]

Notwithstanding that globalization may make critical commercial technologies more available, China's immediate ability to apply and integrate these technologies into fielded military capabilities is questionable. Part of the problem is internal; the civilian and military technology sectors remain bifurcated, and the military technology sector is dominated by state-owned enterprises. The Chinese science and technology system has been traditionally weak in absorbing and dispersing imported technologies. This weakness has been the result of high walls between scientists and research institutes in one bureaucracy and those in another that prevented the exchange of ideas and technology, as well as Beijing's chronic underfunding of the diffusion process. Even in commercial sectors with a relatively direct link to potential military capability, it is hard to find evidence that new skills and technologies have migrated to the defense side of production and made a direct impact on military modernization.[84]

In addition, the structure and shape of global technology flows may limit the ability of the state to direct commercial technologies into military use. Foreign investors want to retain tight control over propriety technology and this concern over control is reflected in the growing preference for wholly foreign-owned enterprise ventures over equity joint venture in China; wholly foreign-owned enterprise ventures are currently preferred to equity joint ventures at a rate of more than two to one.[85] Multinationals are also increasingly relying on licensing agreements and strategic partnerships that may reduce Beijing's ability to control the movement of technology from the civilian to military uses. Moreover, with WTO accession, China has formally committed not to force technology transfer through local content, export performance, or other requirements.

The continued gap between U.S. and Chinese military power may not be a reason for confidence, however, given Beijing's political and strategic concerns over Taiwan's drift toward de jure independence. As Thomas Christensen argues, Beijing does not need to catch up with the United States: "with certain new equipment and certain strategies, China can pose major problems for American security interests, and especially for Taiwan, without the slightest pretense of catching up with the United States by an overall measure of national military power or technology."[86] New technologies and new coercive strategies may allow Beijing to exert greater control over Taiwan's diplomatic choices. In the end, PRC decisions to use force might be based on calculations other than (or in addition to) a simple assessment of the quantity and quality of U.S., Taiwanese, and PRC forces.

Even with Beijing's political and strategic objectives in mind, the likely efficacy of a Chinese IW attack should not be overstated. Despite gains made by the PLA, IW is certainly a dimension in which the United States and also probably Taiwan hold an advantage over China. China is itself extremely vulnerable to an attack on its communications infrastructure, and Taiwan's Communications, Electronics, and Information Bureau is staffed with many of Taiwan's most able computer hackers.[87] In addition, the efficacy of any surprise attack involving short-range ballistic missiles, paratroopers, and IW attacks would be highly dependent on Taiwan's military and political response. PLA and civilian leaders would have to be extremely confident that this type of campaign could achieve its desired military and political objectives. Is it likely that the Taiwanese leadership or population would politically collapse under limited missile and IW attacks? Recent experiences in the Balkans and even in Iraq, where the United States had a greater advantage in information dominance and used much greater firepower, suggest the PLA would have to be skeptical of the success of any strategy highly dependent on the weakness of Taiwanese society.

CONCLUSION

At both the theoretical and policy level, globalization is increasingly a defining (and constraining) condition for Chinese national security.[88] Chinese analysts and scholars have paid greater attention to the question of globalization during the last five years. As Alastair Iain Johnston notes, references to globalization in academic journals have surpassed those of multipolarity.[89] These concerns have been echoed at the highest levels of government. For example, in a 2001 speech, Jiang Zemin argued that globalization was a process "generally conducive to world economic development," but, with improper handling, could bring "a negative impact on developing countries."[90]

It is Jiang's reference to developing economies and to both the positives and negatives inherent in globalization that best captures the interaction of globalization and national security in the Chinese context. For China's leaders, political legitimacy is increasingly dependent on nationalism and economic growth. Although Beijing hopes that greater integration into the world economy will further reform and ensure continued growth, the opposite may be true. Globalization may aggravate many of the social and political cleavages that are the result of economic reforms; globalization may exacerbate weaknesses in the domestic economy, collapsing state-owned enterprises, and aggravating unemployment and social instability. Moreover, the globalization of ITs may strengthen the organizational capabilities of those who oppose the current regime. Falun Gong, democracy advocates, and proponents of Tibetan independence may all use the Internet, text messaging, and satellite television to spread their ideas free of Beijing's control.

After 1989, Beijing saw what happened in Eastern Europe and drew conclusions about what it viewed as the correct relationship between the timing of political and economic reforms. After 1997, policy makers were worried about what had happened in Indonesia and warned about the need to protect the domestic economy from outside forces. Defending China's ability to limit social disruption and control information has become central to security policy, and the state has been unexpectedly resourceful in developing strategies to contain the threat. In the short term at least, Beijing has been able to prevent opponents of the regime from significantly weakening state capacity. The state has been especially resourceful in developing an institutional, political, and technological strategy to prevent the dissemination of controlled information and the mobilization of opposition groups. Recent moves by Beijing to control text messaging suggest that the state remains able to contain the political pressures of globalization and will continue to do so for the near to mid term.

The resiliency of the state, however, should not overshadow the political importance of the globalization of IT and the marketization of the media. The context of decision making has changed as Chinese leaders must now take public opinion into account. Public opinion has not yet forced the public renunciation or reversal of an already announced policy. But in both domestic and foreign policy arenas, policy makers can no longer assume that they monopolize information. As a result, they increasingly have to justify policy decisions and behavior.

The external security consequences of globalization are similarly double-edged. Economic relations across the Taiwan Strait are tightly interlinked and there are few who believe that Taiwan can survive economically without the mainland, but Beijing must feel that the possibility of achieving reunification is more distant than when China began inviting Taiwanese investment in 1979. Economic influence has not been converted into political influence. In fact, economic dependence appears to have polarized Taiwanese identity. If Taiwan drifts closer to independence, and Beijing chooses to respond, China will now have a greater range of coercive choices. But this must provide little comfort to China's leaders who expected economic interdependence to prevent Taiwan from ever reaching that point.

The globalization of commercial technologies provides the Chinese military with greater access to resources, but still the PLA is unlikely to leapfrog to the next generation of advanced military weapons. In fact, the United States is likely to leverage globalization so that the technological gap between the PLA and the U.S. military will probably grow, not narrow.

Beijing carefully tracks the advantages that the United States as hegemon accrues from globalization. Here China exemplifies the response of almost all the other states discussed in this volume. Globalization affects all but not equally, and the concern in Beijing is that the United States is best able to leverage changes in the international system to its advantage. Relative gains are particularly worrying to China because continued economic development, maintained status quo across the Taiwan Strait, and enhanced authority as a regional power all require good relations with Washington.

The hybrid nature of the Chinese case stands out in this volume. In most of the regional or country case studies in this book, globalization appears to make strong states more capable, while further limiting the authority and efficacy of weaker states. China certainly faces threats from globalization, but there are few states that have been as successful in capturing the economic and political benefits of interacting with the global economy. For now, China has decided to further embrace globalization as the best means to achieve its political and economic goals. This is a strategic and paradoxical choice, one that strengthens Beijing at home and abroad but may eventually undermine a political legitimacy increasingly tied to economic performance. The long-term sustainability of this position, balanced on the tip of a double-edged sword, remains uncertain.

NOTES

1. The author thanks Benjamin Brake for excellent research support.
2. Ministry of Commerce, 2003 High Technology Exports Exceed 110 Billion, available at http://kjs.mofcom.gov.cn/article/200401/20040100172807_1.xml.
3. Kirshner, chapter 11 of this volume.
4. Donald Hicks, "Final Report of Defense Science Board Task Force on Globalization and Security" (December 1999), v. Available at http://www.acq.osd.mil/dsb/globalization.pdf (accessed July 2004).
5. Thomas Christensen, "Chinese Realpolitik: Reading Beijing's World-View," *Foreign Affairs* 75(5) (September/October 1996): 37–52.
6. Shi Hongtao, "China Is Rebuilding Its Relationship with the World during SARS Period," *Qingnian Bao,* May 21, 20003, in *Foreign Broadcast Information Services Daily Reports* (hereafter FBIS), May 21, 2003.
7. Wang Yizhou, "Political Stability and International Relations in the Process of Economic Globalization—Another Perspective on Asia's Financial Crisis," (n.d.). Available at http://www.iwep.org.cn/chinese/gerenzhuye/wangyizhou/index.htm.
8. Allen Carlson, *Unifying China, Integrating with the World: Securing Chinese Sovereignty in the Reform Era* (Stanford, CA: Stanford University Press, 2005).
9. Thomas Christensen, "China," in *Strategic Asia, 2002–2003* (Seattle: National Bureau of Asian Research, 2003). Wu Xinbo offers a similar list: sustaining economic growth, preserving territorial integrity, regime security, maintaining favorable strategic balance, and expanding international influence. See his "China: Security Practice of a Modernizing and Ascending Power," in *Asian Security Practices: Material and Ideational Influences,* ed. Muthiah Alagappa (Palo Alto, CA: Stanford University Press, 1998), 127.
10. David Shambaugh, *China's Military Modernization* (Berkeley: University of California Press, 2002), 285.
11. Thomas Moore, "China and Globalization," in *East Asia and Globalization,* ed. Samuel S. Kim (Lanham, MD: Rowman and Littlefield, 2000), 105–131.
12. Zhang Boli, "Economic Globalization is a Double-Edged Sword," *Renmin Ribao* [People's Daily], May 30, 2000.
13. Guo Jingyan, "Economic Globalization and Military Security," *PLA Daily,* January 10, 2001, in FBIS, January 10, 2001.
14. "Globalization Brings Gains and Pains," *China Daily,* December 6, 2001.
15. Guo, "Economic Globalization."
16. Ibid.
17. Thomas Moore, "Globalization and China's Search for Economic Security: Implications for Chinese Foreign Policy and International Relations in East Asia," paper presented to 2001 Hong Kong Convention of the International Studies Association, Hong Kong, July 2001.
18. Wang Yizhou, "New Security Concept in Globalization," *Beijing Review* 7 (February 1999): 15–21.
19. Li Shenming, "Quanqiuhua yu Di San Shijie [Globalization and the Third World]," *Jiefangjun Bao* [PLA Daily, hereafter JFJB], June 7 (part 1), June 8 (part 2), 2000.
20. Yang Xinhua and Hu Changtai, "Informal Discussion of National Security in the Information Age," JFJB, July 24, 2002.

21. Zhang, "Double-Edged Sword."
22. Wu Guoguang, "Legitimacy Crisis, Political Economy, and the Fifteenth Party Congress," in *Dilemmas of Reform in Jiang Zemin's China,* eds. Andrew J. Nathan, Zhaohui Hong, and Steven R. Smith (Boulder, CO: Lynne Rienner Publishers, 1999).
23. Quoted in Joseph Fewsmith, "The Sixteenth National Party Congress: The Succession that Didn't Happen," *China Quarterly* 173 (March 2003): 3.
24. Guo Lianchnag, "Jing Ji Quan Qiu Hua Zhengzhi Xiaoying Lun [The Effects of Globalization]," *Shijie Jingji yu Zhengzhi* [World Politics and Economics], 8 (2000): 42–45.
25. State Council, "China's National Defense in 2000," available at http://www.china. org.cn/e-white/2000/20–2.htm.
26. Xu Kui, "Quan Qiu Hua Liang Chao yu Guo Ji Anquan [Globalization and National Security]," *Shijie Jingji yu Zhengzhi* 3 (2001): 21–25.
27. Xu Zhungzhi, Cao Zhi, and Sun Yanxin, "Quanqiuhau Shidai Renren Yaozuo Guojia Anquan de Shouwangzhe [During the Age of Globalization, Everyone Must Monitor National Security]," *Xinhua wang,* March 13, 2003.
28. Yong Deng and Thomas Moore, "China Views Globalization: Toward a New Great-Power Politics?" *The Washington Quarterly* 27(3) (Summer 2004): 119.
29. Zhang Xudong, "It is Difficult for 'Hot Money' to Create Disturbances through Arbitrage," *Xinhua,* September 8, 2003.
30. "True Lies—Revaluation of the RMB," *Renmin Ribao* [People's Daily], July 23, 2003.
31. "World Development Indicators," World Bank, 2002.
32. Paul Chan, "Asian Internet Sector Rocks in the North; China is Set to Overtake Japan; S Korea is the World's Leading Broadband Nation," *Business Times Singapore,* January 2, 2003.
33. "Analysis Report on the Growth of the Internet in China," CNNIC, available at www.cnnic.net.cn/e-about.shtml.
34. "Asia-Pacific Telecommunication Indicators 2002," International Telecommunications Union, November 2002.
35. Yang and Hu, "Informal Discussion."
36. Xia Lin, "Chuanmei Quanqiuhua Shidai de Guojia Anquan [National Security in the Era of Media Globalization]," *Zhongguo Chuanmei Baogao* [China Media Report] 1 (2003), available at http://ruanzixiao.myrice.com/cmqxhsddgjaq.htm.
37. Luan Juanjun, "Attach Great Importance, Conduct Conscientious Research, and Actively Respond—Investigation and Thoughts on the Impact of China's WTO Accession on the Ideology of Officers and Men," *People's Liberation Army Daily,* March 21, 2002, in FBIS, March 21, 2001.
38. Xiao Qiang, "SARS Impact on Media Control and Governance," Testimony before the U.S.-China Economic and Security Review Commission, June 5, 2003, available at http://www.uscc.gov/qiates.htm.
39. Bill Xia, "SARS Impact on Media Control and Governance," Testimony before the U.S.-China Economic and Security Review Commission, June 5, 2003, available at http://www.uscc.gov/xiates.htm.
40. Maggie Farley, "Hactivists Besiege China," *Los Angeles Times,* January 4, 1999.
41. Clifford Bob, "The Merchants of Morality," *Foreign Policy* (March/April 2002): 36–45.
42. Bu Zhong, "Freedom of the Press in China After SARS: Reform and Retrenchment," Testimony before the Congressional-Executive Commission on China, September 22, 2003, available at http://www.cecc.gov/pages/roundtables/092203/zhong.php.
43. Susan Lawrence and Kathy Chen, "Media Reforms in China Betray Contradictions," *Wall Street Journal,* June 25, 2003.

44. Michael S. Chase and James Mulvenon, *You've Got Dissent* (Santa Monica, CA: RAND, 2002); and Shanthi Kalathil and Taylor C. Boas, "The Internet and State Control in Authoritarian Regimes: China, Cuba, and the Counterrevolution," Carnegie Working Paper No. 21, July 2001.
45. Xiao Qiang, "SARS Impact on Media Control and Governance."
46. Jonathan Zittrain and Benjamin Edelman, "Empirical Analysis of Internet Filtering in China," March 2003, available at http://cyber.law.harvard.edu/filtering/china/.
47. Mark Magnier, "China Clamps Down on Web News Discussion," *Los Angeles Times*, February 26, 2004; "China Issues More Internet Regulations," *South China Morning Post*, June 21, 2004.
48. Joshua Kurlantzick, "Dictatorship.com: The Web Won't Topple Tyranny," *The New Republic*, April 5, 2004.
49. Nina Hachigian, "China's Cyber-Strategy," *Foreign Affairs* 80(2) (March/April 2001): 118–133; John Gittings, "Beijing is Losing the People's War in Cyberspace," *YaleGlobal Online*, July 21, 2003, available at http://yaleglobal.yale.edu/display.article?id=2133.
50. Ronald Deibert, "Dark Guests and Great Firewalls: The Internet and Chinese Security Policy," *Journal of Social Issues* 58(1) (2002): 151.
51. Louisa Lim, "China to Censor Text Messages," *BBC Online*, July 2, 2004, available at http://news.bbc.co.uk/2/hi/asia-pacific/3859403.stm.
52. "China's 'BMW Killer' Case Upheld," *BBC Online*, March 29, 2004. Available at http://news.bbc.co.uk/1/hi/world/asia-pacific/3577829.stm.
53. Charles Hutzler, "Yuppies in China Protest Via the Web—And Get Away With It," *Wall Street Journal*, March 19, 2004.
54. Michael Yahuda, "China's Win-Win Globalization," *YaleGlobal Online*, available at http://yaleglobal.yale.edu/display.article?id=2133.
55. Wu Fenghua, "Jiedu Quanqiuhua Shidai de Zhanzheng [Discussion of Globalization and Contemporary Warfare]," JFJB, January 15, 2003.
56. OECD, Economic Outlook, available at http://www.oecd.org/dataoecd/6/18/2752923.pdf.
57. Benedicte Callan, Sean Costigan, and Kenneth Keller, *Exporting US High Tech: Facts and Fiction about the Globalization of Industrial R&D* (New York: Council on Foreign Relations, 1997), 10.
58. Kathleen Walsh, *Foreign High-Tech R&D in China: Risks, Rewards, and Implications for U.S.-China Relations* (Washington, DC: The Henry Stimson Center, 2003).
59. National Science Board, Science and Engineering Indicators, 2002, quoted in Walsh, *Foreign High-Tech R&D in China*.
60. Harold Brown, Joseph Prueher, and Adam Segal, *Chinese Military Power* (New York: Council on Foreign Relations, 2003).
61. Robert Ross, "The Geography of the Peace: East Asia in the Twenty-First Century," *International Security* 23(4) (Spring 1999): 81–118.
62. Brown, Prueher, and Segal, *Chinese Military Power*.
63. International Crisis Group, *Taiwan Strait III: The Chance of Peace*, Asia Report No. 55 (Washington, DC: International Crisis Group, 2003).
64. Tim Culpan, "IT Hardware Manufacturers Storm into Mainland," *South China Morning Post*, April 30, 2002.
65. Charles Kelley, et al, *High Technology Manufacturing and U.S. Competitiveness* (Santa Monica, CA: RAND, 2004): 70.
66. Chiu Yu Tzu, "Technology Law to Guard Valued Assets," *Taipei Times*, April 17, 2002; Lawrence Chung, "Taiwan Woos Its Companies Back," *Strait Times*, December 12, 2002.
67. Albert Hirschman, *National Power and the Structure of Foreign Trade* (Berkeley: University of California Press, 1945, 1980).

68. Craig Addison, *Silicon Shield: Taiwan's Protection against Chinese Attack* (Irvington, TX: Fusion Press, 2001), 203. See also, "Presidential Office Cautions Mainland over Chi Mei Plant," *China Post*, March 12, 2001.

69. "Qian Qichen Inspects Guangdong, Holds Discussion with Taiwan Businessmen." *Xinhua*, FBIS-CHI, December 8, 2002.

70. James Morrow, "Assessing the Role of Trade as a Source of Costly Signals," in *Economic Interdependence and International Conflict: New Perspectives on Enduring Debate*, eds. Edward D. Mansfield and Brian M. Pollins (Ann Arbor, MI: University of Michigan Press, 2003).

71. Rawi Abdelal and Jonathan Kirshner, "Strategy, Economic Relations, and the Definition of National Interests," *Security Studies* 9 (1999-2000): 119–56.

72. The three *nos* were a Kuomintang or Nationalist Party, policy and were no contact, negotiation, and compromise between Taiwan and China. Chang Kao, *Dalu Jingji yu Liangan Jingmao Guangxi* [Mainland Economic Reform and Cross-Strait Relations] (Taipei: Wu Nan, 1994). Quoted in Tung Chen-yuan, *China's Economic Leverage and Taiwan's Security Concerns with Respect to Cross-Strait Economic Relations* (PhD Dissertation, Johns Hopkins University, May 2002).

73. Mainland Affairs Council, *Dalu Gongzuo Cankao Ziliao* [Reference Documents of Mainland Work], (Taipei: Mainland Affairs Council, 1998). Quoted in Tung, *China's Economic Leverage.*

74. Ralph Clough, *Reaching across the Taiwan Strait: People-to-People Diplomacy* (San Francisco: Westview Press, 1993), 93–95.

75. International Crisis Group, *Taiwan Strait III*, 8.

76. David Rowe, "World Economic Expansion and National Security in Pre-World War I Europe," *International Organization* 53(2) (Spring 1999): 195–232.

77. Brown, Prueher, and Segal, *Chinese Military Power.*

78. Hicks, "Final Report of Defense Science Board," v.

79. Toshi Yoshihara, *Chinese Information Warfare: A Phantom Menace or Emerging Threat* (Strategic Studies Institute, Army War College, Carlisle, PA: November 2001), available at http://www.iwar.org.uk/iwar/resources/china/iw/chininfo.pdf.

80. Brown, Prueher, and Segal, *Chinese Military Power.*

81. Information Warfare Monitor, "Chinese Information Warfare: An Overview," September 23, 2003, available at http://www.infowar-monitor.net/modules.php?op=modload&name=Archive&file=index&req=viewarticle&artid=2&page=5.

82. James Mulvenon, "The PLA and Information Warfare," in *The People's Liberation Army in the Information Age*, eds. James Mulvenon and Richard Yang (Santa Monica, CA: RAND, 1999).

83. Herrera, chapter 3 of this volume.

84. Evan Medeiros, "Analyzing China's Defense Industries and the Implications for Chinese Military Modernization," Presentation to the U.S.-China Economic and Security Review Commission Hearing on Chinese Military Modernization and Cross-Strait Politico-Military Relations, Washington, DC, February 6, 2004.

85. U.S.-China Business Council, Foreign Investment in China, available at http://www.uschina.org/statistics/2003foreigninvestment.html.

86. Thomas Christensen, "Posing Problems without Catching Up: China's Rise and the Challenges for U.S. Security Policy," *International Security* 25(4) (Spring 2001): 5–40.

87. Brown, Prueher, and Segal, *Chinese Military Power.*

88. Thomas Moore and Dixia Yang, "Empowered and Restrained: Chinese Foreign Policy in the Age of Economic Interdependence," in *The Making of Chinese Foreign and Security Policy in the Era of Reform*, ed. David M. Lampton (Palo Alto, CA: Stanford University Press, 2001), 191–229.

89. Alastair Iain Johnston, "Is China a Status Quo Power?" *International Security* 27(4) (Spring 2003), 35.
90. "President Jiang Zemin delivers Speech to APEC CEO Summit," *Xinhua*, October 18, 2001.

11

GLOBALIZATION, POWER, AND PROSPECT

Jonathan Kirshner

WHAT ARE THE CONSEQUENCES OF GLOBALIZATION for national security? The chapters in this volume have collectively made the case that globalization—an array of phenomena that derive from unorganized stateless forces—has transformed the nature of the national security environment that states face, even in the context of a state-centric, traditional definition of national security: issues associated with organized political violence that speaks to the vital interests of at least one state.[1] As a result of this transformation, failure to account for the influence of globalization will make it increasingly difficult to understand changes in the balance of power, the prospects for war, and strategic choices embraced by states.

This conclusion and its implications are too easily lost in a thicket of false controversies, definitional squabbles, and hyperbolic rhetoric; thus some analytical brush clearing is called for in order to clarify what is (and what is not) argued here. In particular, five key qualifications should be reemphasized.

Globalization is not interdependence. As defined in this volume,[2] globalization is not simply an extreme form of interdependence (the political consequences of enmeshed relationships between states). Nor is globalization shorthand for the behavior of subnational, transnational, or supranational actors; though, as the previous chapters have amply demonstrated, globalization can empower such nonstate actors and may affect the nature and consequences of interdependence.

Globalization is not necessarily novel. To observe that it is snowing very heavily is not to deny that there have been blizzards in the past—rather, it is simply to argue that the blizzard matters right now, and we need a better understanding of the consequences of the snow. No claim of novelty is necessary to sustain the conclusion that globalization significantly affects national security; though, to avoid confusion, it should be acknowledged that the contributions to this volume tend to share the view that the interactive and cumulative effects of the processes of contemporary globalization have indeed created a relatively novel security environment.[3]

Globalization is not irreversible. Similarly, the conclusions here do not rest on claims that globalization is irreversible—nor are any such claims advanced. Again, to call attention to the importance of the blizzard is not to insist that it will never stop snowing—it is simply to argue that the snow matters. There is an implicit assumption in these pages that it will continue to snow for a while yet. If contemporary globalization were likely to reverse soon, comprehensively, and with few "hysteresis" effects (that is, if the reversal was more like shutting off a light than putting out a fire), then the stakes for elucidating the effects of globalization on national security would be reduced. Given the likelihood that such a comprehensive reversal of globalization will not occur in the near future, however, it is crucial to understand its consequences for national security.

Globalization is not irresistible. Although many of the pressures brought about by globalization are quite powerful and, as will be discussed further below, tend in aggregate to reduce the capacity and autonomy of states, globalization is not an irresistible force, nor an arbiter of unbending laws. Rather, processes of globalization reshape the costs, benefits, and consequences of pursuing different policy choices. Efforts by states to limit their exposure to globalization—to restrict, for example, the flow of goods, data, money, and people across their borders—remain possible. Globalization does not impose openness; rather, it raises the opportunity costs of closure. States are not defenseless, although the uncoordinated, atomistic, and seemingly organic nature of the forces of globalization suggests that defensive measures by states will not yield once-and-for-all solutions, but will be part of a continuing and dynamic process, as various tactics introduced by states elicit not only intended but also unintended and unanticipated consequences and responses.

Globalization is political. Finally, as should be especially clear from the previous chapters, globalization is rooted in political foundations, and its consequences are not politically neutral. American unipolarity has contributed to an environment more conducive to the advance of globalization than would have likely occurred had the Cold War bipolar order endured, or if an illiberal state, rather than the United States, were the world's preponderant power. And as the biggest fish in a more open pond, the United States often finds itself advantaged by globalization. But, for better or (and) worse, this contributes to the tendency to conflate globalization and Americanization, which have important differences. Moreover, even though the United States has shaped the nature of globalization, this does not prevent the favor from being returned—a reminder that there is a distinction between creating Frankenstein's creature and controlling him.[4] The dominance of Hollywood, for example, is often bemoaned as representing the Americanization of global culture. However, with the major studios now highly dependent on overseas revenues to survive, it may be more accurate to assess with dismay the globalization of American culture.[5] Nor can the economic vulnerabilities expressed by the U.S. trade deficit and financing of its federal budget deficits be easily ignored.

With these qualifications in hand, this concluding chapter proceeds in four parts. First, this section concludes with a brief review of the three general processes of globalization and the three ways in which those processes affect national security. These two triplets lend themselves to a 3 × 3 matrix for considering those consequences. The second section then shows how the contributions of the volume fit into this framework. This is followed by a section that revisits the matrix, shifting from the specific observations of the chapters individually to more general and abstract conclusions offered by the chapters collectively. A final section considers the implications of these findings for contemporary world politics.

This volume has identified three "processes" of globalization: conduits through which the pressures of globalization are transmitted throughout the system: via the intensification of *economic exchange*—including the fragmentation of production and ascension of finance; the flow of *information*—the confluence of innovations such as satellites and cell phones, faxes, and the Internet, that have contributed to the "hypermedia environment"; and *marketization*—the expansion of the set of social relations governed by market forces. Although they are distinct, it is important to recognize that these processes are also mutually reinforcing.

These processes influence national security in three principal ways. First, they affect state *capacity and autonomy*—that is, globalization reshapes the relative power of the state vis-à-vis nonstate actors, social forces, and market pressures. This does not of necessity suggest that the state will be weakened across the board; in some areas, for example, such as surveillance, state power will be enhanced. More generally, the implications of the current information revolution will very much depend on how the new regulatory environment evolves.[6] Second, globalization affects the *balance of power* between states, because of the changes brought about to state autonomy and state capacity—no matter what the nature of those changes are, and even in the case where every state finds itself absolutely less able to advance its interests—there will be a reshuffling of relative capabilities. That is, even if all states are weaker, some will be weakened to a greater or lesser extent, and each will probably be affected in distinct ways. Some states may be relatively empowered by the hypermedia environment; others might be particularly vulnerable to the challenges posed by greater pressures for economic liberalization. Thus, globalization will reshape the relative distribution of capabilities and vulnerabilities between states.[7] Finally, globalization influences the *nature and axes of conflict*—contributing to new sources of conflict and creating distinct opportunities and incentives for political violence.[8] Here the mutually reinforcing aspects of these processes are most apparent. Liberalization and the intensification of economic exchange, for example, present opportunities for transnational criminal groups that in many ways are parallel to the ones afforded to legitimate international business enterprises. Additionally, such criminal groups, given their extralegal nature, may provide natural complementary networks for terrorist organizations and insurgents (who are also taking advantage of contemporary information technology [IT]), and thus empower such movements.[9]

GLOBALIZATION AND NATIONAL SECURITY IN PRACTICE

The chapters in this volume illustrate these three sets of effects that globalization is having on contemporary national security. I consider each effect in turn—autonomy and capacity, balance of power, and the nature and axes of conflict—drawing on some of the examples introduced and considered by the individual chapters. Table 11.1 provides a summary of this discussion.

Autonomy and Capacity

The tendency for globalization to provide opportunities for criminal as well as legitimate business enterprises was one of Alexander Cooley's central themes in chapter 7. Cooley showed how illicit markets for drugs and weapons allowed security agencies in the republics of the Former Soviet Union to freelance, and actively fund their own operations by

Table 11.1 Globalization and National Security in Contemporary World Politics

	Autonomy and Capacity	Balance of Power	Nature and Axes of Conflict
Exchange	Cooley: illicit markets; freelancing Adamson: migratory flows Midford: fragmentation and scale	Mueller: U.S. and allies well positioned Adamson: challenges to weak states Segal: China as hybrid case	Midford: tensions in U.S.-Japan alliance Cooley: criminals, insurgents, separatists Adamson: transnational mobilization, terrorism
Information	Herrera: recalibration of state power Segal: control versus modernization Lynch: demonstration; public opinion	Herrera: U.S. military dominance Mueller: U.S. soft power benefits Herrera: authoritarians challenged	Herrera: cyberwarfare, information warfare Mueller: organizational capacity of terrorists Lynch: resistance to cultural intrusion of West
Marketization	Avant: privatization of force Lynch/Segal: market-driven media Epstein: viability of defense firms	Epstein: European political viability Avant: new challenges to weak Cooley: vulnerability of weak, postimperial	Segal: resistance to U.S., Western culture Epstein: pressures for proliferation Avant: more small wars in weak states

both regulating and participating in these international markets. Weak states—and postimperial settings represent an extreme variant of this—are especially likely to see their limited capacities further reduced by this collusion between local security actors and criminal networks engaging in smuggling, human traffic, money laundering, and drug trade. The resulting blurring of incentives diminishes the capacity of the state to cope with both external and internal security threats as well.

Market incentives put states under pressure even in the absence of such profound security pathologies. Fiona Adamson (chapter 2) observed that many problematic aspects of migratory flows, which are very often responses to economic incentives (that is, perceived opportunities abroad) result from the fact that the "supply" of migrants is greater than the "demand" for immigrants. Paul Midford (chapter 9) described how the global fragmentation of the production process, along with increasing economies of scale in the defense sector, has forced Japan to compromise with regard to its traditional search for "comprehensive" security autonomy. And as Adam Segal (chapter 10) noted, the siren call of the global economy presents China's leadership with the challenge of embracing the opportunities it presents to ensure adequate economic growth; at the same time, the government is under pressure to aptly manage domestic reforms and, of course, to maintain one-party rule. On the one hand, growth depends on continued liberalization; on the other, unmediated economic exchange puts pressure on "economic security" and can contribute to political and social unrest.

As Segal discussed, this double-edged sword is also present with regard to the information revolution. Beijing is convinced that ITs will be essential for growth and modernization; but at the same time, however, this results in a weakening of the state's control of information, and opens the door to Western ideas and lifestyles that the government considers unattractive. The general threat posed by the hypermedia environment to the ability of authoritarian regimes to keep a tight grip on their citizens, as well as to their ability to maintain social cohesion more broadly, is a central theme of Geoffrey Herrera's contribution (chapter 3), and can be seen not only in the Segal chapter but also with Marc Lynch's discussion (chapter 6) of the Middle East. As Lynch argued, the economic pressures of globalization exacerbate the dysfunctions inherent in these relatively sheltered economies (and thus, he cautions, "more" globalization might be even more destabilizing); additionally, access to greater information means that the lower classes are not simply falling behind, but they can see that they are falling behind. And while neither Lynch nor Segal views new media access as inevitably imposing democracy on autocratic regimes, nevertheless they agree that important changes can be observed. In particular, even in nondemocratic regimes, it is increasingly the case that public opinion can no longer be safely ignored.

These new media challenges are a function not only of IT, but also, importantly, of marketization: in both of the cases just discussed, an essential harbinger of this new environment has been the expansion of the media outside of the public sphere and into the private sphere. The consequences of the shift from minimal outlet, state-run—that is, politically responsive—media, to a media environment that is more dispersed and private—that is, market responsive—is profound. As Segal recounts, China now has 2,000 newspapers, 9,000 magazines, and 2,000 TV stations operating in an increasingly private-sector media environment. Similarly, Al Jazeera's market-driven programming was enormously successful in attracting viewers, as well as new entrants and competitors into the market, all at the expense of official media outlets.

Marketization is also obviously at the core of Deborah Avant's consideration (chapter 4) of the marketization of security. This is another example of how globalization does not simply undermine state power uniformly: the autonomy and capacity of some powerful states are enhanced to the extent that they are able to employ private security companies (PSCs) to engage in activities abroad that might not be easily initiated and sustained via standard domestic political processes required to approve the use of force. For weak states, however, the increased prevalence of PSCs can empower opponents and undermine domestic political processes. Cooley's chapter showed how the muddled military environment left in the wake of the Soviet collapse created both an important source of manpower and expertise for this industry (especially from Russia and Ukraine), as well as an important market for PSCs, particularly in the small, weak, central Asian republics.

The challenges of marketization are not limited exclusively to weak or developing states, as Rachel Epstein illustrated with her discussion (chapter 8) of how pressures of privatization as well as increasing economies of scale have placed many European defense firms under significant strain concerning their ability to remain viable and competitive, which in turn has consequences for the political capability of individual European states and of the European Union collectively. These developments confront Europe with the challenge of overcoming internal divisions on foreign and security policy and moving toward greater defense industry integration or facing a serious deterioration of their defense capacity.

Balance of Power

Because states find their autonomy and capacity affected by globalization in differential ways, globalization also affects the balance of power. In general, those states that started out with relatively limited capacity are the most vulnerable. As Adamson argued, weak states are the least likely to be able to cope with large migratory flows and are especially vulnerable to "brain drain" as many talented citizens seek opportunities abroad. Conversely, Karl Mueller (chapter 5) argued that even though globalization has reduced the capacity of the United States and contributed to an environment conducive to the gradual erosion of its hegemony, from a broad strategic perspective America still comes out as a net winner in the balance of power sweepstakes. The United States and its allies, as market-oriented, liberal, open societies, are especially well positioned to thrive under globalization; whereas its principal and potential adversaries—illiberal and authoritarian—are faced with new challenges and even more inhibitions on their range of action. This, as will be discussed further below, may elicit a countervailing political response. Segal argues that China is well aware of these security implications, and he shares the view that liberal states are advantaged by globalization, and that the United States in particular is uniquely positioned to exploit these advantages to its political benefit.

Advances in IT are also strengthening the United States compared to other states, as Herrera emphasized in his chapter. The U.S. lead in IT, and the adoption of these advances by the military, is not only huge but insurmountable for the foreseeable future. Although debates continue as to whether these adaptations have contributed to a true "revolution in military affairs," they have undeniably widened even further the gap implied by the material U.S. military dominance in conventional forms of warfare.[10] Segal traces China's interest in information warfare to the understanding that an important component of U.S. military preponderance derives from its IT advantage.

More generally, as with economic liberalization, the hypermedia environment affects the balance of power because new media puts more pressure on authoritarian regimes than it does those states that already presided over a relatively permissive environment. These challenges relate not just to control of what is seen and heard (though the significance of this should not be underestimated, especially for those regimes that considered it crucial in the past to maintain strict control over access to information), but also to the implications of the process itself, which features competing ideas, commercialized entertainment, and market competition. As Mueller argued, even if U.S. hegemony fades over time, a globalized world is a world in which the United States is comfortable and well positioned to thrive—in the rosiest scenario, this would reflect the ultimate triumph of "soft power"—all the world wanting what America wanted it to want.[11]

Following this argument, it can be seen that marketization also influences the balance of power to the extent that it advantages the values of "the West" at the expense of authoritarian states or simply traditionalist forms of political organization. Avant's chapter offered a more specific illustration of how the proliferation of PSCs leave the weak even weaker and less able to cope with security challenges, while the already strong and able are afforded another arrow in their quivers. Marketization also affects the balance of power within the West. As Epstein argued, greater marketization in the defense industry could have significant ramifications for the relative position of Europe and America. Firms, under market pressure to establish production alliances, do so in ways often divorced from national security policy. Unless the Europeans are able to overcome formidable barriers to much greater cooperation in both defense policy and the coordination of production, the result will not simply be the inevitably diminished capacity of some states. It will also result in continued EU military dependence on the United States and will contribute to the political marginalization of Europe on the world stage and undermine its ability to meet threats by using force.

The Nature and Axes of Conflict

The processes of globalization do not simply alter the balance of power, but the limitations, incentives, and opportunities they create recast the prospects for both the nature of violent political conflict and the axes of those conflicts (see Table 11.1).

Midford argued that disagreements about the management of international financial crises are contributing to increased political tension between Japan and the United States. Additionally, he sees a potentially unsustainable paradox in Japan's efforts to adapt to greater globalization, a bifurcated approach that features greater defense cooperation but increasingly oppositional economic relations with the Americans. Although this tension may ultimately contribute to a political realignment, it should be clear that Midford does not expect militarized conflict between the two states. Many of the other contributions, however, do elucidate changes in the prospects for and nature of war. Cooley anticipates that the reduced capacity of many weak states, coupled with the empowerment of terrorist, separatist, and insurgent groups will be conducive to smaller scale conflicts in these areas. In the environment of globalized exchange, these groups are better able to fund their activities by engaging the illicit market. As he notes, criminal networks raise problems; and criminalized states are not well equipped to deal with them. Failing states, unable to efficiently police or control their own borders, also provide safe havens for terrorist groups and other irregular armed forces. These are complementary to the problems raised by Adamson—the consequences of links between smugglers, illegal migratory networks, and the greater mobility of shadowy political actors—compounded by the opportunities presented by new communications technologies, which provide essential infrastructure for transnational mobilization.

As Herrera explained, the distributed and anonymous nature of many of these communications technologies are also a boon to terrorists or those actors who would challenge the state. He also noted that the information revolution affects the nature and axes of conflict in state-to-state power politics as well. The imposing U.S. lead both in IT and its military applications may contribute to some creative counterbalancing against U.S. power—as some states fearful of vulnerability to U.S. surgical strikes search for novel and asymmetric responses to U.S. power. (Mueller reports this type of paradox as well—globalization enhances American power but at the same time it does much to enable powerful transnational terrorist groups to form and operate, threatening the United States.) Greater interest in (and likely practice of) cyberwarfare and IW more generally is another development suggested by the real and perceived military significance of U.S. dominance in and dependence on IT, a development stressed not only by Herrera but by Segal with regard to China's interest in developing such capabilities.

Segal and especially Lynch also call attention to the ways in which information—especially in media and entertainment flows—can create new sources of conflict due to the fact that such content is often perceived as an unwelcome intrusion of Western culture and norms, eliciting a backlash and providing a rallying point for anti-Western groups. This also touches on the question of marketization and the ways in which pressures for the expansion of the market sphere create new sources of conflict. Whereas it is the regime in Beijing that is especially wary of the encroachment of Western culture and Western values as the market sector expands in China, in the Middle East, the pushback emanates more from nonofficial institutions and sources. The dramatically differential nature of the advance of globalization in much of the Middle East—relatively low in exchange (with the exceptions of migration and remittances) but high with regard to information—puts even more of an edge on the political and economic strains that derive from marketization. The challenge to traditional and religious patterns of activity and the more common tendency to perceive globalization as a form of imperialism contributes to an intellectual middle class response of dissent, a more widespread and oppositional expression of Islamism, and is conducive to both passive and active support for more violent resistance, including terrorism.

Epstein noted that market pressures on defense firms (coupled with the fragmentation of production that increases the likelihood of dual-use issues) undermines efforts to control weapons proliferation as firms scramble to stay profitable. The hallmark of the consequences of marketization on the nature of conflict, however, is most evident in Avant's discussion of the global trend toward the use of markets to allocate security. Not only does this tend, as discussed, to render weak states even more vulnerable, but it suggests a world where small wars are more common. When contracting for force is more accessible, actors within weak states find it easier to challenge the authority of the central government, while strong states are less inhibited from intervening abroad, in support of both ambitious and humanitarian motives.

CONSEQUENCES, PATTERNS, AND TRENDS

Individually, the contributions to this volume illustrate the consequences of globalization for national security across a broad range of issues that pertain to states and regions in every part of the world. Collectively, they also demonstrate that there are identifiable patterns in the ways in which processes of globalization are affecting national security. These abstract effects do not hold equally in every context, but they underscore the transformative changes that are influencing contemporary world politics.

Autonomy and Capacity

One theme that emerges clearly from this volume is that although states remain extraordinarily powerful institutions, and moreover, that some aspects of globalization have enhanced state power, nevertheless, in general and in aggregate, globalization has left states less autonomous and with reduced capacity vis-à-vis nonstate actors, social forces, and market pressures. With regard to economic exchange, the fragmentation of production and the globalization of finance in particular have reduced the coherence of "national" economic policies over trade and investment and have put states on a shorter macroeconomic leash. The more open, integrated global marketplace has created advantages for transnational business enterprises, and this has also unintentionally empowered illicit market networks that often develop natural associations with terrorists, insurgents, and separatist groups, who in turn often finance their activities by participating in the black and gray market economies. The economics of scale implied by global markets also can advantage those firms best able to take advantage of them, and this is especially relevant at the high end of the defense industry.

The consequences of the hypermedia environment are more ambiguous for autonomy and capacity, as the state is especially and uniquely well placed to dominate the information sector, and to manage, manipulate, and take advantage of the ever-increasing amount of information being generated. In particular, the ability of governments to learn about the behavior and activity of their citizens has expanded dramatically. At the same time, however, all states are now less able to control the information that their citizens have access to—despite the measures introduced with varying degrees of success to maintain such control. One consequence of this is the need for all states to be aware of how this information is shaping public opinion; unpopular foreign policies will be even more difficult to sustain than in the past.

Marketization is also putting pressure on the state. The greater role of the market in security spheres that have traditionally been outside the market arena again reduces state capacity and autonomy. Privatized defense firms are less easy to control and may pursue profit-driven activities that do not mesh neatly with national security strategies. Privatized defense forces present states with new security threats and challenges to their authority, but at the same time can enhance the autonomy of powerful governments, to the extent that such states are able to sidestep democratic processes or public opposition that might inhibit smaller scale military adventures abroad. More generally, marketization, the process of bringing additional spheres of social behavior into the market sphere, often comes at the expense of the hand of the government and of traditional norms and customs. Most visibly as part of the information revolution, and with the increase in private as opposed to state-run media, marketization contracts the ability of the state to enforce value systems, pressures that are reinforced by economic liberalization more generally.

Balance of Power

A principal theme that emerges in this volume is that globalization affects traditional security concerns because the processes of globalization influence and reduce states' capacities and autonomy to markedly different degrees, and this in turn significantly affects the balance of power. The continued globalization of exchange and economic liberalization puts pressure on "bunker" states and other regimes that depend on the distribution of rents to survive; states with illiberal economic postures more generally are also less well-positioned to adapt to these developments. Smaller economies are disadvantaged by their relative exposure to the volatile world economy, and weak states are especially vulnerable given their limited institutional capacities to deal with shocks that occur. Thus, although their autonomy and capacity are also, in aggregate, reduced, large politically stable states with robust institutional structures in general, and the United States in particular, are left stronger relative to other states.

The story is very similar with regard to both the consequences of the information revolution and of marketization: the tendency is for illiberal states to be faced with crises of control, for weak states to be confronted with challenges to their capacity to govern, and for large, liberal states, and especially the United States, to find their power, relative to other states, enhanced. Those regimes that have traditionally considered themselves in the business of controlling their citizens' access to news, information, and ideas are now less able to find success in such practices. Private security services tend to make the weak weaker and the strong more capable. Privatization and marketization more generally tend to privilege permissive, individual, consumerist values typically associated with the West. And the integration of new ITs and armed forces has further extended the large U.S. advantage in raw military power.

The Nature and Axes of Conflict

Although globalization tends to reinforce and extend existing disparities in the balance of power between states, it also creates many opportunities for actors to introduce asymmetric strategies of violence against great powers (see Table 11.2). Thus globalization recasts incentive structures in ways that affect the likelihood of different types of wars. The fragmentation of production—which, ceteris paribus, complicates the calculation of the national interest, dilutes the gains from conquest, and increases the opportunity costs of war—creates disincentives for traditional interstate war, especially between leading states in the system. Globalized finance also generates similar disincentives, as some paths to war are foreclosed by anticipatory capital flight.

At the same time, the thriving illicit economy and the eroding capacity of weak states creates fertile ground for terrorists, insurgents, and separatists to thrive; and these prospects and opportunities are

Table 11.2 The Consequences of Globalization for National Security

	Autonomy and Capacity	Balance of Power	Nature and Axes of Conflict
Exchange	State autonomy and capacity tends to be generally reduced	Illiberal states face greater pressure than liberal states	Disincentives to great power war; irregular military groups empowered
Information	States are less able to control information, but also empowered	Authoritarian states pressured; U.S. military power enhanced	Transnational networks empowered; distributional conflicts more salient
Marketization	States increasingly challenged by encroachments on their authority	Weak states are more vulnerable; Western values privileged	Backlash against U.S.; weak states both victims and carriers of violence

complemented and extended by new communications technologies that make it easier for such groups to organize and operate. Moreover, exchange, information, and marketization not only create an environment more hospitable to such organization, they also fuel many of the conflicts generated by globalization. Economic change—even change for the better—disrupts traditional patterns of activity and creates new winners and losers, often suddenly and dramatically. And in the hypermedia environment, losers are more likely to be regularly and explicitly confronted by their relative disempowerment. Marketization in general, but especially when it combines with media and liberalization, also creates new sources of conflict as commercially oriented entertainment flows generate support for movements that sincerely or instrumentally adopt a posture of resistance to Western and American culture and norms. The attractiveness of American culture, as noted above, is one way in which globalization enhances U.S. "soft power"; but its encroachment also elicits an oppositional response.

PROSPECTS AND IMPLICATIONS

Globalization is a political process with political implications. With regard to national security, this chapter has reviewed some of the practical consequences of contemporary globalization and has considered a number of more abstract, theoretical tendencies and pressures. State autonomy is altered and diminished, the balance of power reshaped, and the nature and axes of violent conflict are being transformed. This final section looks ahead to some of the likely effects of this transformation for national security in the years ahead, with an increased emphasis on the role of political responses, implications, and consequences.

Prospectively, there are five trends that will profoundly shape the emerging global security environment. They relate to the prospects for great power war, the fate of weak states, a new fault line of world politics, and to each side of the double-edged consequences of globalization for the United States.

Fewer Prospects for Great Power War

The consequences of globalization have reshaped incentives in ways that make traditional interstate war between relatively advanced, relatively large states less likely. Liberalization in trade and investment and the fragmentation of production, the greater share and significance of knowledge intensive sectors, and globalization of finance have raised the opportunity costs of going to war, reduced the expected gains from territorial conquest, and diluted pristine formulations of the "national interest" that can be effectively advanced by interstate war.[12] To be clear, this is neither a determinist nor an endist argument. Rather, it is the reflection of the way that globalization recalibrates the costs and benefits of interstate war. The bar has been raised, and great power war is less likely. This does not imply, however, that such wars are impossible.[13] Rather, postures, preparations, and prognostications need to be revised to reflect these updated prospects.

The Weak Get Dangerously Weaker

The prospect is much less sunny for weak states and for internal and less traditional forms of violent political conflict. The challenges faced by already weak states due to the various processes of globalization are particularly daunting. Market and media pressures on some authoritarian states in particular, as well as the more widespread atrophy of the political capacity of many weak states, will create an environment more conducive to insurgency, civil war, and violent crises associated with the collapse of state governance.

The inescapable disruptions of globalization, felt most acutely by small economies and vulnerable elements of society, will threaten national cohesion and identity and exacerbate existing regional, distributive, and ethnic conflicts. At the same time, into the void of diminished state capacity will flow participants in the illicit economy, entrepreneurs of violence, criminal gangs, separatist and insurgent groups, and terrorist organizations, all of whom will often find support, or at a minimum crucial tolerant passivity, among those who perceive themselves to be weakened, deprived, or disempowered by globalization. Once established, these irregular military forces will be more easily sustained in a globalized world via external support and remittances and by loosely and closely affiliated transnational networks.[14]

Contemporary globalization will thus contribute to greater violent conflict within weak states, in ways that will also increase new security threats to others. Individually, the behavior of many states will have to be increasingly understood as a consequence of their own weaknesses and vulnerabilities to internal security threats.[15] More generally, world politics are transformed in that globalization not only incubates internal dangers to weak states themselves but also contributes to a hothouse environment for the cultivation of violent transnational political actors and generates safe havens from which such groups are able to operate and strike out at adversaries in very distant lands.[16]

The Clash of Marketization

The determined march of globalization is forging a significant new fault line in world politics, and one that will be an important source of highly charged conflicts, both within and across societies. Just as most economic policies, wise or unsound, create winners and losers, there is also much at stake in the encroachment of the market sphere into areas of human activity that have not traditionally been subject to the whims of unmitigated market allocation. Although "the market"—that is, the operation of the scarcity price mechanism mediating between supply and demand—is amoral, not immoral, marketization does, implicitly and explicitly, act as a carrier for the values of secular capitalism: in particular, universalism, materialism, and consumerism. At times, and to an increasing extent as the cumulative effects of marketization press onward, many alternate value systems, including national, cultural, and social movements, will offer resistance.

Organized religions, with their long-standing traditions, written proscriptions, widespread legitimacy, and legions of followers, will be a natural focal point around which some types of resistance will rally, both sincerely and instrumentally. Ironically, a significant part of this resistance, from all quarters, will manifest in the form of transnational movements empowered by the processes of globalization—and as such will be at the same time an expression of globalization and a reaction to it.[17] In any event, one of the consequences for national security of globalization will be the confrontation of "the market" and its values with a constellation of oppositional value structures: national, cultural, ideological, and religious. These clashes will be an important underlying source of emerging political conflicts between states and will also generate divisions within societies as well.

The United States Remains Preponderant among States

While the United States would be the world's preeminent power for the foreseeable future, one way or the other, globalization further enhances its relative power compared to other states, given its advantages in world finance, information dominance, cultural position and appeal, and the size, attractiveness, and adaptability of its home market. In many areas, such as the exploitation of IT, the opportunities implied by greater economies of scale, and the promise of soft power, globalization acts as a political (and often military) "force multiplier" for the United States, increasing even further its power compared to other states. In these relative terms, the United States is more powerful than any state in history; and, as discussed in chapter 1, such U.S. policy choices must remain part of any understanding of contemporary world politics.

The United States Faces Serious New Threats and Challenges

Despite its dominant position compared to other states, the United States is still (even if relatively less so) constrained by the pressures of globalization in novel ways. For example, although globalized finance has enhanced the relative power of the United States, America is actually at greater risk for a major financial crisis than at any other time since the Second World War.[18] Thus, despite the fact that it is relatively empowered by globalization, just like other states, the United States also faces erosions of its capacity and autonomy.

Another problem for the United States is that its very preponderance will tend to generate resistance to its political goals abroad. An important determinant here will be, again, policy choices made by the United States.[19] In particular, to the extent that it is perceived to engage in supremacy mongering, *political balancing,* even among U.S. allies, will be the result. This is very much not to suggest that the European Union or Japan will arm themselves in anticipation of a militarized confrontation with the United States. Rather, it is the possibility that they will search for greater political space between themselves and the United States and contemplate openly whether their interests are best served by a marginal increase, as opposed to a marginal reduction, in U.S. global influence.[20]

U.S. preponderance, and the resulting extensive engagement in world politics, along with the tendency to conflate globalization with Americanization, all suggest that the United States will be confronted not only with greater political opposition, but with violent resistance as well. Some in the front lines in the clash of marketization will find it easier to take on the corporeal and evocative United States rather than the abstract functioning of the faceless "market"; many others will implicate the United States in local political struggles. In sum, for both germane and nefarious reasons, the United States will be more of a target.[21] These dangers should not be underestimated—globalization is empowering to terrorist groups, which exploit safe havens in weak states, find collaborators among those disenchanted with globalization and America, efficiently employ new ITs, and cooperate with transnational criminal enterprises and other violent organized nonstate actors. Terrorism is also a tactic often associated with asymmetric conflict, which compounds this threat, for while globalization is conducive to terrorism generally, unipolarity makes it especially likely that the United States will be an attractive target.[22] The combination of weak states, the expansion of the illicit economy, the development of irregular military networks, the problem of "loose nukes," and the proliferation of weapons of mass destruction represents a pressing and vital challenge to the United States.[23]

Paradoxically, under contemporary globalization, the United States is at once more powerful than it (or any other state) has ever been; but at the same time, it is the object of more global political opposition than at any other time in its history and more at risk of a catastrophic attack on its homeland.

NOTES

1. As noted in chapter 1 of this volume, this represents a "transformalist" perspective (as distinct from a "hyperglobalist" or "skeptical" position), following the terminology of David Held et al., *Global Transformations: Politics, Economics and Culture* (Palo Alto, CA: Stanford University Press, 1999).

2. This is a crucial modifier that applies generally in this book—as discussed in chapter 1, the definition of *globalization* used here is not the only possible definition, nor do we insist that it is the best definition; rather, it is simply the definition that characterizes this project.

3. It may be that contemporary globalization is also qualitatively different from other periods that featured high levels of global flows. See Michael Bordo, Barry Eichengreen, and Douglas Irwin, *Is Globalization Today Really Different than Globalization a Hundred Years Ago?* NBER Working Paper 7195 (Cambridge, MA: NBER, 1999).

4. Jean-Marie Guehenno, "The Impact of Globalization on Strategy," *Survival* 40(4) (Winter 1998–99): 5–19.

5. See for example Frederick Wasser, "Is Hollywood America? The Transnationalization of the American Film Industry," in *Movies and American Society*, ed. Steven J. Ross (Oxford: Blackwell, 2002).

6. See for example Geoffrey L. Herrera, "The Politics of Bandwidth: International Political Implications of a Global Digital Information Network," *Review of International Studies* 28 (1) (2002): 93–122; and Lawrence Lessig, *Code: And Other Laws of Cyberspace* (New York: Basic Books, 1999).

7. On differential adaptability to the hypermedia environment, see Ronald J. Deibert, *Parchment, Printing and Hypermedia: Communication in World Order Transformation* (New York: Columbia University Press, 1997); on the vulnerability of rent-distributing regimes to liberalization, see Clement M. Henry and Robert Springborg, *Globalization and the Politics of Development in the Middle East* (Cambridge: Cambridge University Press, 2001).

8. Stanley Hoffman, "Clash of Globalizations," *Foreign Affairs* 81(4) (July/August 2002): 104–115; Audrey Kurth Cronin, "Behind the Curve: Globalization and International Terrorism," *International Security* 27(3) (Winter 2002/03): 30–58.

9. Peter Andreas, "Transnational Crime and Economic Globalization," in *Transnational Organized Crime and International Security: Business as Usual?*, eds. M. Berdal and M. Serrano (Boulder, CO: Lynne Reinner, 2002); John Arquilla, David Ronfeldt, and Michele Zanini, "Networks, Netwar and Information-Age Terrorism," in *Strategic Appraisal: The Changing Role of Information Warfare*, eds. Zakmay Khalilzad and John White (Santa Monica, CA: RAND, 1999).

10. Jeremy Shapiro, "Information and War: Is it a Revolution?" in Khalilzad and White, *Strategic Appraisal*.

11. Joseph S. Nye, *Soft Power: The Means to Success in World Politics* (New York: Public Affairs, 2004).

12. Stephen G. Brooks, "The Globalization of Production and the Changing Benefits of Conquest," *Journal of Conflict Resolution* 43(5) (October 1999): 646–670; see also Jonathan Kirshner, "Appeasing Bankers: Financial Caution on the Road to War" (unpublished manuscript).

13. For an earlier statement of this general sentiment, see Charles Kindleberger, *Foreign Trade and the National Economy* (New Haven, CT: Yale University Press, 1962), 241; also Charles Kindleberger, *Economic Growth in France and Britain, 1851–1950* (Cambridge, MA: Harvard University Press, 1964), 324–325, 331.

14. Mary Kaldor, *New and Old Wars: Organized Violence in a Globalized Era* (Palo Alto, CA: Stanford University Press, 2001).

15. Steven David, "Explaining Third World Alignment," *World Politics* 43(2) (1991): 233–256.

16. On the geopolitical consequences of globalization, see Robert O. Keohane, "The Globalization of Informal Violence, Theories of World Politics, and the 'Liberalism of Fear,'" in *Power and Governance in a Partially Globalized World*, ed. Keohane (London: Routledge, 2002).

17. Mustapha Kamal Pasha, "Globalization, Islam and Resistance," in *Globalization and the Politics of Resistance*, ed. Barry K. Gills (New York: St. Martin's Press, 2000); Timur Kuran, "Fundamentalisms and the Economy," in *Fundamentalisms and the State*, eds. Martin E. Marty and R. Scott Appelby (Chicago: University of Chicago Press, 1993).

18. With the United States running massive fiscal and trade deficits year after year, expectations about the value of the dollar—expressed in the inflation rate and the exchange rate—may emerge. In this case, the enormous dollar reserves held abroad—over one trillion dollars—might look less like a sign of American strength than oceans of fuel to be dumped on the fire should a medium-sized financial disturbance emerge in the United States and work its way through the system via the recently deregulated U.S. financial economy and high-flying international capital markets.

19. G. John Ikenberry, "America's Imperial Ambition," *Foreign Affairs* 81(5) (2002): 44–60; Stephen M. Walt, *The Origins of Alliances* (Ithaca, NY: Cornell University Press, 1987), 282.

20. For a discussion of these types of issues, see Robert Pape, "Soft Balancing: How States Pursue Security in a Unipolar World," paper presented at the 100th annual meeting of the American Political Science Association, Chicago, September 2–5, 2004.

21. Martha Crenshaw, "Why America? The Globalization of Civil War," *Current History* (December 2001): 425–432.

22. Arquilla, Ronfeldt, and Zinni, "Networks, Netwar and Information-Age Terrorism," in Khalilzad and White, *Strategic Appraisal*, 79.

23. Graham Allison, *Nuclear Terrorism: The Ultimate Preventable Catastrophe* (New York: Times Books, 2004).

CONTRIBUTORS

Fiona B. Adamson is assistant professor of international relations at University College London, where she is also director of the program in international public policy. She received her Ph.D. from Columbia University in 2002. Her research focuses on transnational actors, migration, diaspora mobilization and security, and has been funded by the SSRC-MacArthur Foundation, the Guggenheim Foundation, and others. She has held fellowships at the Olin Institute for Strategic Studies, Harvard University; the Center for International Security and Cooperation (CISAC), Stanford University; and the Belfer Center for Science and International Affairs (BCSIA), Harvard University. Dr. Adamson is a member of the Consultative Group for the Social Science Research Council (SSRC) project "Reframing the Challenge of Migration and Security;" a founding chair of the Council for European Studies (CES) Immigration Research Group; and cochair of the European Consortium for Political Research (ECPR) Standing Group on Security Issues. Her articles have appeared in *International Security, International Studies Review, Political Science Quarterly, Cambridge Review of International Affairs,* and various edited collections.

Deborah Avant is associate professor of political science and director of the Institute for Global and International Studies at George Washington University's Elliot School of International Affairs. Her research (funded by the John D. and Catherine T. MacArthur Foundation, the Olin Foundation, and the Smith Richardson Foundation, among others) has focused on civil-military relations, military change, and the politics of controlling violence. She is the author of *Political Institutions and Military Change: Lessons From Peripheral Wars* (Ithaca, NY: Cornell University Press, 1994) and *The Market for Force: The Consequences of Privatizing Security* (Cambridge: Cambridge University Press, 2005), along with many articles in such journals as *International Organization,*

International Studies Quarterly, Armed Forces and Society, Review of International Studies, and *Foreign Policy.*

Alexander Cooley is assistant professor of political science at Barnard College, Columbia University. He received his Ph.D. from Columbia University in 1999 and taught for two years at Johns Hopkins University. Professor Cooley's research examines the role of external actors—including multinational oil companies, international financial institutions, globalizing processes, foreign military bases, and nongovernmental organizations—in the political and economic development of postimperial states, with a focus on post-Soviet Central Asia. His articles have appeared in a number of academic and policy-oriented journals such as *International Security, Problems of Post-Communism, Review of International Political Economy,* and *Nations in Transit.* Cooley's book *Logics of Hierarchy: The Organization of Empires, States and Military Occupations* was published by Cornell University Press in 2005. He is currently working on a new book project about the political, economic, and social impact of U.S. military bases abroad.

Rachel Epstein is assistant professor at the Graduate School of International Studies, University of Denver. Since receiving her Ph.D. from the Department of Government at Cornell University in 2001, she has been a Jean Monnet Fellow and a Transatlantic Research Fellow at the European University Institute in Florence. Her research interests include European security, regional economic integration, and the postcommunist transition. Her work has appeared in *Comparative Political Studies, Security Studies,* and *East European Politics and Societies.*

Geoffrey L. Herrera is assistant professor of political science at Temple University. He has published articles in the *Review of International Studies, Millennium: Journal of International Studies,* and the *Journal of Strategic Studies.* His book, *Technology and International Transformation,* is forthcoming in 2006 from SUNY Press. He has held fellowships from the Andrew W. Mellon Foundation, the Olin Institute for Strategic Studies, Harvard University, and the Lindback Foundation.

Jonathan Kirshner is associate professor of government and director of the International Political Economy Program at Cornell University, as well as coeditor of the book series Cornell Studies in Money. He is the author of *Currency and Coercion: The Politics of International Monetary Power* (Princeton, NJ: Princeton University Press, 1995), editor of *Monetary Orders: Ambiguous Economics, Ubiquitous Politics* (Ithaca,

NY: Cornell University Press, 2003), and currently completing the book manuscript "Appeasing Bankers: Financial Caution on the Road to War." From 2000 to 2004, Kirshner was director of the Economics and National Security Program at the John M. Olin Institute for Strategic Studies, Harvard University.

Marc Lynch is associate professor of Political Science at Williams College. He has written widely on the international relations of the Middle East, with a primary focus on the media and the dynamics of transnational public opinion. His first book, *State Interests and Public Spheres: The International Politics of Jordan's Identity*, was published by Columbia University Press in 1999. His second book, *Voices of the New Arab Public: Iraq, al-Jazerra, and Middle East Politics Today*, was published by Columbia University Press in 2006.

Paul Midford is associate professor in the Department of Political Science and Sociology, and director of the Japan Program, at the Norwegian University for Science and Technology in Trondheim. He has published in *International Organization, Security Studies, Asian Survey, The Pacific Review*, and the *International Relations of the Asia-Pacific*. Previously, he taught at Kwansei Gakuin University, Lafayette College, and Kanazawa University. Midford has a Ph.D. in political science from Columbia University.

Karl P. Mueller is a political scientist at the RAND Corporation in Washington, D.C., where he studies strategy, defense, and foreign policy issues for the U.S. Air Force, Army, and other government agencies. He is also an adjunct associate professor in the Security Studies Program of the Walsh School of Foreign Service at Georgetown University. Prior to joining RAND, he served as a professor at the Air Force's graduate school for future strategists, the School of Advanced Airpower Studies (SAAS) at Maxwell Air Force Base, Alabama. Dr. Mueller's publications span a wide variety of national security subjects, including military and economic coercion, nuclear deterrence, terrorism, counterinsurgency, and space weaponization. His recently completed RAND study, *Striking First: Preemptive and Preventive Attack in U.S. National Security Policy*, will be published in 2006. He received his B.A. from the University of Chicago and his Ph.D. in politics from Princeton University.

Adam Segal is the Maurice R. Greenberg Senior Fellow in China Studies at the Council on Foreign Relations. An expert on Chinese domestic politics, technology development, foreign policy, and security issues, he has a Ph.D. and B.A. in government from Cornell University and a MALD in International Relations from the Fletcher School of Law and Diplomacy, Tufts University. Most recently, he was the project director for a Council on Foreign Relations independent task force on Chinese military modernization. Previously, he was an arms control analyst at the Union of Concerned Scientists and a visiting scholar at the Center for International Studies, MIT. He has taught at Vassar College and Columbia University and has been a visiting scholar at the Shanghai Academy of Social Sciences and Qinghua University in Beijing. Dr. Segal has written a book, *Digital Dragon: High-Technology Enterprises in China* (Ithaca, NY: Cornell University Press, 2003), as well as several articles on Chinese technology policy. His work has recently appeared in the *International Herald Tribune, Financial Times, Foreign Affairs, Los Angeles Times,* and *Washington Quarterly.*